PRAISE FOR *GOLDEN BOY*

'At once unputdownable and also unpickupable, because if you pick it up you will eventually finish it, and what are you going to do then?'

ROB SMYTH, *Guardian*

'It made me laugh, it told me things, it reminded me why I love the subject I'm reading about and it put a series of images in my head that I won't ever forget. It's audacious, it's got chutzpah, it's done with a lyrical flourish. I didn't know cricket books could be written like this.'

PHIL WALKER, editor of *Wisden Cricket Monthly*

'It deals with people, with hierarchies, with who has the right to do certain things and what is and isn't legitimate.'

DAISY CHRISTODOULOU, author & educator

'Graphic ... Shocking ... Devastating ... If half of what we read here is true, two Australian legends should hang their heads in shame.'

SIMON WILDE, *Times*

'It's a story of bullying. I think the great genius of this book is the absence not just of Kim Hughes but also of Lillee and Marsh.'

LAWRENCE BOOTH, editor of *Wisden Cricketers' Almanack*

'... Lillee and Marsh declined to speak – as much I suspect out of embarrassment as discretion. This wall of silence forced Ryan, a stubborn man, to look elsewhere. He has written an entirely credible and deeply absorbing account of Test cricket as it really is lived. It is a grim tale.'

STEPHEN FAY, *Wisden Cricketer*

'Heartbreaking to read but such is the quality of Ryan's work you can't stop.'

Daily Telegraph

'Best cricket read of the year.'

KEVIN MITCHELL, *Observer*

'Extraordinary ... A sad tale told splendidly.'

ALEX MASSIE, *Spectator*

'A valuable archive of the professional cricketer's lot during the 1980s – paltry wages, petty officials, vermin-infested hotels and astonishing levels of alcohol consumption ... a fascinating account of Australian cricket's leanest years.'

Times Literary Supplement

'In some ways it's like a great Australian novel.'

WILLIAM FIENNES, author

CHRISTIAN RYAN is also the author of *Feeling is the Thing that Happens in 1000th of a Second*. His essays – appearing in *Wisden*, *The Nightwatchman* and *The Cricket Monthly* – include 'Blew', 'Two Thursdays', 'The Thirty-Ninth Summer of DK Lillee', 'The Unremembered Six', 'Abbamania' and 'Jeff Thomson is Annoyed'. He edited and assembled the literary/photographic cultural sweeps *Rock Country* and *Australia: Story of a Cricket Country*. He lives in Melbourne.

Kim Hughes
and the bad old days of Australian cricket

GOLDEN
BOY

CHRISTIAN RYAN

ALLEN&UNWIN

First published in Australia in 2009 by Allen & Unwin
First published in Great Britain in 2010 by Allen & Unwin
Copyright © Christian Ryan, 2009

The moral right of Christian Ryan to be identified as the author of this work
has been asserted by him in accordance with the Copyright, Designs and
Patents Act of 1988.

Allen & Unwin
c/o Atlantic Books
Ormond House
26–27 Boswell Street
London WC1N 3JZ
Phone: 020 7269 1610
Fax: 020 7430 0916
Email: UK@allenandunwin.com
Web: www.allenandunwin.com/uk

A CIP catalogue record for this book is available from the British Library.

Paperback ISBN 978 1 74237 463 5
E-book ISBN 978 1 92557 545 3

Printed by CPI Group (UK) Ltd, Croydon CR0 4YY

10 9 8 7 6 5 4 3

Contents

PROLOGUE
In the Nets

THE MAN WHO WAS CAPTAIN looked more like a boy. He stood at the far end of the Sydney Cricket Ground practice nets, and as he waited for the bowler his bat banged the ground, impatiently, not nervously. His smile as he leaned forward revealed two rows of gappy, crooked teeth. Not a wrinkle lined his face. His cheeks and elbows had a pinkish glow, the price of playing cricket nearly every summer day for nineteen consecutive summers. He wore his collar upturned and his shirt unbuttoned to the breastbone, and here, in a triangle down his neck and hairless chest, the skin was crimson. His head was a bottlebrush of curls shooting out in so many directions that his green cap could not contain them. The curls were too dark to be blond yet the sun rebounded off them in a way that told you they weren't brown. They were golden.

The bowler the captain was waiting for had seldom if ever been called boyish. His chest hair was ropy and black. His bald spot was round as a beer coaster. Captain and bowler knew each other well.

They first played together nine years earlier, November 1974, Western Australia versus South Australia at the WACA Ground.

Back then, Kim Hughes was feeling giddy about his big-time debut and Dennis Lillee was on a private crusade. Doctors had diagnosed three stress fractures to his back. Critics—'poison typewriters', Lillee called them—had pronounced his career comatose. He had about him an air that would soon become familiar whenever he wished to prove doctors, typewriters or batsmen wrong, a kind of grizzly incredulity.

Hughes was named twelfth man. Twelfth man in those days was more like a butler than a professional cricketer. Bosses' instructions were to be relayed, sweat-drenched gloves replaced, team-mates' peskiest whims respected. But as Western Australia's fieldsmen emerged from a hot morning's toil, their endeavour blunted by openers Woodcock and Sincock, Hughes contented himself with organising a few cold drinks. He wandered off. Twelfth man was usually the last to be seated when the host and visiting players slumped round the same boxy lunchroom. Not Kim. He was one of the first.

'Where's the fuckin' twelfth man?' growled Lillee, bursting through the lunchroom door. 'Come and do your fuckin' job.' Lillee flung back the door behind him.

That's how it was, the first time Kim and Dennis were on the same team. This week in Sydney, though neither knew it just yet, was to be the last. Kim was weeks away from his thirtieth birthday. He had hung on to his teenage habit of cover driving the quickest bowlers off one knee, sometimes at inopportune moments, then loudly congratulating himself on his own ingenuity. 'Shot, Claggy! That's four on any ground in the world.'

Before an innings, he liked making outlandish predictions. 'Today,' he'd exclaim, 'I'm going to hit two hundred before lunch.' Mostly his team-mates laughed. They found it endearing. 'That's Kim,' they would say. Sometimes some of them, the older and more experienced ones, would get a bit annoyed.

Over breakfast in Melbourne, his predecessor as Australian captain confided to him that most players hankered after a new leader. Over dinner in Perth, a senior board man advanced the notion that he give up the captaincy for the good of his batting. Four others, all friends, said he had it in him to be the next Viv Richards; but he could not possibly, they hissed, be the next Viv *and* be captain. One of those four well-meaning friends was fast bowler Wayne Clark. 'If he'd just played cricket,' says Clark, 'just got on and played cricket, he would have gone down in the annals of fucking cricket history.'

Kim dwelt on this, resigned, slept on it, then cancelled his resignation. His vice-captain reckoned him 'very naive' and 'liable to do silly things'. The stand-in vice-captain recommended Kim do an apprenticeship under 'somebody everybody respects'. And as he tapped once more on the popping crease it was as if his cracked and scrubby SS Jumbo, so dotted in red cherry-marks that they blotted out the bottom S of the maker's logo, was a barometer of his relationship with Australian cricket's most powerful men.

But this was New Year's Day, 1984, and great prospects lay in front of Kimberley John Hughes. Tomorrow the Fifth Test against Pakistan would begin. On the second evening Greg Chappell would announce that his wife Judy's long-standing wish—for him to have enough spare time to sweep the leaves off the family tennis court—was about to come true. The next morning Lillee would follow Chappell into retirement. Then Rodney Marsh would let slip his unavailability for the forthcoming Caribbean trip, and spectators knew they were seeing 'Bacchus' devour outside edges, like a bushy-lipped Pac-Man in pads, for the last time in Tests.

After five days Wayne Phillips rolled his wrists over an Azeem Hafeez half-volley and yanked out one stump in celebration. Kim Hughes's Australians had beaten Imran Khan's men 2–0. It was his first series triumph in four attempts as leader. And the three revered legends who had done more than most to make life tricky for him were suddenly out of the picture. Just like that.

Think of it not as the end of an old era, Kim would say in the days to come, but the dawning of a new one. First things first, though. Somehow he had to get through this net session.

•••••

MURRAY BENNETT almost had to remove his dark-tinted spectacles and rub his eyes to believe what he was seeing. The specs gave him the appearance of someone more likely to drive taxis to the airport than batsmen to distraction courtesy of a handily disguised arm ball and some delicate pace variations. But the specs were working fine. A week had blown by since Bennett's unexpected call-up to the squad. Now he found himself bowling in the same net as Dennis Lillee. Except that the moment Kim Hughes arrived for a hit, Lillee stalked away in the opposite direction. Previously he'd been jogging in and unloading off a few yards. Now he crouched far away, roughly two-thirds the length of his full run-up, ball in hand.

Lillee's first ball spat off the pitch and zoomed at Kim's head. So did the second. 'I was thinking: Jesus!' Bennett recalls.

'I couldn't believe it. The two blokes were on the same side. And Lillee seemed to be taking some cheap shots at him.'

Lillee continued. His third and fourth deliveries put his own toes in graver peril than Kim's. 'Every ball was short,' says Bennett. 'I thought, there's something missing here.' Bennett peered around at faces familiar from years of studying them on TV. A few little smiles, maybe. Otherwise nobody seemed to notice. 'I guess I was a bit disgusted. Lillee was a great hero of anyone who had grown up in the game and I was just getting to know him on a personal level. For a bloke of his stature I thought it was way out of line. I didn't think it was very impressive at all. I was thinking to myself, I'm glad I'm not batting in here.'

If Bennett's new team-mates appeared blasé, that was only logical. They had seen it before—not twice or three times, but often. Geoff Lawson was still wincing at the memory of the previous summer's Perth Test against Bob Willis's Englishmen. 'Lillee nearly broke Kim's arm,' says Lawson. 'Just ran in and bowled lightning at him in the nets and Kim had to go off for an X-ray, as I recall. Got hit in the forearm the day before the Ashes started.'

The summer before that, Graeme Wood felt the same mixture of panic and unease pollute an Australian net session. Again it was Test match eve: Pakistan at the Gabba. 'Oh, you know,' says Wood, 'again it was on. I remember Kim getting hit, got him right near the elbow, sort of, the forearm. He had to get ice on it and there was doubt over whether he'd play. Not the great morale booster you need before a Test. Because it's such a bony area, there was concern.'

Other times Wood, a mate of Hughes and Lillee, would joke that he himself was safe in the nets because he and Lillee played for the same club side, Melville. That didn't mean Lillee laid off him completely. 'But you could tell,' says Wood, 'that he wasn't trying to knock my head off.'

Craig Serjeant, former Australian vice-captain, tells of one net session where Lillee let fly his customary bouncer at Kim, followed through, retrieved the ball and looked remorseful.

'Sorry.'

'Oh, that's OK.'

'Sorry I didn't fuckin' hit ya.'

Invariably, though, not a word would be uttered. And Kim would never flinch or grouse. Instead he hooked or ducked or fended away. It made for exhilarating private viewing. During some of the drearier early-eighties interludes, while Kiwi workhorses chugged into seabreezes and subcontinental off-spinners whizzed down their darts, the real spectacle unfolded out of match hours and out of sight. Fiercest were the duels on the WACA practice pitches. There, the bounce was steep—and therefore lethal—but also true, so Kim could trust the ball's trajectory and back himself to hook. Sometimes, say team-mates, the green nets could not seal them in. Lillee would drop short, Kim would skip on to the back foot and top-edged skyers would fizz out of the ground, beyond Nelson Crescent and orbit Gloucester Park trotting track.

The scene at the SCG on New Year's Day 1984 was not dissimilar. 'Kim was fantastic,' Bennett remembers. 'He hooked them off his nose or ducked. Then he picked up the ball, threw it back to Dennis and didn't say a word.'

Bennett was not the only newcomer feeling overjoyed to be there yet slightly puzzled. John Maguire debuted alongside Greg Matthews in Melbourne the week before. Two less alike joint debutants Australia has never known. Medium pacer Maguire was gentle, modest and superfit, a Kangaroo Point cartographer. Allrounder Matthews strummed air guitar between deliveries and wore calf-high black suede boots to the team's pre-Test gathering. He'd happily represent Australia for nothing, he proclaimed, so Greg Chappell ripped up Matthews's paycheque as penance. In Sydney, the dressing-room telephone lingered in Maguire's mind. Some players wrapped it in red electrical tape, dubbed it the rebel-tour hotline and announced: 'We're waiting for the call from South Africa.'

'You know when you're in a side that bonds well together and hangs around together and practises together and everyone encourages each other,' says Maguire. 'It's an intangible thing. But you know when it's not there.'

After surviving his net ordeal Kim romped through the match itself with distinction. Chappell, Lillee and Marsh set about storming the few statistical fortresses they hadn't breached already. Chappell's 120th Test catch equalled Colin Cowdrey's world record, and Kim hugged him tight from the side, fingers beating out a delighted drumbeat on Chappell's ribcage. When Chappell turned and scampered a third overthrow to sweep past Don Bradman's 6996-run pedestal, Kim was up the other end. He switched course, veered diagonally at Chappell and fisted the air as they crossed. Unwitting latecomers might have wondered which one had just eclipsed The Don. Chappell looked merely relieved, shoulders slumped, forehead soaked, like he had stepped out of a mine shaft and into a sunshower. Kim's bliss as he clapped his bat knew no bounds.

Chappell and Lillee were the last ones to leave the dressing room on their final morning. They had been all summer even though administrators, suspecting mutiny, had urged them to please walk out with everybody else. Kim hustled his men into two ragged rows. The retirees were applauded on to the field through a guard of honour. It is possible that Kim resented Lillee for taking potshots at his captain's head during his last full-length net session as an Australian Test cricketer. But the grudge, if it existed, was buried in the pit of Kim's kitbag.

He carried himself with dignity and authority. He batted with his old daredevilry. Feet propelled him so speedily to the pitch of Abdul Qadir's insidious turners that it hardly mattered if he wasn't sure which way they were turning. Out for 76, his average over fourteen months stood at 65. That was better, quite a bit better, than Viv Richards. Who now reckoned him too brash, too impetuous, too immature, too cocky, too silly, too curly haired?

And who doubted his right to be captain? He had been thinking about the job since he was fourteen, not aimlessly like other fourteen-year-olds think about it, but as a realistic possibility, almost a probability, maybe even a certainty. Every Sunday morning, winter and summer, he and a mild-mannered young swing bowler named Graeme Porter would frequent one of three local parks and chuck balls at each other. Every second Sunday or so, their coach Frank Parry would say to the boy Hughes: 'Not only will you play—you'll captain Australia.'

That free-spirited 76 in Sydney was the last time he raised his bat to the crowd for a Test half-century. By the end of 1984, year of great prospects, he was out of the team.

•••••

AUSTRALIA'S CRICKET CAPTAINS, the late Ray Robinson taught us, have been plumbers, graziers, dentists, whisky agents, crime reporters, letter sorters, boot sellers, handicappers, shopkeepers, postmen. They have also been authors. Their book titles—*Captain's Story*, *A Captain's Year*, *Captain's Diary*, *Walking to Victory*—have usually been suggestive of the content, straightforward snapshots of seemingly inevitable glory. Kim Hughes's glories were many and multifaceted. But little about them was inevitable and far too many of them were overshadowed by disasters, disasters which were also many and multifaceted, and which were almost too terrible to mention, let alone write about.

Until now they never have been. Among regular captains of the last half a century, only Kim Hughes has not had a book written by or about him. If he is remembered at all, it is as the captain who cried when he quit at a press conference. All else has lain smothered under the ordinariness of a 37.41 batting average. Yet what a story beckons—the story of a country boy who would leap three, four, five steps down the pitch to bowlers fast or slow. He would go along with the umpire's decision. He would wear a cap not a helmet. He would try to hit the ball out of the ground when within reach of a hundred because this put smiles on people's faces, even if it meant getting out in the nineties, as it often did.

'To create some memories for myself and for other people'— that was always the boy's first aim. Only after accomplishing that would he set his mind to scoring as many runs as he possibly could. This is the reverse of nearly every other cricketer's thinking. Runs and wickets are the thing, smiles and memories happy accidents.

Despite this, and because of this, Kim hit 117 and 84 against England in the Lord's Centenary Test of 1980. For five days no ball was too wide to square cut, no medium pacer too respectable to be hoicked. A year later, Boxing Day 1981, he bludgeoned 100 not out against West Indies in Melbourne when no one else got past 21. He did it against history's meanest speed quartet, on a pitch that alternately skidded and popped, in circumstances that demanded he pre-empt where the ball might land because standing back and waiting for the bowler was tantamount to surrender. It is possible to conceive Don Bradman, acme of batting foolproofness, playing one of these innings. It is hard to imagine any man—except maybe Stan McCabe, another son of the Australian bush—playing all three.

'I've always had enough faith in myself to be different,' the boy once said. 'If I wasn't a cricketer I'd be something like a deep-sea diver.' What he meant was the idea of him being anything else was crazy. Cricket's values, its traditions, ran through him. He was born to cricket. He belonged in cricket. But belonging in cricket, which is a culture, is different from belonging in the Australian cricket team, which is more like a club.

Kim went from captain of the club to out of the club in five weeks of elongated anguish at the end of 1984. Conspiracy theories abounded. What raw material this unwritten book promised. What riches. It even ended in tears. For a short, tantalising while the Kim Hughes story was cricket's block-buster-in-waiting. 'If he lets rip like he once did those cover drives, his book could be not only a real tear-jerker but wickedly and condemningly revealing,' noted Frank Keating, grandmaster of British sportswriting, sitting poolside in Arabia during Kim's last official Australian trip. At the subsequent press conference revealing his leadership of a rebel tour to apartheid South Africa, Kim declined to field questions. 'Like most cricketers I have a book to write,' he explained. 'And I'm sure you'll all want to read it.'

Sportsnight-goers at a Geelong sports store were warned of imminent skulduggery revelations in a forthcoming auto-biography. The *Sydney Morning Herald* reported that the book was 'a few months' away. A few months came and went. By October 1985 publication had been postponed a year. 'I really feel everything will come out in my book, that things will come home to roost.'

Cricket moved on. Allan Border's Australians won the 1987 World Cup. Kim's book still hadn't materialised. 'Those days seem a long time ago. I'll write a book about them one day and it will certainly be very interesting.' That was in November 1987. The idea slid away again.

In 2006 I rang Kim. Yes, he'd read the letter I sent. 'No, I'm not interested in writing a book,' he said flatly. 'I'm fifty-two and I don't need the aggro. It would stir up a lot of people.'

But I had no desire to ghost his life and times. I said I wanted to write an unairbrushed tale of Australian cricket in the Hughes mini-era, told through his experiences, encompassing many voices. I also said there was more to him than a 37.41 average and history should be set aright. He sounded like he was in a hurry.

Five months later, we talked again. He wasn't unhappy to hear from me. But he repeated that he did not want to be the one to 'stir things up'. He had no real objection to me writing it. He just didn't want to be involved. Any book about him would mean big names and controversy and reporters ringing him up all over again. If he were ever going to write his autobiography it would have been when Peter McFarline, the old *Age* cricket correspondent, was alive to help. He said McFarline understood the personalities. When McFarline died in 2002, the chance was gone. And now he had 'turned the other cheek'. He would ask his lawyer, business adviser and family not to speak to me. Others could if they wanted to.

Others did: friends, team-mates, coaches, teachers, officials, close observers. Almost all mentioned Kim's niceness. He addresses people by their first name. He loves being around and encouraging children. He likes being people's best friend. In our second phone conversation, six and a half minutes of me trying to sweet-talk him round, he didn't hang up and he said over and over, warmly, 'It's no slight against you.'

Sometimes affection for Kim came from unlikely sources. 'I don't say this about a lot of blokes,' says Greg Chappell, 'but I love Kim Hughes. I can tell you that now. I admire what he's been through because my life's been very easy compared with Kim Hughes's life, and I think most of us could say that.'

Kim and Dennis and Rod all get along now, people say. You see them out having beers together. Several people add, in swallowed whispers: 'If I was Kim I wouldn't go out drinking with them. Not after everything . . .'

I remembered Kim's own words: that he had 'turned the other cheek'. How much pressure had he been under? How much hurt was there? Why did he never write that book? Was it because he finally felt part of the club—and was afraid of being expelled again?

Late in my research, I discovered a tape of a speech Kim gave at the Australian Cricket Society's annual dinner in August

1990. 'Yes, I've thought about writing a book,' he said that night. 'It would be a bestseller. I would make a lot of money. But I really don't feel deep down that I'd be proud about it. Maybe I'm going to take those things to my grave. Maybe too many other people have made a mistake of getting rid of the old basic values that what was said within the changerooms should stay in the changerooms. Those basics went out the door for a while and people made a lot of money. But Australian cricket paid a price.'

I knew I did not want to 'stir things up' for him too much. I also sensed, more strongly than ever, that you cannot understand Australian cricket in the 1980s, you cannot understand the men who ran the club—the Chappell brothers, Lillee, Marsh—unless you understand what happened to Kim Hughes.

And to understand Kim Hughes, the first thing you have to appreciate is that here was a batsman who had every shot in the book, which can sometimes be a problem, because when you have all the shots you want to play them. And that can get you in trouble.

ONE

'Let Him Stew'

DENNIS LILLEE IS CONCISE with his words and passionate about the Australian XI. Both qualities were evident a year after his retirement when he was asked about his legacy. Would he, wondered the journalist from *Australian Cricket*, go down as 'a Ned Kelly anti-hero' or 'a pure sporting legend in the Bradman mould'?

'If I am remembered,' replied Lillee, 'as someone who gave a hundred per cent at all times, I don't care what else I am remembered for.' In the two decades since, his legend taller and leg-cutter retrospectively deadlier with every passing summer, he has got his wish. Getting what he wishes is a third characteristic of Lillee's.

His wicketkeeping pal Rodney Marsh can be even more concise. Sometimes Marsh's concision turns into gruffness. 'The team is the thing and to devote yourself anything less than one hundred per cent to that team is tantamount to treason,' Marsh once wrote. Should anyone dare accuse him otherwise— 'I'd like to meet the idiot and personally shove the proposition down his throat or up some other orifice.'

Giving a hundred per cent is the most quoted yet least

quantifiable of cricket's prefabricated parrot phrases. It is almost meaningless—a hundred per cent of what?—and was junked anew by Matthew Hayden's twenty-first century pledge of 'one billion per cent' support for Ricky Ponting. It is also immeasurable. The sport of run rates, over rates, strike rates and economy rates knows no such thing as effort rate. All anyone can do is watch a game unfold and interpret what they see. Between May and September of 1981, when Australia toured England, several people saw a lot of things they had trouble interpreting.

•••••

AUSTRALIA'S NEW CAPTAIN was interviewed by John Wiseman on Channel Ten's *Eyewitness News* the day after his appointment. Kim's hair was damp and combed straight—no curls—but as he licked dry lips and swiped Perth's flies out of his face he looked more boyish than ever.

'Kim, first of all congratulations. What do you think of some of this morning's criticism?'

'Well I don't know who's criticising me at all, John, but I suppose one in my position isn't going to please everybody.'

Kim had led Australian Test teams before. That was during the World Series Cricket days when the country's three dozen finest were otherwise engaged as Kerry Packer's so-called circus act. This time the tidings were auspicious, theoretically: a full-strength squad with a winning chance. Theory was one thing. In reality, Western Australia's battle-hardened Bruces—Laird and Yardley—had been left out. Human dynamite sticks Jeff Thomson and Len Pascoe were missing. 'I always thought selectors were idiots,' reasoned Thommo. 'Now I know it.' Record crowds descended on the bar of the Dungog Bowls Club. Not since 1964 had local sweetheart Doug Walters been overlooked for an Ashes trip. 'We would listen on the wireless till 3 a.m. when Doug was playing,' grumbled one irate Dungogian. 'When he hit a four we'd celebrate by opening a cold one. Maybe we're biased but, blimey, it's a bit crook.'

Heading the unlikelier inclusions in Australia's 1981 Ashes squad was Graeme Beard. He'd added folded-finger off-breaks to his repertoire two years earlier when his slow-mediums kept thudding into Tooheys advertising boards at a speed considerably zippier than slow-medium. Youngest of the Chappell trinity, Trevor, was also England-bound. 'The first Australian cricketer to have won a major berth on the strength of his brilliant fielding,' commented McFarline in the *Age*.

Alas, Trevor was a like-for-not-at-all-like swap with Greg. Greg ruled himself out to fellow selectors on a Tuesday. The squad—minus a captain—was announced on the Wednesday. A public explanation was forthcoming, for a fee, on a Thursday-night TV special, *Greg Chappell: Covers Off*. He revealed that his son Stephen no longer knew whether Greg Chappell was his absent father, a famous cricketer, or both. Business interests, including an insurance company, were mounting too. 'March, April, May and in particular June,' he elaborated, 'are vital to the success of the venture.'

On the Friday, Kim was named captain. A newspaperman gave him the good news before anyone from the board did.

Where was Lillee hiding? That was an eventful week's biggest mystery. Six months earlier he and Marsh had each rejected the Western Australian vice-captaincy under Kim. Lillee's name was one of sixteen on the teamsheet for England. But how much was that piece of paper worth? Scuttlebutt crisscrossed the continent from east to west and back again. Finally Perth journalist Ken Casellas found Lillee in the riverside clubrooms of Tompkins Park. It was Saturday night. Lillee was puffed from twenty-five knackering overs for Melville. He was drinking his own version of a shandy—one gulp out of a can of beer, one gulp of lemonade—but there was nothing bubbly about his demeanour. 'I've got an unlisted phone number and it's been changed a few times. Still I get calls day and night from all over the world from people wanting to know whether I'm going on tour. All I want to say is I'm happy the season is over.' The mystery deepened.

Kim celebrated his appointment by popping a couple of balls out of the park in his next innings, an unbeaten 156 in a first-grade semi-final. At the ABC Sportsman of the Year awards, he was asked if he tended to decide on a stroke before the ball was bowled. Confounding the laws of reliable run gathering, Kim answered: 'Yes.' Knowledgeable sorts watching in their living rooms were appalled. But vindication arrived a week before the team's departure when he was listed among *Wisden*'s five cricketers of the year. Inclusion in *Wisden*'s famous five traditionally recognises a season's haystack of runs or wickets. Kim was picked for his two celestial Centenary Test knocks. Anyone who reckoned it impossible to premeditate deliveries and prosper needed only to skim the highlights tape.

The thought of returning to England was sweet. It was tantalising enough for Lillee to decide to go too, although he and Marsh were permitted to skip the pre-tour detour to Sri Lanka. The Australians arrived on day one of the monsoon season. Pitches were custom-built for Sri Lanka's finger-spinning trio. Power was switched off every morning and evening, for the system was hydro-electric and there was a water shortage. On the field, too, it was as if Australia were playing in darkness. Outclassed in the drawn four-dayer, they sneaked the skimpiest of victories in the unofficial limited-overs series, perverse preparation for an English spring.

Really, the twelve-day stopover was a fact-finding mission on behalf of board delegates unsure which way to vote on Sri Lanka's bid for Test status. Australian officials were reportedly seen photographing stadium toilets as evidence for the 'no' case. 'Come on, Aussies, come off it,' pleaded a local newspaper. But all four games were sellouts. Sri Lankan Testhood followed months later. And Kim had not a bad word for the place, the toilets, the tour, or the administrators who devised it. He was equal to the diplomatic challenge posed by one of Rodney Hogg's eccentric contributions to Australian touring folklore. Riled by humidity and his inability to prick a ballooning middle-order partnership, Hogg marked a cross between his eyes and nearly decapitated Ranjan Madugalle with a head-high full toss. The captain strode imperiously across from mid-on: 'That's not on, Rodney.'

England was three-jumper territory. Kim acclaimed the opening net session at Lord's the best first-day workout of any tour he'd been on. This cocktail of good cheer, naivety and overstatement would become a trademark of his public pronouncements, one that bugged some team-mates. But not yet. At Arundel Castle he was out to his first ball of the tour, an Intikhab Alam top-spinner grubbering into his boot. His humour survived. Invited by the ground manager in Swansea to nominate a time for practice, Kim grinned. 'Six o'clock in the morning—the only time it doesn't rain in this country.' Drizzle, sleet, frost and murk gave Kim ample chance to polish his introductory note for the Test brochure:

> As I write this message I know that I am back in England. Once again we are stuck inside the dressing room watching rain stream down the windows. However, I am certain this year's full tour of England will prove to be one of the most exciting in the long history of England versus Australia contests . . . I hope you enjoy watching the cricket and also that I will be able to say 'hello' to as many of you as possible.

Kim's 'hello, everyone' policy extended to travelling Australian scribes. 'We want you to feel part of the team,' he told them. He enquired after their welfare over breakfast and hosted candid off-the-record briefings over drinks. 'Team-mates are singing his praises daily and lauding the great team spirit,' reported Alan 'Sheff' Shiell. 'Australian pressmen will not tolerate a bad word about Hughes the man.' English broadsheet writers stepped the pro-Kim hoopla up several more adjectives. Some felt they'd been shown few courtesies during the furry-bellied Chappell dynasty. They appreciated Kim's plain-speaking eloquence, his insistence that nothing was too bothersome. 'I hope he becomes what he deserves to be—the most popular captain since Lindsay Hassett,' wrote Robin Marlar in the *Sunday Times*. Frank Keating found fault only with the patchy stubble clinging to Kim's chin: 'His clean boy scout's face somehow goes better with the sparkling innocence of his batsmanship. Pulled this way and that by photographers, fringers, high commissioners, low commissioners, book commissioners and hall-porter commissioners, he never stopped being softly obliging.'

Kim's next coup was to oversee Australia's maiden triumph in a one-day series in England. Shivering and rusty, they lost at Lord's then levelled at Edgbaston, where England needed six off the last over and Lillee kept them to three. As Kim walked into the press conference, Australian journalists rose and clapped. At training before the series decider, Trevor Chappell confessed his terror of England's middle order, which had throttled him on wickets made for his glamourless wobblers. Yes, admitted Kim, he felt a bit the same way about Trevor's bowling. But he stuck to the plan. Chappell's three wickets proved suffocating.

Hunches continued hatching fruitfully once the Tests started. Twice Kim called heads and chose to bowl. No Ashes captain had gambled like that before in the first two Tests of a series. Australia won at Trent Bridge and had marginally the better of a soggy Lord's draw. At Trent Bridge, Kim kept the cordon stacked with four slips and the ball in the hand of a 25-year-old debutant with a centipede moustache. Terry Alderman's hula-hooping outswingers knocked nine Englishmen aside. Chasing 132, Australia's seventh-wicket pair were meandering towards victory when Kim joined Alan McGilvray and Christopher Martin-Jenkins in the *Test Match Special* box.

McGILVRAY: Weather good, perfect conditions. Now
    Lawson . . .
HUGHES: Whewwwwsh.

McGILVRAY: There's a big sigh from Kim Hughes. Yes I know how you feel. Now Dilley is on his way to Lawson, and Lawson turns it . . .

HUGHES: ONE MORE.

McGILVRAY: One more, says Kim.

Not for a second did he disguise nerves or excitement.

McGILVRAY: Dilley moves away from us to bowl to Lawson. A full toss and . . .

HUGHES: GOOD SHOT! FOUR! GOODY!

Kim clapped his hands and shouted advice and bellowed over the top of the two commentators.

McGILVRAY: Chappell, you must stay there and pick up these four runs. And Kim, if you'd like to leave anytime . . .

HUGHES: Yeah, I might, ah, just wait one more ball.

A strangled titter.

McGILVRAY: Right, one more ball, all right.

HUGHES: I might just sit in my seat.

CMJ: Terrible isn't it, Kim?

HUGHES: Ay?

CMJ: Terrible isn't it?

HUGHES: Aww, I don't know how anybody can captain for more than a game.

That night it was possible to picture Kim Hughes, twenty-seven, captaining his country for so long as he craved. The Ashes urn had been England's property since 1977. But the handover was nigh, surely. Several uproarious hours later at the team hotel, Marsh, Lillee and Kim were seen deep in discussion, shoulders entwined. Kim cheerfully told anyone who'd listen about how Marsh had held up a glove and halted play with Lillee poised to tear in at Willis.

'You've got all the angles buggered up,' Marsh roared.

'Oh,' said Kim. 'What do you want?'

Marsh reset the field. Deep cover point was relocated twenty-five metres sideways. Two balls later Willis hit straight to him.

'I'm hardly a captain at all,' Kim was saying that night. 'But Hughes, Marsh and Lillee is a bloody good captain.'

•••••

COMING UP TO the Third Test at Headingley, Australia's coach Peter Philpott sensed Kim was in trouble. Over a beer, he voiced his worries to Marsh, the vice-captain.

'Rodney, we've got to try to help him.'

'He's got the job,' said Marsh. 'He's a big boy. Let him stew in it.'

Marsh's words still grate in Philpott's head:

It wasn't a pleasant relationship between Kim and the other two. They thought he was a soft boy. They were two hard men and they didn't have much respect for him. They respected his batting but not his captaincy or him as a human being. I don't think they respected Kim as a man. They didn't hide that. In fact they allowed themselves at times to do just the opposite. You couldn't help but watch and be disappointed at the way they threw the boy to the wolves—threw him to the wolves and didn't throw out a line to help him.

Philpott found Kim faintly immature. 'I think Rodney and Dennis saw him as a kind of little golden boy.' Captaincy was the main volcano of contention. Dennis thought Rodney should be in charge. Rodney thought Rodney should be in charge. It reminded Philpott—up to a point—of Australia's 1957–58 visit to South Africa. A freckle-faced pharmacist still living with his parents led that tour. 'Neil Harvey and Richie Benaud would have been flabbergasted when Ian Craig was appointed captain over them,' says Philpott. 'But they gave him total support. Ian was only a kid and they helped greatly. That didn't happen in 1981.'

With Australia one Test up, the cracks were undetectable to outsiders. Esso scholar Carl Rackemann was borrowed from Surrey's 2nd XI to fortify Australia's sniffling pace attack against Warwickshire. Thirty-six more thrilling hours he'd never known: 'My impression of the dressing room was that everything was pretty positive, pretty good.' Similarly, the reporters who rained a standing ovation upon Kim after the second one-dayer had no inkling of the bloodletting behind slammed doors. In the first match Australia bowled sloppily, fielded scruffily, and Philpott told them so. Second time round they were a team rejuvenated. Henry Blofeld's report in the *Australian* concluded: 'For me, Peter Philpott and Geoff Lawson were the men of the match.'

Blofeld's article whipped round the dressing room. Fair enough, thought the players from New South Wales, Philpott's home state. Bulldust, chorused the rest. 'The Western

Australians, they were livid,' Philpott remembers. 'Kimberley was very upset. And the lines were clearly defined.' To suggest any correlation between Philpott's salvo and the team's salvation was tripe, the players huffed. And if there was . . . Well, if that was the case then the little man in the tracksuit was plainly exceeding his brief.

When Marsh and Lillee addressed Kim by his nickname, something about the way croaky voices draped over the first syllable—'*Claaaaa-gee*'—made others think of grown men patting a boy on the head. Body language—folded arms, rolling eyes—often spoke loudest. Pinpointing what ailed this team wasn't always easy. It was a feeling people got. Lawson believes Lillee and Marsh spent 'nearly every waking hour' undermining Kim. 'I wouldn't have thought that,' counters Wood. 'We were playing very well.' For Graeme Beard: 'We were a bunch of fellas playing cricket for Australia and it was fabulous. I got on well with all the blokes.'

Was it a united side? Beard goes quiet.

'Well. Probably not. A difficult situation.'

And that's all you'll say?

'Mmmm,' says Beard. 'Well. Yeah.'

The cracks were small in those early days on tour but they were there. And they were not like cracks in a vase that could be sealed with putty. These cracks were like a run in a stocking. They were only going to get bigger. They opened up the moment the team left for Sri Lanka minus Marsh and Lillee. 'That was very significant,' says Philpott. 'In the bonding period, they weren't there.'

Philpott planned to build unity through practice, then more practice. But the Sri Lankan leg was hectic. When time did allow for nets, it was too hot to move or too wet to try. Then they hit England. Philpott recalls:

For six weeks we sat in front of the fire and froze. And in that situation the unpleasantness tended to grow. The infection spread. It all made it harder for Kimberley, so much harder. I don't think he was up to handling it. Not many blokes would be. If they'd made Allan Border captain he would have been in much the same position. Rodney and Dennis wouldn't have been so anti-AB, but they wouldn't have supported him greatly because Rodney still would have thought he should have been captaining.

Marsh and Lillee departed eleven days late. Marsh's knees, creaking from years of bending, jolting and fetching, the wicketkeeper's daily lot, appreciated the rest. Lillee had a sinus-clearing operation and deemed Sri Lanka an infection risk. His strategy backfired. He sweated away his first three weeks in a north London hospital's isolation ward. Team-mates donned face masks to visit him. He'd picked up viral pneumonia on the journey with Marsh, or perhaps from his son, who had a chest cold. Either way, chances were his health would have been tiptop had he flown with everyone else, although everyone else probably didn't mention this to Lillee, not even from behind face masks.

Defying medical advice, Lillee played and bowled manfully. Exhausted, he lolled in the outfield between deliveries versus Middlesex. Some observers sensed a sit-down protest against Australia's underperforming batsmen. Admonished by Kim and manager Fred Bennett, Lillee's reply was true to character: 'Have you ever seen me let down Australia in a Test match?'

The bowlers had reason to quibble. Dirk Wellham's 135 at Northampton on 13 July was the first first-class hundred—two months into the tour. Not since 8 September 1880, and Billy Murdoch's 153 against England, had Australians found three figures so elusive so deep into an English summertime. Most dismaying was the captain's form. A 61 at Canterbury, where he drove Bob Woolmer over a refreshments tent, was his only fifty in twenty innings. On seaming wickets he was tiptoeing negligently across the crease and getting suckered lbw. At Lord's for the Second Test, he and Alan McGilvray discussed England's penurious off-spinner John Emburey.

'Watch this fellow, Kim.'

'He can't bowl. I'll take the mickey out of him.'

'Well, I think he can bowl a bit. I'd be wary of him if I were you.'

Square cutting the seamers thrillingly, Kim skipped to 42. Emburey limbered up. Whether his third ball was flat or tossed up no one truly knows, so prematurely did Kim scurry down, as if determined to shovel McGilvray a catch in the commentary box. He didn't middle it. Mid-off caught it.

So often it ended like this. First ball of a new spell. Two minutes before drinks. Third ball after lunch. Last over of the day. It happened too often to be slack concentration. Nor could it be so simple as the reverse: that he was concentrating too hard. It was as if he was twisting between extremes, him and them, between the urge to entertain and the need to consolidate, listening to his instincts but unable to hush the voices all around, believing the whole time that cricket should be a game, but if it was a game did that mean entertaining was the thing or was winning the thing, and when the tempo was raised by a break in play or change in bowling the buzzing in his head got so loud that something had to explode. It had always exasperated team-mates. Now he was captain and still doing it.

Wellham, more compact and elegant than his reputation for stickability suggested, was mooted as a possible twelfth man at Headingley, some promotion for a novice of four Sheffield Shield games. Two days beforehand he was bedridden with flu. Mooching around the nets would only make him sicker. So he left a message and snoozed all day. Upon stirring, Wellham found it had cost him his chance. 'I was a bit annoyed. I supposedly had a black mark. But I was new. They didn't know me so they didn't know whether I was sick or not. I guess nobody asked.'

More unsettling was the aftermath of the Lancashire game at Old Trafford. Wellham persevered through gloomy light—'the first time I saw Michael Holding in real life'—for 19. In the showers afterwards he felt the hot spray of his captain's urine. It was no big surprise. Wellham had been warned about Kim's shower-time habit after a few drinks of unburdening himself over the nearest bystander. But nor was it pleasant. 'Just schoolboy humour,' Wellham recalls. 'I wasn't thrilled. That's OK. It was a juvenile bit of fun. You know, a party trick. I thought it was silly but I thought he was a much better player than I was.'

The trick won Kim few laughs. 'Dennis and Rodney would have thought that was absolutely inappropriate,' says Wellham. 'They would have thought that was more ammunition.' Wellham's response was to stay under that shower and scrub himself clean. 'I thought it was a silly thing for the Australian captain to do. But that was Kim, part of his make-up, part of his reputation, a trick up the armoury.'

Winning has a cohesive effect on teams. Piddling issues drain away. In the Third Test at Headingley, on a wicket jagging every which way but predictably, John Dyson ranked his steadfast 102 the innings of his life. Kim batted four and a half hours, a man in a straitjacket, intent on showing neither extravagance nor weakness. On 89 he was clobbered in the groin. He afforded himself the briefest of convalescences—and got out next ball. He declared at 9–401. 'Four hundred,' said Kim, 'is worth a thousand on this pitch.'

England tumbled for 174. Following on, their seventh wicket fell for 135, lurching towards a 2–0 series scoreline. 'At seven down,' says Beard, 'Steve Rixon and I put the champagne bottles in the bath, ready to lay ice over them.'

●●●●●

ALL THINGS GOOD, UGLY and illusory about this Australian team were contained in Peter Willey's dismissal. Gradually, Kim became aware of Willey's delight in stepping away and skimming the ball over gully. Kim switched Dyson from the slips to a deeper fly slip. Lillee advanced. Willey cut. It was too close for the stroke; arms got tucked up; the ball soared. Dyson froze so still a butterfly could have landed on his shoe. The ball floated into Dyson's chest. 'Superb captaincy,' beamed Richie Benaud in the commentary box. 'One of the best pieces of tactical thinking I've seen in a long time.' England skipper Mike Brearley agreed. 'Such immediate rewards for intelligent and inventive captaincy,' he wrote, 'are rare.'

Benaud and Brearley were alert and astute but not in this instance all-seeing. They missed Lillee requesting a fly slip the moment Willey arrived. No, said Kim. The ball sailed where fly slip would have been. The protagonists mumbled their way through the same rough dialogue.

Can I have one?

You may not.

Sheesh. There it goes again.

The second time it happened, Lillee clamped hands on hips. Marsh wandered over to yarn with the captain. How about a fly slip? The captain gave in. Willey got out. The celebrations over, Kim and Lillee walked the long hike back to the top of his run-up. Never were they closer together than two metres. Both were silent. Kim crept backwards while polishing the ball on his pants. Lillee faced forwards. Neither looked in the same direction or at each other. Eventually Lillee half turned, still walking, and glared at the ball, implying 'give it here'. They reached the top. Kim shook Lillee's hand—a gesture Lillee did not invite or reciprocate—and passed him the ball.

Willey's downfall brought in Ian Botham, playing his first Test since Brearley succeeded him as captain. In his last outing, at Lord's, Botham slithered through the old white gate after a pair of noughts while MCC members all around him avoided eye contact. But the harried look in his face had vanished. He was bearded and carefree. He off-drove classically, edged a couple over fielders' heads, then welcomed incoming No. 9 Graham Dilley: 'Let's give it some humpty.'

Minutes before this, Lillee bet £10 on Australia losing. Ladbrokes' odds were 500–1. Only a mug would let those odds go cold. Marsh, initially reluctant, punted £5. 'That bloody bet. Had Greg been captain they'd never have done it,' believes Adrian McGregor, Chappell's biographer. 'Or if they did it would be a big joke and Greg wouldn't have been happy. He'd have thought it disloyal.'

Nobody thought much at all of it at the time. Nobody considered defeat possible. England were three wickets from despondency and 92 runs shy just of making Australia bat again. Botham had already checked out of the hotel. His swings, misses and top-edges began as defeatism and quickly became something else. Left-hander Dilley, blond-haired and blue-helmeted, clouted crooked deliveries through cover like a Graeme Pollock doppelganger. Botham was either driving majestically or pull-slogging flatfooted. One ball caught the splice and zoomed for the stratosphere. Kim jogged and fetched it, frowning, off a boy in a margarine anorak.

After Dilley came Chris Old. Old studied Lillee, Marsh, Alderman, Kim—'all signalling different fielders to go in different positions'. Botham stuffed England's tuckerbag with 117 runs in partnership with Dilley, then 67 more with Old. That evening, dapper stumper Bob Taylor ducked into the Australian rooms with bats under his arm for autographing. 'Fuck off with your fucking bats,' he was advised.

Irritation had set in. But not despair. At breakfast, Kim and the Sydney *Sun*'s Frank Crook discussed the inevitability of an Australian victory and the improbability of the board reappointing Greg Chappell. 'I don't think they'd dare,' said Kim. Botham ransacked 37 last runs with Willis. He bounded off—to a knighthood, ultimately—149 not out. Australian victory, no longer the only possibility, remained a formality: 130 to get.

The first over was busy. Wood clumped two leg-side boundaries and was judged caught behind when only the bowler appealed: 'A shocker. Must have hit some footmarks.' Dyson and Trevor Chappell travelled serenely to 1–56. Operating uphill and upbreeze, Willis threatened no one. 'Too old for that,' he griped to his captain. Brearley baulked at his uppity fast bowler. Five minutes later he reconsidered, offering Willis the wind and the Kirkstall Lane End.

A ball theoretically too full to endanger brain matter kicked at Chappell's head and he parried a catch to Taylor. Enter Kim, a picture of circumspection for eight scoreless deliveries, until he went fishing outside off and his feet forgot to go with him. It was the last over before lunch. The timing may have provoked wry half-smiles. Half-smiles soon tipped upside down. Graham Yallop guided Willis from his throat into short-leg Mike Gatting's meaty hands. 'I can remember the panic,' says Wellham, an interested spectator, suddenly unable to look away. 'The game had been light-hearted and jovial. Then we hit the wall and couldn't contain it. If you've got a more subdued leader, you've got a less attacking leader. But you might have someone better able to withstand the barrage.' Lunch was served—and barely picked over—at 4–58.

Border failed to impede a massive Old in-ducker. Dyson hooked and gloved. Marsh hooked from outside off stump and picked out long leg. There seemed an intangible aimlessness about the batting. Bright and Lillee pulled and slashed for four commonsense overs, worth 35 runs. Willis kept banging the ball in and seeing it jump. His reward was 8–43. Nine wickets melted for 55. Australia lost by 18. Nobody quite understood how. The haunting sensation was heightened by the sight of the flop-haired Willis, his eyes vacant and lifeless, hanging loosely in their sockets, like the imperilled damsel in a Mario Bava film.

So ended history's only Test known by a suburb and two digits: Headingley '81. Kim's errors have become legend, part of the mystique. Once Botham attained blast-off Kim was too slow to spot the tipping point, too gung-ho to retract his fieldsmen, too reluctant to rest Lillee or Alderman. Ray Bright dropped hints. Yet not until 8–309—174 runs later—did Kim summon Bright's slow left-armers. Trevor Chappell maintains he wasn't even consulted; it seems trying a part-timer either never entered Kim's head or fell out of it very quickly. Then there was his enforcing of the follow-on, sentencing Australia to bat last on an under-watered pitch. The theories have multiplied with hindsight.

All evidence suggests Kim did fret about batting last. After winning the toss he took ten minutes and two pitch inspections, accompanied by Marsh and Lillee, to make up his mind. The follow-on was simply irresistible. Bright was Victoria's last Test spinner until Shane Warne's emergence. But there, resemblances end. Bright's trajectory was generally flat, his turn measured less in inches than in figments of a batsman's imagination. Kim did overbowl Lillee and Alderman. But he'd been successfully overbowling them for two entire Tests and three-fifths of another. Besides, his only other frontline quick, Lawson, fell over a foothole and wrenched his back.

Blaming Kim for Headingley '81 underplays another significant factor. Luck. Botham's 149 might rightly be considered a once-every-130-years event. How his windmill wind-ups—those that connected, those that didn't—evaded hands and stumps so repeatedly defies rational explanation. 'Bloody lucky innings,' Lillee called it. 'I expected to get him virtually every ball.' England's turnaround was so fast, so implausible to the fieldsmen in the middle, that it became almost an hallucinatory experience, as if they were onlookers not participants. 'I still have nightmares about that Test,' Wood admits. 'All along we thought we'd win. So we didn't question it.' Too late, the faint prospect of defeat dawned. 'We started thinking we should have tried something different,' says Wood. 'But Kim probably thought Lillee and Alderman were having great tours and eventually Botham would nick one and get out. It just didn't happen. It kept rolling on and on and on. Horrible experience.'

Or as Lawson puts it: 'Twenty-seven years later people still ask me what would you do differently at Headingley? Well, apart from maybe giving Ray Bright a few more overs, what else could we have done?'

Kim reached the same conclusion in minutes. Outside the pavilion, his fine words were generously acclaimed by a delirious crowd. 'I'm proud the Australian team has been part of one of the greatest Tests of all. Of course I'm disappointed we didn't win. But we know we gave immense enjoyment.' Later, among reporters, good manners deserted him. 'We didn't do much wrong except lose.' And Botham? 'He is a player who wins games and the only one England have got.' That was skipping a little too conveniently over his own team's frailties, of both the cricket and the human kind.

•••••

WHEN PRINCE CHARLES married Diana Spencer on 29 July, Kim was not among the estimated billion watching a TV set. He had a tour to run. He glanced at the replay while unwinding in his eighth-floor room of the Albany Hotel in

Birmingham, scene of the Fourth Test. The match would prove the noisiest ever played in England, reckoned the home players, as if the wedding guests had decamped from St Paul's Cathedral and flocked to Edgbaston for the reception.

The cricket was worthy of the din. England were skittled for 189 and Australia responded with 258. Kim's boundary-laden 47 was top score. At England physio Bernard Thomas's garden party, he told Brearley: 'I only hope we don't have 130 to get again.' England stuttered obligingly to 8–167, 98 ahead. Then Emburey and Old, a nudger and a swiper, hoisted 50 more in one of the tour's most telling half-hours.

If Australia's chase of 130 at Headingley reeked of aimlessness, a touch of catatonia pervaded their pursuit of 151. Border camped three and a half hours for 40, Yallop two hours for 30, Kent 68 minutes for 10. Kim's hook stroke on 5—slammed flat and hard off one leg, his posture geometrically impeccable—summed up the man. 'Ah,' purred the BBC's Mike Smith, 'it's a beautiful shot.' Smith paused to admire the ball's flight. 'But straight down that man's throat. A beautiful-*looking* stroke . . .'

Botham's 5–1 in 28 deliveries applied the finishing gloss. Australia all out 121. Kim's kicked-puppy demeanour inspired one of Richie Benaud's shiniest lines: 'Hughes there, looking like he's just been sandbagged.' Bob Taylor likened him to 'a shellshocked soldier . . . Not for the first time I found myself wondering how much respect he was given by the former Packer players.'

While Kim grieved publicly, Marsh sought refuge alone in the downstairs dressing room. 'I don't recall the tears welling up inside,' Marsh wrote later. 'But suddenly I was sobbing.' As he sat and he wept, Marsh reflected on Australia's batsmen. Mostly he thought about Kim. 'I thought what might have happened if Hughes had not played a stupid hook shot when the Poms had two men stationed out in the deep. Christ, a captain is supposed to lead by example.'

Trailing 1–2 when he might have led 3–0, Kim finished that night dancing on a table at Bob Willis's benefit function. Resilience was one of Kim's less appreciated but undying characteristics. Memorable was his conversation with Brearley: 'I suppose me mum'll speak to me. Reckon me dad will too. And my wife. But who else?' Kim neither excused nor apologised for hooking. 'I'm a natural strokeplayer. That time it didn't come off.'

Brearley agreed with his logic. 'And I admired his dignity.'

Kim and Lillee were unlikely holidaymakers together on the Isle of Man, house guests of racehorse mogul Robert Sangster and his socialite wife Susan. It was a kaleidoscope of race meets and casino jaunts. The series resumed in Manchester with the Ashes alive, the spirit a cropper.

•••••

THE AFTERNOON BEFORE his Test debut, Mike Whitney was handed his room key at Manchester's Grand Hotel and told to settle in. Be back in the foyer in one hour for the press conference announcing your selection, team manager Fred Bennett instructed. Whitney went upstairs. He unlocked the door. Cricket gear was strewn everywhere. 'There were more pills in the room than a fuckin' pharmacy.' He wondered who his room-mate could be. Then he realised. In the corner was a suitcase, sumptuously crafted, adorned with the letters *D.K. Lillee*.

Whitney flopped on the bed. He could actually feel his own eyes bulging. 'Here he is. My hero. You've got to remember, back then Dennis was D.K. Lillee, man.' Several times that night, Whitney woke and snuck a peek at the sleeping body across the room. 'I've gotta be dreaming. Nup. There he is.'

Next day, Test match morning, Whitney couldn't see the other players anywhere. 'Where's the bus?'

'It's fuckin' gone,' said Lillee.

'You what?'

'Nah you're cool. You're with me.'

A mate of Lillee's drove them to Old Trafford. Whitney was wearing jeans and one of John Dyson's tracksuit tops. 'Who are you?' the gateman demanded.

'I'm playing. Mike Whitney.'

'Who?'

Getting in was Whitney's second biggest worry. His main thought was to find Kim, fast. Ascending the staircase, he elbowed past Geoff Boycott—'Cor, lad! Ah, young Whitney'— in his scramble to the visitors' dressing room. There was Kim.

'Oh, mate . . .'

Kim stopped him. 'You're with Dennis, aren't you?'

'Yeah.'

'That's no excuse. But if you think it's special, it's not. Dennis does this to every debutant on their first day.'

Whitney's story set him apart from other debutants. A left-arm quick with a broad chest and big heart, he grew up on Sydney's beaches and played for Randwick fourths in 1976. His progress was slow. A reputation for disappearing on the second weekend of grade games when the surf was up didn't help. You could almost see the sea-salt specks in his black curls. Plucked by New

South Wales after three-quarters of a season in first grade, Whitney took 11 wickets in four games and followed the sea to England, playing league cricket for the fishing village of Fleetwood.

His pace and late swerve won him a county call-up for Gloucestershire. Eight overs in a Sunday league game against Surrey changed his life. Whitney took 2–9. Watching on TV were the touring Australians, hobbled by injuries to Hogg, Lawson and first-choice replacement Rackemann. Three days later, Bennett rang. Whitney was on the balcony at Cheltenham, anxiously surveying the early overs against Hampshire. He dismissed the phone call as a scam: 'Listen man, Malcolm Marshall's hit two guys already and I've got to bat today.' He hung up.

Bennett tried again. 'Fred Bennett here, from Balmain club in Sydney.'

'Fred,' gasped Whitney. 'It *is* you.'

Whitney drove the hundred miles to Manchester. 'How ya going, Mr Hughes?'

'Call me Kim.'

'Call me Whit.'

He felt both starstruck and at home. Introduced in a bar to champion fast bowler John Snow, Whitney blurted: 'Hey, you're the bloke they threw beer cans at at the SCG. I was there.' Kim could not have helped more. Nor could Lillee. One night Lillee invited the self-described 'young punk fast bowler' to a party in Chelsea. 'There were chicks running around everywhere,' Whitney remembers. 'A lot of married couples as well. And the house was fantastic.'

Lillee asked the owner of the house if he knew the Kim Carnes song 'Bette Davis Eyes'. Lillee sang a bit to him: '*And*

she'll tease you; she'll unease you; all the better just to please ya . . .'
The guy knew the song well. In fact, he had the cassette tape in
the music room.

So Dennis and I walk through this door and into this
massive room. Big stereo. Tapes everywhere. Dennis puts
the tape in, turns it up, the guy flicks a few switches and
suddenly it's all through the house. *Bette Davis eyes. Da-da-
da-da-da-da-da.* Dennis was dancing on his own. For me,
coming from Matraville, the son of a truck driver and a
mother who never had a pair of shoes till she was twelve—
she came from a real poor family in Paddington—this was
outrageous.

Whitney witnessed strange on-field occurrences too. He'd
see Kim make a field change and Marsh shake his head for
several seconds before letting out a big sigh. 'That's heavy shit
on the field,' says Whitney. 'It's like, oh, hang on, Rodney
doesn't agree.' Once the field was set, Marsh would sometimes
whistle—'and move the guy back five metres. Now, that's
completely usurping the captain's authority.'

Whitney would watch Kim attempt to give Lillee a breather.
Lillee would fume. 'I can just imagine Dennis: *Fuck that, I'm
not going off. I'll get a fuckin' wicket here. Gimme back the ball.'*
Whitney would be dumbfounded. 'Is that Dennis saying:
*You can't tell me when to stop. I don't care who the fuck you are.
I'm D.K.?'*

Whitney slanted one across Botham to have him
caught behind. It was his third Test wicket. It felt like a big
one, putting a cork in the run rate and keeping Australia's

chances afloat. Marsh caught it, lifted one hand in gentle appeal, saw the umpire's finger rise and then frowned, flicking the ball from glove to glove, not a ghost of a smile. Whitney recalls:

I'm running down the wicket going 'Yessss!' Then I've realised there's no joyous celebration. And so I've just sort of walked back to my mark. Man, what went on there? Botham was carving us up and I got him out. I thought I'd get a pat on the back. I don't know why Rodney did that. I don't know whether he told Kim 'don't take the second new ball', or 'we should have a different field'. But I remember he took the catch and stood there with his hands on his hips. Amazing. I'll never forget it. I thought I'd done something wrong. I really did.

Whitney's Test call-up startled others besides him. 'Graeme Beard must have felt snubbed to be passed over,' wrote Brearley in *Phoenix from the Ashes*. Actually, Beard felt no such injustice. He'd been trundling off-breaks since Colombo. Australia needed a firebrand. 'If Dyso and Woody got a couple of broken fingers,' he points out, 'they wouldn't have said: "Let's put Beardy in to open".'

Beard never added to his three Tests and two limited-overs internationals. His lower-order brio and frugal, multi-pronged bowling might nearly have made him a half-the-horsepower Andrew Symonds prototype. Except: 'I didn't like playing one-day cricket.' He felt uncomfortable equating dot balls with good balls. Bowling against New Zealand in the 1980–81 one-day finals, he fizzed down a leg-cutter, elicited an outside edge and watched it roll for four. 'Jeez,' thought Beard. 'That's not a good delivery at all.'

His last ball in international cricket was Trevor Chappell's underarm to Brian McKechnie at the MCG. 'That was worse than Headingley,' says Beard. 'It really wasn't in the best cricketing spirit.' Beard was on the square-leg fence. Had he been bowling, he suspects he'd have lacked the chutzpah to refuse Greg Chappell's underarm request. 'I think Greg was astute enough not to ask somebody he thought wouldn't do it.'

Six months after the 1981 Ashes tour, Beard retired. He was thirty-one. He'd started at New South Wales on $12 a day and always relied on a schoolteacher's wage. But he never pictured himself in the classroom at forty. He contacted Frank Mitchell, general secretary of the Australian Workers' Union and father-in-law of cricket writer Jim Woodward. 'I didn't have an industrial background,' says Beard. 'I went along purely for the experience of a job interview, expecting they wanted a Labor Party member.'

But Mitchell said: 'I know about you. We'll give you six months—and if you like it, fine.'

The other thing Mitchell said was: 'I can't give you time off for first-class cricket.'

It was only out of courtesy to his wife that Beard didn't say yes on the spot. The job was national industrial officer in the Sydney office. He's still there today. 'A fellow who had been there twelve years said he woke up each morning and wondered what was on his desk. That appealed to me.' In the following two seasons the first-class careers of three friends—Ian Davis, Peter Toohey, Trevor Chappell—wound down prematurely and unceremoniously. Beard felt glad he'd got out. He remains grateful to have played in the era he did. For today's cricketers the game is a job, with the choices, commitment and risk that entails. 'These days,' says Beard, 'I wouldn't have had enough confidence in my cricket ability to have taken the punt.'

After farewelling the people he had known fleetingly as Test team-mates, Mike Whitney returned to Fleetwood. 'Welcome home, Mike!' trumpeted a banner across the village's main road. Years later, a member of Allan Border's triumphant Australian sides, he finally felt able to see the 1981 tour in perspective. It was his most amazing adventure. It was also 'the maximum lack of respect to the Australian captain. Rod and Dennis gave Kim no support at all . . . Looking back now, he was under enormous pressure, getting squeezed from all angles.'

In a career spanning a dozen years and 118 first-class matches, Whitney was never late again. 'Never late for training, never missed a plane, never missed a bus, never missed a warm-up session. Because I didn't think it was the right thing. The only time I did it I was with my hero on my first day of Test cricket.'

•••••

CATATONIA TURNED TO RECKLESSNESS in that Fifth Test. Kim's three-ball innings set the pattern. First he played and missed. Next he blasted over Willis's head for four. Third ball he shuffled indeterminately in the vicinity of an off-cutter and was lbw. The modest seam trio of Willis, Botham and Paul Allott tweezered Australia out for 130—that number again—in 30.2 overs.

Dual punishment followed: the cane from Botham, blitzing 118 in two hours, and Chinese water torture in the shape of Chris Tavare, whose 78 occupied seven. Fans grateful for past miracles granted Botham a standing ovation to the wicket, little realising his masterwork was nigh. Three singles decorated his first thirty deliveries. He strolled to 28 off 53. Kim called up the second new ball. And, as Brearley phrased it, the sky was Botham's target not limit.

Going from 28 to 100 took 33 balls. As an echo of his Headingley humdinger, it lacked only the element of chance. Two blind hooks were possibly unique. Confronted by perfect Lillee bouncers, Botham swivelled to hook then ducked late, eyes to the ground, but carried through with the shot anyway. Twice fine-leg Whitney thought the ball struck Botham's unhelmeted head. Twice the ball bounced off Botham's bat—a paddlepop stick compared with today's superspringy megawillow—and into the crowd. The bowling was nearly as culpable as the batting was breathtaking. Lillee and Alderman, as at Headingley, erred wide of off stump. The space liberated Botham. Scorer Wendy Wimbush's wagonwheel pencilled a picture. Other than one swept and three hooked sixes, Botham's leg-side scoring strokes amounted to three singles and a two.

Set 506, Australia mustered 402. The unlosable Ashes were lost. Awaiting his second innings, Kim sat on the balcony, pads on, not watching openers Dyson and Wood. He was reading the Screws—*News of the World*—shrouded in newspaper. Just visible over the top were his green cap and right index finger. The finger drilled hard into his temple.

There was little point feigning comradeship now. One clique, the World Series Cricket camp, tended to drink in one corner. Kim and others drank in another. A few floaters drifted in between. Wellham found Kim chatty and helpful but tried not to talk to incoming or outgoing batsmen. During one moribund run chase, it was suggested the batsmen should bat carefully—anathema to Wellham, who'd been educated to play balls on their merits. 'I was told to shut up, to get back in my box,' Wellham recalls. 'That was by AB.'

At Edgbaston, Yallop's arrival provoked three Willis bouncers. Kim announced, 'I'll take Willis,' and shepherded the strike. 'Just Kim being his usual confident self,' says Lawson. He did not want to lose a wicket. He considered Yallop vulnerable. So he turned his back on clear-cut singles. Willis tore through the creaseline unleashing deliberate no-balls at Kim's skull instead. Kim slapped him through gully and snicked him between slips, clapping hands mockingly, and screeching at himself: '*Concentrate.*'

Yallop was first off at lunchtime, humiliated and furious. And not alone. As Wellham recalled the dressing-room scene when Kim ambled in: 'Lillee and Marsh were threatening mutiny . . . I had always felt the Australian team was one for all and all for one. The latter part of that phrase seemed to be more appropriate than the first.'

Willis was not the only fast bowler hunting Kim. 'In the nets,' says Lawson, 'Dennis would bowl bouncer after bouncer at Kim on dodgy practice wickets.' As the tour unravelled, the bouncers increased. Lawson's bewilderment grew:

If it was once he might be doing it for a good cricket reason. But it happened a number of times in '81. I don't think it happened every time. But often. Often Dennis would wait to see which net Kim was going to bat in and then go and bowl at him. He might have been bowling line and length at Border. Then Kim would come in and it would be a different kettle of fish. It was pointed and obvious and I don't think it served much purpose. It didn't serve any positive purpose for Kim. And the team certainly didn't think it was very positive. But no one was going to say: 'Dennis, you shouldn't do that.' Because he was Dennis. He did what he wanted. The person who should have stopped Dennis was Rod. And he didn't do it.

The run in the stocking was a gaping tear.

•••••

IN A DIVIDED cricket team, responsibility for fixing the divisions falls on the captain. If the captain is raw and himself the prime target of the divisions, then the senior players might do something. If the most senior duo happens to be chief instigator of the divisions, then the coach usually intervenes. But Peter Philpott had his own traumas.

For starters, he was not called 'coach'. His job should have been prestigious: the first appointed coach of an Australian touring party. Yet his title was 'cricket manager', or sometimes 'assistant manager'. New South Wales players admired the way cricket's spirit, technicalities and arcane charms roamed Philpott's veins. Western Australians were split between those who reckoned a coach had four wheels, not two legs, and those who expected him to come from the state where real men resided. 'The West Australians were very unhappy,' says

Lawson. 'All of them. Their view was, we win the Shield every year, we should have Daryl Foster.'

An effervescent exponent of and crusader for the slumbering art of leg-spin, 'Percy' Philpott played eight Tests in the mid-sixties. Since 1978–79 he'd coached New South Wales. During the New Year's Test against India, Greg Chappell invited him backstage and suggested he apply for the Ashes tour. They chatted for hours. Philpott felt torn. He was a happy housemaster, cricket coach, rugby coach, English and history teacher at the King's School in Parramatta. But he was not one to decline opportunities—especially when cricket called.

He'd lived life fast since he was four. That was when rheumatic fever left him with a damaged aortic valve and doctors fearful he wouldn't live past thirty-five. Philpott says: 'It was like I was trying to stack two lives into my first thirty-five years, to get my full life finished before I went.' This urgency partly explains, he believes, the open heart surgery he underwent in 1980, aged forty-six. He'd bounced back since then. Of course he told Chappell yes. He went to the headmaster and arranged leave without pay.

Two things happened next. Chappell chose to stay home: a blow, because although Philpott rated Kim a gorgeous batsman they barely knew one another. Then, two weeks before departure, the board decided Fred Bennett and Philpott should share a player's salary. 'Instead of earning $16,000,' says Philpott, 'it was $8000'—a squeeze for a family man heading abroad for four months. 'Had it not been so late I would have made myself unavailable.' But school leave had been sorted. And there was England, an Ashes summer, cricket to look forward to.

His first conversation with Kim occurred on the plane.

Differences soon emerged. Philpott felt Chappell craved a coach in all but title: a confidant, a strategic and technical adviser, a practice mastermind. Kim seemed to want a managerial dogsbody. When Kim glued Lillee to one bowling end and Alderman to the other, Philpott warned a captain must treat his bowlers like precious trinkets to extract their best. 'Very early in the piece I'd say Bright, Hogg, Lawson and Beard felt unwanted. Poor old Dennis at times couldn't stand up. It wasn't an attack at all. It was two bowlers.' Kim would listen politely and do nothing.

On the team bus one night a chant started up. '*Perr-cy's a tourist, Perr-cy's a tourist, Perr-cy's a tourist.*' Whitney was one who didn't join in. 'I couldn't work out why they were calling him a tourist. I was like, well, I'm a tourist too. I'm in England. On tour.' Philpott, it emerged, had taken his mum and fiancee to Ireland for a week's break. Some players were half-joking, Philpott thinks. 'But there would have been a couple who were being nasty. I was too well aware by then of what was happening to get myself upset about that. I felt terribly disappointed and sorry. It was all such a sorry mess.'

Kim, he felt certain, wanted Daryl Foster, coach of Western Australia. They'd worked together since Kim was sixteen. Philpott suspected Alderman and Wood were Foster men too. Wood thrived on hard physical work. Philpott was a non-believer in sand-dune sprints and cross-country shows of endurance. 'A lot of fitness-oriented coaches I see are covering up a lack of technical knowledge of the game,' he says.

Animosity revolved around states' rights more than coaching wrongs. The seventeen-man squad included five West Australians and seven New South Welshmen if you counted latecomer Whitney. Philpott, manager Bennett and scorer Dave Sherwood added up to five against ten. Yet WA had won six of the last ten Sheffield Shields, New South Wales none. Secede or get nasty is the dilemma millions of Western Australians, believing themselves rich in gold and minerals but poor in legislative clout, have confronted since European settlement in 1829. In 1981 Western Australia's cricketers, some of them, got nasty.

'Oh dear,' says Foster. 'That's the first I have ever heard of that. Honestly. I always accepted that I would never ever coach Australia.' It is a job he would have cherished, he says, and one to which he aspired. 'But quietly, within myself, without ever overtly promoting myself. It would have been lovely.' Foster is serious, soft-spoken, dazzlingly successful and has never had one conversation with a single person of influence about the Australian coaching job. He knows why. He'd been hearing why his whole career. One wintertime he offered to help opener Bruce Laird devise ways of rotating the strike against the West Indian quicks.

'Stumpy,' said Foster, 'why don't you learn to cut? I reckon it's one or four runs every time against these guys.'

And Laird replied, in the nicest possible way: 'Foss, how many Tests did you play?'

Philpott did not feel hurt that certain players preferred Foster. What hurt was that when Foster missed out they did not get behind the man in the job. It was a replica of the captaincy shambles. Once Marsh wasn't named captain he and Lillee could have backed Kim doubly loyally, lest anyone accuse them of putting a grudge ahead of Australian cricket's best interests. Instead, feels Philpott: 'They weren't disappointed at

Kim failing.' And they weren't shy about letting their lack of disappointment show. 'I don't think they set out to destroy him. Basically, they just did. When things were going bad he needed their support and there was no active attempt to help the boy.'

Philpott felt powerless. He had no rapport with Kim and no agreement about his own job description. He set up practice nets, monitored warm-ups, assisted individuals who asked. He wishes now that he'd said to Kim: let me help you. He wishes he'd sat Lillee and Marsh down and threatened to drop them from the team. He thought nobody would listen. He wishes he'd more quickly overcome his disappointment about Chappell not touring. He wishes Kim had been willing to embrace him.

> In the long run I was able to walk away and go back to teaching. Kimberley couldn't. Kim had a cricket career which he couldn't just walk away from. All the divisions and nastiness . . . He must have been hurt, must have been hurt, if he was able to recognise what was happening. I've always prided myself on bringing sides together and making them happy. This was the only time I didn't feel that happen. And I'm talking about hundreds of teams in cricket and rugby where you all suffer together and laugh together and enjoy it together. It was the only time I haven't felt totally at home and part of a team. And I still don't bloody know what I could have done about it.

Apparently oblivious to all of this was Fred Bennett. At tour's end he congratulated Philpott on a job well done. 'You available for the next one?' he asked.

'Whaddya mean, Freddy?' Philpott replied. 'Is the board offering me a contract?'

'No. You'd have to apply tour by tour.'

That settled it in Philpott's mind: 'The board had no bloody idea. *No* idea.' Didn't they realise he had a living to make?

'Oh no,' said Philpott. 'No way. Go away. Never again.'

•••••

BETWEEN THEIR BLUSTER about giving one hundred per cent, cricketers regale us with the wonders that abound once they 'cross the line'. 'When we got on the field,' says Lawson, 'when we crossed the line, my memory is there was nothing negative. I wouldn't put losing down to the dynamic between Dennis, Kim and Rod. I put it down to Beefy Botham playing well and the cricket gods being on England's side.'

Had effort rate been invented, Lillee and Marsh might nearly have topped the tables. Lillee uprooted thirty-nine batsmen in six Tests despite snuffling, wheezing and nipping off for more changes of clothes than a pop diva. Marsh's 23 catches propelled him past Alan Knott's world wicketkeeping record. We delivered our hundred, they can comfort each other in old age. Page 311 of the relevant *Wisden* says so.

Camaraderie, trust, empathy, mutual respect, good humour and desire to see your team-mates succeed are not recorded in scorebooks. What does it cost a side if these elements are missing? A hundred runs? Fifty? Thirty would have been enough to overturn the Headingley and Edgbaston defeats. Conqueror of the Poms: that could have been Kim. Is not being disappointed when the captain fails, as Philpott alleges of Lillee and Marsh, the same as being happy, even subconsciously happy, to see the team struggle? Rob Steen and Alastair McLellan touched on this in their book *500–1: The Miracle of Headingley '81*. 'Might it possibly be,' they asked, 'that heads made promises hearts were unable to keep?'

Intriguing questions, ones that the pair whose reputations have furthest to sink may never countenance. Upon his confetti-free 1987 comeback to cricket, Lillee consented to TV interviews on two conditions: no questions about a possible Test return, and none about you know who. Lillee's reticence remains undimmed. 'I have spoken to Kim Hughes regarding your book. As it is unauthorised, I am unable to help out.' Marsh's reply arrived a day earlier—oddly, as if the two of them had conferred. 'Thank you for the invitation to participate in your venture,' wrote Marsh. 'I have no desire to do so but wish you luck.'

All we can do is listen to those who were there. Even to many who weren't, something rotten and malignant inside this Australian team was apparent. Leg-spinner Tony Mann, always chipper, and fond of Kim, Lillee and Marsh, followed the series at home in Perth's Swan Valley. 'It happened because they weren't all there with one aim in mind,' says Mann. 'Obviously I'm about tenth-hand on this. But it was almost as if they said: "Oh well, Kim's had his day and we won't support him and we'll get rid of him."' Philpott has no doubt that issues only loosely connected to cricket helped lose Australia the Ashes. 'The divisions? Oh yes. Particularly after Headingley. I've never seen an Australian side drop its bundle like they did. Our body language went down the bloody hill.'

Returns dollied rather than slung into the keeper's gloves; players leaving a bar as others entered; Marsh's frown when Botham got out. Little things had a seeping effect. 'The team has to function as one unit, otherwise energies are lost out the side door,' says Whitney. 'Even off the field those things damage you. It's a mental game. If you've got things wavering through your head that aren't plain and succinct—this is how we're going, this is what we're doing—then the team starts to go through the motions.'

We are still in the fields of the subconscious here. On the fields of play, nobody suggests Lillee and Marsh did other than bustle and sweat. Even so, certain curiosities stick out. The TV commentators thought Lillee's Headingley line of attack—one foot outside Botham's off stump—peculiar. They were mystified when he repeated the tactic at Old Trafford. Alec Bedser, England selector and a plonk-it-on-a-sixpence medium pacer himself, remarked: 'Lillee bowled like an idiot to Dilley and allowed him to get fifty. It makes me wonder about Lillee. Why did he keep bowling outside the off stump?' Dilley wondered likewise, before deciding his Englishman's inferiority complex was playing tricks on him.

Marsh's kamikaze contributions to Australia's two shambolic run chases are worth recording. He made 4 both times. At Headingley he was caught hooking from outside off stump. At Edgbaston he heaved across the line and missed an inswinger, also from outside off, forty minutes before weeping tears over the captain's 'stupid hook shot'. No one thinks Marsh got out intentionally. Acts of wantonness routinely scarred his batting around this period. But could Marsh and Lillee's failings in Australia's hours of greatest tumult have been unwittingly connected to their lack of disappointment at seeing Kim Hughes go belly up?

Their 500–1 wager muddies matters. It reflected nothing more sinister than temptation, naivety and disrespect for the captain. Lillee has promised he did not bowl to lose and pledged to 'flatten anyone' who says he did. He has rightly explained that had he known Australia's fate he would not have bet ten quid. He'd have bet his house. His first thought, as it happens, was to bet £100, but team-mates talked him down, and in 1981 a £100 bet, for a £50,000 profit, would indeed have got him a house, a big one, with Indian Ocean views.

A draw at The Oval ended the series, Kim's batting travails turning vaudevillian. First he trod softly enough on his stumps to run three before realising he was out. In the second innings both the timing (last over before stumps) and mode of dismissal (lbw for the seventh time in the series) seemed apt. 'Getting out lbw is an easy fault to rectify,' he'd chirped beforehand. Consistent only in his inconsistency, Kim collected single and double-figure scores in every Test—7 and 22, 42 and 4, 89 and 0, 47 and 5, 4 and 43, 31 and 6—a prank matched only by South Africa's Russell Endean in series of five games or more.

Englishman Alan Ross, connoisseur of Baudelaire and batsmanship, concluded: 'Boyish and unassertive as captain he was never dull; the Australian batting sometimes was, largely because he was rarely there long enough to put a proper gloss on it.' Back home, Greg Chappell savoured family time and rounds of golf at Indooroopilly and Royal Queensland. During tense periods in the cricket he paced the house as he watched on TV. Chappell told Adrian McGregor he consulted 'Rod, Dennis and other England tourists' about the captaincy. Their verdict 'was universal'. They allegedly said: 'For God's sake take it. If you'd seen what happened in England. Don't bail out on us.' It's a version of history which Lawson disputes:

I certainly didn't say that to Greg, I can assure you. I mean, Greg wasn't a very warm kind of person and you didn't confide in him. Maybe Rod and Dennis did because they were all mates from the seventies, but I can't believe anyone else in that team would do that. They would not go to Greg and say: 'We don't like Kim Hughes as captain.' I find that incredibly hard to believe.

One final chore beckoned before everyone could go home. A day–night game was scheduled on a synthetic pitch under cheapskate floodlights at a football field, Cheltenham's Prince of Wales Stadium. It was a 40-overs-a-side ghost match, ignored by most newspapers, granted not one word in *Wisden*, with only a couple of internet scorecard relics to say it ever happened. The Australians wished it wasn't happening. The pseudo-lights were suitable for a drive-in, not cricket. Wellham, a debut centurion at The Oval, took the field, annoyed, with a pulled leg muscle. 'When I said I couldn't play my word wasn't valued because I was a junior.' Australia got rolled in 24.4 overs and Gloucestershire won easily.

Exactly what happened afterwards remains hazy. This much seems certain: Kim and Lillee had a disagreement. They wrestled each other. They came close to hitting each other. And Kim walked back to the team hotel in his underpants. Wood's recollection is that 'Dennis went to the bar and fuelled up' before his turn to bat—which may have angered Kim. Alternatively, Lillee may have been the angry one after Kim won the toss and elected to bat last in semi-darkness. Or maybe it was simply the end of a long tour.

Lillee appears to refer obliquely to the incident in his book *My Life in Cricket*. But, for reasons unknown, he says it happened after the Fourth Test and consisted of a 'mess-around all-in wrestle' between several players. He makes no mention of his own involvement. He lends a jocular air to proceedings. It was 'quite humorous' and 'a funny day'. The way Lawson tells it:

> The plane was going that night and we all went for a drink. Kim and Dennis tore the clothes off each other in a public bar. It was bizarre. It was quite physical, yet no one hit anyone. They just tore the clothes off each other, tore their shirts off, and Kim walked two hundred yards to the Waldorf Hotel in his jocks. We were all thinking, well, these West Australians are funny people. It was really Kim saying to Dennis: 'I don't care what you do to me—I'm going to do it back to you.' It wasn't necessarily a cricket thing. It was a maintain-your-ego, maintain-your-status, look-after-your-self-esteem thing. They did a bit of wrestling but they didn't throw any punches. They didn't do anything really nasty. It was incredible really. The red mist came down and they just tore each other's clothes off.

Wood's recollection differs only in that, the way he remembers it, Kim and Lillee were screaming at each other. 'We were laughing at the start,' says Wood. 'But in the end it wasn't too pretty.'

It was the story of the tour.

TWO

Rare Thing

TWO TEACHERS SAT in Geraldton's Queens Hotel on a Friday afternoon in 1964 for one of their regular after-school meetings. Rudy Rybarczyk, of Allendale Primary, was telling Bob Bryant, of Geraldton Primary, about Kim Hughes. This boy was new in town and ten years old, so undergrown that the knee rolls of his cricket pads came up to his thighs and his box toppled out of his shorts. Not that he needed protective equipment. He barely seemed to own a defensive repertoire. This boy Kim swung ominously from the beginning, balls cannoning off a blade fifteen centimetres too long for him. He played that way for fun, not to dominate, bringing others in, cheering them on, making sure everyone got a hit. One lunchtime he bowled to the supervising teacher: a short ball, a foot outside off. The teacher reached out and flicked it past square leg.

'Mr Rybarczyk, when a ball is that wide outside the off stump you do not pull it behind square.'

'But I hit it for four, Kim.'

'Well, you won't hit the next one for four.'

Lunchboxes were emptied and play began swiftly most days. Allendale could not afford cricket nets. Children played on the school oval's concrete pitch. For Friday sport a couple of coir mats—luxury—got rolled out. Allendale and Geraldton Primary were renowned on-field enemies and Bob listened half-believingly to Rudy's stories at the pub. This boy will represent Western Australia before he turns twenty-one, said Rybarczyk. They bet a carton of Swan Lager on it.

Kim Hughes was born on 26 January 1954 and the symbolism of this stayed with him. A proud Australian, born on Australia Day, he'd say again and again. He wore wristbands the colour of wattle blossom in his first full Test series. He beseeched the entire team to sport baggy green caps in Antigua in 1984. That brainwave was cottoned on to by Allan Border years later and became official policy under Mark Taylor and Steve Waugh. Waugh felt it lifted his men's spirits and 'gave us an aura'; Kim's men lost by an innings and floppy sunhats were making a comeback by Jamaica. When Alan Bond's *Australia II* won the America's Cup—'the greatest day of my life'—Kim drank more than he intended over lunch, bought miniature flags on the way home and sat down in front of two replays of the race. His two-year-old twins, Simon and Sean, sang as he watched: 'Good onya Bondy, good onya Bondy.'

Stan and Ruth Hughes arrived as newlyweds in Kudardup, home of 161 people and a one-teacher school. Stan was the teacher. Enlightening two dozen students of various sizes across seven grades in the intricacies of the universe must have been worrisome. Stan handled it with jolliness and a soft touch, though he'd sometimes cane the boys. 'He tapped me on the hand once with a ruler,' remembers Julia Matthews, who was nine, 'and I dissolved into heaps of tears. Because he touched me in anger. And because we all adored him.'

Thirty-six kilometres away at Margaret River, the nearest hospital, Ruth gave birth to Kimmy, as everyone in Kudardup knew him. He was their first child, although Ruth was soon seen as a kind of second mum to Stan's students. She brought in milk and cocoa. When Stan took the boys for craft sessions, she taught the girls sewing. Lessons were usually held in the poky schoolroom, Ruth wheeling Kimmy across in his pram, the girls cuddling him and changing his nappy while mum wielded knitting needles. Other times they'd go to the Hughes family's little house, a minute's walk away, and gasbag with Kimmy in the middle.

About 250 tumbledown one- or two-teacher schools flecked Western Australia's miles of orange dirt. These schools fostered an intimacy treasured at the time and long since withered. Big children watched over little ones. Girls learned to dance with their fathers. Everybody went out together. In Kudardup they'd hold cabaret nights, six or eight to a table, all bringing their own food. They'd sway to Frank Wake's band—a piano, a violin, a saxophone—in nearby Karridale, at the old timber dance hall, later wrecked in the 1961 bushfires. 'To dance on that floor was like dancing on ice,' remembers family friend George 'Pud' Challis. 'A beautiful, beautiful floor to dance on.'

Stan was king and court jester of that dancefloor. 'Harmony Hughes', they called him. He liked to dance, party and smoke, even if he rarely seemed to buy his own. 'George, my boy, have you got a smoke on you?' was his standard greeting to Pud Challis. Stan was fond of a drink, too. 'On Monday mornings we used to love it,' says Julia's cousin Yvonne, 'because Sunday was football day and Stan did the football. And of course he was feeling so hungover on Monday morning that we always got to do nature walks. We'd take off all day in the bush. He was a fabulous teacher.'

Coach, captain and centre half-forward at Karridale, Stan was enjoying a sizzling streak: four flags in six seasons in assorted country competitions. Long before that he played forty games for Subiaco, an emergency selection in 1942 when poliomyelitis left giant-leaping regular forward John Hetherington a paraplegic. War enlistments restricted the Western Australian National Football League to under-18s. Stan was sixteen, a schoolboy tennis champ and cricketer at Wesley College—and a virtual one-man forward line. Picked for Subiaco's last five games that season, he booted 25 goals while everyone else managed 21 between them. It was enough to colour in his son's daydreams. From the instant he could kick, hit or throw, Kim's heroes were footballers.

Two young brothers for playmates, Don and Glenn, were soon followed by sisters Robyn and Christeen. One-teacher school families led lives enriching but transient. Teachers got moved on every two or three years, the Hugheses hopscotching their way round the state's south-west triangle, from Kudardup to Ballidu to Pinjarra and finally Geraldton. The tiny school at Ballidu, where streets were named after varieties of wheat, had chewed up something like eleven teachers in a rush. Pud Challis remembers Stan telling him two troublemaking brothers were to blame. On Stan's first morning he was sitting at his desk. One brother rose unannounced, sauntered towards the window, then turned to his classmates and winked. It was a silent pact to break the new guy.

Stan's response was surefooted. He hauled both brothers away. He tossed off his jacket. He said he'd show them who was boss of Ballidu Primary School. 'And George, my boy,' he told Challis, 'I gave those pair the biggest thrashin' they ever had. After that I never had one iota of trouble.' Years later a motorbike pulled up outside the Hugheses' Pinjarra home: the same two lads, grown up and clean-cut. They had come to thank him. Getting belted by Stan Hughes, they said, was the luckiest break of their lives.

Kim's footballing passions were by then booming and twofold. He barracked for Subi and pretended to be Austin Robertson, their deadeye drop-punter. It mattered not that Subiaco's last premiership was in 1924 or that Robertson kicked with his right foot, Kim with his left. Technique wasn't what made Kim swoon. It was Robertson's charisma, his main-man status at Subiaco. When Kim was eight Robertson headed the WANFL's goalkicking charts, a feat he'd repeat seven times in ten seasons. Kim stitched the number 16—Robertson's number—on the back of his jumper. 'I just wanted to be Robertson . . . Robertson was my hero.'

Football was not the only thing going on in Kim's head. When he was nine he rode the streets of Pinjarra on his bicycle, a packed lunch on his back, collecting recyclable bottles. He stopped when he had enough money for his first bat: two pounds, ten shillings. It was a Bradman-autographed Slazenger. He wouldn't let anyone else use it. He would oil it then pinprick it so that the oil oozed right in. He took this task seriously. He was determined to make the bat last.

•••••

LETTER WRITERS to the *Geraldton Guardian* made childhood sound a desolate existence in a wheat-growing, sheep-farming, mineral-rich port city of twelve thousand. So many hooligans, so few playgrounds. No bowling alley, no skating rink, no modern theatre. Just socials and dances—hick ones, and not to everybody's taste. 'Most teenage girls have illegitimate children through having nothing to do,' speculated one correspondent. Boys, when not knocking up girls, hit balls on streets. That meant trampled gardens, snapped wires, shattered windows and the mind-twisting banging of balls on walls, a curse of modern mothers who in going to work had lost grip on their sons. One gentleman motorist calling himself 'Hard Luck on Cricket' despaired: 'Only this week I had to dodge the "stumps"—two petrol drums in the street—and then the ball hit the windscreen. Luckily it was a tennis ball . . . Is there not a law about playing cricket?'

More irritating than cricket on Geraldton's streets was Aboriginal children pissing on them, the subject of a 1965 report to the town council. Mr W. Gillam, senior health inspector, found: 'This is an age-old problem and one of the main causes of complaint by all people interested in the assimilation of colored persons into modern white society. There does not appear to be a ready solution and until the native himself is made to understand and obey the white man's laws, there is little chance of him enforcing the same law on to his children.' One unusual aspect of this report was that the *Guardian* mentioned it. 'Coloreds' or 'natives' were seldom portrayed in the life of the town. When they were, they were social nuisances or fluffy nonentities. A December 1966 headline—'Happy Time for Colored Folk Last Monday'—was typical.

The letter writers obsessed with bored youth were almost certainly fuddy-duddies, their corrugated brows not to be taken seriously. Randolph Stow, poet and novelist, was born in Geraldton in 1935 and went to Geraldton Primary. A salty wonder infuses his descriptions of childhood. Seashells, sandalwood, sunflowers, ant-orchids, surfboards, gulls, sand-hills—'and brief subtle things that a child does not realise, horses and porpoises, aloes and clematis'. In *Sea Children*, a poem about Geraldton, Stow wrote:

> For the children the sea was deeper, and the dive
> longer, the things to be found in the tangled weed
> richer and stranger: coral, writhing, alive;
> a hairclip formed like a bow, or a coloured bead
> —rare things . . .

For the Hughes children, arriving for the 1964 school year, newfangled curiosities were on offer too. 'The Wild One'—Johnny O'Keefe—defied a sore throat to pack out the Radio Theatre for Geraldton's inaugural rock concert. Locals stamped feet to 'Shout' and scratched heads at the abrupt finale, 'Advance Australia Fair' starting up as O'Keefe fled the stage. 6GE disc jockey Warren Kalajzich was plotting his successful assault on the national continuous announcing record: sixty and a quarter hours. The annual Sunshine Festival entered its sixth year, a log-cutting competition and sheepdog exhibition among the attractions.

Stan's new job was a big one—headmaster at Allendale, with a full roll-call of teachers—but not so lucrative that the father of a young family could relax on weekends. One mother, new to town, warmed to the gentle, funny man, a roll-up ciggie spinning somersaults out the corner of his mouth, who shifted her family's furniture from the back of a truck. She was startled on Monday morning to discover that the moonlighting furniture removalist was headmaster at her children's new school.

Breadwinning aside, sport came first, second and third in the Hughes household. Chasing golf balls was the limit of Stan's on-field exploits. But the passion of his speeches, hair aflutter, cigarette ablaze, rallied fans, children and bemused passers-by round three-quarter-time huddles at Brigades, the football club he coached. Stan was a thinker, not a ranter, with a vision that went beyond humping the ball long and a measured yet quietly insistent manner of asserting himself. He coached the town's representative side, unbeaten all season. Not to be outdone, Ruth shone at tennis and was women's champion at Geraldton Golf Club. Before bedtime, Kim and the little ones would help get mum ready. 'They'd all polish her shoes,' remembers Marianne Murray, Year 1 teacher at Allendale. 'That was the feeling: a real happy family. They didn't let egos go to their heads. They bounced off each other. Kim had huge family support to be whatever he wanted to be.'

On tour in 1980, drizzle drove Kim indoors and on to a squash court in Nottingham. Spin bowler Ashley Mallett volunteered to join him. Mallett cannot be certain of the first-set scoreline. He thinks Kim won 21–0. It's possible Mallett scored once when Kim flashed and missed.

'I think we better play fair,' said Kim.

'How's that?'

'I'll play left-handed.'

Mallett wasn't sure whether to be amused or affronted: 'Look, I don't want to take advantage of you.'

Kim won 21–2 with his left hand.

Signs of a precocious sporting versatility were evident in Kim as a ten-year-old. He was no runner: a temporary design flaw. Little legs, as they were then, could generate only so much steam. Saturday mornings consisted of hockey for one of Allendale's two sides. Kim was listed among the best afield most weekends, dazzling in a losing grand final and pocketing the team's best-and-fairest prize. In tennis he was classy enough at ten to reach the under-12 boys' semi-finals at Geraldton's annual tournament. 'Whew, Kim's playing tennis,' fellow junior cricketer Geoff Gallop tut-tutted to himself. 'He'll bat with a cross-bat. He'll lose his technique.'

Had his racquet endangered his kicking motion, Kim might well have retired it. For he remained adamant that nothing would block his path to Australian Rules stardom. He, Don and Glenn—who had graduated from crawling and aped whatever Kim did—were full-time hangers-on at the end of Stan's arm whenever he took the men of Brigades for practice. Training was twice a week at Maitland Park or the Recreation Ground, and the Hugheses came clad in Brigades colours, gold with blue trim, three daffodils in a field of beanstalks, hoping to be noticed, until one of the beanstalks would beckon them over for a bit of kick-to-kick.

For a ten-year-old, slight of build, getting your name and initials in a cricket scorebook was trickier. Matches were recorded in Geraldton as early as 1866. After the turn of the century rival sheep-shearing stations would play each other on hillsides, with dirt pitches and bats chiselled from pick-handles and corkwood trees. By the 1960s, philosophical differences over whether cricket matches should be afternoons of simmering combat or of beery frivolity triggered a split. A breakaway Social

Association began playing on Sundays alongside Geraldton's regular club competition. The volume of cricket had never been higher. It meant nothing to Kim. Under-16s was still the only junior league in town. Kim's bulging quiver of strokes was seen to best effect on the street with friends or in the backyard at 20 Christie Street. They played, in a nod to the pioneers, with a tree trunk for a wicket.

It was around this time that Kim read Don Bradman's *The Art of Cricket*, published in 1958. It seems a reasonable guess that he skimmed whole chapters. 'No batsman should attempt to pull a ball which is over-pitched or of good length—this is courting disaster,' was one Bradman sermon that did not sink in. 'It is unwise for a batsman to specifically make up his mind before a ball is bowled where he will hit it,' was another. Some of The Don's devotion rubbed off. Kim fixed a ball to a string and hooked it up to the clothesline. Hour after hour he hit that ball. 'Practising with the ball on the string,' Kim believed, 'was a great help.'

The first solid memory anyone claims to have of Kim batting in an organised match was at a carnival involving neighbouring townships. Kim went along to watch. What happened next will be familiar to readers of cricketing folk tales and biographies. One of the home team's players fails to show; ten sets of eyes scan the horizon in desperation; boy prodigy is reluctantly invited to make up the numbers; boy prodigy astounds all present with his bravery and hard hitting. Kim's story deviated from the script only in that someone hollered for an abdominal protector to be sent out. Kim had tried one on earlier; it was too big.

This was a nuisance that soon became a hindrance. He was eleven when he started playing for Bluff Point No. 1 in the under-16s. He would later rue his oversized pads and the box that fell out when he ran between wickets, ensuring he was run out as often as all other methods of dismissal combined. Newspaper archives prove he was not alone. One weekend, Bluff Point's 90 against Postals was pockmarked by seven run-outs. The *Geraldton Guardian*'s first mention of K. Hughes, cricketer, was on 27 November 1965. Bowling his accurate but slower-than-very-slow-mediums—'donkey lobs on the stumps' is how Kim described them—he captured 3–2 as Postals tallied 73. Bluff Point made 57, 23 of them Kim's, as opener.

Five days later a short notice announced Junior Country Week trials: nine o'clock, the next two Saturdays, on Geraldton High School oval. Any lad under sixteen was welcome, the paper added. 'The competition gives country boys a chance to play on top-class turf wickets in Perth over a week in January.'

Kim was grateful for his upbringing on ramshackle pitches in unpampered surroundings. That was where he developed his flair. Years later he remarked: 'I see so many youngsters being taught how to play cricket on turf. The ball pops here and there and dad's saying: "Son, get in behind the ball." He doesn't want to get in behind it because he's going to get hit.'

Bluff Point under-16s played on malthoid wickets hard, straight and true, wickets not unlike the ones Reg Sewell would have encountered in the thirties. Sewell, in the eyes of old-time resident Con Culloton, was the prince of Geraldton batsmen. Culloton told how one day, against highly fancied Naraling, Sewell and opening partner Jimmy Wells set off in chase of 180. They got there unscathed. Sewell made every run bar four. From the first over he had the Naraling fieldsmen spreadeagled. By the last he was still thrashing boundaries, only now he was doing it with half a bat, the other half having splintered and fallen away in his hands and Sewell having declined a replacement because the game was as good as won.

Suddenly Reg Sewell had some competition. Kim Hughes, aged eleven, littlest and youngest of all who flocked to the high school oval, was named in Geraldton's squad of thirteen for Junior Country Week.

•••••

HE TOOK A DAY to make an impression. He was twelfth man for the opening match with Morawa–Mullewa–Carnamah at Abbett Park, close enough to Scarborough Beach that you could breathe in the seaweed. On a sweltering afternoon Kim zigzagged by the sidelines, biffing a ball and overdosing on Coca-Cola. Geraldton won by five runs. Coach Jeff Carr drove half the players back to their accommodation. The rest returned in the sleek ministerial car of Les Logan, cricket enthusiast and staid, no-nonsense Country Party member for the Geraldton region. The game was so gripping, the sunshine so sapping and Kim, so little, had guzzled so many soft drinks; and as Les Logan's black car whirred along Stirling Highway, Kim quietly chundered. 'Everyone understood,' Carr remembers. 'And Les wouldn't have been too upset. He would have put the car in the government garage and someone would have cleaned it for him.'

They were away nine days. Before Kim went, Ruth discreetly rang Ian and Marianne Murray, who had left Geraldton for the city. 'She was very anxious that Kim be looked after and that his clothes were washed and that his whites were whiter than Omo-white,' says Ian. Marianne reports that she appeased Ruth's laundry concerns. 'His mother was worried because he had never left home before. She asked us to keep an eye on him. He didn't really want an eye kept on him—he'd have been horrified.'

They stayed at Crystal Palace guesthouse, near Perth's old town hall, and played on fields greener and neater than any they'd seen: Hale School, Perth Oval, Claremont Oval, the WACA Ground. On their weekend off some headed for the beach. Others watched a grade game. Smoking was the main harmless mischief. For every cricket-mad boy in every dust-caked dot on a map, Junior Country Week was first rung up a tall ladder. It was no place to slip up.

The standard was competitive. Sheffield Shield players sometimes umpired. Geraldton's vice-captain Geoff Gallop, future premier of Western Australia, recalls Tony Lock giving him out lbw. They won five, lost one and finished B-section runners-up. Fast bowler Gary Margetic and allrounder Peter Scott showed promise. Kim radiated something more than promise: an unbreakable self-confidence. Coach Carr didn't dare tamper. 'Kim had a straighter bat at eleven,' says Carr, 'than I ever had.'

Gallop showed a straight bat too. With Kim, though, a straight bat was a springboard for vivacious self-expression and the savaging of bowlers' reputations. Gallop's straight bat was his start, middle and finish. 'I was a blocker'—and, at a pinch, a stopgap leg-spinner. Gallop's fantasy was sports commentary. His first break came on Sunday afternoons as a thirteen-year-old scorer for Geraldton's A-grade competition. He'd keep records, collate averages, rank star performers and present his handi-work to the ABC. There he met Englishman Bill Phillips, head

of the ABC in Perth. Phillips favoured British minimalism—
'*Stiles/Ball/Charlton*'—over the verb-spattered verbosity of
Australian football commentators. He set Gallop exercises. A
British Open wrap. A WANFL preview. Gallop remembers:

> I'd write it out, go into the ABC on a Saturday morning,
> tape it, and then he'd play it back to me. He'd talk about the
> commentator's role and what emphasis you put on things.
> I thought I was pretty good. I was seriously thinking about
> becoming a sports commentator. Then my academic career
> got the better of me and I didn't do it.

Kim's destiny seemed clearer to Gallop than his own. 'The
mental picture I have,' says Gallop, 'is of a very small guy coming
out and hitting the ball all over the place. Confident. He'd get
twenties and thirties—that was Kim's little thing—then he'd get
caught at mid-off.'

Twenties and thirties eluded Kim that first week in Perth.
Some of the *West Australian*'s most anticipated column inches
all year out bush were the daily potted scorelines during junior
and senior Country Week. Kim, an eleven-year-old among
fifteen-year-olds, was not expected to figure in dispatches, and
didn't. 'And yet,' says Carr, 'he was matching it with them.'

He sprouted a little in time for Junior Country Week
1966–67, legs lanky enough to secure him third place in the
boy's high jump at Allendale Primary's annual sports day. He
top-scored with 31 against Narrogin. But Geraldton lacked
one sturdy opener to partner Peter Scott. They lost twice and
slid out of contention. Carr arrived at Hale School for the final
match with a proposition: how did Kim fancy opening?

Kim paused. He wasn't at all sure. His thirteenth birthday was a fortnight away. The opposition attack looked sharp.

Carr persisted. None of their bowlers are any nastier than Margetic or Scott, he promised. 'And Kim said "all right"—a bit reluctant, but "all right".'

Merredin hoisted a respectable 8–171. Kim confronted the first stern test of his cricketing life. Hopes were that straight bat of his might hold perpendicular for half an hour while Scott made merry at the other end. The impressive thing was the way Kim stuck to the plan. Scott was there at the finish, 94 not out, but it was the teenager-to-be who had team-mates buzzing. He made 34 in a century partnership. In retrospect, the arresting detail is that he was comfortably outscored. He did the team thing. Blazing instincts were spurned and a barricade built.

Gallop believes a state selector, Allan Edwards or Lawrie Sawle, was in attendance. A whisper went round: 'They've come to watch Kim. He's the one.' Sawle cannot remember this. Carr can't either, though he doesn't rule it out. He does recall being at the WACA Ground that night with the late Les Logan, who was tweaking the lapels of any cricket administrator with any selectorial influence and rhapsodising about Geraldton's new boy opener.

In the schoolyard Kim was head boy in Year 7. He suffered little of the stigma that sometimes dogs the headmaster's son. But, then, Stan wasn't a crusty or unpopular boss. He dispensed with formalities, empowered his teachers and personally helped troubled children. Stan's friendliness was as renowned as his dancing was infamous. He'd be first to fire up the record player and challenge the ladies to step up, a trait enshrined in a rhyme, *Twinkletoes*, written by staff for the end-of-year booklet:

A sportsman keen is Stanny Hughes
And keen on manly fitness,
Who follows all the sporting news
I think you'll all bear witness.
We all say, 'Liar', when he says,
'Too old! I can't stay with 'em.'
For we have seen the twinkling toes'
Reaction to hot rhythm.

Kim's own twinkling toes would eventually fetch him even greater infamy. For the moment, his tonsils were as noteworthy as his toes. He was an enthusiastic singer in the school choir. 'Kim probably wouldn't like to hear this,' says Rudy Rybarczyk. 'But he actually had quite a good voice, a sweet voice. His brother Don had a really good voice. They must have got it from their mother.' Friendly rivalry could be a foggy concept between Western Australian country schools. In Geraldton's mid-year eisteddfod it was an oxymoron. Ambition was fierce and practice relentless: twice weekly initially, four times a week by the business end, all during school hours. Five-year-olds longed for the day they would reach senior classes and qualify for choir selection. The emphasis changed later, until participation was the thing. In Kim's day, victory over Bluff Point or Geraldton Primary sparked semester-long celebrations.

Choirmistress was Joan Gliddon, Kim's Year 6 teacher, a former violinist with Perth Symphony Orchestra. To get to school every morning she travelled through low-lying scrub and past two Aboriginal town camps. Wonthella, the suburb Allendale served, was on Geraldton's barren outskirts. Gliddon was conscious on arrival in 1961 that academic standards were 'not considered very high' and that many of the children's schooldays would be over at fourteen. 'The main aim,' she felt, 'was for them to leave with a reasonable knowledge of how to speak, read and write English, and to have an understanding of figures and elementary maths. I set about achieving this.'

Rudy Rybarczyk took Kim for Year 7. These things stood out: his confidence, his competitiveness—'second best was never really good enough for Kim'—and his conversation. 'He wasn't afraid to debate social issues with you, even as a twelve-year-old. It might be on a Monday morning, when you talked about the weekend's events. But he would never step over the mark. He always had that element of respect.' As head boy, Kim would volunteer to look after Mrs Murray's Year 1s. He had a head for maths and a love of composing short stories. *A Car Crash*, which Rybarczyk has hung on to all these years, went like this:

The screeching of wheels and smell of burning rubber broke the dead silence on a cold winter's night. It was a mass of broken glass and jagged bits of tin. People rushed frantically to and fro, trying to put out the blazing fire; for twenty minutes this went on until it began to smoulder out very slowly.

Then through the action-packed air came a whining sound of an ambulance, rushing through the gloomy streets. With a sudden jolt, the ambulance halted beside the mangled bits and pieces of iron. In a second, the ambulance officers were carrying away the blood-stained body of an elderly man in his early sixties from the scene of the accident.

The mess was later swept away by gigantic sweepers.

The macabre detail and fatal twist seem at odds with Kim's usual sunny optimism. But the staccato rhythm of the sentences would become a trademark of future press conferences.

•••••

KIM FINISHED PRIMARY SCHOOL, the family moved to Perth and within two years he was facing Dennis Lillee in the nets for the first time. Ambulances and gigantic sweepers may not have been far from Kim's thoughts. He was fifteen, dressed in shorts and a pathetically thin thigh pad. 'I don't know why I wore it.' Lillee was nineteen. He had the breeze at his back, a new cherry in hand. His legs were going at full tilt. The ball pitched short and Kim saw it fizz by. He didn't sight it clearly enough to profess to have left it. So fast was it flying that the ball embedded itself—stuck—in the wire mesh. 'So I knocked it out and gave it back to him with a great big smile and he thought I was being a little so-and-so,' Kim recalled. 'And the more I smiled, the quicker he bowled.' Thirty years later, telling the story of that first ball from Lillee, Kim said: 'I vividly remember it.'

Tiffs over drinks-waiter duties were then undreamt of. Lillee was on the verge of first-class cricket, his crackle and pop having put a pile-up of club openers off their breakfasts. Kim was in the state colts squad, whose weekly sessions in the WACA nets coincided with senior squad practice. He played for Floreat Park under-16s. His 555 runs at 46, including his first century, outscored everyone else in the competition in 1968–69. His donkey lobs made asses of more batsmen than seemed plausible. Twenty-eight wickets at 6 apiece shaded future Test bowler

Wayne Clark's 27 at 10. Two years before Garry Sobers's 2000 runs–200 wickets Test double, Kim contributed 70 of Floreat Park's 154 then took 4–3 to singlehandedly rout Perth in the under-16 grand final.

He made his first-grade entrance the summer after. He was close to full height—5ft 11¼in—but had an adolescent's scrawniness. Floreat Park, sister club of Subiaco, played only as high as B-grade, where Kim rustled up an opening-round 40. He was summonsed to appear in the Subiaco nets and slung into Des Hoare's first-grade XI that weekend. There was no hoo-ha. Journalists, preoccupied with Mt Lawley's barnstorming No. 3 Bruce Duperouzel, seemed not to notice Subiaco's dimple-cheeked No. 4.

Kim breezed on to Rosalie Park at 2–54, soon 3–56, in dawdling pursuit of 230. Two Sheffield Shield squad fringe dwellers, Trevor Bidstrup and East Perth ruckman John Daniel, spearheaded Mt Lawley's attack. Richard Wilberforce was batting up the other end. Kim made a bystander of him. Gazing out from the tiny audience, disbelief rising, was practice partner Graeme Porter. Kim was square cutting Bidstrup and Daniel with the same belligerence he showered on Porter's Sunday morning throwdowns. 'Daniel was a big strong fellow who did a lot of bowling,' Porter remembers. 'And Kim played him easily, with real command.'

Out for 36, Kim waited two Saturdays for his next dig, a duck against Fremantle. Next day, a colts knockout stoush at Fletcher Park, he exploded off the mark with three fours and a six. Watching transfixed, long-serving Fremantle secretary Bob Ballantine pronounced Kim a Test prospect—the first person to say so publicly, though Kim's coach Frank Parry had said it privately a hundred times. 'High praise for a fifteen-year-old,' noted Jack Lee, unshakeably pro-West in every word he ever wrote. 'But I have seen rasher predictions fulfilled.'

Back in first grade Kim strung together 42 against Nedlands, 31 against University and 75 against Claremont–Cottesloe. Jack Lee's monthly round-up in *Australian Cricket* charted Kim's ascension: from 'Subiaco's pride and joy' in the December 1969 issue, to 'batting prodigy' in January, and 'star of the future' by February. The memory of Kim's 31 has stayed with University's leg-spinning allrounder Graham House, who dismissed him lbw:

> That was my introduction to this young whippersnapper everyone was talking about. All the senior guys in my team seemed jealous. He looked a lovely player. But he was a pretty cocky little fella and I think that got up the noses of the older guys, who expected him to show more respect. They tried a bit of sledging. He'd have a couple of words back and almost laugh at them. Then bang! The next ball would go for four.

Kim went to Melbourne in January for the inaugural national under-19 carnival, later a hothouse for myriad Test players. The 1969–70 crop lodged at Scotch College in Hawthorn for $25 each. Kim was youngest—something he was getting used to—in a WA side captained by Ric Charlesworth and starring Mike Fitzpatrick, future Rhodes scholar and big cheese in Australian football. 'Kim was the prodigy, our best batsman, in some ways the hope of the team,' Charlesworth remembers. 'He was the most gifted junior cricketer I ever saw. No one was even close.'

It rained a lot. Pitches were substandard and Kim's output mediocre: three failures, a 20 and a 25 against Victoria's crack attack of Rod Hogg, Brendan McArdle and Ray Bright. 'Kim was wild,' says Charlesworth. 'He was away from home. Maybe things were pretty strict there.' Charlesworth suspects Kim's thimbleful of runs gave him some grief. If so, he rebounded quickly.

His next innings was his first against Lillee. Perth made 145. Evening fell, bringing two late Subiaco wickets. 'Kim just had to survive,' Geoff Gallop recalls. 'And Lillee was absolutely belting in at him.' Gallop, on university holidays, had ventured down for a look at his old team-mate. 'I remember thinking: God, Kim. No helmets back then.' Kim made 40, thrusting his neck behind the line for every one, in a matchwinning stand with George Young. 'Lillee used to come off the longest run-up I've ever seen,' says Young. 'I would have been petrified. And I was five years older. Imagine how Kim felt.'

Kim felt he'd achieved something. So far his runs were more eyecatching than plentiful, his fame narrow enough for Saturday afternoon's *Daily News* to report that 'Tim Hughes' was 33 not out against Midland–Guildford. The paper never repeated that mistake. By second edition Tim was Kim and not out 63. Subiaco's 2nd XI, playing on the adjoining field at Rosalie, virtually downed balls and bats. 'As soon as Kim came out we were watching him,' says second-grade captain Con Tsokos. 'It was unbelievable. We could see the bat going, the shots flowing.'

It was Kim's seventh first-grade game, his first since his sixteenth birthday. Rosalie Park's pitch was the rottenest in town and Midland's attack the most dreaded. Respected quicks Stan Wilson and Mike O'Shaughnessy had three past and future Test players for back-up: Bruce Yardley (bowling swingers), Keith Slater (offies) and Norm O'Neill (leggies). Dropped twice early, Kim batted flawlessly thereafter. He went to bed that night 104 not out. Hitting his hundredth run was as emotional for Kim as his Centenary Test ton a decade later. For Keith Slater, whose mate Des Hoare had been 'driving me mad telling me how good this young bloke was', it was awe at first sight:

> Midland ruled the roost in those days and anyone who made runs against us we rated pretty highly. Stan Wilson was frightening at grade level. But Kim handled it with aplomb. He was technically as correct as you could possibly be and his temperament was quite incredible. He had a lovely outward confidence. He wasn't over the top; he just believed he had the game to do the job. And he did. It was obvious to everybody there that this was something a bit special.

Midland's captain-coach Tony Mann was away on state duty that first Saturday. Earbashed at training about the amazing child-batsman emu-stepping his way down the wicket at Stan Wilson, Mann resolved to have a go himself when 'the little bugger' resumed batting. Mann's third ball spun; Kim pushed forward. 'He never was prepared to accept that spinners could bowl,' says Mann. First slip O'Neill caught him for 112.

Smalltown Perth's sporting obsession exceeded its sporting accomplishments in those days. Overnight Kim became a big shot: by reputation, and by batting inclination. The following weekend he was mixing with the cream in a sixteen-man double wicket knockout, a fundraiser for Perth's Test match appeal. He and partner Ian Brayshaw beat Ross Edwards and Bob Massie to the $80 first prize. Kim topped Subiaco's averages that blissful, freewheeling summer. George Young accompanied him in several bountiful partnerships. 'We were mesmerised by this kid who could belt the ball so hard to so many different areas of the ground,' says Young. The boy's square cutting gleamed brightest. 'Third man, gully, point—whoever—they never got within cooee.' Almost as impressive was his refusal to get riled, however clodhopping the provocation. Young recalls:

> On-field sledging was rife and Kim grew up against some shrewd old customers, wily people who had played district cricket for twenty years. They loved having a crack at a young bloke like Kim, and I wasn't much older. They jumped at the chance to upset us. But Kim didn't retaliate verbally. He copped it sweet and put it on the scoreboard. Most batsmen would be happy to fend them off, but Kim, he took them on, even at fifteen. He took 'em on and nine times out of ten won the battle.

Backyard battles at 10 Clanmel Road, Floreat Park, were intensifying too. Youngest brother Glenn was increasingly the aggressor, hissing and hectoring as he ran in. Beamers were as legitimate as bouncers. Mum Ruth often stood as umpire and peacemaker. They played with a tennis ball and a gum tree for stumps. Here a fourteen-year-old Kim is said to have announced to his family, a touch pompously, if these were indeed his exact words: 'I will one day wear the green and gold Test cap and walk the hallowed turf of Lord's.'

Stationed close on the leg-side were a picket fence and a flowerbed. Hit the fence on the full or land one in the flowers and you were out. Kim's cuts and cover drives blossomed accordingly. The family dog, a black cocker spaniel, was the boys' most loyal spectator, and sometimes an obstacle. The dog would plonk himself down mid-pitch. This was not the last time someone would get in the way of Kim's yearnings on a cricket field, and for those who delight in coincidences, the cocker spaniel's name was Rodney.

THREE

'Dead Animals, Bloody Turds, Old Apples, Sponge Cakes . . .'

A FANTASTICAL SCENE awaited Daryl Foster on his first afternoon at Rosalie Park. It was the tailend of the 1970–71 season and he had come to inspect the headquarters of the cricket club he was contemplating coaching. A short man's booming voice roused his attention.

'Jeepers, champ!' the voice bellowed. 'Fantastic shot. Beautiful shot. *Ho, magnificent!*'

The man was in his mid-forties, perhaps. He was looping slow full tosses at a boy. The boy was hammering these full tosses into the side net. Nothing could be simpler. Yet the man's hysteria rose with every blow. Foster supposed, on reflection, that it was a useful exercise: how often, sprung unawares, do batsmen mishit full tosses? But at the time he was bewildered. That's Kim Hughes batting, someone said. And the fellow with him? That's Frank Parry, Kim's coach.

'Oh,' said Foster. 'Gee.'

The late Grant McLennan, singer-songwriter of Brisbane band The Go-Betweens, was once asked why he dropped Grant and called himself G.W. McLennan on his first solo record. Vanity? Literary aspirations? Pretentiousness? 'I think ambition and arrogance are two very lovely attributes in a man,' McLennan replied. 'But, especially in this country, people mistrust vaulting ambition. People mistrust you trying to achieve things. They just don't like it.' Kim's ambition vaulted out of every net he lit up and every interview he gave, but politely, seldom boastfully, with a flash of head boy's charm. How much of his self-assurance was inbuilt and how much it metastasised under Mr Parry and his endless hosannas was hard to tell. But people, and not just opponents, did not like it.

At Subiaco older, worldlier team-mates would meddle with Kim's towel before his shower. Once Kim was underwater they would wait for his hair to lather up, shampoo streaming down his cheeks and into his eyes until he could barely see, then several of them would urinate on him. They stuffed his kitbag with all things vile. 'Dead animals, bloody turds, old apples, sponge cakes from afternoon tea,' says George Young. 'You could only get away with it with Kim. Anyone else would react a little bit. That's how green he was. Kim was the whipping boy, you could say, for the Subi Cricket Club.'

Everybody would laugh, Kim included, and the boy who played strokes that others couldn't draw a picture of would be lopped down to a more satisfactory size. Thus were upheld two fundamental club principles: that team morale is paramount, and every player, however gifted, must be equal to the rest.

Rosalie Park today is as tranquil as it sounds, a lunchtime sanctuary from Thomas Street traffic, a vast sweep of sun-browned playing fields encircled by log fences. Lacrosse, tennis, junior soccer and suburban turf cricket are played here. There are four well-kept nets. Peaceful now, they were once no place for a batsman to be. The nets are narrow. When all were in operation it felt as if batsmen were taking strike on top of each other. Bursting out of a tree-lined dusk came Des Hoare, Dennis Baker, Jim Hubble, state bowlers all. Each had his own new rock. None delivered from the full twenty-two yards. Invited to try out for Subiaco, Geoff Gallop never returned. 'It was terrifying,' says Gallop. 'It was actually quite ridiculous. There was bloody Des, flying them in at you from eighteen yards. I went to training for a week and Des Hoare tried to kill me.'

Mustering what authority he had as second-grade captain, Con Tsokos sometimes interjected: 'At least bowl from twenty yards.' The request always went unacknowledged. Back heels sailed once more past the popping crease. It was no tea party for any batsman. And for Kim? 'It was special treatment,' Tsokos confirms.

He made net bowling baffling. Defensive strokes were rare, half-hearted ones unheard of. Getting out did not fuss him. Facing Test or state bowlers never cowed him. No note of humility or apology affixed itself to his shotmaking. He just wanted to slam the ball past them faster than it came at him. Bowlers got the impression he rated them inferior, when really he was thinking of the bowlers hardly at all. He was enjoying himself. But they would get in a tizz. He must have noticed, so in this respect it's arguable that he brought their wrath and bouncers on himself. Other causes of aggravation were beyond Kim's control. 'He had a baby face and blond hair,' says Tsokos. 'So they'd give him buggery.'

Sam Gannon remembers bowling at Kim during a 60 against Scarborough in his debut season. The time he had to play the ball that day ran into aeons. Cockiness was the other characteristic Gannon never forgot, and liked: 'He didn't say anything. It was

his mannerisms; he carried on as if he were a veteran of the crease.'
Bruce Duperouzel captained Kim on a 1972–73 colts tour. 'An
extravagance which pushed the bounds of acceptability' stood
out. 'In the early seventies things were still very conservative,' says
Duperouzel. 'The old guard didn't appreciate people pushing the
boundaries. And Hughesy, if he could invent a shot, he would.'
Craig Serjeant went on the same colts trip:

> That brashness got senior players offside throughout his
> career. But hey, that was Kim the man. Take that away and
> you take a lot of his batting force away. He had this attitude
> that some bowlers couldn't bowl and no matter what they
> threw up he was going to dispatch it. That's probably
> what alienated him at the start against some senior figures.
> People objected to the brashness they saw—that brashness
> as a person which manifested itself in his batting.

Gallop has another theory. 'Always, he was younger than his
playing partners. And somehow they never adjusted.'

It was true at Junior Country Week. 'He used to rub up
against some of the older guys,' Gallop recalls. 'There's a big
difference between someone approaching sixteen and someone
who's twelve. And he was chirpy, a bit sort of gauche, a bit
of a nuisance, and some of the older ones would think, oh,
bloody Kim.' It was true when he became Test captain. He
was the golden boy still. 'People can be cruel, and he copped
all the cruel comments and just marched on. Nothing hugely
significant. But he was always nippin' round the heels.'

Hard as he strained to fit in at Subiaco in his mid-teens,
Kim uttered no regret, only gratitude, for things that happened.

Batting in the middle was a doddle once he knew he could survive a Subiaco net session unbloodied. He added the club's shower-room hijinks to his own repertoire. He built a lifelong friendship with his first captain, Des Hoare, twenty years his senior. For Kim, standing beside Hoare in the slips was an on-the-job crash course in tactics and the dedication required. Hoare, in turn, showed a honeyed appreciation of Kim's uniqueness. 'I have most admired him,' Hoare once said, 'because he has had the courage and ability not to become ordinary.'

Three words recur at mention of Hoare's name: 'mad', 'fiery' and 'bastard'. He claimed to have been sledged mercilessly by Sam Loxton during his first Sheffield Shield innings and conducted the rest of his career as if thirsty for vengeance. His one Test was against West Indies in 1960–61. Moving from Fremantle to Subiaco, he brought with him high-class swing and a ginger ant's sting. Bodies accustomed to light stretching threatened to snap under Hoare's commando-style pre-season drills. Approaching middle age he turned himself into a spinner and opening bat, despite having limited obvious knack for either, as if by willpower. Tsokos remembers batting with him against Lillee, who had to leave at teatime for a wedding. Lillee pinged Tsokos's shoulder and let loose a wasp's nest of bouncers around Hoare's ears. Tea was called and Hoare kicked over the stumps, spitting: 'I'll fucking kill that bastard.'

Coach Foster joined captain Hoare in 1971–72. 'Daryl was the brains and Des was the blood and guts man,' is how George Young puts it. Pennantless since 1946–47, Subiaco cleaned up twice in three seasons. Young was also an elegant left-footer who counted killer instinct, fed into him by Hoare, among his strengths. Four times he led St Kilda Football Club's goalkicking. Yet Subiaco's 1971–72 cricket premiership remains Young's shiniest playing memory. It was such a close-knit team, old and young, all challenging and encouraging and enjoying each other. Was that how Kim saw it too?

The Hughes family was part of the furniture. Stan was club president, though seldom spotted boundaryside when Kim was batting. He'd get so anxious for his son that he made himself genuinely ill. He worried Kim might catch the vibrations out in the middle. Maybe there was something in it. Ruth dragged Stan to a grade game once, in 1980–81, and Kim and Glenn both made ducks. When Stan did go, just for a peep, he'd stand in the shadows, feigning invisibility, stubby in hand. Ruth didn't like missing an innings of Kim's. If she knew Subiaco were batting she'd get there early, bringing the children, and a plate for afternoon tea, as many of the women did.

After play the men might fetch barbecued chickens and an eighteen-gallon keg of beer. Occasionally some were still carousing past midnight. Another keg would have materialised. It wasn't just cricket's culture. Tsokos remembers his country footy days, rare nights when players abstained from drinking before a big game. The hooter would sound next day and they'd have lost control over shellshocked nerves and muscles they'd forgotten they had. Kim at fifteen was no drinker. And when he drank he got drunk, something Ric Charlesworth noticed at the under-19 carnival. 'He couldn't hold his grog. And he was always a prankster. He'd be throwing beers at people and doing silly things.'

Being liked mattered to Kim. Being liked was as important as making runs, maybe even more important, and the wish to be liked never faded, it only ever got stronger. 'Kim refrained for a fair while but eventually they get you in,' says Tsokos. 'I think Kim felt that if he had a drink with the boys, well, maybe they would accept him.'

Kim was not the only Hughes who got a going-over at Subiaco. It was all done with the intention of sending team morale skywards, explains George Young:

> Old Stan, we used to fill him up with ink. He was one of those funny drunks. He loved making speeches. We'd get him up as president—'C'mon, Stan, have a few words to the boys'—when he was three parts pissed. And of course he didn't make any sense. He had a bit of a stutter, and he sort of stuttered his way through speeches. The boys would keep encouraging him: 'You're our president and we're going places with you.' He was just happy to be part of the club. And he loved Kim. I think he took all these roles on because he loved seeing Kim advance through the stages.

Everyone agrees that Stan drank too much, and that this probably did not do his oldest son much good.

•••••

FRANK PARRY ALWAYS called Kim 'champ', like he was training Cassius Clay. Champ, he'd say, you need four kinds of ability to be an Australian Test cricketer. 'One you already got from your parents. That's natural ability.' Frank would whiz through the three remaining must-haves. Technical ability. Physical ability. Thinking ability. 'Kimbo,' he'd say, which was the other name he had for him. 'Kimbo, your technical ability's up here and your physical ability's there. And your thinking ability, well, that's down here, champ.'

Sessions with Frank involved copious underarm work. Kim rehearsed specific strokes. Sometimes Frank simulated a spinner's flight and Kim had to charge at Frank, reach the ball before it bounced and pulverise it. Often Frank tossed the ball hip-high and Kim pulled or hooked for minutes on end. Frank talked as he threw. He believed that if you were balanced and could hit to the on-side, you could hit the ball anywhere. In a favourite routine, away from the nets, Frank underarmed and Kim struck then chased the ball, so that his body weight followed through with the shot. Balance—getting your head and feet just so—that was the secret, and for as long as he played cricket Kim carried a skipping rope in his kitbag. Skip for ten minutes before an innings and he believed his feet would move instinctively into position from the first delivery.

He was foxing rather than pulverising balls for Frank the first Sunday they met at Floreat Park Oval. Kim was fourteen and Frank forty-three. A couple of other lads were on the receiving end of Frank's horse sense and underarms. Kim fetched and watched curiously. He'd never had any real coaching himself. After two hours Frank said: 'Look, son, if you want to be here next Sunday around nine o'clock we'll give you a hit.' Kim was there by seven, wearing whites, and he turned up almost every Sunday after for the next seven years.

Floreat Park Oval was three blocks from Frank's house and one block from Kim's. Some Sundays they alternated at Rosalie Park or at a little oval behind Jolimont School in the next suburb. Frank's sons Rob and Geoff might come. A boy called Ross Dickinson joined in for a while. Usually, though, there were three: Frank, Kim and Graeme Porter. Both boys went to City Beach High School. Porter was a year younger, tall and trim, talented enough to go to the 1979 World Cup. He rated himself 'a scrubber' beside Kim: 'I think Frank needed someone else to throw the balls, so he needed two. They were really enjoyable sessions. I remember them fondly.'

Kim did almost nothing but bat. Porter liked batting but preferred his medium pacers, though Frank offered little in the way of tuition. 'I don't think Frank was keen on me bowling.' He suggested Porter put batting first and supplement it with leg-breaks. When they didn't take off, Frank let him be. Frank himself was a former first-grade batsman for Mt Lawley, Ashley Mallett's old club. 'Frank always wore his box on the outside of his strides at practice,' Mallett remembers. 'And he bowled huge leg-breaks off the wrong foot. Honestly, they were the biggest turning leg-breaks I've seen in my life.' These leg-breaks of Frank's spun more than a metre but were seldom aired outside the nets.

Frank was the oldest son of a wood machinist who opened a small furniture factory in Leederville in 1934. Toil and innovation got Frank Parry senior through the Depression years. He constructed spindle moulders, thicknessers and other arcane woodworking gadgets out of old bicycle parts. Frank junior eventually took over running the company, which had switched from building to selling furniture. Parry's Furniture Factory became Parry's Department Store. When Frank started a discount and finance business he left the family firm in brother Kevin's hands, paving the way for Parry Corp. Kevin later recalled of the family's furniture struggles: 'We had to cut our staff to four, and for some reason I was the guy elected to tell the rest they had to go . . . It was a bitter pill.'

A hotshot baseballer who dabbled in property, TV networks, resources and technology, Kevin followed the arc of many a self-made Perth megamillionaire. He carved out a fortune, borrowed a bigger one, then saw it all go kaput in the 1987 stockmarket crash. At the height of his might he beat Alan Bond for the right to defend the America's Cup. *Kookaburra III* was trounced and Kevin Parry achieved the distinction, unique even in Perth, of losing not only his empire but the America's Cup too.

Frank's trajectory was less cataclysmic, equally diverse. He was a trade unionist, an entrepreneur, a promoter of numerous causes. He campaigned for friendly societies pharmacies. He imported one of the earliest prototype electric cars into Western Australia. He bankrolled research into the zinc-bromine battery, initially as a way of making the car run, later as a long-life, high-energy, green-friendly alternative to conventional lead-acid batteries, one with rich possibilities for his company ZBB Energy Corporation. Frank was a doer: earthy, kind, passionate, unflappable, optimistic. He had smiling eyes. He loved cricket and Bradman was his hero. In Kim, it was like he'd tripped across a superpowered teenage version of himself.

'They fitted each other,' says Porter. 'Their personalities were the same. Frank became a father figure to Kim; well, to both of us.' Geoff Marsh, who was best friends with Glenn Hughes, says: 'Frank was like a real second father. He loved Kim—that was it. He believed Kim was a great player and no one else was as good and he kept telling Kim that.' Frank passed away in 2003, aged seventy-eight. The following death notice ran in the *West Australian*:

My second Dad! So much fun, so many dreams and memories. Your spirit will always live on coach! What a champ!

It was signed, *Kimbo*.

Early in their relationship, Kim admitted to a quandary against bouncers. Planting his front foot forward to everything wasn't working. Frank gave him a lesson in playing back and across, expecting Kim to take eighteen months to catch on, like most youngsters he'd seen. Kim got the knack in three weeks. Usually Frank's tips were not so specific. 'Watch it and hit it'—frequently followed by, 'And have fun!' The things Frank said were less important than their constant reinforcement, the round-the-clock vote of confidence in his boys, the sheer multitude of underarms he threw—enough to snap the arms off a gibbon. 'I don't know what he did for a living in the end,' says Sam Gannon, who lived nearby. 'All I ever saw him doing was throwing balls to Kim. He was totally obsessed with Kim.'

Sunday sessions were sacrosanct, save for a fleeting winter recess. On weekdays Frank might wheel balls at Kim for an hour before Subiaco training, then hover in the wings to sum up afterwards. On Saturdays the trio occasionally gathered pre-match, Frank staying on to watch Kim bat. One Saturday he rang the WACA and announced he was moving the game to Rosalie Park's No. 2 ground. The No. 1 wicket was too awful for 'my boys' to bat on.

Distinguished visitors came some Sundays, partly as guest experts, partly to promote Frank's two shining wares. One Saturday night Frank spied John Rutherford, Western Australia's first born-and-bred Test player, who was down from Merredin and staying with his sister.

'Can you ring her?'

'Why?'

'Stay the night with us. I've got someone I want you to look at.'

The dawn wake-up next morning was worthwhile. Kim had 'an eye like a hawk'. 'If you keep employing that technique,' Rutherford told him, 'you'll make a heap of runs.'

For three years, from 1970–71 to 1972–73, Kim might have settled for a hillock of runs. After nine first-grade games he was flung into WA's Sheffield Shield squad and hailed by Rodney Marsh as 'a technically perfect batsman'. Playing for Lock's XI versus Inverarity's XI in the state trial, he clasped three catches—at slip, point and a screamer behind square leg. He was sixteen years old. 'A level-headed youngster who eats, drinks and breathes cricket, he seems destined for a great career,' wrote Jack Lee. 'Hughes may even be blooded in a Shield game this season.'

It was the summer of Perth's inaugural Test, years in the making, a triumph of city and country folk, who auctioned whales and harvested surplus barley crops to raise money for the WACA Ground's fabled new 'Test Stand'. Kim was one of 23,057 day three spectators who witnessed Greg Chappell's serene 108 on debut. As he cheered, he may have entertained a grand daydream or two. The gap between dreams and reality was becoming a gulf. All that season in first grade, Kim passed 33 twice. Speculation abounded that he was having trouble with his stance, that he was bothered by school exams. 'Things were coming into my life,' he'd later reflect. 'My peers were going to hotels and doing different things.'

And it was the old familiar story. People liked seeing a bright youngster get ahead, but not ahead of them. Kim sensed it in the things they said, things like 'you'll get found out', or 'it's gunna be tough', or 'beware second-year blues'. 'I began to have the second-year blues,' said Kim. 'I listened to these things and these things began happening.' He averaged 23, 29 and 20 those three seasons in first grade. State trial invitations dried up. Others overtook him in the precocity stakes. He tipped out of the state squad. The summer of 1972–73 was a mausoleum of Kim's own making. Run out three times in a row early on, he finished with 1, 0, 1, 0 and 2.

'Son, how'd you go today?' Stan asked one night at dinner.

'Not too good, Dad. Got a duck.'

'Jesus, that's not too flash at all.'

The telephone rang about 7.30. Only one person could be ringing at 7.30 on a Saturday night—the same person who rang that time most Saturday nights.

'Champ, how are you feeling?'

Kim lied. He was feeling pretty good, he said.

And Frank said: 'Your left elbow was right, your head was fantastic, your footwork was great. As a matter of fact it was the best-made duck I've ever seen in my whole life.' There was more. 'You were perfect. There's only you and Donald Bradman.'

It could be that these were not Frank's exact words; the story is one of Kim's after-dinner favourites. For sure, though, Kim caught the tang of it.

'Who was that?' Stan asked, not that he needed to.

'Oh. That's Frank.'

'Well, how does he think you're batting?'

Deep breath. 'Jesus, Dad. There's only me and Bradman. The rest can't bat.'

Stan said they were both idiots. Many who knew them would go along with that. But Kim went to sleep feeling something more than merely reassured: he was filled with hope. Because Frank was correct. Yes, he made nought. But he did do plenty right. 'I was up next morning, Sunday morning, at seven o'clock, excited to get down there and build on that duck.'

Falling under the spell of a risk-taker, a self-believer, a super-optimist—another him—was the moment in childhood on which everything turned. Frank took tender care of the straggly excesses others might have chainsawed. Daryl Foster never knew what Frank was teaching but could tell it was sound: you only had to look at the boy's feet and straight bat. Frank was never an ogre from the pickets. All he ever did was applaud. 'If Kim wanted to hit one over the bowler's head, he could,' says Wayne Clark. 'A lot of coaches would say you gotta keep it along the ground, or don't go down on one knee to hit a cover drive. Frank encouraged Kim to be different because he realised Kim had the skill to do it.'

But is being different enough? 'It was all positive and probably a bit too over the top in some regards,' is Clark's conclusion. 'If he had some restraint early, he could have been even greater.'

A batsman who knew better how not to get out when well set might have made more runs. 'I'm not sure there wasn't a detrimental side,' says Gannon. 'Frank never stopped telling Kim how good he was. Just go and smash them. Tear them apart. In hindsight he could have given Kim guidance on being more circumspect, so if he came across a good spell of bowling he saw it off. Frank's attitude was the next bowler's just another bowler and you hop into him.'

Stan and Ruth worried about the psychological damage in later life should Kim not fulfil Frank's expectations. Frank's conviction that Kim would captain Australia: that was embarrassing. His visions of leadership genius in a child: they were absurd. And Frank rarely shut up about it. Even Kim did not truly believe it. He liked hearing it though. It beat becoming a schoolteacher like his dad and grandmother. Porter remembers Frank regularly mentioning Kim and the captaincy. 'And I don't recall him saying it about me.'

Every Boxing Day, the Hughes and Porter families visited Frank's house at 85 Evandale Street for a shindig. The Porters walked down with a carton of beer. There'd be a barbecue, and cricket in the driveway, and cackles at the tales of Frank's union pals. Kim played Test cricket during the small window in history when player Q&As were common as sausages. PBL, Kerry Packer's publishing and marketing arm, fattened magazines with them. Top players were asked around thirty-five questions each—the same thirty-five questions. Their answers tended to look the same too. Like many players, Kim's favourite TV show was always *The Winners*. He enjoyed eating 'rare pepper steak' and listening to 'middle of the road' music. His preferred holiday resort was 'home' and his superstitions 'none'. Every summer he'd pinpoint 'disloyal people' or 'false people' as his biggest dislike. And his luckiest break was always 'meeting Frank Parry':

> I developed a relationship with a fellow who I suppose has been the reason why I have been a survivor, why I've played the game the way I have played it, with a tremendous amount of love. I've dared to be different because someone brought

out that individuality which is within us all . . . Frank could see something in me. He had a dream or a vision that some day I would be different . . . It was his dream to start with, but if someone who is around you believes in you often enough, in the end what happens is you begin to believe in it yourself.

•••••

THE MILLIONAIRE BATSMAN with the scatterbrain streak was sometimes known as 'Howie', after the scatterbrained millionaire Howard Hughes. He was occasionally called 'Billy', after Prime Minister Billy Hughes, whose biographer L.F. Fitzhardinge once noted: 'Almost the whole of Hughes's life was passed in an atmosphere of controversy, to which his own temperament and methods contributed not a little.' The other similarity was their surname. 'Motormouth' caught on briefly, a crack at Kim's unguardedness in the company of pressmen. 'Jekyll and Hyde' was bestowed by team-mates who sensed some connection between the irregularity of his runmaking and the fitfulness of his moods on tour.

None of these nicknames assumed any permanency. Only 'Clag' stuck. He shared it with the little tubs of thick glue omnipresent in Australian classrooms. The relevance to Kim has long been a puzzle. Schooldays team-mates put it about that it described his sticky-fingered slips catching. Others guessed a schoolroom allusion. One former Test team-mate believes it related to wet dreams and 'sticky sheets'. Another, Jeff Thomson, claimed in *Thommo Declares* that it originated 'because, well, he was a bit soft. Not a real macho type, really, was he?'

Actually, Kim and some colts team-mates visited Adelaide's Glenelg Beach one day. It was the week before his nineteenth birthday. He was in the water with a couple of girls. He was very excited. There was a bit of foam about from the ripples; a lot of foam, as a matter of fact, for what really were quite small ripples. Unflattering as the name sounds, Kim never disowned it, often murmuring 'Clag' or 'Claggy' at the crease to will himself on. When he gave his nickname as 'Howard' or 'Billy' in those Channel Nine tour guide Q&As, that was because he was a gentleman.

His glittery panache on successive colts tours kept his name thereabouts in Australia's coming cricketing firmament. Western Australia's colts, or under-23s, took their first steps on the Melbourne Cricket Ground and Adelaide Oval in January 1973. Wavy-haired Bruce Duperouzel was snapped in short pants in the *Age* and with flannels unbuttoned to his navel in the *Advertiser*. But the 'sensational prospect' singled out in Peter McFarline's preview was Kim. It was the first of McFarline's many pro-Kim trumpet blasts, and he was soon questioning the intelligence of his spies out west. Kim made 39 first up, then scrounged 15 in 95 minutes on the second evening, McFarline wailing as Kim wallowed: 'The inventor of colts cricket matches would have jackknifed in his grave.'

Victoria's attack was potent. Graham House recalls a volcanic Rod Hogg 'hitting the bat before I had time to think'. Duperouzel remembers young sports journalist Patrick Smith as taller, fire-breathing and even faster. 'And Kim had a day out.' On a steamy third morning he thumped eleven boundaries, exquisitely timed drives, until his proximity to three figures and the sacredness of the location awakened in him the urge to do something truly memorable. He lashed at Hogg and holed out on the fence for 97. A complicated relationship with the MCG, scene of his mightiest innings and his meek Test exit, always his favourite place to play with a full house crammed in, was born.

Kim cracked a couple of seventies on the return expedition twelve months later. Nearly four years had elapsed without a first-grade hundred. 'We tried to curb his flamboyance,' George Young believes now. Subiaco liked batting first and squirrelling three runs an over, knowing Baker, Porter, Hoare and Hubble would strangle the opposition to two. 'I guess it was totally contrary to the way Kim wanted to play,' says Young. 'It was silly. We just didn't know how good he was going to be.'

The Rosalie Park pitch did Kim even fewer favours. Rain landed thirty-one weekends out of thirty-three up to Christmas 1973, which was as unlikely in Perth as Martians landing. Rosalie's inhospitable alien terrain—humps, craters, spongy thickets—would have made them feel at home. Opener Graeme Watson was struck four times in one over against North Perth and the match shifted to Hale School. There, 1407 days after his dreamlike maiden hundred against Midland–Guildford, Kim hit another.

Old head boy at Allendale was City Beach High's head boy in his final year. Student council presidency of Graylands Teachers College completed the hat-trick. Kim was training to be a primary school teacher. Graylands was a corro-and-asbestos mishmash, located near a mental hospital on a derelict army camp that later served as a migrant holding centre. Always intended to be temporary, Graylands had survived two decades on a mix of government inertia and student camaraderie, known as the Graylands spirit. *This Day Tonight*, the ABC's biting current affairs show, chewed over its plight on 28 June 1974. It was Kim's TV debut. The deep voice, the clipped turn of phrase, the way he let his interrogator finish before speaking himself, the firm yet disarming air which told viewers he cared deeply but posed no menace; all these soon-to-be-familiar characteristics sparkled as President Kim pronounced: 'We feel that we're missing out.'

Adversity and small numbers—five hundred in Kim's day—bound students together. The focus was on grooming practical classroom teachers not textbook academics. The only thing dusty about Graylands was the falling-down walls. Termites periodically plundered the locker room. Science was taught in a broom closet. Students ate lunch in their cars. Lectures were staged outside because ventilation was non-existent inside. 'During summer you can't concentrate because it's far too hot,' said Kim. 'And during winter you freeze. It doesn't lend itself to the learning situation at all.' His forehead as he sat before *This Day Tonight*'s camera was clammy with sweat, as if to prove his point. But it was wintertime, and nervousness was the likeliest cause.

He was a dashing sight at twenty, natty V-neck sweater complementing his crisp paisley shirt. Golden curls were bushy, almost a beehive. Wispy sideburns dangled down to his jawbone and blond specks feathered his upper lip. His words added to the picture of boyishness, right down to the way he complained: 'You do get boredom here because there's nothing to do, no playgrounds to go to.' As for the state of the corrugated-iron outhouses:

I feel they're absolutely disgusting. If you look at the women's and male toilets, the staff ones, they're a disgrace to the education department. And they should be ashamed with what we've got to put up with. The same with the boys' and girls' toilets. Country towns wouldn't have it as bad as this.

Ten years later, almost to the day, he'd say something similar about cricketers' wages. Perhaps his earnestness swayed the departmental bean counters. Airconditioners and new toilets were installed in 1975. A practice cricket pitch sprung up behind the tennis courts—a year too late for Kim, and too little too late overall. Graylands shut down in 1979.

Resemblances to Austin Robertson had become something more than Kim's imagination. On consecutive weekends for Floreat Park under-18s he kicked seventeen goals from full-forward, eleven from centre half-forward and seven as ruck-rover. Named fairest and best in the district, he won a $1000 scholarship—it bought him his first car, a blue Hillman Super Minx—to play for WANFL side Claremont. The Tigers had a prospective new saviour in coach Verdun Howell, an adventurous half-back flanker in St Kilda's flag-winning team of '66. Howell was surveying Claremont's under-21s one Saturday when Kim snagged six goals. 'Great ball skills, brilliant hand-eye coordination and a very, very reliable kick,' was Howell's first impression. 'And he showed courage. He went full throttle at the ball and didn't look for a second option.'

That evening, Howell invited Kim to seniors practice. He said: 'I believe you could go as far as you want in football.'

Howell did have one anxiety: that Kim should not flirt with his two favourite sports and jilt one or both. He found it ludicrous when Duperouzel skipped the football season's opening fortnight to play first-grade cricket finals. That situation simply couldn't last, and didn't. After five Sheffield Shield matches on $12.50 a day, Duperouzel was offered $5000 a year at St Kilda. 'There really wasn't even a decision to be made,' Duperouzel recalls. 'Long-term, cricket just seemed pointless.' George Young chose football only two games into an even more promising first-class career. He hit a tantalising 125 against South Australia by way of farewell and boarded an aeroplane bound for Melbourne—and stardom—two days later. 'Football was the main game as far as popularity and ego and everything else went,' says Young. But cricket, pitting himself against eleven others and relying on no one, gave him the greatest pleasure. Young remembers his captain John Inverarity saying he was silly to choose football. 'And yeah, I often wonder . . .' The man he replaced in those two Shield games, Bruce Laird, eventually opened Australia's batting.

After a couple of weeks of seniors training they reconvened for a long chat. 'I'm very much looking towards cricket,' said Kim.

'That,' replied Howell, 'is a decision only you can make.'

Everyone at Claremont enjoyed Kim's company and enthusiasm. He even coached Floreat Park's under-11s. 'And he was such a presentable young man,' says Howell. A seven-goal bundle in the under-21s earned him a promotion to the reserves on 9 June 1973. He kicked a goal in a 37-point defeat to West Perth. At teachers college the next week he fell off a desk and broke his neck. Three weeks in hospital turned into three months in a neck brace. It was a funny kind of confirmation that he'd chosen the right career trail.

Sixty-six goals was Kim's full-forward's harvest in eleven under-21 games next season. He played out the rest of 1974 as a centreman in the reserves, strong overhead, swift underfoot. 'When the ball hit the ground he had good recovery and very good goal sense,' says team-mate Terry Waldron. 'He could judge the flight of the ball.' He could read what was happening upfield too. 'He had that inbuilt cunningness to break at the right time, to establish a lead,' says Howell. Skills-wise, Howell believes Kim had what high-flying Claremont clubmates Duperouzel, Graham Moss and Colin Tully had. But Kim didn't test himself. He never did play a league game. 'If cricket was his go,' says Howell, 'he owed it to himself to make that decision.'

It soon seemed a wise one. A dashing 112 versus Midland–Guildford catapulted him into Western Australia's twelve for the Shield match with South Australia. Those Swan Lager cans looked like Rudy Rybarczyk's after all. Selection had come four years later than Kim's truest believers recommended. But on the *West Australian*'s back page of 20 November 1974, his only discernible emotion as he strapped on a pad was joy.

Robbie Langer pipped him for the last batting spot. Kim spent hours fielding as twelfth man. His first appearance on a first-class scorecard was dramatic—'a magnificent overhead catch' in the gully, wrote Ken Casellas, to dismiss Gary Cosier off Lillee. When Mike Denness's Englishmen visited he was twelfth man again. WA's batting was reportedly 'painstaking', 'dreary' and bleached by 'periods of inactivity'. Kim, the least painstaking batsman in the state, was conceivably as bored as the spectators. The selectors didn't mind though. Kim was named twelfth man a third time against Queensland. He must have felt frustrated. But he was so close now. He must have known that.

•••••

ANGUISH, BEWILDERMENT AND RELIEF showed on the faces of the evacuees crowding Adelaide airport in the week after Christmas Eve, when Cyclone Tracy felled Darwin. Some had measles, scabies, snapped limbs or diarrhoea. Many had skin infections after getting sliced by flying glass or iron. Two weeks after Christmas Eve, Kim Hughes wandered into Adelaide. Scuffs to his pride were his only injury. Anguish was definitely one of his emotions, bewilderment perhaps another. And maybe he was relieved—relieved that he'd got out of Perth.

Certainly he left in a hurry. The Queensland game finished on the 23rd. He took Christmas off, played for Subiaco on the 28th, captained a colts XI against the WA Cricket Union on the 29th, and fled town on January 7th. Fled is the best word for it. 'He came to see me at my home and we had a lovely chat for an hour or so,' John Inverarity remembers. 'I strongly encouraged him to stay. I thought it was in his interests to stay and to break into a strong side. Then I didn't hear from him for a day or two, and the next thing I read in the newspaper was that he was already in Adelaide.'

Captain and impatient prodigy had a couple of earlier conversations too. 'My guess,' says Inverarity, 'is Kim thought he should have been in the side. And good on him. He was a young man seeking fame and fortune because it wasn't coming quickly enough.' Inverarity wasn't peeved. Moving to Adelaide was in step with Kim's self-belief, his impetuousness—'a very engaging side of him'—and his youth.

It was also unprecedented—and not far off unfathomable. What young cricketer in the twelve of one team ever hopped interstate mid-season in the hope of cracking the eleven of another when no promise or guarantee had been made? No cricketer. No one has done it since or is likely to again. Little was made of it at the time. And Kim never properly explained himself. He did say, much later: 'I just couldn't see myself getting into the WA side so I decided to try my luck in South Australia.' If that was the only reason, the risks outweighed the sense. Was there something else? Were a team-mate's words—'where's the fuckin' twelfth man?'—making his eardrums itch?

Chinaman bowler Daryl Lambert was on the committee at East Torrens, the club that recruited Kim. He doesn't recall how it happened. Nobody does, it seems. Lambert wonders if a visiting South Australian planted the idea, advertising the plentiful opportunities over east, during that first Shield game in November. If so, if Kim was already open to deserting Perth, then it wasn't three stints as twelfth man that made him despair. He was feeling uneasy or unwelcome or unloved—un*something*—from the beginning.

'Why the hell would he be doing that?' was fellow colt Graham House's first thought when he heard Kim was coming. Coincidentally House had moved to East Torrens, seeking spin-friendlier pastures, at the start of that 1974–75 summer. 'Kimmy bounced into town,' House remembers, 'as hyper as he always is.' His first net session at Campbelltown Oval's dewy practice wickets was on a Tuesday evening:

> Kim batted after me. Normally you walk out, flip your pads off and go about your business. This time I thought, I'll just watch Kim. There were two A-grade bowlers, one a fairly skiddy sort, and he absolutely carved them up. It was

magnificent. He put on a net exhibition. The two nets beside him shut down and by the end of his session a whole host of people gathered at the bottom. They were standing there watching these dancing feet. A couple of second-graders and third-graders tried their luck, and they got dispatched high and wide. Whoever rolled up he kept on belting. Balls were going everywhere. It was quite an occasion. I said to the person next to me: 'Yeah, I think he can bat.'

Kim lived in a room at the house of George Dickinson, the club's 69-year-old president. A kindly ex-boxer, Dickinson managed teams and refereed bouts at three Olympics. He still had plenty of vim about him. Before one end-of-season trip to Whyalla a railway official disallowed the crate of beer amidst the team baggage. Dickinson upended the spoilsport with a straight left. The trip was a cracker. The club history *Parade to Paradise* records Dickinson had 'at least four marriages, several of which were charged with controversy'. His house seemed as good a place as any to stay, and East Torrens a club more splendid than most. Joe Darling, Jack Lyons, Clem Hill and Les Favell headed the batting alumni. Fourteen A-grade flags, though none since 1934–35, swelled supporters' chests. And Kim was right about one thing. A South Australian top seven of Woodcock, Drewer, Chappell I, Cosier, Nash, Jenner and Clements looked very breachable.

On his first weekend, Kim hit 15 not out on Saturday and top-scored with 34 on Sunday in a one-day semi-final. Selection was not forthcoming in the following week's Shield game at the Gabba. 'I remember seeing he was at East Torrens,' says Ashley Mallett, 'and thinking why in the hell isn't this bloke being picked?' A twenty-first birthday party was thrown for Kim on Dickinson's back lawn at Klemzig, with its clothesline in the middle and roulette wheels, blackjack tables and poker machine in the shed. Adelaide's best-known resident, Don Bradman, rang to say happy birthday. At Linden Park Primary School, Kim began a teaching job. 'I saw him make his way to the staff room for morning tea on his first day of teaching,' recalls Barry Nicholls, a cricket-smitten twelve-year-old. 'He looked young and fit and moved quickly. There was no sign of the nerves most new teachers have.'

He taught in the classroom closest to the toilet block. Kim's kids were an unusual mob: a mix of grade 5s, 6s and 7s, about twenty of them, many with few English skills and little enthusiasm for being there. Kim built on what interests they had. One boy, Michael, had a mouse obsession. Kim let the boy's favourite mouse perch in a shirt pocket. He got the boy writing mice stories, giving class presentations on mice. Pretty soon they were all building mouse houses. The boy's confidence soared. 'Now Michael,' Kim announced one maths time, 'if three mice have three mice, how many mice have we got?'

Kim regularly marched his class outside for games of continuous cricket. He coached the school team—good news for Nicholls, who'd envied Kim's kids their continuous cricket jollies and was voted team captain. Net sessions were rare. Kim liked taking his boys out on the oval. He'd teach them to use a skipping rope—he was like a human willy-willy—and tell them they had to be light on their feet. He'd show them how to swing a bat, gesturing with his hands, saying: 'It's like rocking a baby in a cradle.' Fielding and catching routines were a priority. You'll spend a lot of your life fielding, he'd say.

Often Kim lingered half an hour after practice. Once it was to fine-tune Nicholls's calling between wickets. 'Shout loud enough for the whole school to hear,' Kim ordered. Nicholls did, several times, puzzling passers-by and embarrassing himself. But his calling improved. Another time, Kim stayed back to face one delivery from Linden Park's football coach. Mr Hudson was a slinger and a dragger and was bowling with a red compo ball. Kim had no pads and a child-size bat. The ball clanged into a metal fence beyond the midwicket boundary before the football coach completed his follow through.

Tonking Mr Hudson wasn't getting Mr Hughes where he wanted to be. Late February came and bottom-placed South Australia still hadn't phoned. Kim wasn't even invited to state squad practice. 'We had a shocking batting line-up,' says Mallett. 'It was Ian Chappell and the rest were tail-enders. Hughes could have batted blindfolded and got more runs than some of the blokes. And he didn't get picked. It was a ridiculous circumstance.' State selectors were Phil Ridings, Les Favell and Geff Noblet. None are alive to answer back. Bob Blewett, captain-coach of East Torrens, believes they took a long look at Kim early and stopped looking later. 'And I think Kim was probably aware of that.' Out west, where Western Australia were hosting Victoria, Ross Edwards injured himself fielding and created a vacancy that would almost certainly have been Kim's. He was probably aware of that, too.

Runs did not so much trickle as sneeze from Kim's bat, in loud, sporadic gusts. He'd bat in his familiar millionaire's way and donate his wicket for a song. Soft, blotchy pitches discouraged strokeplay. Yet Kim would be casting his cares to the wind just as other batsmen were putting on an extra cardigan. The Campbelltown Oval wicket was grislier than most, based on inferior red clay. Still Kim would not adjust. A trotting track circumnavigated the ground, like a noose.

'He almost had too much ability, because there wasn't anything he didn't believe he could do,' says Blewett. 'There wasn't a shot he didn't think he could play. I suppose what I tried to do was tighten him up. It was like starting a horse in the Melbourne Cup: you had to sort of put him on hold for a while.' When reputation got him nowhere, Kim's only hope was to pile runs so high the state selectors couldn't see past them. But in eleven innings his best was 38 and his average 17. East Torrens met Adelaide in the final, Mike Coward diagnosing in the *'Tiser*: 'There could not be a better time for Kim Hughes to play the big innings he has often threatened.' On a cloudy day at an almost empty Adelaide Oval, a bare-headed Kim made 5 in a total of 52 all out.

Gary Cosier was in Ian Chappell's South Australian side. He'd moved from Melbourne to Adelaide and got picked straightaway. 'So there was a precedent,' he points out. Actually there were six—himself, Mallett, Jenner, House, Yagmich, Hendricks—all interstate stowaways, all in South Australia's XI. And yet they made an exception out of Kim. 'He came over with such a splash that the older heads probably resented it a little,' says Cosier. 'The South Australian guys were pretty insular. They kept their group pretty tight. Anyone built up to be anything special without showing they were special was quickly brought down to earth.' Cosier got the feeling that: 'The fit wasn't too good—and that probably haunted Kim all the way through his career.'

Blewett dragged East Torrens from bottom to second in one season after leaving Prospect. 'Captain Bligh', Rodney Hogg called him—'Captain of the Bounty, wasn't he? I think Hoggy thought I was a hard prick.' Blewett bowled unslayable finger spin, hung tough with the bat, caught everything and demanded similar of others. Belatedly picked for South Australia at thirty-two, he later heard secondhand that selectors Bradman and Favell reckoned him a slogger. This seems curious. Favell himself called his autobiography *By Hook or By Cut* and knew no way in between. Yet something similar happened to Kim, Blewett believes: 'It's South Australian cricket, it's South Australian administration, the committees, the old school tie system.'

Blewett went on to captain the state. He'd have wanted Kim had he been skipper in 1974–75. Kim could have been anything, given the chance, on Adelaide Oval, with its pitch so true, its square boundaries so near. He eventually hit two of his nine Test centuries there. 'Someone should have had the guts to say let's see what we've got here,' says Blewett. No one did, and it ached:

He was so disappointed. He got down in the dumps. But Kim's one of these blokes, you'll walk around the corner worrying about him, then you'll walk back and give him a kick up the backside and throw a few balls at him and all of a sudden there's a few hitting the middle of the bat again and he's back.

Blewett tried to persuade him to stay. Kim spent time in the Blewett backyard with future Test batsman Greg, aged three. Kim was grateful to Bob for developing his front-foot play. But the golden boy was not really a boy anymore. He was twenty-one. And all the things he wished for seemed further away than they had at sixteen. He trained a handful of nights with Norwood Football Club. He saw out term two at Linden Park Primary. And within four months of arriving in Adelaide, he'd bounced away again. 'I'm missing my family,' he said. 'I realise now there's no place like home.'

FOUR

The Crumb-Eaters

THE FREMANTLE DOCTOR floated in from the south-west minutes before Kim did on 2 November 1975, his first day as a first-class batsman. Although the afternoon was cool he rolled his long white sleeves up past his elbows. The exposed arms looked puny, all bone, no meat. The New South Wales fieldsmen stared. He couldn't be any older than fourteen. He won't hold us up for long, they thought.

Lunch was forty-nine minutes away, Western Australia a squeaky 2–68. Straightaway Kim surged on to the front foot. The bowlers tried aiming shorter, flatter, fuller, wider. They should have tried nails and a hammer. Nothing would still Kim's leaping feet. Once his feet landed there was no whirling backlift. Instead he blocked, or drove past the bowler for a couple, or pinpricked an off-side gap for one. Nothing went in the air or across the line and everything was hit off the front foot and the bat's middle. It was risk-free and purposeful. He kept this going until lunchtime.

Since leaving Adelaide he'd joined North Perth as captain-coach. Few so callow have wielded so much clout at an Australian cricket club. Kim had his players running laps of

Charles Veryard Sports Ground then sprinting twos and threes in full batting clobber. 'Ironman training,' the press dubbed it. His 61 in the state trial was sweetly timed in every way. Two days later Ross Edwards, doughty batsman and nimbler cover field, quit for work and family reasons. Years spent stooped over and dribbling hockey balls had caused a degenerating spine and stolen an inch off his height. 'People think I'm a bloody good fieldsman but I'm not really,' said Edwards the day he retired. 'I cannot bend down so I throw myself to the ground, which *looks* spectacular.'

Kim played a Gillette Cup one-dayer against Victoria. He lasted two minutes for nought. He looked a more apt incumbent of Edwards's boots when the Shield match began. Kim's acrobatics in the covers were proclaimed a rare bright spot on a sedate first day, New South Wales declaring at 8–285. He went to lunch on day two 22 not out: flying without rushing. After an hour's batting he was 32.

'The best start to an innings I've ever seen,' says Keith Slater, who was commentating on radio station 6WF. 'It is printed indelibly in my mind. He was 32 after the first hour and he hadn't hit one boundary. When you see something as perfect as that you get excited. And I got pretty excited.'

With the hour up, Kim introduced a new dimension to his play: visible haste. Drives and cuts still clung to the ground. But he was hitting them harder. Len Pascoe went for almost four an over; Gary Gilmour and Dave Colley for nearly six; Kerry O'Keeffe for seven. Fieldsmen revised their condescending first impressions. 'We couldn't believe the way he was playing,' David Hourn recalls. 'He was running down the wicket to Lenny and Gilmour and Colley. I'd never seen anyone do that. With fast bowlers you always stay in your crease. He was the first bloke I'd seen who jumped down.'

Portentous times, they were, nine days before Gough Whitlam's overthrow, his government locked in a barney with the opposition over the release of treasury funds. Nothing the bowlers tried could block Kim's supply. Captain Doug Walters gave himself a turn. His golden arm proved decidedly yellow. His eyes were a snapshot of shellshock. 'I will never forget the look on Doug's face,' says Hourn. Walters staggered up to him.

'Jeez, Cracker, do you wanna have a go?'

'I'll do my best.'

Hourn bowled chinamans. He was the owner of a wrong'un that verged on indecipherable whilst rattling nerves more than stumps, so steepling was its bounce. He'd never bowled in Perth. Spinning it wasn't Hourn's priority today. He was having enough trouble making the ball pitch. The kid wanted to turn everything into a full toss. 'He just ran down the wicket at me. And if he couldn't quite get to me, he'd simply cut me backward of point.' Kim was dropped once, a hooked skyer, on 69. The bespectacled culprit Hourn—'my eyesight was a bit like Devon Malcolm's'—glimpsed it once in front of the old police building. He next saw it on the grass. At least one other stroke was cavalier: Kim pranced, knelt and walloped over mid-on's head and on to the next morning's back pages. Another lofted drive, straighter, took him to a hundred.

Graeme Porter, sitting with his father in the crowd, ranks it alongside Lord's and Melbourne in a trilogy of Hughes masterpieces. 'I doubt whether even Greg Chappell could have been so perfect,' says Keith Slater. 'When I'm explaining to kids how to start an innings I always refer to Kim Hughes's first knock for Western Australia.' It was the first of several Hughes–Hourn duels. 'Amazing, amazing innings,' says Hourn. 'That century was and still is the best and most dynamic innings I've seen in first-class cricket.'

But, think—you bowled to the Chappells, to Viv and Barry Richards:

> Kim was the hardest bloke I ever had to bowl to. Easily the hardest. He was intimidating. I bowled against Greg a couple of times and Ian three or four times. I was always far more nervous and pumped up bowling to Hughes. I played against Barry Richards once and he got 178, but he tended to play the ball on its merits rather than jumping down. With Kim, every ball was a challenge. A day of bowling to Hughes left me mentally and physically drained. I'd bowl quick as I could just to keep him in his crease. There was no way in the world you'd throw the ball up because you knew it would go for four or six. Maybe six.

The one sadness was the paucity of witnesses: a Sunday crowd of 5558, Test selector Neil Harvey among them. The local ABC showed a *Four Corners* re-run, *The Drover's Wife* and *The Sky Bike*. They crossed to the WACA Ground at 4.15 p.m., eighteen minutes after Alan Turner caught Kim on the long-on boundary in the last over before tea. He'd stampeded Hourn once too often. 'Nearly knocked Turner over the fence,' says Hourn. 'If he wasn't there it would have been six and probably killed a spectator to boot.' Ian Brayshaw, watching from the pavilion, remembers the cheeks of Turner's backside almost touching the pickets. Six runs and Kim would have hit 103 in the session.

Out for 119, he made a masher, Robbie Langer, look a mouse in their 205-run stand. John Inverarity went up to him afterwards. 'Congratulations, Kim. Well played. That was brilliant,' he said. 'But you shouldn't have got out just before tea. Think of others apart from yourself.'

Inverarity, bound for a teaching job in England, had recently stepped aside to let Rodney Marsh captain. Inverarity says Kim's team-mates were thrilled for him. But his dismissal required a fresh batsman to weather the session's final deliveries. Inverarity wanted to remind Kim of his responsibilities to the team. 'He was probably a bit surprised,' Inverarity reflects now. 'And it was probably a bit mean.'

•••••

A SESSION'S BATTING was all it took for Western Australians to know they had never produced another like Kim. For much of the last century, Fremantle Harbour or Perth Airport was the first sight the world's cricketers had of Australia. For many, their biggest surprise will have been their lack of surprise. They discovered a place of sand dunes, freeways and spotless streets. Blowflies in your mouth were a commoner phenomenon than rain on your shoes. They noticed the warmth, seabreeze and scintillating light, as if a chandelier swung from every stringybark. On arriving at the WACA Ground they marvelled at the glassy outfield and bouncy pitch, hard and white like limestone, the superabundance of brawny fast bowlers. Only one stereotype of Australian geography, meteorology and cricket lay unturned. Where were all the audacious batsmen?

In the eighty-three years between Western Australia's first-class entry and Kim's debut, only three homegrown batsmen managed as many as half a dozen Tests. Ross Edwards's twentieth and last Test ended two months before Kim turned up. Barry Shepherd, burly and pugnacious, played fourteen. Inverarity, grasshopper-lean and cautious—'Inforeverity', E.W. Swanton christened him—played six. Jack Lee blamed insufficient competition. 'Our West Australian batsmen lack that killer instinct,' he theorised as late as 1971. 'The complete and utter dedication necessary in other places cannot be developed in the more leisurely atmosphere of Perth.' That was as simplistic as saying exposure to too much sunshine fried batsmen's minds. Living in a beach-going suburban pleasure paradise never lulled Nugget Coombs, Polly Farmer, Edith Cowan, Rolf Harris, Bon Scott, Bob Hawke or Dennis Lillee into being happy with mediocrity. And yet it was as if Western Australians had been batting in black and white. Kim's arrival was as dazzling to the senses as the switch to colour TV.

'He was a precursor to the modern game,' says Tony Mann. 'In WA we had blokes like Inverarity and Charlesworth, dour batsmen who eked out their runs. Then Kim said, this is how I'm going to play. Bang, bang, bang!' Mann knows something of Western Australia's cricket pedigree. His father was the creator of Houghton's white burgundy—'You can exist without table wines,' Jack Mann contended, 'but you cannot live'—and a champion bowler of underarms, a variety which lingered longer in Perth than most centres. Overarm bowling was more typical fare by Jack Mann's wrist-twitching pomp of the twenties and thirties. Batsmen underperformed against both. Swan River Colony was founded in 1829 and cricket first mentioned in

1835. Fifty-four years went by until Bill Bateman of Fremantle hit the initial century. Another forty-four years elapsed before Ernie 'Slogger' Bromley was picked for the fourth Bodyline Test. He'd moved to Melbourne months beforehand in the hope a selector might notice him.

John Rutherford is the 79-year-old keeper of the dominant themes of Western Australian cricket's first 125 years: isolation, disadvantage, prejudice, poverty, extortion, bitterness, resentment, jealousy and hate. On Mondays he minds Merredin's old railway station museum in the state's wheatbelt. In the course of four hours one July afternoon not a single tourist passed through to distract him from his memories or his irritation, which time has not quite extinguished. He was the first West Australian to win Test selection while playing for the state. But even within Western Australia, getting noticed was never a cinch for Rutherford.

At eighteen he came to the city from Bruce Rock and asked state captain-coach Keith Carmody to take a look at him. It was 1948, the year after WA's Sheffield Shield admittance. Carmody was busy coaching ten-year-olds. Ten-year-olds he could do something about; it was too late to fix Rutherford. 'You've got so many faults it's not even funny,' said Carmody. So no, he wouldn't take a look at him. He had no objection to Rutherford watching from behind the nets, and this Rutherford did daily for three months, until one day he and Carmody were the only ones there. 'All the other kids were flying kites or had gone swimming out at Scarborough,' says Rutherford. Carmody had nothing to do. So he tossed Rutherford a few balls.

'You've got one thing,' he said at last. 'You've got ball sense.

If I throw this ball you know where it's going to finish up. But as for hitting it, you wouldn't have the first idea.'

Rutherford instinctively thought 'get rooted'. Instead he said: 'Give me the first idea.'

A ball hung from a cord. Carmody demonstrated how to hit it off the front foot, then went whack off the back. It rocketed round the loop and slammed into the back of Rutherford's head. Carmody sent him away to find his own ball and cord. Come back in a year, he said. Rutherford was studying for a science degree. He attached a ball to a tree. He woke at six, batted an hour, breakfasted, batted twenty minutes, went to lectures, came back for lunch, batted ten minutes, returned to lectures, batted two hours, ate his tea, then batted an hour until the light went. He did this for a week.

'Got something to show you.'

Carmody winced. Rutherford persisted. He grabbed a bat and began swinging. Front foot. Back foot. 'Jesus,' said Carmody. 'You have learnt in one week what I thought would take you a year.'

Rutherford was opening in first grade when summer came and for Western Australia by 1952–53. Shortly before selection of the 1956 Ashes squad he played a Test trial at the Sydney Cricket Ground: Ian Johnson's XI versus Ray Lindwall's XI. 'Had to have someone from Western Australia, didn't they?' says Rutherford. 'So I polished my bat, got on the plane and over I went. I got there and there was no bastard to meet me.'

No one was drinking at the pub near the players' lodgings either. And no one thought to alert Rutherford to the practice net that had been arranged. He cabbed it to the SCG. Bradman, a selector, enthused about how wonderful it was to see him:

'This could be a very important match for you.' Bradman had a list. 'I'll put your name down here and you'll get a hit. Just join in.' Rutherford trundled a few. He breathed it all in: the theatre, the occasion, the two hundred swarming spectators. And without a word the players decided practice was over. 'Didn't give me a hit. Oh no. The bastards didn't want to waste their time bowling to me.'

What Rutherford did next says something about the character of the early West Australian cricketers. He put on his pads and gloves and perched unblinking on a practice strip. 'I would have stood there till the next day,' he says. 'I'd still be there.' The other twenty-one players were vanishing into the pavilion. Only Len Maddocks glanced over his shoulder. He ascertained that Rutherford had missed out and sought to set things aright. 'So my practice before taking the first ball from Ray Lindwall next morning,' says Rutherford, 'was to have the No. 2 wicketkeeper roll me up a few leggies.'

Resolve stiffened, Rutherford ground out 113. His rivals for an Ashes berth, Les Favell and Sid Carroll, made 4 and 2. Late on the final afternoon Johnson gave Rutherford a bowl. Neil Harvey was 96. Rutherford feels certain the intention was to embarrass him: for Harvey to bring up his century off Rutherford. Harvey didn't get past 96. Rutherford knocked him over.

'Hey! You're not supposed to be taking wickets.'

'That's right. Isn't it a funny game?'

Rutherford could not now justifiably miss the Ashes tour, and didn't. The Board of Control's original cost-shaving plan, he says, was for him to skip the warm-up games in Tasmania and get scooped aboard as the *Himalaya* left Fremantle. Word reached Rutherford that Alf Randell, WA's lone board delegate, had claimed Rutherford, a schoolteacher, wouldn't wish to miss classes. 'When I heard this I was ropeable,' says Rutherford. He complained to a very high-up board official. The very high-up official, it transpired, was no big admirer of Western Australians. Rutherford's recollection of their conversation goes like this. The very high-up official said: 'We have forty opening batsmen in Victoria who can do the job better. But for some unknown reason the Australian selectors have picked you.' The next thing the very high-up official said was:

> I'm going to give you some advice. First thing is, no word you say is worth a cracker until you've been in the side at least five years. And God help us that doesn't happen. The second thing is that in the meantime you should just eat at the crumbs that fall from the masters' table.

Rutherford took his protest to Bradman and Johnson, the captain. He joined the team from the outset. As they stepped off the plane in Launceston, Rutherford remembers everybody being introduced one by one.

First, Keith Miller. 'Good to see you back here, Keith . . .'

Ray Lindwall. 'Oh Ray, I remember the day when you . . .'

Len Maddocks. 'Oh Lenny, good to have you on our soil, absolutely tremendous . . .'

John Rutherford. 'John who?'

Rutherford was a statue of obstinacy. It was becoming his regular pose. 'The name's Rutherford.'

'You're not here.'

Silence. 'Well, it looks to me like I am.'

'Look, go and get yourself a ticket back to Perth or Fremantle or wherever you've come from.'

Board chairman Frank Cush informed Rutherford he couldn't stay at the team hotel. No beds were left. Rutherford asked for the pavilion keys. He'd doss there and be first at the ground when he woke. Not allowed, said Cush. 'Go down the wharf. There's some places there you could possibly get in.' Luckily, an eavesdropping Harvey ordered an extra bed up to his and Maddocks's room.

Bamboozled by the curving ball, Rutherford struggled once in England. He did play what he considers the innings of his life in Southampton. As Rutherford tells it, Johnson was holidaying and Miller escorted all bar five players to London to see *The Pajama Game*. Miller's promised early-morning return didn't eventuate. Only five Australians were present with play against Hampshire due to start. It was a case of bat first or face pandemonium. The coin spun and Lindwall grunted loudly—but indiscernibly. The coin landed. 'Tails it is,' swooped Lindwall. 'We'll bat.' Hampshire captain Desmond Eagar objected. Lindwall, says Rutherford, asked Eagar whom people would likelier believe: 'Ray Lindwall, or you?'

Rutherford opened with Ken Mackay under instructions to survive until reinforcements arrived. The problem was that curving ball. Ten weeks in England and Rutherford still hadn't acclimatised. Derek Shackleton was starting it outside off and finishing on leg. Rutherford kept nicking into his pads, balls ballooning off them precariously. 'Six times I was missed in the leg trap'—fingernail chances, but chances. Somehow he made it to 30, mission completed, then finally fell caught. Miller and his merry men entered the pavilion at the same time as Rutherford.

'That was a shocking shot, Rutherford,' said Miller. 'When I get out there I'll show you how you should have played that.'

Rutherford just looked at him. 'I thought, you bastard.' As for his cherished 30, he still remembers reading Lindsay Hassett's description of it as the worst of Rutherford's many bad innings in England. 'Hassett didn't have a clue. If I'd got out . . .'

The Australians sailed the long way home, Rutherford substituting for Colin McDonald in Bombay for his one and only Test. Again he made 30; again acclimatisation was a problem. He swept Subhash Gupte and momentarily forgot the heat. 'Stupid me ran four,' says Rutherford. 'It was the last running I did. I had double vision. *Double vision.*' He faced up, hazarded a pull at what appeared to be two balls, and bottom-edged to the keeper. There was no second innings or chance.

Western Australia's first Test tourist found advice non-existent and anti-WA chitchat rife. Incompetent Perth umpiring was the topic of general bewailing one rainy day in England. That got Rutherford really steamed. 'Whenever we go over there,' someone said, 'we've got to get Rutherford out three times.'

A very high-up board official, who Rutherford had met before, led him aside. 'John,' he said, 'I tried to save you from this.' Then, those familiar words again. 'I tell you, nobody's interested in anything you say—and also, you should eat at the crumbs that fall from the masters' table.'

Rutherford waited for him to finish. 'You better get used to the way I speak,' said Rutherford. 'Very soon half the Australian XI will be made up of West Australians.'

'And that,' replied the very high-up official, 'only shows how stupid you are.'

•••••

BASTARDS, as John Rutherford calls them, gets spat out a lot when Westralian cricket folk talk about eastern staters, another favourite phrase. When Bob Simpson endured a fallow few weeks upon moving to Perth in 1956–57 he was tagged *the ex-New South Wales player*. 'As soon as I started getting runs,' Simpson recalls, 'I became *the West Australian*. Then when I went back to Sydney it was *New South Wales batsman Bob Simpson failed today* when I failed, and *ex-West Australian Bob Simpson* when I succeeded.' It shocked him at first. Simpson had grown up among a people who considered themselves part of Australia. 'Around that time in WA they were talking about setting up a separate country. I put it down to the isolation. I got used to it.'

Rutherford's calamities were not the lot of every sandgroper to make it big. Keith Slater, selected in the Test twelve against England in 1958–59, got greeted at the airport and ushered to the MCG for the last day of Victoria–New South Wales. Richie Benaud spied Slater before the old players' pavilion and stopped setting his field. Play halted for five minutes while Benaud shook Slater's hand and chaperoned him into the Victorian dressing room: 'Look after this guy, he's over here to play for Australia.' Slater felt adrift because so many team-mates were strangers. Otherwise his anxieties were the typical newcomer's. For example, only after playing once and being twelfth man twice did he know not to address wicketkeeper Wally Grout as Grouty—'or he'd punch you in the face. You could call him Griz or Wal but not Grouty.'

'Griz' was short for 'Grizzler', a tribute to Grout's incessant geeing-up of bowlers and fielders. Grizzler summed up several West Australians too. Grizzliness was not unwarranted. They were denied Sheffield Shield status until twenty-one years after Queensland and fifty-five years after South Australia. Champions that first season, they remained part-time underlings for the next eight. To go full-time they had to pay the extra travel costs of the other states in trekking west annually instead of biennially. This arrangement—The Subsidy—swallowed up to 10 per cent of income and reigned from 1956 to '66. It might have folded sooner had the WACA's voice amounted to more than a squeak. Alas they, like Tasmania, occupied one of thirteen seats round the board's table, meaning a one-thirteenth helping of profits and one-thirteenth of a say in proceedings.

The players were loosely aware of the financial particulars. But to see the implications they had only to look in a mirror. Eleven squirming vegemite scarecrows stared back at them. In *Garth*, his charming biography of fast bowler Graham McKenzie, Ed Jaggard paints a gruesome picture:

> Caps were described by one player as 'inverted saucepans with cardboard inside the peaks' . . . Sweaters were fine knit rather than the distinctive cable knit of true cricket sweaters. The blazers came from another era. Black, trimmed with wide gold braid, these monstrosities could be spotted a kilometre away . . . Representing Western Australia wasn't much fun.

Western Australia's inaugural 1947–48 triumph—they won on percentages, playing half as many games—was part mathematical quirk. Certainly it was an aberration. They inhabited the bottom three for the next seventeen seasons. They played as if awestruck. And cricket is a hard game to master on bended knees. Switch off your radios, commentator Ron Halcombe used to exhort the citizens of Perth: *'Nothing is happening!'* Barry Shepherd's captaincy brought a turnaround. When Shepherd picked and clubbed Benaud's top-spinner he didn't give the embarrassed smile that Benaud detected years earlier as a west coast tic. Instead, Shepherd growled: 'Take that you bastard.' Opponents became bastards from the east. A woe-is-us mentality turned into a them-and-us obsession.

Cricket was not alone in this transformation. 'Bastards from the east' was the catchcry when people rang a commercial TV station after hours and got a recorded message because the programming funnelled out of Sydney or Melbourne and everyone had gone home. Reporting on the Perth Royal Show was less about fairy floss than pointscoring. 'You'd ask an expert whether our pigs were as good as the ones from the east,' journalist Norman Aisbett once explained. 'And if he said Perth pigs were better it was a guarantee of getting your story in the paper.'

Comparing swine and swearing at the phone were petty pastimes. In cricket, resenting the bastards helped win matches. It was a positive force. And it became almost intrinsic. Men like McKenzie, Inverarity, Edwards and Charlesworth learnt it from their fathers, who'd played in the lickspittle pre-Sheffield Shield days. It was bequeathed from team to team. The Subsidy was a powerful cudgel. Captains of the fifties and sixties could thunder: 'We're paying for these bastards. Now let's make *them* pay.' The Subsidy had dwindled to $572 in total by its final year. In retrospect, they were 572 dollars well spent.

Rutherford's premonition became fact sooner than even he envisaged. Six of Australia's eleven at The Oval in 1972 were West Australians. At Lord's, Bob Massie and Dennis Lillee looted all twenty wickets. They were not just eating at the masters' table. They built and laid it. But those 572 dollars and all they stood for had not been forgotten. In Anthony Barker's WACA history, Lillee vouched: 'Playing for WA was an all-consuming passion. I'd have died out on the pitch for the team. I never believed in saving for the second innings, for the new ball, for the next day, for a tour that might be coming up.'

The captaincy passed from Tony Lock to Inverarity. 'You gave your all for WA,' said Lillee, 'but then you gave a little bit more for Inver. Teams under him were very, very passionate . . . I've never known team spirit in any team, ever, like that.' WA won the Shield ten times in eighteen years. Ruling the roost did not stop them rueing the east. Decades after 'us' had caught up with and overtaken 'them', Western Australian cricketers still felt furious and indignant.

Other states dreaded the six-hour flight westward. It wasn't just the likelihood of defeat. It was the lack of banter. If your ball landed in WA's net it got kicked away not tossed back. John Rogers left behind his life as a New South Wales selector and University of NSW captain-coach to become the WACA's first general manager in 1979. He discovered a foreign country. The New South Wales way was the rugby way: compete hard, get along afterwards. 'Western Australians,' says Rogers, 'play cricket in an AFL fashion. The opposition are the enemy. You don't fraternise beforehand, you don't fraternise during, you don't fraternise after.' A gut grizzliness simmered on through the eighties. 'Daryl Foster fostered it,' says Rogers. 'Non-drinking academic that he is, he got all the blokes in the palm of his hand. He fostered this thing of them and us.'

On his first day in Western Australia, Foster rumbled cross the Nullarbor in a white Falcon with a vinyl top and a back seat loaded with cots and prams. He was headed for Perth to study physical education. 'We're playing a Shield game there this weekend,' were Northcote team-mate Bill Lawry's last words to him. 'Come down.' Foster parked outside the WACA Ground:

I talked my way in as the thirteenth Victorian man and got in for nothing. The Farley Stand was still there, the old wooden one, and I heard this roar as I went in. Good grief, I thought, this sounds like a footy game. I rushed up the embankment and saw seven or eight thousand people. Lawry had just been dismissed—caught somebody, bowled McKenzie—and as he left the middle they yelled and screamed the whole way: 'You've had it, Phantom.' So it was there. I've noticed it all my life here. I think it drives success in Western Australian sport. I won't say I didn't foster it—but it was certainly latent.

Lackadaisical gatekeepers have gone the way of the Farley Stand. Secession whispers are the preserve of nutty conservative politicians, proffered half-heartedly, like a great-aunt with her tray of Iced Vo Vos. Even isolation isn't what it used to be. Thanks to the internet, Perth really feels three thousand kilometres from anywhere. Before, it was like going to Venus, and almost as hot. If obscene house prices and a couple of AFL teams are badges of nationhood, Western Australians could even be considered quintessentially Australian. West Coast Eagles' 1992 premiership victory might have been the moment when resentment died. Because it's hard to feel smug and resentful. Interestingly, in the sixteen years since, Western Australia have won the Sheffield Shield competition only twice. Smashing eastern staters still gives people pleasure, but it's a fleeting pleasure, a frisson, not the overpowering obsession it was in John Rutherford's world.

When Kim Hughes entered that world, extortion was a thing of the past. Disadvantage and prejudice were getting increasingly difficult to prove. Bitterness, resentment, jealousy and hate lived on.

•••••

KIM GOT PAID $16.25 a day in his first match. Extortion wasn't stone dead after all. It was $3.75 more than the previous season's allowance but still only 36 cents a run, once you added his second-innings 60 to his 119. Money was tight all right—too tight not to mention. During Kim's next game, against Queensland, Eric Beecher's *Cricketer* magazine surveyed the top dozen players from each Shield state. Fifty-eight out of sixty reckoned the financial rewards were insufficient. More than two-thirds feared those pittances could persuade them to quit cricket. Kim's feelings were probably more tangled than most.

'I have always played the game because I've loved the game,' he'd later philosophise, 'not because of how much money I can make out of it.' But there was something else to consider. He was fourteen when he saw a gaggle of girls burst through the quadrangle at City Beach High. He asked his friend who was the one with the luscious blonde hair and the skirt down to her ankles. That's Jenny Davidson, the friend said, and pretty soon they were catching the bus to dance classes at Gilkisons and Jenny's anxious father was pacing a hole in the porch. Playing for Australia was Kim's dream. Yet he wanted to support a family some day. It would not be the last time that dilemma intruded.

The Queensland game is one he still dwells on. Jeff Thomson was menacing as a sasquatch, so quick as to be mathematically unexplainable. Scientists calculated that when Thommo let rip his ultrafast one the batsman needed 0.3 seconds to analyse it plus 0.3 seconds to execute a stroke. Yet the ball arrived in 0.438 seconds—leaving him minus 0.162 seconds. On Roy Abbott's WACA pitch it didn't feel that long. Abbott was a former insurance clerk, cattle-station hand and prisoner of war on Crete. Sent to the WACA by the Commonwealth Employment Office for three months' casual work, he stayed thirty-three years. He lived at the ground, in a cottage, first to rise and last to shut the gates after trotting meets, stirring in darkness when it rained unexpectedly to lay down the covers with wife Tina. Nothing about Perth was so otherworldly as the pitch Roy built. Hard, true, rearing and—in certain bowlers' hands—dangerous. Abbott and Thomson were a duo whose deadliness rivalled Lillee and Thomson.

'You'll kill 'em today, champ,' was Frank Parry's message as Kim passed him at the bottom of the stairs, thirty minutes before stumps. Bruce Laird's first words were less heartening. 'Now Kim,' said Laird, 'someone's gunna get hurt here.' Kim took guard on leg stump. He pulled away; keeper John Maclean was back on the sightscreen. Why wasn't he getting into position? Quickly Kim twigged. Maclean was in position. He survived both and saw neither of Thomson's first two balls. A straight one rattled his bat and rolled into a gap. Kim took off. A guttural roar resounded. '*Geddback.*' Another lesson: no singles would be run tonight. Kim faced every ball of Thommo's four overs. Laird took genial Geoff Dymock.

There was a second century that summer against the touring West Indians. Kim made a first-ball duck then watched 23-year-old Vivian Richards massacre 175. Ball left bat like a thunderclap. Three in a row off poor Bob Paulsen cleared the long-on fence. Balls cascaded over but nowhere near a thankful Charlesworth in the covers. Richards replicated such bowler battery on a hundred occasions. The significance this time was the effect on an impressionable youth. That's how I want to play, Kim decided, and in the second innings he bolted to 102 in a couple of hours: dancing, driving, sweeping, pulling. Richie Benaud, taking his first look, thought Kim 'most promising'. Shrewd old Percy Beames, in his final season on the *Age* cricket beat, asserted: 'Hughes is a batsman with possibilities.'

Possibilities were undone by rashness more often than not that first season. He'd play around a medium pacer's straight ball. Or he'd misread a googly, apparently uninterested in watching the bowler's hand. Occasionally it worked. Joined by Brayshaw at 6–62, hunting 150, on a last-day Adelaide turner, Kim swept two foxes in Mallett and Jenner theatrically, repeatedly, almost obsessively. First slip Ian Chappell thought Kim desperate, his tactics doomed. But although he wasn't watching the hand, he was judging the length. Every sweep stayed down. Every boundary jabbed Mallett's blood pressure up. Western Australia won easily. Afterwards Chappell met Kim for the first time in the South Australian dressing room: 'I was left with the impression that here was a young man who didn't lack confidence in his own ability.'

The life of a full-time cricketer appealed. A hoped-for winter of county or Lancashire League cricket in 1975 wasn't to be. But Edinburgh-based Watsonians were keen for the 1976 season. A Wiltshire gentleman, an agent, who sent the club handwritten briefings about potential imports on Basildon Bond notepaper, recommended him. Watsonians captain Brian Adair liked the sound of this Kim Hughes whose destiny it was to play for Australia. His wife Mona had struck up a regular correspondence with another antipodean swashbuckler, Keith Miller, as a schoolgirl. Mona was bewitched after seeing Miller play. Miller responded, intrigued, for he'd seen Scotland during the war and assumed the Scots cared little for cricket.

They agreed terms: £1000 or so for the season. Or so Adair thought. Kim's promised letter of confirmation didn't arrive. Adair heard no more of it. In a meeting one day a call came through. Watsonians' new Australian had touched down. Could someone please fetch him? Adair didn't bust his neck to get there. The lad could have said something. 'I found him sprawled on the roundabout at our little airport,' Adair remembers. 'He was clad in a denim suit and open-necked shirt. Blond hair.'

Adair drove Kim to his new home, the boarding house at George Watson's College. He was surprised when the jetlagged new pro chose practice ahead of bed that first evening. The wicket was muddy and slow, batting torture. The rain broke long enough for practice to proceed. And when he got home,

Adair told Mona he had just seen an amazing batsman. Kim's confirmation note showed up six weeks later. He'd sent it sea mail.

Jim Hubble was the last first-class West Australian to embark on a Scottish dalliance. Hubble brought an ankle strain. He saw the rain, the practice pitch marked out of ordinary grass, the waterlogged run-up and the miracles expected of him. He repacked his bags and flew home. Kim and Watsonians looked assured of bonnier times. Kim went with an open mind, a spirit of adventure and the two qualities that helped wherever he went: a desire to be liked and a determination to see good in people. His first game was at Selkirk, in the Scottish borders, with a field of cows for a sightscreen. Kim didn't grouch. He adjusted. Almost bowled for nought, he sped to triple figures then enquired whether it was the done thing to retire. Carry on, everyone trilled, carry on.

One night at practice he used the edge of his bat only. He invited anyone game to penetrate his defence. Wally Hammond used to perform an identical trick in pre-season nets at Gloucestershire, not that Kim realised this or knew who Wally Hammond was. The result was identical, too. Like Hammond, Kim didn't miss one.

Team-mates were enchanted, opponents perplexed. Was that a Welsh accent? Kim saw Dublin, where he and another player bet on themselves being first to kiss a girl when they stepped out of the hotel. Nuns were the first females encountered. The bet's outcome, says club historian Stewart Oliver, is still unknown. Kim guest-skippered against Malahide. 'A day he will never forget,' reported the *Watsonian*. He hit a century then watched seven catches go kerplunk, his crinkled brow showing 'the strain the club's captains usually feel'. In all he souvenired five hundreds and 1711 runs—club records, both. A sublime 79 for the wandering Irish Leprechauns against Keith Fletcher's Essex was another highlight. If only winter would never end.

'He was one of the nicest and most exciting cricketers Watsonians have ever had,' says Adair. 'He was always asking for advice on all manner of subjects. There was a very close bond between us, even though I was forty-one to his twenty-two. He must have seen me as a father figure.' Only one batting peccadillo is today remembered: 'He'd decide what he was going to do to the ball before it was bowled.'

For the last game at Forthill, Adair sent himself and Kim in first. Sentiment swayed that decision. They proved inseparable: 232 they put on, another club record, Adair's contribution 41. 'My role,' he says, 'was to count to five and run like hell on the sixth.' Kim's unbeaten 218 took under three hours. Watsonians, a humble club of ex-George Watson's pupils that had won nothing since the 1890s, achieved the double: East League and Masterton Trophy champions. Presented with a Royal Stewart tartan kilt at the end-of-season dinner, Kim wore it proudly. Forty of his new friends farewelled him at the airport. Adair posted a letter to Australian Cricket Board secretary Alan Barnes, who was sufficiently impressed to run off fourteen copies, one for each board delegate. The letter read:

The Scots as a race are not given to extravagant praise, but . . . the attraction of his style brought a lot of spectators to our games. You are extremely lucky in Australia to have such fine, uninhibited and technically correct strokeplayers . . . Kim behaved both on and off the field with exemplary sportsmanship, and his conduct was at all times a credit to Australia and the Australian cricket authorities. In these days when the manners of cricket players leave a lot to be desired, it is encouraging to see a fiercely competitive player acting properly.

Dicey wickets made Kim watch the ball and play with bat nearer pad. Being his team's greatest hope educated him in the art of building, not frittering, an innings. These changes Kim detected in himself. After falling cheaply against out-of-towners one sodden afternoon he was quick to check it didn't count towards the official averages—as if the cold hardened him, briefly. A year later he rejoined the team on their trip to Corfu. He loved it, reminiscing long after his Test days were over: 'Sipping ouzo and coke on the side. Twirling your arm over and having a bit of a dash. That was life.'

And that was the real legacy: a place and people he would return to again and again. 'Possibly the best six months of my life.'

•••••

SIX OF KIM'S most cherished months were soon followed by five of his most sought-after days. The afternoon before Christmas 1976, in the scramble to catch Zaheer Abbas's spooned pull, Jeff Thomson and Alan Turner bumped shoulders. Thomson dislocated his, five agonising centimetres separating bone from joint, with no guarantee that lightning would strike from it ever again. At the Parry household's Boxing Day shindig the mood was festive. For that was the day selectors

Harvey, Ridings and Loxton held their phone hook-up to discuss Thomson's replacement for the Second Test.

Kim joined the team on a Thursday night and batted in the MCG nets on Friday. He was bareheaded and wore mitten gloves. Next morning, New Year's Day, he landed the twelfth man's job, catching Asif Iqbal off Gilmour. A dressing room run-in between a glass shard and Ian Davis's foot meant he substituted again on a perfunctory fifth morning, Australia eyeing three last Pakistani wickets. Stationed at mid-off in Lillee's first over, Kim tumbled on his right shoulder in a futile and ungainly effort to catch Imran Khan. Out snapped the collarbone: a minor version of Thomson's injury. Team physio Barry Richardson prescribed a week's rest. It was as drab an international audition as that. Retelling it to the Melbourne Cricket Club years later, Kim sprayed a sprinkling of poetry to go with his graceless motion:

> Dennis went back to the sightscreen, pretending to push off from the wheels. Well, Bay 13 were screaming, chanting 'Kill, Kill, Kill'. Dennis steamed in and they built up to a crescendo. As he let the ball go you could hear the air being sucked out of the MCG. I wanted to kill someone. There was that much adrenalin pumping through me, I just wanted to do something. And I did something. I crashed into the ground and injured my shoulder.

The post-Chappelli era was two Tests old. Already Greg was running a grey-socked kind of outfit compared with Ian's polka-dotted banditti. In the game where Thommo maimed himself they looked keener on escaping defeat than inflicting it. Marsh and Cosier sidestepped a victory chase of 56 runs in 15 eight-ball overs. An Adelaide audience more accustomed to patting cats than howling catcalls was outraged. It wasn't the Australian way. It certainly wasn't Kim's way. And it wasn't Kim's 39 average after fourteen first-class matches that people craved. They craved his class, his cheek.

It was a confounding summer, 1976–77, the game caught between flux and gridlock. Western Australia ditched black caps for gold caps to evoke pizzazz. The Perth Building Society tossed $10,000 into the players' pot. A step towards 'adequate and full sponsorship', Rodney Marsh called it. Yet when Kerry Packer offered the Australian Cricket Board half a million a year for the exclusive TV rights he elicited smacked gobs, then a shrug, and finally a brush-off.

Kim's position mirrored Australian cricket's. In one corner sat those who delighted in his fluidity; in the other, those who wished to dam it. A week in October illustrated his conundrum. It started with a 40-over grade tussle conducted more like a car-chase scene. South African superbat Barry Richards, in his first home game for Midland–Guildford, slugged a 100-ball century. Kim retaliated with a 102-ball century, beating Richards to the man-of-the-match prize. Five days later WA's Shield team gathered at Adelaide's Arkaba Court Motel for their pre-game meeting. Captain Marsh kept Kim behind afterwards. Team honchos Lillee, Brayshaw and Foster stayed seated too. Together they itemised the golden chances blown during Kim's debut season: his dill's hoist off Geoff Attenborough; the Malcolm Francke googly that hoodwinked him; the Alan Hurst half-tracker that clean-bowled him. Each time he'd been well set.

'You need to bat for periods,' said Marsh. 'Bat for drinks, for lunch, for drinks again, for tea.' Marsh stressed the importance of planning. A sensible plan for you, he suggested, would be to score centuries in 240 minutes. Lecture over.

'Right,' said Marsh, wrapping up. 'You bat for drinks . . .' Kim nodded.

'You bat for lunch . . .' Another nod.

'And finally you've been batting 240 minutes. How many are you?'

Kim looked at the ceiling. 'Eight hundred.'

It's possible Kim was playing for laughs. The way Brayshaw remembers it: 'A wicked grin creased his young face.' It's plausible, too, that he was signalling, in the guise of a jest, that he wouldn't be heeding Marsh's advice, that his plan was to have no plan. Only Kim knows. What we know is he batted once that game. He cantered to 59 then got out trying to loft Terry Jenner over the Victor Richardson Gates.

An unconquered 137 in 167 balls against Pakistan, spiriting Western Australia to a late-evening victory, did not comply with Marsh's specifications either. It was opportune, though: four days before Thomson's shoulder went bang instead of its customary whang. 'Rarely has a batsman of his limited experience been seen in a more majestic performance,' wrote the *Australian*'s Phil Wilkins. 'The timing and power of his drives and cuts had to be seen to be believed, but he also hooked and pulled with the confidence of a champion.' Kim's loudest backer was Keith Slater's *Sunday Times* column, once you flicked past the girls in unfeasibly small bikinis marvelling at Perth's improbably warm sunshine to find it. Slater's glee rose week by week. Forget normal runs-on-the-board policy. Kim wasn't normal: 'He should be selected for Australia immediately . . . I believe Hughes will be Australia's next great No. 3.' Slater rated Kim his country's most exciting batsman since a young Norm O'Neill, and that was as exciting as could be.

Kim's next innings were under a green cap, not gold. His dislocated collarbone excused him from Third Test sub-fielding duties. But he went on the two-Test tour of New Zealand. Greg Chappell, thwarted 1–1 by Pakistan and not satisfied, introduced early-morning fitness runs. Chappell's own unscripted dashes after willowy-bottomed streakers in Christchurch and Auckland provided a forgettable tour's two unforgettable images. With Kim, he followed Marsh's interventionist approach. Try batting long periods, Chappell recommended. Acquaint yourself with conditions. Wait for a loose one.

This time, Kim obliged. His first official knock for Australia was an hour-long 22 against Northern Districts. A second-innings 76 showcased more of his several personalities. He ran out Rick McCosker by half the pitch, loitered two hours over twenty runs, then hammered boundaries left, right and straight to set up a declaration and victory. He collected eight runs in his next four innings and was a spectator at both Tests. Back home, Adelaide's David Hookes was racking up hundreds like he was tying up shoelaces, five in six innings over that same month-long stretch. Home was a place Kim thought about a lot.

'He was green and homesick,' tour manager Roger Wotton recalls. 'He was the junior of the squad and he was made to seem as such . . . They were pretty tough blokes to be involved with, Lillee and Marsh and Chappell.'

That was not all. 'He was very much in love. He was missing his girlfriend, obviously.'

Kim's non-cricketing exploits both impressed and bewildered. Mike Sheahan, later an Australian Rules reporter of lordly influence, watched a post-practice kickaround at Christchurch's Linwood High School and fantasised: 'If young Hughes ever drops cricket for football . . .' A night of shaggy-dog poker naivety intrigued the *New Zealand Herald*'s Don Cameron. Kim delved into his pocket. His hand reappeared full of $10 notes, a rolled-up wad of them—'thick enough,' Cameron noticed, 'to choke a donkey'. But he kept putting his faith in two pairs. The journos kept taking his money. Cameron felt a pang or two. At breakfast, Cameron had no chance to explain before Wotton cut in: 'Serves him right. Cocky bloke. Thinks two pairs will always win.'

Popular and respected, Wotton was nonetheless on his one and only expedition as manager. For he had a day job—state member for Burrendong in rural New South Wales—and Country Party leader Leon Punch wasn't pleased. Six weeks in New Zealand while parliament was sitting, Punch fumed, equalled untold masses of votes squandered. 'Well,' says Wotton, 'he'd be surprised how many bloody votes it won for me. I supplied a few locals with tickets and got great publicity in the bush papers. That won me more votes than sitting in parliament listening to boring debates.'

Sprucing up player appearances is one achievement Wotton lays claims to. Recent unofficial dress policy had been that anything clingy, stripy or spotty which didn't lend itself to being tucked in was a winner. For Otago's centenary dinner, Wotton requested that everyone don coats: 'Well, they came in all sorts of coats. But at least they wore them.' He also advocated that wide-brimmed sunhats with the green underside replace the mismatched terry-towelling beach gear that adorned most heads.

The team flew home and to Melbourne for the Centenary Test against England. Hookes filled the slot that could have been Kim's. On cricket's most glittering stage in a hundred years, Hookes booked his place in larrikin folklore with five gunbarrel fours off five Tony Greig off-breaks. Approximately 55,300 fewer spectators saw Kim hit 33 for North Perth. The Test ended with Kim's selection in Australia's seventeen-man Ashes squad. Eight days later he and Jenny—charming, vivacious, unfailingly supportive—got married. Swing bowler Mick Malone was best man. Four weeks were all the newlyweds had together. Four and a half months in faraway England beckoned.

Wotton would have liked to be on that plane but there was no way. Six weeks he could get away with. To go to England he'd have to quit parliament. Len Maddocks went instead. In retrospect, Wotton is glad it wasn't him. Overseeing the 1977 Ashes tour turned out to be the most joyless, thankless, pointless job any Australian cricket manager ever had. The signs were there in New Zealand, nothing too foreboding, nothing you could really point at, just a couple of shadowy presences, Austin Robertson and John Cornell, in the players' ears and up their nostrils. David Lord, of Channel Seven and *David Lord's World of Cricket Monthly*, noticed it too. Players kept ducking into an alcove beneath the Eden Park grandstand, where Robertson and Cornell were sitting. 'They were disappearing two by two, like Noah's ark,' says Lord.

There was nothing so unusual about Robertson hovering around, Wotton supposed. Journalist, wasn't he? Ex-*Daily News* man? The players all seemed to know him. Presumably he was writing something. More mysterious was the omnipresence of Cornell, an unmistakable figure even without the surf lifesaver's cap he wore as dunderheaded Strop on *The Paul Hogan Show*. And another funny thing—although Wotton kept seeing Cornell, they were never actually introduced, never exchanged a word. 'Every time I walked into a room,' Wotton remembers, 'Cornell was just leaving . . .'

FIVE

'You're the Fred Astaire
of Cricket'

LATE ON A SUNDAY, Geoff Dymock retired to his room at Hove's Dudley Hotel and wrote his diary entry for 8 May 1977.

> Slept in. Up at 10 a.m. Beer at Lamb's Inn with Gary Cosier. Lunch at restaurant near Ifield. Watched cricket on TV in p.m. and rested. A couple of beers in pubs at Brighton with Greg C, Ray B, Gary C . . . Takeaway chicken and chips in hotel and to bed about 11.30. Team professional group news released and problems for players.

Dymock had never kept a tour diary before. After two weeks his prose and his bowling already had something in common: a knack for making the potentially devastating appear run-of-the-mill.

'Team professional group news' was upgraded to 'greatest cricket show on earth' in Monday's papers. Even then, the greatest cricket scoop on earth caught editors snoozing. Peter McFarline's *Age* yarn was shoehorned on to an inside sports page. Alan Shiell regrets not ringing the *Australian*'s office to explain just how big was the boom about to erupt. 'In those days,' he laments, 'we didn't use the phone as much.' They pooled information before leaving Australia. Shiell knew slightly more than McFarline and they both knew enough by the Saturday night of Tony Greig's party, thrown in a marquee on his Brighton lawn. A leisurely Sunday's golf with McFarline kept the *Sydney Morning Herald*'s Brian Mossop uncontactable by phone and the scoop, by blind luck or otherwise, safe with two. A bunch of Australians had signed up for a bunch of breakaway games against a world side. They were to go on Kerry Packer's payroll, their deeds to be televised on his Nine network. Among them were thirteen of Australia's seventeen Ashes tourists.

For Packer, World Series Cricket delivered bottomless summer hours of high-rating, low-budget TV with inbuilt ad breaks each over and advertising smorgasbords whenever a wicket fell. For the game itself, cameras from both ends, helmets, white balls, coloured costumes, triangular tournaments and abbreviated nocturnal matches became life's essentials. These upheavals, probably inevitable, now happened not in dribs and drabs but in the blink of a tycoon's eyelashes. For the thirteen Ashes tourists who enlisted, WSC meant swankier hotels, pay packets unimaginably fatter than $400 a Test, and a feeling of justice. For the four who didn't—Serjeant, Dymock, Cosier, Hughes—the changes were less dramatic but ultimately, perhaps, more profound. For them, 'problems for players', as Dymock put it, was a candidate for greatest cricket understatement on earth.

Serjeant's debut 81 at Lord's earned him a belated approach from Packer's people. But he rated his hospital job paramount and his cricket job a bonus. He politely declined. Dymock and Cosier didn't sign because they weren't asked. Doing the asking was Austin Robertson. Doing the picking was Packer's captain-to-be Ian Chappell. 'Now who do you want in this fucking team of yours?' was one of Packer's first sentences to him. Brother Greg, Marsh, Lillee, Robertson, Cornell and Packer himself chimed in. But they were no selection panel. It was Ian's team. Ian was a man any aspiring Australian cricketer wanted as an admirer. Not an enemy.

'I always believed Ian Chappell didn't think I could play,' says Dymock. He has fond memories of his second Test, a hard day's bowling in Wellington. He and Max Walker chugged in tirelessly, lucklessly, and were rewarded with an escape clause from that night's team function. 'Go have a hot bath,' said Ian. It made Dymock feel valued. And yet: 'I never thought that he thought I was good enough.'

Cosier was ticklishly placed with two Chappells. A long-ago interview on Channel Seven's *World of Sport*, when Greg suggested this promising newcomer should perform away from Adelaide Oval before anyone got too excited, was a nick on Cosier's memory banks. 'He didn't say it softly,' Cosier recalls. 'He really made a point of it.' Within a year—Melbourne, 1975–76—Cosier was playing his first Test. Greg was captain. Cosier joined him at the crease late afternoon. Andy Roberts took the second new ball and Cosier got the feeling Greg wasn't unhappy at seeing the anxious debutant cop most of the strike. Did his captain wish him to fail? 'He certainly didn't help me succeed,' is Cosier's conclusion. Anxious debutant survived and proceeded to 109 next day. 'I messed him up and stayed in.'

Cosier's rapport with the older Chappell felt sturdier. Yet even Ian publicly questioned Cosier's physique (too fat) and diligence (too thin). 'If Ian thought I wasn't serious about my cricket it was because I was with him in the bar,' says Cosier. 'We'd sit together on Shield tours until one or two in the morning, having a drink and talking about fast bowling, spin bowling, field placements. There's no better person to learn off.'

What about Kim: was Ian an admirer or enemy? They'd never played together and opposed each other twice, most recently when Ian encountered a youngster 'who didn't lack confidence in his own ability'. Was that a compliment? After all, Ian himself oozed confidence, stepping inside the line and hooking bouncers off his moustache as an expression of his own indomitableness. Or was it a tart way of saying the kid's full of himself? Ian captained South Australia during 1974–75, Kim's half-season in Adelaide, when no vacancy arose at state training. Nor could Ian find space in the 1977 Ashes squad he nominated for *Cricketer*. He lumped Kim with seven other also-rans who showed 'very little in the way of grafting ability'.

Kim and Ian sat at distant ends of Australian cricket's family tree. If Kim was the golden boy, Ian was the bronzed renegade, lowering his pants at the crease and holding a megaphone to player grievances. Kim wasn't a bloke, not in the way Hogan and Cornell—Hoges and Strop—championed blokedom. As Gideon Haigh observed: 'Their TV sketch comedy echoed the era as faithfully as Ian Chappell's cricketers . . . The pair lionised lairs and wags whose street-smart charm redeemed them.' Kim wasn't a wag or a lair. He wasn't terribly street-smart, either.

Kim publicly maintains he was invited to play World Series Cricket, not that he has mentioned it publicly even a handful of times. After taking a night-time phone call in London he confided to McFarline: 'I have been approached to join World Series but I told them I want to captain Australia.' *Sun* journalist Tom Prior heard Kim say something similar, that the Packer defections would 'clear the way' for his ascension to the captaincy. McFarline trusted Kim when he said he'd been asked. 'That approach has been the subject of much bitter debate . . . but I believe Hughes.'

The asker—Robertson—is the same Austin Robertson whose number 16 Kim stitched on his jumper. Did he ever talk to Kim about World Series Cricket? 'He says I did and I say I didn't,' Robertson replies. 'So you can believe who you like. I know who I approached and who I didn't approach and I think Mr Packer would have been very annoyed with me if I had approached Kim Hughes, who was not on the list.'

By the 'list', Robertson means Ian Chappell's list. 'Now, I'm telling you he wasn't there,' Robertson continues. 'They will all tell you he wasn't there.'

By 'they', he means Lillee and the Chappells. 'They are all great friends of mine. He wasn't there. So there you go. There's a story for you.'

There is much to ask Robertson. Was Kim's name mentioned? Who said what? And if not Robertson, who was it that made the approach Kim believed he received? But Robertson will not elaborate. 'The last time I chatted over the phone with a journo—and this is no reflection on you—I got misquoted. So I don't do interviews over the phone.' Email me, he says. A page of questions is dispatched by email. Robertson doesn't reply. Then a second email. No response.

There is a lot to ask Ian Chappell about too. That lost half-season in Adelaide. World Series Cricket. All those years in the commentary box—when Ian didn't sound to many ears like an admirer of Kim's. But Ian declined the invitation to talk about

Kim Hughes: 'I don't really have a lot to say on the matter so if you don't mind I'd prefer to leave it.'

Greg Chappell does recall a conversation with Robertson about Kim's possible recruitment. 'I was asked my opinion,' says Greg. 'And I said he wasn't ready. There were other players we would suggest before him. That's what happened, yep. Kim's been quoted as saying he was offered a contract and turned it down. That is not true. I know that for a fact.'

Kim has made occasional mention of a casual approach from Lillee, not in England but inside Perth's Floreat Hotel. Kim apparently told Lillee he wasn't interested, and the discussion ended. This contradicts Lillee's account in his book *Over and Out!* Lillee's ghostwriter—Austin Robertson, just to thicken the stew—had Lillee saying: 'If he was approached, it was done by someone who had no authority . . . I was close enough to WSC to know that the three captains chose their own sides and Ian Chappell did not pick Hughes at any stage of the operation . . . Hughes was given a big miss.' In 1996 Kim seemed to tell WACA historian Anthony Barker that he did not receive an offer but would have got one had he not foreshadowed his lack of interest. This was not quite consistent with anything any of them have said before.

Unoffered contracts. Faltering memories. Who cares? Kim cared, Cosier too. Twenty-eight Australians played WSC Supertests, one-dayers or up-country Cavaliers matches. Some were battlers: Bruce Laird, Robbie Langer. Several were obscure choices whose Test prospects looked dim: Dennis Yagmich, Wayne Prior, Graeme Watson. A few were old salts: Graham McKenzie, Ian Redpath, Ross Edwards. One was a relative: Trevor Chappell. Half a dozen others rejected invitations. For a

Test squad member to be judged inferior to all of them felt like more than an oddity. It felt like peer rejection. It was public, hurtful and not a little demeaning.

'There were people playing World Series who I can't even remember now, some really strange names,' says Cosier. 'They might have been in the B team but at least they got an offer.' One selection in particular perplexed Cosier. 'I was OK with Hookesy and those guys being involved, but I got a bit pissed off about Trevor and all that. Not that he wasn't a good player. He became very good, Trevor. But at that stage he was a struggling Shield cricketer. There was a big mates thing, I think. Guys who hadn't got any money out of the game; if they were mates, they were offered a contract.' For the record, Cosier had played eight of Australia's last nine matches and had a Test average of 46 at the time of his WSC snub:

> How many people went to World Series? Thirty? Forty? If you're playing for Australia and you can't get in the top thirty of the others then I'm not quite sure where that sits. It either means the three Australian selectors were really wrong or Ian was really right. I mean, they could be wrong a little bit. You wouldn't think they were going to be 300 per cent wrong.

Victorian Graham Yallop also had cause for befuddlement. Three Tests against West Indies had left him with a 44 average and a hunch that the doorbitch at the Chappells' club was gunning for him. 'I have no doubts,' felt Yallop, 'that certain members of that team wanted me to fail.' The selectors hadn't knocked since. Austin Robertson didn't either.

Kim did not have a Test average yet. But other qualities of his came dear. Youth. Blue eyes. Daredevilry. Chutzpah. *Hookesy's clearin' pickets* ran one line in WSC's anthem 'C'mon, Aussie, C'mon'. Well, Kim could clear those too. Hookes was of like age, similar instincts, the same unruliness of hair. Loosely translated he was a left-handed Kim Hughes, only more susceptible to spin bowling. Yet Packer, Robertson and the Chappells were immune to Kim's charms and desperate to buy Hookes's.

Desperate and buy is precisely what they were and did. Robertson has previously described Hookes's signing as essential: 'There was no doubt we brought back some older players who had retired . . . Hookes was a huge, bright star on the horizon.' And the language in which they lured him was strictly monetary. For Hookes, they stumped up two-thirds rather than the standard half of his first-year salary up front. When Hookes wanted out, queasy about all the Test cricket he was forsaking, Packer did not open his own wallet. Packer put his hand in Hookes's wallet.

At an emergency summit in his Dorchester Hotel penthouse, the speech bubble out of Packer's mouth contained the phrases 'lives will not be worth living' and 'every court in the land'. Hookes told Kerry O'Keeffe in the lift going up that he might bail out. Once inside, O'Keeffe watched Hookes slide 'so far down his leather chair he resembled a slow-moving oil slick'. Back home, nerve regained, Hookes confronted Packer at last. 'If David pulls out,' Packer replied, 'he will spend the rest of his life paying me back what I sue him for.'

One upshot was that Hookes missed the 1979 Indian tour on which Kim and Border honed their street-sassiness against spin. Thus could it be reasonably claimed that Hookes's Test career, not that he regretted much, was butchered under duress. It is curious in the circumstances that Kim wasn't heavied. Or even wanted. He was the shop-window dummy nobody was looking at.

Tony Greig, captain and head drumroller of the World XI, cannot be sure whether he'd have approached Kim. But he does say: 'Good young players are decidedly better in a situation like World Series Cricket. I speak first hand about this: I was thirty-two. You are better off having youngsters who haven't been terrorised by Holding and Roberts and Lillee and Thomson than an older player who's wearing a few scars.'

Serjeant was approached again: at home, by Marsh, less formally. If this lends plausibility to Kim's alleged Floreat Hotel rendezvous with Lillee, Graeme Wood takes it away again. 'I was twenty-one and all I wanted to do was play cricket for Australia,' says Wood. 'So I said no a couple of times. But they just kept knocking on the door, knocking on the door, and in the end it became an offer I couldn't refuse.'

That was not Kim's experience—unless everyone in the WSC recruitment department is fibbing. It's far-fetched, but possible. Maybe they dreaded the public relations hit of a cricketer as appealing as Kim telling them no, and so denied everything. Or maybe, easier to understand, Kim talked himself into believing he had been approached. Believing he was approached meant not wondering why he wasn't. And Kim was sensitive, in a way most dressing-room inhabitants weren't. Kim hurt, Kim cried. He wanted to be liked.

Twenty-sixth of September 1977 was the day of a peculiar press announcement. Doing the talking was Perth accountant

Bert Hewitt, Kim's business adviser at the time. Their purpose was to support establishment cricket and to state on the record that Packer's people had indeed dangled before Kim their box of baubles. 'It is wrong to imagine,' said Hewitt, 'that no approaches have been made to Kim concerning the new cricket venture, either before or since the recent tour of England. The fact is Kim's driving ambition has always been to represent his state and country.' Hewitt then read from a statement Kim prepared earlier:

> It is completely understandable that players approaching retirement or even past players should avail themselves of an opportunity to capitalise on their skills. It is rather like a person looking for a good form of business to enter. I sincerely wish each of the players concerned in the new cricketing venture well . . . The necessity for all young players—and we do have some brilliant ones knocking on the door—is to dedicate, train long and hard . . . That is what I propose to do. That is exactly where I stand.

Senior Australian players never forgot it. And they never let Kim forget it.

•••••

BEFORE PACKER, BEFORE ENGLAND, before contracts and the yeah-I-was-invited-oh-no-you-were-effing-not rig-marole, Greg Chappell got his first peep inside Kim Hughes's head. Greg was twenty-eight, Kim twenty-three. The team was dining at a lousy motel in New Zealand's backblocks.

Everything about the night was tiny: the town—Hamilton, was it, or Nelson?—the motel, the restaurant, the menu.

The waitress didn't see it that way. Some cricketers in gaudy shirts with rainforests for lips were eating in. She was the only one on tonight. She was the only one on every night. She hadn't been waitressing long, hadn't handled a mob this big, hadn't stopped scribbling and fetching and whirling and clanging stuff all night. Ever dreamt Marshall's peppering your teeth, Garner's arrowing at your knuckles, Croft's trundling warm-up beam balls and Holding's touching his toes at fine leg? That's the night this waitress was having. At least the guy in charge—the captain?—noticed. He could tell, could read a situation. Then another cricketer sat down.

Sat down? Sort of bounced down. He had no moustache—a tuft of blond fluff maybe—but gee he could eat. Bread, he wanted. What else did he ask for? Hard to remember now. Fresh cutlery. Drinks. A napkin. His steak done just so. Did someone say: listen, mate, go easy on the girl? Might have. Hard to be sure. He should have noticed anyway. Not that he meant trouble. He would have been mortified to know he was ruining her night. He was, though. It was embarrassing. Chappell says:

I just remember putting it in the back of my mind. Whew, OK, here's a kid who's going to need a little bit of management because he's not worldly-wise. He didn't read that situation well. And I'm here to tell you, if you don't read situations well off the field, I've never seen someone read situations well on the field.

Was he ready for a world outside Perth? For adulthood? For fickle, mean men's cricket? Fair questions.

How much do 28-year-olds really know; as opposed to *think* they know? Can a 28-year-old judge a 23-year-old? When is someone immature and when are they merely different? Are their actions the wrong way or simply not your way? Is being in a team about embracing, sculpting or jettisoning personalities that do not fit in a box? These are reasonable questions too.

•••••

'YOU'RE THE FRED ASTAIRE of cricket.' Len Pascoe was referring to Kim's batting swagger. Kim was the song and dance man of Australia's 1977 Ashes squad. Trouble was, Chappell wanted plumbers and bricklayers—Brayshaws, Inverarities—blokes canny at sealing cracks and laying foundations. 'Kim,' says Chappell, 'was young, enthusiastic, gung-ho, wanting to break down the barricades, burst the walls and take 'em on up the front. Sometimes you need to skirt around the sides and set up an ambush.'

It wasn't just that. 'His mercurial sort of personality required a lot of management. He was high maintenance.' Chappell found Kim loveable, a hoot to be around, but in need of experience: 'Experience of the tour, more than of Test cricket.' Chappell beseeched the selectors not to clog his squad with greenhorns. Eight youngsters with five Tests between them was the selectors' response. Chappell would have picked only one, Hookes. Even he lugged an unusual burden. Other 22-year-old maiden voyagers have felt like homesick impostors but never in circumstances like these. 'We thirteen players who signed with World Series Cricket,' Hookes firmly believed, 'should have been sent home.'

Such a step would have barely scratched the paintwork on the series scoreline. England might have triumphed 4–0 instead of 3–0. And everyone would have had more fun. Never before on an Ashes tour had fun been so scarce. 'The first step on London soil is the big moment in any Australian's life,' reckoned Jack Fingleton. Chappell's Packer-bound Australians landed with dollar signs on the brain and sunglasses over their eyes.

Certain rituals of an England tour were tolerated. Politicians Malcolm Fraser and Andrew Peacock were foisted on the players at Lord's. The players foisted themselves on Miss Australia Karen Pini at London's Penthouse Club. Mostly the pomp and pleasures passed them by. Lancashire legend Ken Grieves had zero takers for his trip to an historic northern brewery. Dymock and McCosker alone joined Sir Bernard Lovell for sherry, dinner and a gander at the Milky Way through Jodrell Bank Observatory's telescope. Only three players lingered more than a few minutes at the traditional singalong with Swansea's Pontarddulais Male Voice Choir. Among them were Cosier and Kim, tears swimming down their cheeks as they belted out 'Land of Our Fathers'.

Tears drizzled almost as plentifully as raindrops that bleak English summer. 'An awful, awful tour,' says Cosier. 'There were arguments all the time.' In the first week Kim wore his Australian blazer to a British Commonwealth Society dinner. Dark green, with the coat of arms on the left pocket, it fulfilled a teenage fantasy. 'Mum and I would talk about how all I wanted to do was wear the Australian blazer and play in England where you met the Queen.' But team-mates weren't about to cloak themselves in the kangaroo and emu. They were mentally trying Packer's three-black-stumps-and-a-red-ball logo on for size. Kim was anxious for acceptance. So he wore what they wore: tracksuits. 'I wanted to wear my blazer to bed and down to breakfast. But no one ever wore it because that wasn't the done thing,' he regretted years later. 'I found that very difficult. Not to be able to wear the blazer or feel proud of your blazer, that was something I really struggled with.'

The uninvited four often fretted together. 'Couldn't find any other bastard to talk to,' says Cosier. They would enter a doorway and hear hubbub turn to silence. Room-mates would pick up a ringing telephone then say nothing into the receiver. Wordlessness was catching. 'Can't talk, can't talk,' flapped Dymock, backtracking on a story-sharing arrangement with the *National Times*'s newly arrived Adrian McGregor. Tension was catching too. Fieldsmen weren't. Seventeen chances they muffed in five Tests. Chappell blamed the light, the poor sighting on English grounds, the positioning of the slips, the opposition batsmen's loose wrists. Burying truths was easier than facing them. 'Whatever's missing, I can't pinpoint it,' Chappell told his tour co-author David Frith as Australia went one down at Old Trafford. Perhaps it was the shabby digs, old-fashioned bathtubs, lack of TV sets. 'It's not the Packer business.'

Team meetings grew frequent, and heated. Hush, the old guard would soothe, our single concern is retaining the Ashes. 'They would say that,' Dymock recalls, 'then the next day you'd be on the bus and thirteen blokes would get a package from Packer while the four of us twiddled our thumbs.' Two days after the Ashes were squandered, Cosier wandered into the Waldorf bar for a team get-together only to find thirteen of the team gone. They were Dorchester-bound to see Packer and hadn't mentioned it. 'That,' says Cosier, 'was the lowlight. This other matter was so strong that it was imposing itself on the conduct, the togetherness and certainly the happiness of the team.'

Packer-aligned juniors floundered too. O'Keeffe found himself overindulging at the bar, underperforming with the ball. The eerie calm of the Old Trafford lunchroom spooked Hookes. Never did he imagine an Australian XI so nonchalant in defeat. Players were desensitised to losing, super-sensitive to criticism. Travelling wives—Jenny among them—were muttered to be hindering comradeship. Tit-for-tat denunciations circled. Older players weren't offering enough guidance. Younger players weren't savvy enough to learn from their mistakes. Older players should try harder in tour games. Younger players should try respecting their elders.

Old and young turned on manager Len Maddocks: too keen to socialise, too soft on indiscretions, too quick to abandon the Packer contingent. At one meeting Maddocks disparaged Chappell's captaincy and Marsh reportedly volunteered to biff him. Tom Prior got the story. O'Keeffe wondered how. Prior explained that, being a former CIA agent, he'd scaled a ladder and held a drinking glass to the window. Actually, physio Syd McRae leaked. But O'Keeffe was soon heard urging team-mates to beware CIA trickery. 'To say there was tension and ill-feeling is a massive understatement,' Prior later recalled. 'Most times you could cut the atmosphere with a knife—and there was always a knife available, sticking out of someone's back.'

Maddocks is eighty-two. 'How good do you think my memory is?' He remembers the knives. He remembers Packer's thirteen as protective of their secrets, determined to keep the four others at a distance. 'There were times,' says Maddocks, 'when I thought some of those guys should have been picked to play and weren't.' But the on-tour selectors—Chappell, Marsh, Walters—were appointed long before. 'I couldn't kick them out,' says Maddocks. 'Nobody could.' Maddocks resigned himself to powerlessness, irrelevancy:

> It wasn't the easiest thing to be managing two separate teams in the same changeroom. Any number of times there would be something that affected the Packer signatories, and they'd all be in one corner, with the other four left for dead up the other end. It was uncomfortable. They were on their first tour of England and they were effectively being dumped . . . How can I put it? I just hope it never happens to any other young players. Because the senior blokes did dud them.

Were they deliberately dudded? 'I couldn't see in anybody's minds. But I'm certain in my own mind it was intentional.'

Close-up observers got the same impression. 'They were like lepers within a team that wasn't winning,' says David Lord. 'The others would go into the bus for a meeting while those four stood waiting in the gutter.' Lord's job was as rocky as Maddocks's, but merrier. He was personal manager of the planet's least manageable cricketer. Or as Lord puts it: 'When Thommo got in the shit'—sports shops going bust, one Maserati too many—'he rang me. I couldn't say I was his manager. Mainly I was like toilet paper, just cleaning up at the end.' Jeff Thomson's latest misfire was to jeopardise his $633,000 4IP radio contract by signing with Packer.

Lord interviewed Packer, supposedly for Rex Mossop's *Sports World*, the day WSC broke. Three thirty-minute reels went unaired. Opposition freebies were not chief of staff Bob Johnson's idea of good TV. 'That,' says Lord, 'set up this unbelievable Packer versus Lord crap.' Lord told Thomson he couldn't keep signing contracts until his biro snapped. Packer took Lord to the High Court. The press match in sleepy Harrogate reunited them. Packer came by helicopter—'straight out of Harrods, spic and span, wearing the schmick number one gear'—and caught the English board's Peter Lush off Lord's bowling. 'A rozna of a catch,' says Lord, 'low to his right.' Neighbours in slips, an edge dribbled between them and they crashed shoulders in the chase. Lord was surprised by Packer's speed for a big man. He was struck, too, by the attitudes of Australian cricket's senior trio.

'They were strung with consciences about what they were doing,' Lord believes, battling with the paradox that their actions were right for cricket yet hurting Test cricket, and oblivious to those sinking under them:

> Greg Chappell wasn't half the man he is now. He was a weak captain and he didn't lead by example. He, Marsh and Lillee were like the Three Musketeers. They were of no earthly use. They did as they pleased. The three of them since then have been absolutely fantastic blokes. But in that period they didn't honour their obligations to Australian cricket.

Among the players a crude joke circulated. 'What are those shoes?'

'They're Richie's boots hanging out of Bacchus's arse.'

Certain people felt certain others—Richie Robinson, for example—were getting a gold-dusted run from selectors at the non-Packer quartet's expense. Serjeant's 81 in his first Test didn't save him from expulsion after two. Cosier, swerving inswingers, took 5–18 in the second one-day game and wasn't sighted again. Dymock became Queensland's first Ashes tourist since 1964 on the strength of a three-and-a-half-hour spell in a forty-degree WACA furnace. Upon reaching England he bowled 192 overs—three weekends' worth—in 130 days. He didn't play a Test either. Yet none sensed a pro-Packer bias. Serjeant felt out of form and knew that Chappell knew it. When an all-Packer XI was named for the Third Test, the accusation that they'd rigged it that way shocked Chappell: 'Bacchus, Bacchus, you know what those bastards in the press are saying?' Cosier, composing team songs on Marsh's bed, out of sight, heard the horror in Chappell's voice.

Kim added the six-hitting panache of a George Bonnor to his Fred Astaire routine. Scores of 2 and 3 in the one-dayers were harbingers of a strangely mediocre career in a kind of cricket for which Kim's swishing Slazenger seemed heaven-sent. A 60 against MCC top-scored on his first outing at Lord's. An 80 in Canterbury charmed the *Times*'s John Woodcock: 'I have a nasty feeling Hughes may be a thorn in future England sides. He is quick on his feet, watchful and a fine, free striker.' Four sixes lit up his 54 at The Parks, where law student Peter Roebuck watched Kim charge and clout yonder seemingly the first ball of every over. Four more followed against Lancashire and three in his 95 against Nottinghamshire, one blow shattering a window of Trent Bridge's Cyril Lowater Suite, something no man had done before.

The finest young cricketer I have ever seen, a senior Australian player told Woodcock. Alas, he cannot remember who. Woodcock was surprised when Kim—'a man of destiny'—missed the First Test. Fingleton recommended Kim open—'his defence is very sound'—in the Second. The closest he got to some excitement in the Third was when Ian Davis's boot spikes trampled a TV cable, terminating the *Bugs Bunny* cartoon Kim and Malone were watching. For the Ashes-deciding Fourth Test his selection seemed almost mandatory. McFarline wanted Robinson's scalp and Fingleton that of Walters—'an enigmatic, phlegmatic character who doesn't enthuse over anything'. Walters was also a tour selector. Kim may have been one more thing Walters was unenthusiastic about. He didn't play.

Kim was every bit as convinced as his press fanciers. 'He certainly didn't hide his feelings,' says Chappell. 'But there was never any antagonism, no backdooring, he wasn't sniping and undercutting behind your back. I always found Kim, much like his batting, very upfront.'

He was in particularly upfront mood before that Fourth Test. 'Gimme a go,' he urged Marsh. 'I'm a technician. I'll get in there and work hard.'

Marsh told Chappell. Chappell disagreed. Kim, he considered, was more a blaster and hoper. 'The blast-and-hope mentality wasn't what we needed,' says Chappell. 'Kim was seeing himself in a better light than I was.'

Old death wishes lingered on. His addiction to bringing up hundreds with a starburst of sixes got in the way of him bringing them up at all. Four times he fell swinging in the nineties or eighties. There were ten single-digit scores. No hundreds. Statistics vindicated Chappell's doubts. Statistics, as ever with Kim, concealed as much as they illustrated. They didn't tell you that he'd given up.

To outsiders he was familiar, irrepressible Kim. So colossal was his natural confidence that disappointments big and small loomed like mosquitoes on a crocodile's snout. Rod Eddington, a Rhodes scholar and old colts rival, remembers yakking with him in Oxford: 'He'd always stop and say hello, even though I was a journeyman grade cricketer.' Those with him daily saw someone longing for guidance, explanations, belonging. At the Trent Bridge Test, the tour's halfway point, still not playing, Kim and Serjeant spent time jogging together, filling space. 'He felt dispirited and disheartened and I don't think his heart was in the rest of the tour,' Serjeant recalls.

Give up, he did. 'With Kim,' says Serjeant, 'you can see it. He'd spend less time in the nets, more time out social-ising. He wouldn't be bothered watching the game, or out having a practice, or doing the things you expect someone busting their guts to get in the team to be doing. He wasn't doing that.'

•••••

WHAT CRICKETER WHO EVER LIVED wasn't overjoyed at the news he'd been picked to play for his country? Harold Gimblett of Somerset wasn't:

> I can remember listening to the twelve names announced on the radio. The names were given in alphabetical order and I prayed that I wouldn't be included. Far from throwing my hat in the air, I was terrified. Suddenly I realised the fearful responsibilities resting on my shoulders. The telephone started ringing, cars arrived, the usual nonsense. I just

wanted to go away and get lost. I didn't want to play for England. In desperation I jumped on my bicycle and went in search of Rita.

David Foot's soulful biography of Gimblett was subtitled 'Tormented Genius of Cricket'. Gimblett was a crowd thriller, like Kim. Gimblett lofted a six when Queen Elizabeth II was crowned, the sort of proud, premeditated showmanship Kim might have gone for. Team-mate Horace Hazell thought Gimblett the definitive Jekyll and Hyde. Gimblett's first-class average was 36.17, Kim's 36.52. Barely one-third of one run split them. The similarities should not be exaggerated. Gimblett could be morose. 'The undisputed captain of cricket's hypochondriacs,' Foot called him. Kim entered cricket's dressing rooms like a peacock. You could almost hear distant champagne corks popping. They shared something else though. Kim was as unhappy about his Test debut as Gimblett was.

Norm Tasker found Kim alone in a London bar on the night Australia's team for the Fifth Test at The Oval was announced. Tasker offered his warmest congratulations.

'Isn't that great, Kim?'

Kim barely lifted his head. 'Those pricks,' he said. 'Now they've made me part of the failure.'

Kim wasn't frightened like Gimblett. Kim was bitter. Tasker, covering the tour for Sydney's *Sun* newspaper, wondered at the volatility, turmoil and complexity within. 'He was on his own and very much down in the dumps,' says Tasker. 'I remember that conversation as if it were yesterday. It was a fairly happy night, the tour was drawing to a close and Kim's depressed state was out of kilter with everything else.'

Your Test debut occupies a sacred place in cricket's mythology. Even Chris Brand, the fictitious veteran in Malcolm Knox's novel *A Private Man*, so boiled by sun and singed by cameras that he can hardly feel anything anymore, feels compelled to somehow mark the occasion of young Nathan Such's first game. 'Let's stuff these cunts then,' says Brand to Such, as they approach the gate. Did anyone think to mark Kim's occasion?

Day one was rained out. Serjeant does not recall even being aware that it was Kim's debut. On day two Australia fielded. Kim's friend Malone took five wickets in 43 boundaryless overs on his first day as a Test cricketer. England made 214. On the third afternoon Serjeant—surprised to be playing, annoyed to be opening—was lbw in virtual blackness. It rained some more.

A draw was predestined and Kim hadn't yet batted. His chance arose at 12.58 p.m. on day four, Australia 2–54, McCosker his partner, The Oval stacked with pale Londoners reacquainting skin with sunshine on a bright Bank Holiday Monday. Derek Underwood beat Kim first ball and appealed for lbw. Kim dead-batted the next two. Was this the technician people were promised? He sat on maidens from Underwood, Lever, Hendrick. David Frith wrote down: 'Hughes went on showing scant interest in making his first Test run, though it must have been the most pressing of needs.' Lunch was taken. Thirty-four minutes' batting and nought to show for it.

'They threw him to the wolves,' says Dymock. 'To me, it was doing the wrong thing by a bloke who'd never played a Test—to pick him when he's out of form after you didn't pick him when he was in form.' Chappell figured that with the series shot, here was something to gain. 'Pretty much everyone else had been given a go. It was time to give Kim a chance to back his words up with some action. Well, OK, you fancy your chances: let's have a look at you.'

After forty-seven minutes and thirty-four balls he hit Hendrick into the covers and ran a single. His thirty-seventh delivery was a Hendrick away-seamer, which he sparred at, and he departed for 1.

•••••

THE MOOD AMONG the rejecters—those who rebuffed the establishment, the status quo, the only kind of cricket they'd ever aspired to—was nearly as hangdog as that of the rejected. For Rodney Marsh, the tour was 'the worst I went on', he told Keith Butler. Not knowing if he'd represent his state or country again was a strain. Strewth, he wasn't even thirty. Then there was the bumbling Maddocks, the overabundance of kid cricketers, the sanctimonious scribes. Tom Prior gave Marsh three out of ten in his tour ratings—and 'Marsh threatened to rip my head off and use it as an ashtray'.

Worst was the Richie Robinson business, the insinuations of favouritism towards a mate. At Lord's Robinson, ever willing, addressed the new ball like a farmer skinning a buffalo with secateurs. Young Kim confronted Marsh, saying Robinson should never have opened. He said this round a table at Leeds's Post House Hotel, in front of others. 'We'd probably,' says Cosier, 'had nine thousand beers . . . With or without alcohol, that stuff was going to come out.'

Then Kim said: 'Skull thinks so too.'

O'Keeffe hadn't expected that. 'Well,' he said, when Marsh challenged him, 'as a matter of fact I do.'

Was Kim sloshed? 'We were sitting down,' says Cosier. 'So it was hard to know who could stand up.' Marsh could. He rose from the table and stumped out. Chappell, coming in, almost got bowled over. Marsh was crying.

Days later Australia lost that Leeds Test, and with it the Ashes. The final stroke was Marsh's, getting the toe of his bat to an attempted six off Hendrick. Extra cover Derek Randall caught it, hurled it and did a cartwheel. The arc of Randall's upturned body as his hands and feet hit the ground matched Marsh's furry frown.

Another nuisance irritating Marsh all tour was the way people tied Kim's non-selection to his non-Packer man status. It happened whenever he, Greg and Douggie picked a team. 'The reason Hughes didn't get chosen,' Marsh fumed, 'was because he didn't make any bloody runs.'

SIX

Hungry? 'I've Had Twenty Malt Sandwiches'

THE FAMILY FARM at Wandering was an hour and a bit's drive from Perth. Seventeen-year-old Geoff Marsh knew the road well. A driver could get some thinking done on that road. One Friday night, the night before his first encounter with the world's most famous bowler, his head was full of Lillee. 'Keep thinking about it and he'll get you out,' Marsh told himself. He pulled over at a pub, bought three stubbies and drove on. 'Every bloody time I think of Dennis,' he promised, 'I've got to have a sip of beer.' The three stubbies were drained before he got halfway to Perth. Next day Lillee couldn't shift him, 79 not out he made. But in his head he'd imagined Lillee and brave Bruce Laird and the entire Western Australian team as gods. The whole state had. Righting old injustices, smashing the eastern staters, they were brilliant cricketers and beaut blokes. And Kim was one of them.

Lillee and Rodney Marsh rejoiced in him. His arrival dumbfounded them. Suddenly, it seemed, there were three. 'The larrikin in Kim,' Ian Brayshaw recalls, 'appealed to the larrikin in Rod and Dennis.' Kim was funny and chirpy, bringing bounce to the flattest social occasion, a forceful character among strong-willed personalities. 'He was well loved,' says Inverarity. 'He had a generous heart and was a great optimist. He was fun-loving and fun-seeking and easily excitable.' He was passionate about cricket. He knew he was good at it. He let others know that he knew. That was just like Rod and Dennis too.

'Mad gambler,' says Tony Mann. Kim would bound up to team-mates and say: 'Toss you for fifty.' Mann played along just once. The coin landed right side up and Mann pouched the $50 note. 'Thanks very much.'

'No, no, we gotta keep going.'

'Rubbish.'

His poker resembled his batting. Cocky, a bluffer, he never owned up to a dud hand. Near-penniless newcomers were hopelessly outflanked. Kim would chuck another twenty on the table and 'nah I'm out' Geoff Marsh would sigh, even when his hand was stronger. Once on an away trip, at Devonport's Sunrise Motor Inn, Marsh had a dream hand. All he lacked were the facial muscles to disguise it. When Kim tried to bluff him out of it, Marsh bluffed back. 'Is that you, Dad?' he whispered into the phone, pretending to ring Wandering. 'Dad, how much did we get for the wheat crop last year?'

'Wheat crop!' whooped Kim, slapping down his cards and joining his team-mates in a hysterical heap.

Word of this unshrinkable free spirit reached the Australian dressing room. 'Kim was built up by Rod and Dennis as the next Bradman,' says Cosier. 'They didn't say it in those terms because they didn't like Bradman. But they were always talking about Claggy and what he did and how good he was gunna be. They thought he'd be one of the greats.' Marsh saw plenty of himself in Kim. Sir Rod Eddington, who after finishing at

Oxford ran British Airways and myriad multinational boards, used to roll out his left-arm orthodox in the University of Western Australia's nets. His good friend Marsh would wallop him into Reid Library, at the opposite end of the oval. 'Rod, as a batsman, played absolutely like Kim,' says Eddington. 'It was premeditated, measured aggression. It was, I will not let these bowlers dictate. My memories of Marshy are that he recognised Kim as a very special player.'

That opinion never budged. But reservations soon mounted. One afternoon Kim was treating the WACA Ground like an amusement park, swinging Rodney Hogg to all corners. Eventually Serjeant got down the striker's end. Incredulity dawned: Hogg was raining down meteor showers. Seeing the ball was problematic, hitting it a lottery. The lower order would be wiped out in minutes. 'Mate,' said Serjeant, 'they won't want to face this.' He calculated that Hogg might last eight overs. Kim made mincemeat of the sixth. 'Two to go,' Serjeant reminded him. Hogg bowled only one more, making way for a part-timer, whom Kim cut instantly to first slip. Hogg came back and Serjeant's fears came true. 'We had an obligation,' says Serjeant, 'to ensure those other players weren't exposed. Kim entertained the crowd and was magnificent. But was it good for the team? Uh-uh. And that's Kim the man. He wouldn't change.'

Team-mates say Inverarity would admonish Kim privately, strategically. Rodney Marsh and others would openly fume: 'Why the fuck did you do that you silly prick?' Taming Kim was the subject of regular chatter. Kim would nod. Then he'd do things his way. Would he listen? He'd listen to Frank Parry. And Frank was telling him to keep on entertaining. The Western

Australian public adored him, the players less so, some of them anyway. 'I think players better than me,' says Ric Charlesworth, 'might have felt threatened by him and resented his flamboyance and brilliance.'

Kim's approach won matches and spread joy. They just wished he'd spread less joy and win more matches. Lillee and Marsh, hellbent on victory, wished it with gusto. 'Kim played as though every new match was another chance to go have a whack and some fun,' says Mann. 'And good luck to him. But I think Dennis and Rod felt he wasn't switched on to being successful. There was certainly something different about them all. They didn't get on.'

Lillee and Marsh stopped forewarning others of the golden boy just over the horizon. Then Kerry Packer helicoptered in. 'Anybody who had two eyes in his head would have had Kim Hughes playing World Series Cricket if they wanted the best players,' says Charlesworth. Then Kim announced that he hadn't joined because he didn't care to. And a once happy relationship wilted some more.

•••••

MARSH WEARS A WARRIOR'S SMILE and bandages round his aching right knee in a photograph in his 1982 book *The Gloves of Irony*. The caption reads: 'Sometimes it hurts—but the paycheque eases the pain!' It was an unusual sentiment for a cricketer to put his name to. Even now, when their paycheques contain sufficient zeros to soothe most kinds of suffering, players cite honour and mateship as motivation before they mention money. Late in the summer of 1982–83,

Lillee muttered 'clap you bastards' to the Adelaide members as he hobbled off, a throwaway grumble from a sore fast bowler. Yet it was symbolic, too, as if he finally found the words to sum up the lack of gratitude he reckoned he'd been shown for a quarter of a lifetime's footslogging.

Like all Test cricketers, Marsh and Lillee felt chuffed to be among the chosen few. But they felt something else too. They felt cricket owed them. Marsh banked a tenth of what his golfing brother Graham did. For Lillee, whose happy childhood had nonetheless involved 'a struggle to make ends meet', the struggle continued. One kindly doctor said he could pay a dollar a week off the medical bills for his back. Such was the lot of the Australian cricketer. For a century they'd had reason to feel short-changed; 'raped', trade union leader Bob Hawke called it. Usually the prestige outweighed the grievance. With Marsh and Lillee it was hard to tell. Their winning bet against Australia at Headingley was a squaring up of sorts. When Lillee tugged an aluminium bat out in 1979–80 it was in the hope that the business he'd co-founded might sell a few thousand more of them. Asked to explain themselves, their response never varies. I gave, says Lillee, more than I took, thus introducing yet another statistic to a game replete with them.

Some traditionalists found them repulsive. Wicketkeeper Bob Taylor liked Lillee after hours. On the field he turned into 'a moron' cultivating the persona of a 'male chauvinist pig'. E.W. Swanton, who wanted Lillee jailed for manslaughter should his throat-tickling of English tailender Geoff Arnold prove fatal, pointedly excluded Lillee and Ian Chappell from his essay collection *As I Said at the Time*. 'The reader,' wrote Swanton, 'must draw his own conclusions as to my reasons.'

Kim never took any objections he had to Marsh and Lillee's faces. But remember his words? 'I have always played the game because I've loved the game, not because of how much money I can make.' Long, long after, his own pockets full of rebel rand, Kim's disquiet rumbled: 'When people are making large sums of money the game gets away from the basics. Australian sporting heroes or teams have been built around the colours you wear. And I believe what happened was there were people who maybe got a bit carried away with their own importance.'

It is ironic that by the time Marsh and Lillee wearied of talking Kim up, they had planted in some the urge to tear him down. 'It put others offside,' says Cosier. 'He wasn't embraced quite so much as he should have been, not quite so closely as maybe others were. They didn't appreciate the building up of this kid before he'd actually done anything ... There was an element that was almost anti-Claggy because of the West Australian push for him.'

Marsh's own absorption into the national side could not have happened more differently. He arrived a nerve-addled stranger for the Gabba Test of 1970–71. The afternoon before the game, Ian Chappell invited him for a round of golf with Doug Walters and the great Ray Lindwall. The four of them downed some clubhouse beers beforehand. They sank a few more afterwards. Then they dined out with Lindwall's wife Peg. At 11 p.m., maybe a little later, Marsh floated back into his room. 'I owe—and will always owe—a hefty debt of gratitude to Chappell and Walters for making me feel ... that I belonged,' he wrote. 'I'll never forget that.' Did it slip his mind in 1977, before the Oval Test? Where was Kim's welcome mat that black night in London?

Lillee always treasured the kindnesses of Tony Lock, his first state captain. 'The old campaigner was like a father to me, encouraging me to bowl fast and never criticising me for inaccuracy as long as I was fast.' Who among Kim's teammates said similar, that he should keep bombarding boundary fences and not fret overmuch about the odd foolhardy dismissal?

Ian Chappell built the Australian team and culture that Greg Chappell inherited and Kim walked into. Ian had taken to wearing cowboy-style boots off the field. Jackboots remained popular dressing-room apparel among senior players. Cosier recalls:

> As progressive and different as the Chappell era was from the eras that had gone before, they still had the same hangover from Benaud, Simpson, Lawry. Sit down, shut up and we'll tell you when to speak. And if you get a couple of hundreds and start to look all right then we'll let you talk sometimes. And if you're really good then you can open your mouth whenever you want to. All right? There was still that really hardline ethic that you had to earn your stripes.

To earn his stripes, Kim had to change his spots. And that was never likely. 'If Dennis and Rod were demeaning him from a cricket or personal point of view, he didn't take any backward steps,' says Geoff Lawson. 'And both those guys didn't like people standing up to them. So that made it worse. But that's Dennis and Rod's fault rather than Kim's.'

Opponents got put in the freezer for failing to greet senior Australian players by their Christian names. Kerry O'Keeffe wrote: 'If, say, Rod Marsh, on passing Glenn Turner at the pre-game nets, offered "Good morning, Glenn, how are you?" and only received "Morning, all right?" Marsh would feel aggrieved.' It was what Mike Whitney did utter that bothered Marsh during the first innings of the inaugural Sheffield Shield final in 1982–83. Marsh hooked one bouncer for four and the next into Steve Smith's lap. 'Fuck off,' recommended Whitney, pointing directions to the WACA pavilion, a route Marsh knew like the back of his Kookaburra gloves.

'Pardon?'

One muscular chest bobbed towards the other. 'You think I'm scared of you?' said Whitney. 'Get off the ground you fuckin' prick.'

Had Marsh lifted his bat in anger, Whitney believes he would have punched him. That night, feeling apologetic, Whitney held out a hand not a fist. Marsh told him to clear off: 'You think you're a big fuckin' whirl. But you can't fuckin' play.' Whitney yanked back his hand. The instinct to deck Marsh bubbled again. Before he could, the manager dragged Whitney to the visitors' dressing room and locked him in. 'Rod and I didn't speak for nearly ten years after that.'

The confrontation reveals something of Marsh's beliefs concerning proper deportment for junior players. Marsh wrote: 'Michael is yet young and will no doubt learn in time that such conduct is, by tradition, the privilege of the superstars, the Dennis Lillees, if you like. It is certainly not the stuff expected from apprentices.' If that reads like double standards, hypocrisy of another kind bugged Whitney. 'Rodney thought me telling him to fuck off after I bounced him out was a terrible thing, that I'd showed absolutely no respect. Yet they didn't think what they did to Kim in England in 1981 was bad. How,' asks Whitney, 'could they be so right there and so disgusted with my behaviour?'

That first Shield final was a classic of the genre. Twenty of the twenty-two players represented Australia. Swear words outnumbered dot balls. 'It was like the end of the world,' Geoff Marsh remembers. Momentum seesawed until the fifth afternoon, Kim's studious half-century navigating Western Australia to within 113 of victory. On the short stroll to lunch Kim scoffed at New South Wales captain Rick McCosker: 'There is no fucking way you blokes can bowl us out. You're not good enough and never will be.' He'd bullseyed the wrong target. McCosker was too gentlemanly to return lip, too shrewd not to pass Kim's message on. Eleven stirred-up New South Welshmen steamrollered the last six wickets after lunch. Kim went first, slashing at Lawson's second delivery with the new ball. 'A real loose cannon,' reflects Tony Mann. 'As a youngster growing up you could see he was going to have a very turbulent sort of career. And it did turn out that way.'

Whitney caught Wayne Clark at mid-off to seal a poignant New South Wales victory: by 54 runs, on hostile terrain, against their bloodthirstiest rivals. He heard his name called out and trotted up to accept his winner's memento, a medallion in a brown box. The West Australians sat all in a row. As Whitney sauntered back past them he flicked open the brown box and snapped it shut in Marsh's face. In the return game next season he succumbed in the old familiar way—caught Marsh, bowled Lillee—and heard an old familiar voice. 'How ya going now, tough boy?'

Whitney stripped off his gloves, helmet, dropped his bat and exploded. 'Who wants to go first? Or do you both wanna come round the back together?'

Lillee told him not to carry on, said it was all part of the game. Whitney said it wasn't. 'I was going to leather them,' says Whitney. 'Because I was an idiot. And because I was aggressive. And because I really took offence at the way they played the game.'

•••••

AT EVERY STEP—first grade, first class, Test cricket—the pattern repeated. Kim had to prove himself to grizzly, sceptical men who had heard plenty about him before they met him. He had to be spectacular and unique or else they'd reckon him overhyped. Then they would never respect him. But he also had to fit in, to not stand out. So he had to be unique but the same. Grog was an added complication. People drank when they won, they drank when they lost. Grog soothed, rehydrated, helped you forget, made you get along, filled hours, oiled conversations and hid you from the ever-gaping public. It gurgled out of cracks in dressing-room walls. The higher the standard, the bigger the schooners.

'The Sheffield Shield tour was laced with alcohol,' says Charlesworth, one of the WA team's few non-drinkers. 'You played, you drunk, you played, you drunk, you played, you drunk. Then you'd have three days off and you went to the next place.'

The Test scene was the same—only without the three-day break if you were on tour. On Kim's first Test trip the pinnacle was Doug Walters's 250 in Christchurch. 'Freddie had the usual Freddie night the night before and the previous night and the night previous to that,' Cosier recalls. Cosier's demise for 23 brought Walters moseying out at 4–112 on an up-and-down wicket, the sky cloaked in cloud. Instantly Walters saw only stars. In delayed response to a Richard Hadlee bouncer he toppled backwards and lay slug-like. 'We thought Douggie had been killed or had a heart attack,' says Cosier. 'Then he dusted himself off and didn't miss another ball. It was like he'd woken out of a stupor.'

Unbeaten on 129, Walters drank from stumps to 2 a.m. with batting partner Gary Gilmour, slurping out of Kiwi beer bottles on Kerry O'Keeffe's bed, humbugging him to join them. O'Keeffe estimated their blood alcohol levels at 0.25 per cent when the partnership resumed. Under the weather, they bunted over the infield, which saved gallivanting singles. The 217 they put on remains a seventh-wicket record. The trend had been set early.

On Kim's next tour the journey was longer so the bingeing started sooner. Walters swigged forty-four tinnies and Marsh forty-three aboard the Qantas flight to Heathrow. Points were awarded and tallies monitored on a sick bag. 'Does it have to be beer?' asked Kim. It didn't, and Kim promptly consumed six, a dozen, twenty-one or twenty-two brandy and dries, depending on whose foggy written recollection you trust. Kim himself remembers having 'eleven or twelve', the ratio of dry to brandy decreasing as he gulped. What is agreed is that Kim was winning as they flew over Queensland and sleeping thereafter. He'd passed out—blotto—on his first long-haul flight for Australia.

The players landed squiffy but unsated. In Bath, Dymock remembers Marsh and Walters being late to bed and rewarded with light fielding duties, Walters loping from fine leg to fine leg. 'I don't think Kim would go along with that way of playing cricket,' says Dymock. In Dublin, the Australians outswilled the Irish. 'Never in the history of Australian sport,' McFarline recorded, 'has so much hospitality been enjoyed by so few in such a short time.' Dymock's diary entry captures the flavour:

> Arrived about midday. Driven in cars to Shelbourne Hotel where we had couple of Guinness pints. Went to Guinness brewery in cars at about 1.30. Few drinks, then lunch at about 3 p.m. Few more beers, then back to hotel. Changed and then in cars to Phoenix Park races. Few more drinks, a few bets, etc, till about 9 p.m. Met Lord Killanin at races. Returned to hotel, had hamburger with Ray Bright and couple more drinks. Retired about 12 o'clock.

Kim drank like he batted, with a swagger. He was fast to get into it, fast to get wobbly, fast to get out. Brandy and dry was his favourite. The Western Australian guys, wives too, often visited each other's houses. 'Haven't you got any wine in the place?' Mann asked one evening at Kim's Drabble Road home in City Beach. Kim suggested the pantry, where Mann, Clark and Malone found and refrigerated several untouched relics from old man-of-the-match awards. Three or four bottles later Kim asked if it was any good.

''78 Veuve Clicquot,' Mann replied.

'Was that one 150 bucks a bottle?' asked Malone.

'Nah,' said Mann. 'I think it's only 140 bucks.'

'What!' Kim was thunderstruck. 'Give us a taste.'

In *Chappelli Speaks Out*, written by old friend Ashley Mallett, Ian Chappell outlined his philosophy towards cricket and drinking:

> I always used to say to Rodney Marsh, 'Mate, when you win you drink to celebrate and when you lose you drink to drown your sorrows and after about four or five beers you are not quite sure what you are doing anyhow.' I always thought it was very important to celebrate a victory, because you work your butt off to win, and I couldn't see any point in working so hard to win, then just coming into the dressing room, throwing all your gear together and saying, 'Bye guys, see you next time' . . . And I realised after a time that they would be sort of saying to themselves, 'Gee, this is fun when we win, we have a bit of a party, so the more times we win the more parties we have,' so that became a bit of a psychological ploy.

When in Chappelli's team, most tended to do as Chappelli did. When O'Keeffe didn't, heeding Keith Stackpole's tip that if he 'sucked piss with Douggie' he'd blow cold next morning, he found Walters lying in wait on his return from the movies. 'Skull,' Walters would crackle, 'what flavoured milkshake did you have at intermission? Chocolate or vanilla?' Lawson debuted the season after Ian Chappell retired. His teetotalism confounded older team-mates whose shout it was, resulting in unsupped beer glasses gathering grime on the hotel bars of several countries.

Nobody imbibed Chappell's advice so wholeheartedly as its original recipient. Yarns of Rodney Marsh's drinking prowess are recounted slack-jawed: of the night he disappeared into an outside shed in England and Lillee found him sitting on a mop bucket, complaining 'Every time I try to get off this toilet something grabs me by the balls'; of how he mislaid his room key in Launceston and gashed an arm smashing a window to get in; of the way he'd say 'I've had twenty malt sandwiches' when reminded that he hadn't eaten since the teabreak. Some people use the phrase 'Chappelli clone'. Then along came Kim. 'Kim was, if you like, a product of Rod Marsh,' says Daryl Foster. 'Kim was one who socialised a lot and enjoyed socialising. He was a very, very fine socialiser.'

Kim's state debut was Marsh's first game as captain. Foster sensed the culture evolving, the nights lengthening. 'Especially when we were away,' Foster recalls, 'I had to hang around the dressing rooms until about 9.30, pack Rod's gear up, get him in a taxi, get him over to the pub, or if we'd finished the game get him ready to get on a plane.' For junior players, too, the working day continued after the clock struck six. There were beers to be ferried from fridge to senior players. Stories were handed down, advice passed on: nuggets and beer was a diet on which the young cricketer could learn plenty. 'It was very instructive for them,' says Foster. 'But I think the destructive part might have been that they'd get drunk, or even if they didn't get drunk a lot of alcohol was consumed.'

Many drank sensibly. 'You knew when to say no, when to go to bed, how much sleep you needed,' says Geoff Marsh. 'You just knew.' Lillee, if he was bowling next day, upped the coke content in his Bacardi and coke. Lillee was shrewd, and older. 'So many young players who didn't have the capacity of a Rodney Marsh fell by the roadside,' says Foster. 'Their careers were considerably shortened, in my opinion, by the fact that they played up too much, the alcohol consumption was too much.'

The question of how much equalled too much was seldom raised, let alone scientifically investigated. Rodney Marsh's batting started off puckish and grew notoriously skittish. He averaged 33 in the first half of his Test career, 19 in the second half. 'I used to think Rod used his drinking exploits and his late nights and his failure to eat proper food as a crutch—to really perform on the field,' says Foster. 'OK, I had a few last night, but I will never be slow up to the wicket, I will never stop diving.' Marsh blamed his batting decline on the preoccupation West Indian fast bowlers had with his windpipe: 'I just don't know how to combat it.' And that was quite plausible.

Foster wondered, as well, about Kim, whom he found emotional, delightful, sensitive, vulnerable, vivacious, someone people flocked around at parties, and happy to be so, because that meant they liked him. 'He had a very good cricket brain but I think somehow or other he got a little bit lost; lost in what was really expected of an Australian captain.'

'Daryl didn't drink,' says Geoff Marsh. 'He never drank beer. So . . . nah.' He disagrees that the culture changed. Blokes drank before; blokes drank after. 'Still the best times I've ever had in my cricket career have been in the West Australian dressing room when we've won a game or a Shield.' Geoff Marsh recognised the good in playing, drinking, learning, bonding together. His experience of the dressing room almost paraphrases the vision Ian Chappell had. Marsh says:

Guys just had this thing about this dressing room. You played for each other, for the team, for the moment in the dressing room. That's the thing everyone loved doing—getting in that dressing room after a good day and having a couple of drinks and a laugh. They were my great memories . . . sitting in the dressing room and talking to your Inverarities and Chappells . . . When you got the opportunity to sit and listen to them you just did. You didn't open your mouth until the right time and you did a lot of listening in those days. And that's when you learnt.

Guys also had a thing about aeroplanes, something those who over-indulged or oversaw proceedings have occasionally wished to forget. Greg Chappell, Ashes captain in 1977, was majestically coy about Walters's 44–43 victory in his post-tour book. 'It is,' Chappell wrote, 'a long flight, twenty-odd hours, and with the players trying to get some sleep and watching movies, it was, I'm glad to report, quite uneventful.' David Boon's feelings lie somewhere in the mudflats between denial and pride. Quiet as granite about the 52-can marathon fellow passengers witnessed in 1989, he willingly lends his body to Victoria Bitter commercials. His talking 'Boony Doll', a plastic insomniac on the mantelpieces of VB-buying households, emits prerecorded wisecracks such as: 'I'd go to the pub if I could walk.'

Boon's fifty-two beers beat Rodney Marsh's inflight record, not his forty-three of 1977 but his forty-five of 1983, en route to the World Cup, when his captain was an emotional, delightful, sensitive, vulnerable and vivacious young man who hoped to be liked and whose challenge was to be different yet the same.

KIM'S ALL-WHITE UNIFORM, right down to his sweat-bands, was the only thing not colourful about his time in the two-year war between old cricket and Packer cricket. Needing to fight fire with fire in the divided summer of 1977–78, the establishment rubbed two sticks together. They brought out one touring side, India, whose five Tests and zero one-day internationals were sticky-taped over three months. Bishan Bedi's men saw more of Australia than most Australians, every state capital plus Port Lincoln, Hastings, Griffith, Nambour, Wongan Hills, Launceston, Newcastle, Canberra, Geelong. They came laden with graceful batsmen who played geometrically conventional strokes, plus multiple slow bowling varieties: Bedi's butterfly-like left-arm orthodox, Bhagwat Chandrasekhar's whirligig wrong'uns and toppies, the off-spin of Erapalli Prasanna and Srinivasaraghavan Venkataraghavan. This was cricket not just traditional but unusually pure, a strength and weakness in the battle to woo the terry-towelling masses.

Razzmatazz, Kim knew, counted plenty. Dancing feet rushed him to and got him out for 99 in the tour match, attempting to swat Prasanna over the long-on pickets when ordinary batsmen might have contented themselves with tip-and-run. Kim was unrepentant. 'I'm a pretty happy sort of bloke and I enjoy my cricket, and seeing we've got opposition I am conscious of providing entertainment for the public. Cricketers now have a duty.'

Rated a sure thing for his first home Test at the Gabba, he was named twelfth man after breakfast. Picked instead were Peter Toohey, captain Bob Simpson's Western Suburbs clubmate, and

Victorian Paul Hibbert, whom Simpson likened to a beloved old opening comrade: 'He reminds me so much of Bill Lawry it's embarrassing.' Tony Mann was another Gabba debutant. 'Kim carried on in the rooms like a pork chop,' Mann remembers. 'Just typical Kim Hughes.' Disappointed maybe, but easygoing too, assured of a starring role in the future, whatever the future might be.

The series moved to Perth. Kim was in. He took centre stage in the *West Australian*'s full-colour wraparound, plucking a sitter off the slips cradle to the mock amazement of team-mates and catching the equally appreciative eye of chief cricket writer Ken Casellas. 'For sheer uninhibited skill,' wrote Casellas, 'Hughes ranks as Australia's most exciting strokemaker.' Dropped twice in two deliveries on his way to 28, he retreated first ball in the second innings and was lbw to Madan Lal. Twelfth man duties were resumed in Melbourne.

Sydney was the setting for a tantalising 22-minute duel with Bedi. Watching from side-on in the old Bob Stand was twelve-year-old Steve Waugh. Almost thirty years later, Waugh recalled Kim's on-driven six into the gutter of the members' top balcony as 'an astonishing blow'. But Bedi was an artist of once-a-generation cunning. The first time Englishman Derek Randall faced Bedi he excavated two runs in ninety minutes while waiting for a bad ball. The second time he reversed his strategy and was immediately out slogging. For their third encounter Randall resolved to scamper and smother: 'I ran out to meet the first ball, fell head over heels and saw myself stumped in undignified confusion.'

Kim had even fewer clues to go on. So barren was Australia's spin landscape that Jack Fingleton wanted Malcolm Dolman, a teenage club chinaman bowler from Adelaide, in the Test side. But Kim had enjoyed the sight of that six. 'He thought if he could do it once,' Sam Gannon remembers, 'he'd do it every time.' Two balls later he straight-drove Bedi for four. Next he shaped to cut. Off stump almost caught fire. 'Didn't know Bish bowled a quicker ball,' says Craig Serjeant. 'No one in Australia had seen it and it wasn't discussed in team meetings. You knew he may have a slightly faster, flatter one—but this came out like a rocket.' All the same, a twelve-year-old might have predicted Bedi would try something devious. 'A victory,' Waugh deduced, 'for brains over brawn.'

Scores of 17 and 19 guaranteed the return of twelfth man brackets in Adelaide. In, out, in, out, in, out: Kim still hadn't played two Tests in a row. The series was a slow-burning thriller. The Indians landed down under for their first tour in ten years complaining that the bright light made competent fielding impossible. They blew two Tests narrowly, won the next two comfortably and were 6–415, seeking 493 for victory, in the last. Then Kim, substituting at gully, thrust two hands at a ball that looked like decapitating him, the series-swinging catch, snuffing out Karsan Ghavri's ominous stand with Syed Kirmani. 'One of the great Test series of all time,' says Simpson, 'and a great, great tour. We killed World Series as far as crowd attendances and public interest went. That was very satisfying.' Australia's 3–2 triumph was completed on the extra sixth day, Simpson's birthday, his forty-second, no less.

Bradman's example swayed Simpson. Bradman was thirty-eight when he resumed Australia's postwar captaincy after an eight-year hiatus. Simpson, three years older, had been out of the game two years longer, not that he advertised this to bowlers. 'I never get tired when I bat,' he commented after his gargantuan 176 in his second Test back. Simpson's state comeback game presented his first up-close glimpse of Kim, who responded with a characteristically hyperactive 85. 'Immature,' was Simpson's impression. Then he laughs. 'Well, everyone was immature.'

Twelve freshmen, some unlikelier than others, wore baggy green that Packer-ravaged summer. Lively left-armer Sam Gannon had returned from a Greek islands holiday with wife Jill after being bumped from Western Australia's winter practice squad. He reaped 7–161 in his hometown Test debut then headed to Melbourne, where he had Sunil Gavaskar dropped in single figures. 'Soon after that,' Gannon recalls, 'Simmo was saying he wanted me to bowl negatively to Gavaskar, just prevent him scoring, don't try to get him out.' It muddled Gannon's mind. If he followed instinct ahead of instructions, would that spell the end for him? 'I thought, hang on a minute, I've got to try and survive here. So I bowled in a negative way and Gavaskar ended up getting 118.'

For Tony Mann, seventeen eventful years had elapsed since his maiden first-grade season at fourteen, when three cheap wickets didn't stop the Claremont Oval tea lady denying him cake: 'Sorry son, men first.' Thrilled to be playing, Mann was slightly miffed by the choice of leader. 'The obvious captain,' he says, 'was Inverarity. Obvious captain. And they brought back bloody old Simmo, who to his credit did quite well. From my point of view it was a disaster because I hardly bowled.' Mann trundled 552 balls in four Tests, fellow leggie Simpson 524 in five. His first international spell netted him 3–12. 'Piece of piss, this Test cricket,' thought Mann. In the subsequent tour match he felt every Indian batsman's eyes on every delivery he let go. Any air of mystery was history. 'Gavaskar played me with a stump virtually. Quite often he didn't pick my wrong'un, but he had such skill and got so far back that he'd just zip me round the corner. I sit back years later when Shane Warne's got 0–150 on debut and I think, well, they're bloody hard people to bowl to.'

Mann's muscular, matchwinning 105 as nightwatchman was the sensation of the Second Test. He got to Melbourne for the Third Test and saw a banner strung across Bay 13: 'HIGGS A CERTAINTY'. In Sydney he went wicketless and runless, out second ball each dig, and was never picked again. He didn't make enough of opportunities, Mann is quick to admit, although one of the few cricketing keepsakes on display at his home is a framed Allan Langoulant cartoon from Perth's *Daily News*. As a baggy-eyed Simpson stomps off, turbaned Indians whooping it up in the background, a cherubic fellow who looks a lot like Tony Mann asks: 'Tell me, Simmo, if Chandrasekhar was in your team would you give *him* a bowl?'

Out of the XI for the decisive Adelaide Test, Kim was among those visiting that city's health department on Australia Day, his twenty-fourth birthday, for yellow fever injections. Simpson's fifteen-man squad arrived in the Caribbean to the standard rum-punch-and-steel-band reception. Instantly Kim began pounding a drum of his own. In the first net session at St John's his snappy footwork before two thousand locals impressed John Benaud, batting dynamo turned newspaperman. Benaud declared the Hughes–Serjeant middle order showdown 'a no-contest'.

The team flew to St Kitts, Kim chalked in at No. 3 for the tour opener against Leeward Islands. A stomach ache made him think he'd swallowed contaminated water. On the morning before the game a doctor dished out anti-nausea pills. At training in the afternoon Kim flopped himself down on the cool Warner Park grass. Night fell. The pain intensified. Manager Fred Bennett summoned a doctor, a different doctor. Along narrow stone streets in the hotel manager's car, Kim was bustled to Basseterre's Joseph N. France General Hospital for an emergency operation on something pre-tour jabs could not have forestalled: a gangrenous appendix.

The appendix came out. Kim felt better, well enough to slouch boundary-side for the third day's play. His temperature zoomed and he returned to hospital. 'I can't take a trick,' he told visiting team-mates. 'I'm either twelfth man or sick or injured.' Years later he'd recall: 'I was frozen with fear and pain.' He felt far from home, unsure what was wrong, shacked up at the Antigua Beach Hotel and Trinidad Hilton on a largely futile antibiotics course. 'Kim was in a dirty pool in Trinidad,' says Serjeant, 'and his wound became infected and was pouring out pus three days later.' Serjeant, a pharmacist, was a rapt observer of the Caribbean hospital system's idiosyncrasies. Twice the appendix wound was reopened, drained of pus, resealed. 'I remember them squeezing it and filling up a bottle with this gangrenous stuff,' says Wayne Clark.

The tour management considered sending Kim home. He pleaded with them to let him stay. Kim was anxious not to let down his family and supporters. The management relented. He first graced an outfield one month into the tour, spilling two catches against Barbados as replacement fielder. His misfield at point in Georgetown enabled Larry Gomes to run three for his maiden Test hundred. After six weeks the outlook brightened.

In dismissing Guyana's Sew Shivnarine—caught Ogilvie, bowled Hughes—he joined Freddie Stocks of Nottinghamshire as the only men to score a hundred in their first first-class innings and take a wicket with their first first-class ball.

At picturesque St George's, against Windward Islands, on a pitch dry, brown and speckled with little hills, Kim entered at 4–40 and square cut treachery to tatters. 'I guess his sheer majesty in the circumstances,' John Benaud recalls, 'might have been a tiny preview of those couple of brilliant digs at the MCG and Lord's.' On 30 he square cut once too often, swaying back and missing Hubert Annibaffa's arm ball. He'd fallen the same way in Guyana. 'This bloke just doesn't learn'—or words similar—remarked Simpson, within earshot of others.

Crabbier words were heard as the Australians readied themselves to bat a second time in the Barbados Test. 'Arse of the team.' 'Just an arse.' That was Simpson's plain-spoken verdict on Kim, say Wood, Clark and Serjeant. Kim wasn't playing. Wood remembers Kim hearing it and leaving the room: 'He said it in front of him, that's my recollection. And Kim actually walked out and sat with the photographers.' Simpson cannot remember it and does not believe it: 'I wouldn't have said it. No way in the world.' But several people say it happened. 'Who are the several?' wonders Simpson. 'Western Australians?'

Simpson's supposed anti-WA chip was a fable handed down the decades, along with the evil Subsidy, inverted saucepans for caps and blinkered eastern-seaboard selectors. Before he even knew Simpson, Clark was warned: 'Just be careful walking down the stairs in front of him.' Its origins harked back to Simpson's five seasons in the west in the fifties and sixties. Its reasons are unclear. Perth, after all, was where the national selectors finally noticed Simpson, where in twenty-four career matches he averaged 85. Simpson speaks fondly of the long unroped boundary, where outfield returns sometimes necessitated three men if the Doctor was blowing, and of the light: 'You could almost read the Kookaburra brand on the new ball.' Him resenting WA cricketers is pure fiction, says Simpson, not that it surprises or worries him. 'I've always felt West Australians have more trouble than the rest in settling into an Australian team. They feel the world's against them. Or they did in those days.'

Misgivings about the captain were not merely geographical but generational. Young batsmen taught to get bodies behind fast bowling thought they spotted fear in Simpson's method of creeping to leg and cutting or letting balls roar over stumps. Spectators hooted, bowlers pawed the turf, team-mates har-rumphed among themselves. What they were really seeing was time-tested pragmatism. 'You was never going to get hit, man, because you was never there,' said Wes Hall, a phantom from Simpson's first Test life. Simpson's 102 against Barbados echoed his 117 against the same opponents thirteen years earlier. He'd legside-swiggled his runs then too, Hall confirmed. 'I had total admiration,' says Wood, Australia's bravest batsman in 1978 and half Simpson's age. 'The guy was forty-two and up against the quickest bowlers, wearing the baggy green for protection.'

Some saw Simpson as a competitor not a mentor, blaming others rather than his own shortcomings, expecting everyone to match his exacting standards, suspicious of media darlings. 'Kim's ego and Simmo's ego was an enormous match-up,' says Cosier. Wood feels Kim and Simpson 'didn't get on . . . they certainly didn't see eye to eye'. 'Divide and conquer' is how Cosier describes Simpson's leadership style. Players were unsure where they stood. 'One minute he's patting you on the back,' says Clark, 'and then you hear he's nailing you behind your back . . . You just thought, fuck, what sort of captain's this?' Serjeant confronted Simpson about it at the behest of four or five others. 'I'm probably more of a diplomat than some of them were,' Serjeant explains. The conversation didn't go well. 'He sort of listened,' says Serjeant. 'But afterwards our relationship wasn't like it was previously.'

Future detractors would collect near-identical grievances about Simpson the coach. Complaints always mingle with praise for the purpose and discipline he entrenched, for his salvaging of players' true potentials, for the gutbusting fielding drills. As Mike Whitney says: 'I've seen guys collapse and vomit on the practice area and Simmo's still hitting balls at them, saying "get up, get up!"' At pre-game training in Gwalior in 1986, wicketkeeper Tim Zoehrer pouched skyer after skyer, lunging wider and higher, Simpson pinning him back, back, back, until finally he reverse-tumbled into three rolls of barbed wire and got hooked in mid-air. Zoehrer recalls: 'I was hanging off a barbed wire fence in India with blood pouring out of my back and two army blokes trying to rescue me, their machine guns whacking me in the head. It's not a pleasant thing.'

Players certainly noticed when Simpson didn't take training. At Sabina Park on the 1991 tour he was bitten by a mosquito and bedridden with an infected leg. Whitney remembers Allan Border plonking his men down after practice and revealing that Simpson had a list. 'So I'm telling everyone,' said Border, 'you better go up and say: "Hey Simmo, how you going, hope you're feeling OK." Just five minutes. Because there's going to be a lot of ticks and one cross for anyone who doesn't go.'

Whitney went with Greg Matthews. 'Hey Bobby, how you feeling, how's the leg?' But Simpson was doing the asking, not the answering.

'How did training go today?'

'Yeah really good.'

'How did Veletta go?'

'Yeah great. Waggy was in there, y'know, batting hard, fielding.'

'What about Tub? How'd Tub go? Tub do a lot of catching?'

'Yeah man. He was there doing his slips stuff . . . OK Bob, we're gunna head. Yep, yep Bob, yep, yep, good to see you.'

Shuffling out, they passed the Waugh twins shuffling in: 'How was it?'

'Well, he's going to hit you with a shitload of questions about who's puttin' in and who's not puttin' in.'

'OK, cool.'

Says Whitney: 'Like AB said, he had a list. He was sticking names on. How bizarre is that? But that's the way he ran the thing.'

Back in the final fortnight of the 1978 tour, Kim missed selection for the Jamaica match and therefore the last Test too. 'Kim Hughes is the most frustrated, disillusioned young man in the West Indies today, and with good reason,' reported Alan Shiell. 'Hughes will continue his familiar role of spectator/ amateur photographer . . . Never at any stage has Simpson considered Hughes a Test prospect.' Shiell went on to quote Simpson's explanation: 'We are here to win a Test. We are not a benevolence society.'

Simpson stands by what he did and said. 'You don't give a person a game just because they're disappointed. You're not there to hand out caps. No one on that tour believed Kim was fit enough. Talent didn't come into it. In retrospect he probably should have been sent home to recuperate.' Eighteen months after Australia's 3–1 defeat, Simpson wrote in *Australian Cricket* that the Kim he'd captained possessed 'too much natural ability' and 'played by numbers': 'It got to the stage that I was able to nominate the ball and shot he would get out to.'

That wasn't Simpson being a competitor rather than a mentor. It was the truth. 'Simmo,' says Serjeant, 'was doing what Lillee and Marsh wanted to do, imposing some discipline, because he had the power to do it, saying you're not going to play because you don't fit my team rules. And I don't think you can argue with that.' Simpson reflects:

> You don't have generation gaps, you know. You don't have trouble with young players. You have trouble with players at the end of their careers. So in that regard it was a reasonably good, happy tour. I always felt I had huge respect from the players. They respected me for making the comeback to help Australia—and also, I suppose, to help them.

Simpson spent much of his cricketing middle age, the eight years between captaining and coaching Australia, as a newspaper columnist. He was no likelier to file a puff piece than he was to clap a misfield. And he found fault with many a pratfall of Kim's. Yet he also wrote admiringly of Kim's ability. He did so consistently, uncharacteristically, even extravagantly. You had to read between the lines, but you could almost sense affection there. As for Kim, he once observed of Simpson:

Simmo was always on about attitude . . . He was a classic example of always batting at practice as he wanted to in the middle. Many of the young Australians learnt from him. He taught us that Test cricket was a game for people with the best mental attitude.

'That,' says Simpson, 'was the right lesson.'

•••••

FEARLESS PRONOUNCEMENTS BOUNCED out of Kim's mouth as the Ashes summer of 1978–79 got into swing. He plundered 127 against Queensland when nobody else got to 25 and proclaimed it his 'most important' innings. A 48 against Victoria was his 'most satisfying' because of the classy attack. He spoke reverentially of Yorkshireman Geoff Boycott's stonewalling capacities. He had heeded advice from Barry Richards about grinding out an innings, premeditating nothing. Six appeal, he now realised, had distracted him. He'd 'done myself an injustice' by shooting skywards instead of along the ground. And no longer would he see off the rottweilers only to lose concentration against the labradors. 'I have found I am most often out to fellows who bowl ordinary medium pace, and wide,' said Kim.

Now a new tendency emerged: to declare a lesson learned before the lesson was over. Kim was 4 not out when Botham came on in the First Test in Brisbane. He steadfastly ignored three juicy outswingers. He drove at the fourth and snicked it.

Bill O'Reilly judged Australia's 116 all out above par in seamier conditions than any he remembered in forty-seven years of playing and watching Tests in Australia. England's batsmen coped well enough, chiselling 286. Kim reappeared at the crease on the third afternoon thinking it could be his last international innings for many moons. He wore his green cap and mitten gloves. Straightaway he looked better balanced and more assured than his helmeted new captain Graham Yallop. He hooked Willis on to the Gabba dog track, normally Kim's cue to swipe all Willis bouncers for attempted sixes. But Brearley posted a second man in the deep and he didn't risk it again. Botham, slower, was a different matter. At fine leg Boycott heard a whistling coming at him—'like a shell'. He was still twelve yards away when it clanged the advertising sign on the full. 'Had I got in the way,' Boycott reflected, 'it would have taken me with it.'

Kim hooked and pulled a couple more like that. Others he ducked. Slow bowling meant fast scoring in Kim's head. Yet he greeted Geoff Miller's looping straight-breaks with a bat even straighter, crouching low. When he attacked, he often lunged. He never quite flowed. Forty minutes he spent in the nineties. Forty times, conceivably, he visualised the buzz among spectators if he were to loft them a catch and hoist his hundred in one blow.

Singles carried him from 97 to 99. In Old's next over he blocked six balls. The seventh angled in from outside off stump and he paddled it for two. He took off his cap, ruffled a curl above his forehead. He lifted his bat to the crowd—once, quickly—then dragged it down, fossicking at some imaginary pitch debris. He looked shy.

Instead of raising his ton with a six, Kim celebrated with one. He took three strides at Miller, landed two strides short, but still cleared the dog track and clattered the concrete outside the members' bar. It did not save a Test but it gave the Poms something to chase. He was last out for 129. Apart from Yallop's 102 no one else reached 20. Kim hoarded fifty-two singles and batted four minutes shy of eight hours. Never before in his life had he lasted five hours. 'They didn't,' said Kim, 'serve up much tripe.'

At once he became a big hit among children. Kim made cricket look like serious fun, not hard work. And he was himself so childlike. He could pass for head boy, still. He was especially popular in bush households, so faraway from the brain cortices of Kerry Packer's henchmen that they could have been living in the Bavarian wilderness. They didn't get Channel Nine and missed every ball of World Series Cricket. Australian Cricket Board cricket was the only cricket they knew.

Those qualities that enchanted children were not necessarily good for Kim's average. Promoted from five to three in the order, he returned to ways less Boycottian. A switch of bowler, a scheduled interval, an approaching milestone: all of these heralded doom. Twice he flung himself overboard on 48 and once on 46. The Third Test was a lark: out first ball in the first innings, out first ball of a new Botham spell in the second. In the Fourth Test he ran at Willis, drove gaily and picked out cover first ball after lunch. 'Some sort of mental seizure,' diagnosed Frank Tyson, christening him 'Impetuosity Hughes'. Flailing again towards cover, he succumbed second delivery with the new ball in the Fifth Test. In the Sixth he nibbled at ball one of a fresh Willis spell.

All that was missing from his 48 in Melbourne was a spinning bow tie and a water-squirting flower in his buttonhole. For once in a bowler's summer he had seemingly hit on the right mix of aggression and tact. Hendrick bowled four consecutive maidens at Kim then excused himself to replace a broken bootlace. Botham stepped up. 'Bowl Hendo's length,' chirped Boycott; not full, but not quite short, though Botham's only thought clip-clopping in was to get the first one up and straight. It was neither. Yet the stupefied roar Hendrick heard from the dressing room could mean only one thing, a wide floating loosener, which Kim had pranced at and cuffed to extra cover. It was as typical of Kim as it was of Botham. 'No wonder they call you Golden Bollocks,' Hendrick offered in congratulations, musing afterwards: 'How many times has he bowled crap, come off at 0–60 and ended up with 6–90?'

Many on their couches pined for a Brearley–Inverarity captaincy duel, two grey-headed chess grandmasters cracking knuckles. The only pawns Yallop moved were his slips, operating under an innovative but ill-fated rota system. 'It would have been nice if it happened,' says Inverarity. 'But it didn't, and that was that. It was never a point of great disappointment.' Inverarity admired Yallop's batsmanship. 'But there was no evidence at all that he was a good captain. In terms of the aggregate talent, it was not that England were better than Australia but that they were very well led and Australia were not well led.'

The 6–0 victory Yallop foreshadowed at his Eagle Farm airport press conference petered out to a 5–1 defeat. In Perth he asked Cosier to sledge Boycott from silly point. When Cosier baulked, Yallop repeated the order. 'So I went up there,' Cosier recalls, 'and I hardly said boo. I'd been brought up in an era when an average player doesn't sledge a good player.' While Cosier was standing there, Hogg asked him to ask the captain for a leg gully.

'You ask him,' Cosier replied. 'He's just there.'

'I'm not talking to that prick. You ask him.'

A series low-grade but high in spectacle was energised by Hogg's 41 wickets and the Dalek-like qualities—bulletproof, pitiless, staccato—he assumed in Boycott's mind. At one point on tour Boycott endured 857 boundaryless minutes. 'Hey Geoff,' cracked Hogg before the WACA Test, 'you'd better have some good insect repellent tomorrow because I have a couple of trained flies who are going to land in your eyes every time I bowl to you.' Allan Border debuted in Melbourne. On his first Test day he hit a single off the last ball of the penultimate over when Wood was 97. For perhaps the only time in sixteen seasons, Border was roundly booed. Wood was chiefly responsible for another amazing stat: the run-out of an Australian opener in every Test. His habit of advancing several speechless strides, whether running or not, was the cricketing equivalent of the hangman's itchy nose. 'It began to look as if the wicket could do with traffic lights,' wrote Ray Robinson.

Kim's series average bottomed out at 29. When Western Australia played in the Gillette Cup one-day final at Hobart's TCA Ground, Kim nodded towards Mount Wellington. 'I'll put one over the top of that,' he told team-mates. 'I can't resist having a go at that.' A single got him off the mark. It was time to make good his promise. Down the track he hopped, blasting Jack Simmons a return catch. WA lost.

Gentlemen of influence in Australian cricket saw in this young man the characteristics of a leader. Just a week later Kim succeeded John Maclean as Australia's vice-captain, their sixth in twelve games. Autumn arrived. Pakistan lurched into Perth for the last of two Tests. Yallop pulled a calf muscle batting for Richmond. Kim was captain of Australia.

•••••

TEN GAMES as North Perth skipper was the extent of his leadership experience in adult cricket. Nine times Kim-led teams went belly up. Outdoing West Perth four Christmases ago saved him from an imperfect ten. But he wasn't daunted, merely nervous, and not so nervous that it inhibited creative thinking. He made players who barely knew each other room together. He called extra team meetings. He trained his men from mid-afternoon till dusk. The idea was to grow spirit, vigour and purpose where before sloth and aimlessness had flourished. Advice poured out of him, some of it unusual. Left-hander Jeff Moss, about to play his first Test, was surprised to hear his new captain mention to the batsmen: 'Don't pick the ball up.'

Anything went in a series Imran Khan rated the ugliest he'd known. Pitch-gardening in the First Test, Hogg's green thumb triggered the umpire's raised finger when Javed Miandad broke the stumps and appealed, an old Karachi street cricket trick. Kim's 84 and Border's maiden hundred swept Australia to within 77 of the 382 required. Sarfraz Nawaz, swinging a wrecking ball that looked more like a beach ball through Australia's innings, demolished those aspirations with 7–1 in 33 deliveries.

That was then. This, Kim announced, was 'a new era'. It sure looked unfamiliar: eleven Australians boasted sixty-one Tests between them. Needing only to draw the Second Test, Mushtaq Mohammad instructed his team to aim no higher. That was Kim's first stroke of luck. And he was at home. On his side was a whole city. In his corner was a friend, Daryl Foster, temporarily filling the new gopher-style position of team liaison officer. At his fingertips was a commemorative silver coin marking Western Australia's 150th birthday. With it, Kim won the toss, inserted Pakistan and smiled as they slid to 5–90 at lunch.

Concentrating was difficult when there was so much to think about. He stationed himself at second slip. Twice he dropped Javed: sitters, both. Javed proceeded to 129. Bat in his hand, Kim flicked at a straight ball from Sikander Bakht and missed, lbw for 9. Australia's Border-fortified 327 put them 50 in front. In the nets on the third morning Kim was bowling at his batsmen, filling in the minutes, when he trod on a ball, tripped and didn't get up. The right ankle was sprained, and badly, the rest day reducing neither swelling nor pain. Fielding on it was a no-no. 'There is no point in me trying to be a foolish hero,' said Kim, a captain rendered lame in all but quotability.

While Kim was away the alleycats played. Asif Iqbal, dealing in threes and ones, engineered a pesky last-wicket stand with Sikander. 'I was on the boundary,' says Moss, 'and if the ball came down I had to let it go for four rather than let them have a single, so we could get the other bloke on strike.' That didn't work. Pakistan's lead mounted. Twelfth man Trevor Laughlin, fielding in Kim's stead, had another idea. Thanks to some improbably swift singles, Sikander had faced only three balls in thirty-nine minutes. A batting rabbit who knew how to hare, he was leaving the non-striker's end long before the ball did. Laughlin told bowler Hurst. Bowler Hurst removed bails. Sikander was 'Mankaded'—by metres, and without warning. Would Kim have instigated it? He did not condemn it.

'It was just part of cricket,' said Kim.

Payback was on Pakistani minds when Rick Darling's gentle drive rolled to mid-off Sikander, whose even gentler return eluded the bowler. Andrew Hilditch, three Tests old and a caretaker captain already, picked up the ball to spare Sarfraz the bother. Instead of 'thank you', Sarfraz said 'howzat?'

'It just wasn't cricket,' said Kim. Umpire Tony Crafter, a Mankad and handled-the-ball virgin two days before, suddenly had one of each for the scrapbook.

Australia began the final 15 overs with rain beckoning, the sky blackening, 68 needed and Kim preparing to don pads should things get desperate. A six off Imran eased the pressure. 'Just one of my normal ones over midwicket,' says Moss. 'Just a front-foot, ah, slog.' Moss was nine years old when ex-Test opener Leo O'Brien discovered him at Lindsay Hassett's Elwood coaching school. He joined Melbourne as 'a ten-year-old with a fat backside who used to get in the way at practice', in the words of club committeeman Clive Fairbairn. Now thirty-one, Moss turned Mudassar Nazar to fine leg, becoming the first player since Frank Penn in 1880 to hit the winning stroke in his one and only Test. 'I didn't think you were up to it when you were selected,' Moss's room-mate and new friend Geoff Dymock confided that night. 'But you did well.'

The Fourex and soft-drink bottles Kim brought into the opposition rooms went untouched by pursed Pakistani lips. The winners hadn't all been grinners either. Hilditch's well-meaning bowling counsel provoked directions—from his own men—as to where he could stick those three Tests' worth of wisdom. But if not for his ankle, Kim could have jumped with joy. There was the congratulatory prime ministerial telegram from Malcolm Fraser. There was the page one team photo, all beers and flashing teeth, with Kim and Border hugging up front, future captain, future champion. It was possible to believe that Kim's new era he'd mentioned was something to rejoice in.

•••••

MIKE COWARD is no fisherman—'not interested'—which explains how he got chatting with the Travelodge Motel maid. It was the rest day, mid-morning. Fellow broadsheet scribes McFarline and Mossop—'the morning mafia', the afternoon tabloid contingent called them—had left at 4 a.m. in pursuit of marlin off Rottnest Island. Most of the players headed to Rottnest too. Coward was working in his room. Catch of the day came to him. 'Oh,' said the maid, 'nice old bunfight last night.'

A party, it transpired, had been held on the sixth floor where the Australians were rooming. Some Pakistan players joined them from the third. The party was a ripper. Beer bottles were tossed from balconies into the swimming pool and car park. Broken glass dappled the concrete. A car was damaged, a motel door broken. Parents stopped children from approaching the pool. Several guests complained to the motel manager.

Coward's instinct was to leave it alone. Earlier that summer an exploded TV set and a flaming hotel curtain had gone unreported. But this was different. This time, Coward points out, police were summoned:

The newspapermen in those days were very much prepared to take a sympathetic view. We didn't react like the English papers, and probably our papers, would react today.

199

Perhaps we were wrong but that's the way it was. A different world. But once the police were involved you knew you had a responsibility, because if suddenly there was a court appearance and you hadn't done your job properly you'd be in more trouble than the early settlers.

A delegation of players sought unsuccessfully to stop the story. The journalists were discreet, writing a ripple not a splash, but it was enough for one or two players to fear exorcism from the forthcoming World Cup in England. Kim rang board chairman Bob Parish, pleading alternative punishments. Kim apologised to the motel manager. The motel manager delivered a ticking off. The busted door was paid for—$140.

Jeff Moss missed it all. He ate out with his wife and brother. And Kim departed for his own home well before the end. Word was that, before bed, he left proof of how much jollity had been had on his driveway. Was this the new era? It was the night of his third day as Australian Test captain.

SEVEN
The View From the Scrapheap

IN THE CITY with the most sparkling light for playing cricket, six planks of electric lights sprout out of the main cricket oval. They resemble cigarette lighters more than candlesticks: purely functional, strictly inelegant, grey and thick, butchering river views from street corners miles away. Their shadows dangle over the school next door, Trinity College, permanent reminders to teacher Graeme Porter of days he might nearly have forgotten. 'In so many respects that part of my life is finished,' he says. 'It's over. And it's interesting, I don't have a lot of memorabilia at home. It kind of happened, that little brief moment for me, and it's over, over and done with. Nice, but it's gone.'

Some of it was nice, at least, like being picked for the 1979 World Cup. He got called out of class on a Friday to answer the phone—Robbie Burns from the *Daily News*. 'You're going to England.' No, no, Porter tried explaining. He'd wintered there before but was staying put this time. 'No,' Burns interrupted, 'you're going to England,' and Porter started setting him straight again when Burns said for the third time: 'You're going to England *because* . . .'

And not long after that his Cannington Senior High maths class was huddled round his feet, over his shoulders and pulling chimpanzee grins for the press photographer. Porter had played fourteen first-class matches, never done better than four-for. But the selectors calculated that in English conditions he might swing the ball so far it boomeranged. They were desperate, too. 'I had never thought about it—never even gave it one thought. At all. I think people sort of said, well, who the heck's he?'

The World Cup was Kim's first adventure as full-time captain. Porter got married a fortnight before departure. One warm-up match was drowned out, he missed the next two, then played against Hampshire; 6–2–6–1 read Porter's figures when rain sent everyone scurrying. 'All I remember is being basically awestruck, enjoying every moment.' It didn't win him a berth against England at Lord's, scene of four Australian run outs and a six-wicket hammering. But the night before the Pakistan game Kim confided that Hogg was either crook, injured or both. 'Interesting person to tour with,' says Dymock. 'Hoggy didn't turn up to first practice. Too bloody cold. Didn't get out of bed.' Porter emerged from sleep filled with curiosity. Then, on the way to the nets, it happened. 'Kim just mentioned it: "You'll play!"'

It was Jeff Moss's limited-overs debut too. He got to 7, knelt to sweep and missed, the ball trickling off his pad. He was still on bended knee when Hilditch—shrieking 'Yes! Yes!'—was sixteen yards down the track. 'I probably should have said no,' Moss concedes. 'But he'd been in a while and that's how you were brought up. If someone's calling yes, you go.' Out by half the pitch, Moss's one-day career really would have lasted one day, had rain not forced a spillover on to a reserve day. But that was later. First, Kim won the toss and threw the new ball to Porter:

There wasn't a lot of guidance, I have to say. I don't recall anyone coming up to me, even through my spell, and saying we're going to try this or that or whatever. I don't think anything special was said. It almost felt like just another game, just another grade game, except we were at Trent Bridge and there were lots of people around.

The nerves that hovered he kept hidden. Bowling at Dickie Bird's end helped. 'He would chat to me,' says Porter. 'I was getting in close to the danger area and he'd say "you gotta keep outta here". But in a nice way. It was relaxing.' Uprooting Sadiq Mohammad relaxed him some more. Alan Hurst dropped short and was whacked high. Porter switched ends and pared back. By seventies standards Pakistan's 7–286 verged on mountainous. Porter's 1–20 off 12 overs kept them, briefly, to a molehill. Defeat by 89 runs tipped Australia over the cliff.

There was nothing to gain and dignity to lose against Canada. Glenroy Sealy, thirty-eight and unknown, hustled four fours in four balls to end Hogg's opening over. Hurst's five wickets put a brake on bedlam. Porter's six overs and 2–13 capped one of the cucumber-coolest initiations in limited-overs legend. 'I was really quite chuffed, quite confident,' he says.

Now there was the long shot of a six-Test trip to India to consider. While they were in England a settlement had been reached. Packer's wish—the TV rights—was granted, his players to return to cricket's official stage. But not yet. War was over, a truce declared; however with Packer players unavailable until the following home summer, selectorial rations remained in force. Porter was going to India.

'We should have a few laughs about India,' says Hogg. 'But we don't talk about it much. We went everywhere. It wasn't one of these little six-week tours that Australia go on and stay in the best hotels. It wasn't really an Australian cricket tour at all. It was like one of those Channel Nine *Getaway* shows—and throw some Test matches and a bit of cricket in.' Porter bowled just 78 overs in 78 days, each one longer and more excruciating than the day before. Seldom was he picked. It didn't feel as if he was even being looked at. He couldn't practise during matches because the practice strips were on the field. So he sat. The guidance that hadn't been forthcoming still wasn't, and he began to crave it:

I lost confidence. I lost total belief. I felt I shouldn't have been there and I lost the belief that I could actually play, almost to the point where I didn't want to play. There certainly wasn't any help, no 'you're close here, all you have to do is this'. There was none of that, none whatsoever. I don't have any fond memories of India, to be perfectly frank, because of the state of mind I finished up in when I got back.

Was he doing something wrong? Was he a chance of playing? He didn't know. Should he ask? He knew he lacked the self-confidence for that. But still he grappled with whether the expectation was for him to say something or to keep worries inside. 'What do I do?' The thought spun round and round.

He did not talk to Bob Merriman, managing his first Australian squad. 'I didn't find Bob that easy to sometimes chat to.' He did not approach Kim. Not so long before, he'd watched late-night Wimbledon finals at the Hughes family home. 'Mmmm. Yeah, I don't know. I guess I felt Kim had his own troubles, trying to lead the side. No. I don't know. That's a tough one to answer.' Only Border offered anything, in the Delhi nets. He showed Porter how to sweep spinners from down low instead of standing up.

Others battled. Graeme Wood opened in the First Test. By the Sixth Test Hilditch, Darling, Yallop and Yardley were preferred openers. 'That tour was one I tried to erase from the memory banks,' says Wood. 'When I first went to India I couldn't stand it. I hated it. I hated the food, I hated the place, I hated the environment.' Porter was wonderstruck inside the Taj Mahal and on snow-tipped mountains near Srinagar. He liked the hotels. And on the tour's sixty-first day, against East Zone in Cuttack, he finally took his first wicket. It was also his last. Batting in the second innings, a lengthy stay in the offing, he had just settled in when the other batsman got out and Kim declared. Kim declared so fast that Rick Darling was already walking the drinks out and had to turn back. Porter recalls:

I thought, I've obviously got no hope here, have I, of pushing my claims? A little bit of anger did well up in me—to think, well, clearly I'm not thought of on this tour. I walked past and I threw my bat into my bag. And that was it. That was the end for me. Shattered—yeah, I suppose that's probably a good word. It took me a long while, a good couple of years, to recover from that.

Nine days after he got home, with Packer's men back and jousting for their official cricketing lives, Western Australia met Victoria in a McDonald's Cup one-dayer. Wood was in bed when he discovered his green Australian blazer didn't entitle him to a yellow WA cap. His dad Mal read it in the paper and banged on the bedroom door: 'Mate, you're not in the side.' Porter was named in a fourteen-man squad. He arrived at the ground, 13,581 people there, on match morning. 'You know how you walk into a room and you get a feeling? Well, I got a feeling that I wasn't in this team.' The selectors confirmed it half an hour before play. 'As soon as the game started and the selectors had gone I picked up my bags and left.'

Did he cry? Porter goes quiet. 'I don't know. I may have. I may have.' He laughs—a warm laugh. 'Look, I don't recall, but I think I probably would have.'

He became WA's sometimes anywhere man, in, out, bowling second-change, batting at nearly every cranny from one to eleven. That went on for a couple of seasons. His head still hadn't left India. 'I was still wondering whether I was good enough.' He'd scour the small print for his name. One day his father said: 'Just get out of thinking about what's happened and what's passed and just enjoy playing with your team-mates.' And that's what he did. For four years he was a Saturday club cricketer. In 1985–86, Fremantle versus Melville, he helped bowl Melville out, walked off and was led aside by state selector Allan Edwards.

'Are you interested in playing the one-day games?'

'Absolutely.'

Western Australia won that year's McDonald's Cup and reached the semis the next year. Across two seasons Porter conceded 2.56 runs an over. Ungetawayable. And ungetdownable. And just like that he bowed out, happy. He knew how close he'd gone to fading out.

He never spoke to Frank about India. He is sure Kim has no inkling either. He never felt tempted to tell him. 'Can't do anything about it. No, it's over. I've never had the urge or the feeling to talk about it with anybody. Apart from now.'

He wears a Trinity College badge during school hours: 'GRAEME PORTER'. So that *is* how you spell it. He sighs. 'I've actually rung a couple of places. There was one on the web, might have been Cricinfo, and they had my name incorrect. They had a "contact us" sort of thing so I wrote to them and got a response and it was changed. I know it's a little thing but I really do get annoyed.' He still gets 'Graham' in various WACA publications, despite mentioning it to Western Australia's stats guru Bill Reynolds. He gets it in all kinds of places where editors should know better: *Wisden Australia*'s births and deaths section, the *Penguin History of Australian Cricket*, Bill Frindall's book of one-day scorecards. 'I'll try again. I do, as I say, I do get annoyed with that.'

•••••

WAYNE CLARK WAS EIGHT when the future started to make sense. He had a fast bowler for a teacher in grades 3 and 4, Laurie Mayne, whose craft took him to the West Indies, India, South Africa. 'Heck,' thought Clark, 'that's what I want to do—if I'm not playing league footy.' The revelation brought clarity. The clarity proved long-lasting. When Packer's persuaders came poaching, Clark rang the Australian Cricket

Board enquiring how far away was Test selection. The board said not far so Clark stuck with the board. Seven weeks later he was opening Australia's attack against India and outstriking Jeff Thomson with 28 wickets in five Tests. His bowling action, reckoned dubious by some, was filmed and cleared.

Chucking—and ducking—were bones, frequently broken ones, of contention on the Caribbean tour immediately afterwards. Peter Toohey was pinged on the forehead by Andy Roberts and incoming batsman Steve Rixon took guard in a puddle of blood. The astronaut strolling into battle in Bridgetown was actually Graham Yallop under a batting helmet, Test cricket's first. He benched it in the subsequent tour game, incentive enough for Colin Croft to break Yallop's jaw in two places. When Cosier's thumb was chipped in Grenada in the tour's eighth week, John Benaud drily recorded: 'It gave manager Bennett the chance to keep intact his record of visiting a hospital in every centre the Australians played.'

Australian eyes locked on West Indian elbows, Croft's and Garner's especially. Watching Croft's arms was like deciphering the brand name on helicopter propellers. Bruce Yardley, inching wider and wider of leg stump, square cut him to a stupor against Guyana, then began tapping his own elbow and lecturing: 'Keep your arm straight.' Croft silently resolved to knock Yardley off his podium. 'Crofty's eyes were always glazed,' batting partner Cosier recalls. 'But this time they looked like they were spinning. He went off his tree. Next ball he's gone back and Bruce's left foot is on the uncut grass, three feet outside leg stump. And Crofty's hit him in the back of the head. It would have clipped the peak of short leg's cap. Bruce went down like a sack of spuds, doing the dead-fish flap on the wicket.' Blood was sponged and jelly legs tested. In the distance skulked Croft, hands in pockets.

Croft wasn't umpire Douglas Sang Hue's concern during the First Test. 'He came in at lunchtime,' Clark remembers, 'and said he was going to call me.' Clark swapped ends. Nothing happened. He played the next three Tests. 'I never doubted I was all right.' But he did think back to the previous summer's film footage. 'Once the mud's thrown, it sticks a bit.'

If Laurie Mayne fired young Clark's mind, watching Graham McKenzie bowl taught him where to put his feet, legs and chest. Clark was strong, side-on, streamlined. But stress fractures had forced some subtle restructuring. 'Because I had such a side-on action—a bit like McKenzie, I always set myself on him—I probably opened up a bit.' Clark's bouncer, a mean one, was the worry. When Sang Hue returned for the tour match in Jamaica, and so the grapevine had it the Fifth Test, Clark took a breather. 'I had a crook back,' he says. 'But I probably could have played.'

Sang Hue had signed up to umpire Packer's Supertests. Simpson's Australians didn't trust him as far as Charlie Griffith—whom Sang Hue declined to no-ball in 1965—could have thrown him. Acting Australian skipper against Jamaica was Jeff Thomson, who had outlined his personal philosophy on captaincy two years earlier. 'It would interfere too much with my social life . . . Imagine coming back to the motel to a bundle of messages—from blokes.' After a couple of hours Thomson introduced Yardley to the attack: 'Maddie [Ian Callen] is fucked and I'm fucked so you and Higgsy will have to bowl all day.' Yardley had received the same Sang Hue note of caution as Clark during the First Test. Now, Sang Hue no-balled Yardley's fifth—'try bowling the rest with a straight arm,' advocated Thommo—and seventh deliveries.

Clark's 'crook back' was timely. But time, unbeknownst to him, was running out. A Peter McFarline article over the winter read a lot like his Test obituary. Clark rang him: 'What the fuck are you talking about?'

'Well,' he heard McFarline say, 'your name and Yardley's name have gone to the International Cricket Conference. There's an agreement going back to the Bradman days. You won't play against England.' He would, McFarline added, play in the two-Test series against Pakistan afterwards.

Clark phoned the board. 'They were weak as piss. Ray Steele I talked to. No one would give you an answer. The press blokes knew more than anyone.'

Clark was picked against Pakistan, as foretold. He did not go to England for the World Cup. Neither did Yardley—who wasn't required for England trips in 1980, 1981 or 1983 either. And in the long Ashes summer of 1978–79, Clark watched Australia's 5–1 extermination on TV:

> I was pretty bitter. Because everything McFarline said came true. We were getting belted and the wickets were absolutely ideal for me—and you had Dymock coming in and fuck knows who else. That did make me pretty annoyed. I've very rarely spoken about it to anybody. Not too many people know that happened. I just got on with it. No good being a bloody sook. But deep down it really hurt. Because I'd stayed with traditional cricket and hadn't gone to World Series I thought there might be more support. But they just washed their hands of me. That was the bit that really

pissed me off. There was no real explanation, no effort. It couldn't have been because I wasn't performing. I'd proved I could play at that level . . .

His voice trails away. 'Anyway, next question.' Not once was Wayne Clark no-balled for chucking.

•••••

AN EXPLANATION, any explanation, would have helped Craig Serjeant too. Over coffee at the Waldorf in 1977 he and Kim had pondered what the galaxy might look like minus Packer's stars. I'll be captain, bragged one. Nah it'll be me, retorted the other. 'Banter. That's all it was,' says Serjeant. 'Certainly on my part.' But it was a time when no notion was too harebrained. When they got home Serjeant was named vice-captain against India. He'd played three Tests in his life and flunked two of them. He had no leadership ambitions, no experience either. But did a single selector or board messenger discuss his appointment with him? 'No,' says Serjeant. 'Not one.'

He saw the words 'heir apparent' in a newspaper report. 'That scared me. I grappled with that.' Simpson was the emergency captain. Simpson was turning forty-two. 'If you're the heir apparent, what does that mean?' says Serjeant. 'How long's this guy around for? Is it one series? Is it four series? You know, what is it? That was mentally tough for me and I didn't deal with it. It was the worst thing that happened to me in my career. If you're inexperienced at that level you've got to deal with one thing—playing. And I had this other thing going round my head.'

Three more things were soon circling: Bedi, Prasanna and Chandrasekhar, three trinkets out of a cereal box he had never opened. Balls bounced on the wickets out west on which Serjeant grew up. They rarely spun. Two ducks in the First Test in Brisbane gave him three in a row. The going got little smoother thereafter. He lost his spot by series end and his vice-captaincy for the 1978 West Indies tour—'a terribly hard tour but really enjoyable', now that heir apparency was some other sucker's burden. Serjeant hit a Test hundred in Georgetown, hotfooting singles with Wood, their 251-run partnership resuscitating Australia from 3–22 to 362 tense and far-fetched runs for victory. While they were batting Kim sketched a graph on a shred of paper, crossing off every logic-defying run. 'You bit them up and chewed them into little pieces out there,' hoorayed Simpson.

Wayne Clark is thankful for the ten Tests he did play. Serjeant is perhaps the only cricketer who said no to Kerry Packer and wishes he hadn't:

My decision was based on my preconceptions of me being a professional person first and a cricketer second. I made the conservative decision. In hindsight it wouldn't have had any impact on my professional career and it was the wrong decision. I actually made the wrong decision. I should have joined World Series. I think I would have been a better cricketer. As a professional cricketer you get more time to practise. Parts of my game would have changed. I would have spent more time doing different things. Wonderful in hindsight.

Runs were scarce on his return from the Caribbean. The position he vacated was gone forever. The World Series Cricket era took many wicked twists. Serjeant's twelve single-figure scores in twenty-three Test innings seem particularly unfair. 'In the end my confidence just fell apart,' he says. 'If I'd had Kim's confidence maybe it wouldn't have.'

•••••

DISAPPOINTMENTS LANDED IN THREES for Gary Cosier before the Gabba Test of 1978–79. 'I was actually a bit disappointed when they announced the captaincy,' he says, 'because I thought I could have been a better captain than Graham Yallop.' Cosier had guest-skippered South Australia on occasion. He liked Yallop. But when the selectors asked Cosier to share his on-field nous with Yallop, his first thought was: 'Well, fuck me, if they want me to help Graham they could have made me captain and he could have helped me.' News that Cosier was to open the innings, never his natural habitat, was his second disappointment. And then he realised who he'd be opening with. Graeme Wood patted the fifth ball of the summer to cover-point David Gower and bolted. Cosier responded, and kept running, all the way to the pavilion.

From there, disappointments piled up and became career threatening. First ball of the second innings, he drove, missed and was bowled by Willis's half-pace full toss. Fourth evening of the Second Test, journalist Dick Tucker mentioned over a beer that Cosier was already dropped from the next game. Something similar happened to John Benaud during the Melbourne Test of 1972–73, except that Benaud's guillotining was official, not bar-room tattle. What's a cricketer dumped mid-match to do, Benaud would later reflect. 'Expect his captain to ring up the chairman of selectors? Confront the selectors himself? Go out and get pissed, maybe? Call Lifeline?' What Benaud did was middle everything on his way to a century next day. And Cosier had Benaud on his mind as he dashed to 47. Then he swept at Geoff Miller—'got hit in the middle of the chest'—and was adjudged lbw.

He took some while to get up and leave. His replacement in the team was a diligent left-hander with a greengrocer's friendly moustache. 'I went out and Allan Border came in. Worst decision of all time.'

Cosier's 46 Test average before World Series Cricket wriggled its way to an eventual standstill at 28. 'It kind of ruined the way I played,' he says. 'I went from being an aggressive player to a bloody stupidly aggressive player. There were all these World Series promos—Hookesy's clearin' pickets, that sort of stuff—and I thought, bugger this, these people are here to watch us. Let's give them something to watch. That was a personal decision and it was stupid.'

Maybe a World Cup could prove not just his salvation but his making. 'I reckon Cosier will eat bowlers like Miller for breakfast,' was captain Kim's pre-tournament tip. But Cosier found himself batting low, bowling plenty. He was run out for 6 against England. 'Trevor Laughlin turned his back on me. I'll never ever let him forget it. He said "yes", I got halfway down, and he just turned his back and put his bat down.' Against Pakistan, Cosier lasted one ball—long enough, almost, for his red hair to go grey:

Majid Khan was bowling and Majid was the gentlest off-spinner that's ever, ever bowled. He bowled a half-tracker, it was super-slow and I spooned it straight back to him. First ball. Javed went crazy in the outfield. It was unbelievable. I don't think I'd ever played a shot like that in my life. Normally I would have gone whack over the top. But I guess I wanted to consolidate myself.

He did not bat against Canada. The worst stroke of his international cricketing life was his last. 'Just a shocking shot,' says Cosier. 'Just awful. A three-year-old wouldn't have hit it back to him. Anyway, so be it.'

For some, World Series Cricket was a beautiful golden coach, carrying them to Test matches they would otherwise never have played. For others, it was a pumpkin, with pips.

EIGHT

'Like the Biggest Neon Sign Up at Kings Cross'

RODNEY MARSH ONCE REMARKED that he had captained Australia for years. What he meant was he could hear a game's heartbeat from behind the stumps. He could 'work out the angles' better than anyone. He said this near the end of his playing days. 'I'm not being egotistical,' he added. The truth was that in thirteen years, ninety-six Tests and ninety-two limited-overs internationals Marsh ran things for two days, in the Adelaide Test of 1981–82, when Greg Chappell broke a knuckle and Kim Hughes a toe. It bothered Marsh that when Greg was not around Kim was captain. It bothered Marsh that he himself wasn't.

September 1975 was a month of potentially seismic upheaval in Australian cricket. Ian Chappell relinquished the captaincy during the Oval Test: 'I've had enough . . . enough of the pressure, and enough of the glory, too.' Keith Stackpole backed his old opening pal Ian Redpath as successor. Few others did. And nobody was backing Marsh. Catching balls kept Marsh's hands full already; and besides, wrote Bill Lawry in *Cricketer*, smashing 'the Chappell stranglehold' would be spiteful. September came and went not with an earthquake but

Seashells, sandalwood, sunflowers . . . and a cricket bat. Geraldton, Year 7. Kim, in cap, is third from left, front row. *Rudy Rybarczyk*

State squad new boys, Kim Hughes and Bruce Laird, September 1970.
The West Australian

The West's new Test foursome: Wayne Clark, Kim, Craig Serjeant and Tony Mann, November 1977. *The West Australian*

Woodlands Golf Course, 1979.
Fairfax Photo Library

Home from Edinburgh—'best six months of my life'—1976.
The West Australian

'I'm vice-captain!' . . . Kevin Wright, Jenny and Kim on the night he got the good news, January 1979. *Bruce Postle, Fairfax Photo Library*

Pom-bashers unite: Kim and Greg Chappell, SCG dressing room, 1980. *Fairfax Photo Library*

Hooking Holding, MCG, 1979. *Bruce Postle, Fairfax Photo Library*

Greeting the Queen and WA Premier Charles Court at Government House, Perth, 1981. *Fairfax Photo Library*

The 1981 Australians in England. *Patrick Eagar*

By 1984 Kim had hooked his way into Bob Hawke's re-election campaign.
Geoff Pryor, National Library of Australia

Conversation about tactics. With Rod Marsh and Dennis Lillee, Lord's, 1981.
Patrick Eagar

Conversation about field settings. With Lillee, SCG, 1983.
Fairfax Photo Library

Not talking to Ian Chappell after the toss, SCG, 1984. *Fairfax Photo Library*

'A good photo.
A very good photo.'
Congratulating Rodney
Hogg on a wicket,
Port-of-Spain, 1984.
Ray Titus, News Limited

Gone with the Windies, 1984 . . . In the spa with Clive
Lloyd; weeping goodbye to the captaincy; leaving Test cricket
for the last time. Lbw, bowled Garner, 0. *Fairfax Photo Library*

Flogging Botham. Revenge . . . MCG, 1982. *Fairfax Photo Library*

Four off Garner brings
up the hundred. MCG,
Boxing Day, 1981.
News Limited

'How do
you spell
repertoire?'
Lord's,
Centenary
Test, 1980.
Patrick Eagar

Next page:
Spinners
are for
slaughtering,
SCG, 1983.
Patrick Eagar

with the rustling of leaves on a tree, a family tree. The captaincy passed from Ian to Greg.

It felt obvious. Leadership adjectives had long clung to Greg. No pen-portrait was complete without the words regal or princely. Yet he did not so much rule kingdoms as bat in a kingdom of one. Others were let in rarely and on his say-so. So nonchalantly did he demoralise bowlers that they wondered what he might do to them if he exerted himself. 'He batted like Michael Holding bowled,' says Rodney Hogg. The sensation that everyone else was moving in slo-mo followed Greg wherever he went on a cricket field. Marsh once bet Greg could go a whole tour without bouncing a return to the keeper—and won. Gary Cosier remembers him catching Tony Greig three inches above grass in an Edgbaston one-dayer. 'As Greiggy played it,' says Cosier, 'he stepped out of his crease. Greg took the catch, threw down middle stump and the ball bounced back to him at short cover. So he'd caught him, run him out and got the ball back again . . . Egos are justified, I guess.'

Seldom did the miraculous prove routine as captain. Greg spoke tetchily and often of the ringing telephone, of the strain on wife Judy. 'Cricket is definitely a game for single, unemployed people. Divorce is the alternative,' he commented weeks after retiring. Greg made no claims to tactical genius. He considered his rapport with players inferior to Ian's. He could not inspire like Ian either. He confessed to getting 'snaky' with lesser colleagues who 'let themselves and the team down because of their own stupidity'. A schoolmaster, not a friend, that was the commonest complaint, one repeated by India's cricketers of the twenty-first century when Greg became their coach.

Cosier's feeling that Greg wished him to fail on debut also found an echo in Geoff Lawson's Gabba initiation of 1980–81. Any ball less than unplayable seemed to provoke a teapot posture from the foreman at first slip, and a glare that told Lawson: 'Don't bowl that crap, son.'

Figures of 3–65 earned Lawson the axe. 'Well,' thought Lawson, 'Greg's got his way, hasn't he?' Lawson recalls:

> Greg certainly didn't help me. He hardly spoke to me off the field and on the field he gave the impression I wasn't good enough to be there. Fortunately I didn't get that impression from Dennis and Rod, who were very positive. But Greg obviously didn't want me in the team. It became obvious with each reaction when I bowled a half-bad delivery. And I didn't bowl too many; I didn't get that many overs. He didn't think I should be there and therefore I wasn't getting his support.

Lawson mentioned some of this in a book he wrote. Greg read it, and when next he saw Lawson he remarked: 'Oh.' 'He didn't realise he was like that,' says Lawson. 'It was one of those cracks in his subconscious.'

Chappell's rule was interrupted. He captained two seasons before World Series Cricket, four seasons afterwards. His respectable record of twenty-one wins in forty-eight Tests flatters him. Most were on home soil. Tours that might have defined his reign—a vulnerable England in 1981, a formidable Pakistan in 1982, a crackerjack World Cup in 1983—he skipped. As a result, when people talk of the Chappell era they tend to mean Ian's, primarily.

There was an alternative. Mike Brearley, squeezer of green-and-gold pressure points for much of the period, pictured a more imaginative captain in Marsh. '[His] trenchant exterior,' observed Brearley in 2005, 'only partly concealed a thoughtful, empathic and dynamic person.' Few could see the leader within the geezer when destiny knocked in 1975. 'Greg Chappell was a fantastic talent,' says Marsh's friend Sam Gannon. 'But to me the logical bloke to take over the Australian captaincy when Ian stepped down was Rod. He would have been an unbelievable captain.'

From rejection came perhaps the first faint stirrings of bitterness. 'Bacchus hurt over that,' says Craig Serjeant. 'I think he took that as a massive slap in the face and really hurt. I think that was the start of it.' Then it happened again. And again. Again. Again.

•••••

JOHN INVERARITY, Marsh's University Cricket Club captain in the sixties, used to hold Thursday night planning meetings after training. He and three or four others would brainstorm ways to dismiss specific opponents. A run out was the strategy concocted for Ian Brayshaw on the Thursday before the 1965–66 grand final against Claremont–Cottesloe. Inverarity knew Brayshaw, a flyer, liked taking two to third man. He told Tony Mann, 'You'll go to third man, Rocket'—so-called for his torpedo arm—'and when Sticks goes for his second run I'll be at the bowler's end. OK?'

On the third afternoon Laurie Bedford carved one in Mann's direction. 'Two!' hollered Brayshaw. Loping his second, bound for the safe end, Brayshaw craned his neck to see Mann's throw make its predictable journey to the wicketkeeper. 'Instead,' says Mann, 'it whistled straight over his head to Inver at the bowler's end. Sticks was run out by five yards. Worked perfectly. Inver knew every batsman backwards.'

Inverarity's brain distanced him from some. 'He's got a grandstand named after him at the WACA and he only played six Tests for goodness' sake,' notes Hogg, who toiled under Inverarity in South Australia. 'You're in the presence of someone who knows he's smarter than you.' Most praise Inverarity's approachability. He identified and articulated players' individual roles. This promoted belonging, empowerment. He was expert in chemistry, in who should bowl at who. He even attended a good school. 'We have a bit of a thing in WA,' says Mann. 'The private school boys have always been looked after in the captaincy stakes. It's because the selectors and WACA hierarchy usually come from Aquinas and these places.' Inverarity went to Scotch College; Marsh graced the somewhat less manicured lawns of Armadale High.

The state captaincy eluded Marsh until 1975–76, year of the national vacancy. 'Oh Rodney, Rodney!' quaked Richie Benaud after his third Shield game in control. Benaud took exception to Marsh's needling of Victorian rookie Trevor Laughlin for repeatedly hanging his bat out. 'Heavens, you've got some hide, fellas,' Benaud wrote, 'particularly you Rod. It's tough as old boots. The number of times I have seen you play, Rod, and miss outside off stump would blow the insides out of an adding machine.'

As wicketkeeper-captain he had an odd, piercing habit. A glove would cover his face when he was displeased. Occasionally two gloves went up. Sometimes they stayed there. By his second year Marsh extracted absolute devotion from his men. Like Inverarity he had a scheme for every bowler, batsman and occasion, governing not by iron hand but by dimpled leather glove. 'You'd see him put his face into his glove,' says Gannon, 'and you knew damn well he wasn't happy with the line you were bowling.' Gannon rated himself a 10 per cent better bowler under Marsh. 'He wouldn't take any shit,' says Wayne Clark. 'He'd give you instructions on what he wanted and if you didn't deliver he'd give you a pay—a pay you knew you deserved. But he'd also be the first one to pat you on the arse and say you're doing a good job.'

Mann describes Marsh as a 'go out there and belt the shitter out of them' captain. 'Had he been an officer in the First World War,' says Rod Eddington, 'he would have been the first bloke over the top. And you couldn't help but follow him. He was absolutely fearless.' Marsh was likelier to contrive a batsman's downfall on his feet than on a Thursday night. The result was the same. Inverarity himself believes: 'There are a number of good but very few outstanding captains. Rod was certainly one. People respected him and responded to him. He had an outstanding reading of the game and the tactics. If you worked out ten criteria for captaining a cricket team he had a tick in every box.'

Men who sat on boards struggled to see past the crosses. Increasingly he was Rod, not Rodney. Cricket captains of Australia were traditionally Bills, Bobs, Harrys, Herbies, Vics, Dons or Ians. Whoever heeded instructions from a Rod? Rod sounded like a publican, or a bookie. And this was a Rod whose inflight beer can average exceeded his batting average and who once wagered against Australia winning a Test in which he was playing.

Rod's roly-poliness obscured the nimbleness of his cricket brain. The advent of pitch microphones acquainted TV viewers with the gnarled excesses of his vocabulary. Those at the grounds had been hearing and lip-reading him for years. He became the face of *Parade* magazine in *Sunday Times* ads back home, his baggy green and larrikin smirk cresting the latest month's busty covergirl:

> rod marsh says parade magazine is a man's best buy. in february parade read about king hugh and his amazing sex secrets. dolly parton reveals what men like and penthouse centrefold joanne tells . . .

Captain of Western Australia one scorching Sydney day in 1979–80, he flung open a big Cottee's ice chest. The ice chest was bare. Still in his keeper's pads, sweat dripping, Marsh marched into the committee room and addressed a gathering of men in suits, cigars in their mouths: 'Where are our *fucking* drinks?'

It was as if he desired the job so much that he did not want them to see how much. Reasons not to appoint Marsh mounted. They festered beside officialdom's standard reluctance to overburden a wicketkeeper. Discounting stand-ins Billy Murdoch, Barry Jarman and Adam Gilchrist, only Jack Blackham has occupied both jobs for Australia, from 1892 to 1894, the one captain in Test cricket's first hundred years to enforce a follow-on and lose. Blackham's men took to calling him 'The Caged Lion'. 'He was,' decided Ray Robinson, 'too highly strung for the cares of captaincy. If his batsmen were failing he would pace up and down the room, fists clenched and beard on chest.' Among Marsh's contemporaries, Bob Taylor led Derbyshire for two seasons, too snakebitten with anxieties about the team bus's non-reclining seats, broken stereo, falling-down TV set and ropy accelerator to keep wickets sprucely. 'A keeper,' sighed Taylor, 'should be captain only on the rarest occasions in first-class cricket. The mental strains are just too much.'

A fundamental contradiction in job descriptions applies too. Stirring captains stamp contests with their own runs and wickets. A sound wicketkeeper is virtually invisible. Taylor's rule had one exception. 'Marsh was such a powerful, positive thinker that I don't believe his work behind the stumps would have suffered. But the Rod Marshes of this world are few and far between.'

Seldom has Marsh let sorrow show. He once told Jack Egan that had he been captain he would not have retired with Lillee and Chappell in 1983–84. He would have toured the West Indies then played the following home season. Friends believe he would have thrived and reloaded, continuing for two, three more years. This book would have a different ending. Some see Marsh's snubbing as payback for World Series Cricket. But they made Greg Chappell captain, didn't they? 'I had one point left to prove and I was never allowed to get around to it,' Marsh recorded in *Gloves, Sweat and Tears*. It looms more than ever, now that his subsequent careers as coach, mentor and selector have underlined what an innovator he could have been, as the calamity of his cricketing life.

'Rod would have loved to captain Australia. I know he would have,' says Greg Chappell. 'He desperately wanted it,' says Mann. 'He will carry it,' says Serjeant, 'to his grave.'

In some ways Marsh had a point: he did 'captain' Australia for years. The view from the top of Lillee and Thomson's run-ups during the 1974–75 Ashes wipeout often consisted of Marsh hoisting one glove high—sign language for a bouncer—or pinching his left toe, cue for a sandshoe crusher. In 1982, when Greg was captain, manager Alan Crompton watched the players stick to Marsh in dressing rooms across New Zealand. 'Like bees round a honeypot,' says Crompton. Twenty minutes of Marsh deputising in Auckland left a lasting impression on Kiwi captain Geoff Howarth. 'The game,' Howarth noticed, 'turned from a relatively quiet scene to a highly charged battle.' Six months later in Pakistan, under Kim, Mike Coward was eyewitness to a tour in danger of unspooling. 'Marsh organised soccer games—it was like being in school camp—and kept morale up,' says Coward. 'It was Marsh who was demonstrably in charge.'

Back at pre-season practice in Perth, old leg-breaker Tony Mann had apprentice keeper Tim Zoehrer bamboozled. Marsh grabbed a bat. 'Wrong'un,' he yelled, meeting the ball on the full and clearing midwicket. 'Leggie,' he roared, slugging another. Zoehrer, who whispered Marsh's name to himself as a teenager plucking blinders off a backyard wall, was picking Mann out of the hand within minutes. 'I was,' Zoehrer recalls, 'in total awe.'

Adelaide Oval was the dreamy, red-roofed setting for Marsh's one shot as Australia's captain on 3 February 1982. It was the last day of the international summer. Australia began it one Test up and 190 ahead, 4–341 in their second innings. A rare series win over a Clive Lloyd-led team looked a breeze from here. Word reached the West Indians that champagne bottles were loaded into Australian dressing-room coolers. Marsh was first man out that morning, driving. In twenty balls Joel Garner took 4–5. Australia lost 6–24. West Indies needed 236. A simple draw would suit Australia. But Marsh missed stumping Viv Richards on 32. He dropped Lloyd on 18. Batsmen toppled steadily as Marsh marshalled a Lillee-less attack.

And then, suddenly, he sought to suffocate runs. He removed men from catching positions. In the press box, Bob Simpson wondered why. Border's fingertips grazed another Lloyd edge that went between him and Marsh. If there were two slips Border could have cuddled it. Several others narrowly missed hands. And as the sky turned pink, Australia lost.

•••••

PLAYING FOR AUSTRALIA is a boy's fantasy. Captaining Australia? Nice if it happens. Kind of a bonus. Not a dream you have. Kim had those daydreams, a lot. Realising, too late, that others tend not to have them, he has tried to deny them, saying captaincy was never a specific longing, saying oh, if only it happened eight years later. He would have lasted longer, averaged higher. 'I just turned up in the wrong era.' Really, circumstances were only partly to blame.

If captaincy was an urge Marsh brooded over but kept quiet, the opposite was true of Kim. Kim talked about it all the time without properly thinking it through. He talked so often and openly about becoming captain that worried team-mates wondered where this big dipper might take him. It wasn't mere aspiration. It was expectation: a lifelong head boy's predestination. Graeme Wood calls it infatuation. Certainly it came from Kim's heart, not head. 'His mistake was his infatuation with being captain, no matter what level,' says Wood. 'He wanted to be captain of Western Australia. He wanted to be captain of Australia. If you were close to him it was obvious. It was a real burning desire. It was huge. I think it really drove him.' He did not stop to think that it might burn him.

He was on a telephone in a corner of an MCG changeroom, twenty minutes after a day's play against Victoria, when he found out he was Australia's new vice-captain. 'You beauty, Pop,' he shouted, for wicketkeeper Kevin 'Pop' Wright was to debut in the same Test. Graeme Porter was in that changeroom. He remembers Kim beaming, dazed, saying: *I'm vice-captain.* 'He looked really alive,' says Porter. Outside, Wright and Kim, with Jenny in the middle, strolled arm in arm towards *Age* photographer Bruce Postle's camera. Kim, a stripy shirt tucked into black slacks, crinkly eyes, looks friendly, carefree, excited. It is one of the sunniest images ever taken of him without a bat in hand.

'Captain of Australia!' he was soon saying out loud, trying out the sound of it, as if test-driving a sports car. *'Captain of Australia!'* Frank Parry, Frank's son Rob and Kim's own family shared his desire. Frank's cuckoo prophecies might have embarrassed Stan and Ruth when Kim was fourteen. But when he got the job, brother Glenn said the family celebrated for a week.

Kim's wish that came true was something he shared with Ian Chappell. Chappell was sixteen when Test bowler Geff Noblet led a South Australian schoolboys side round the Adelaide Oval dressing rooms, encouraging the boys to carry their ambitions in their wallets as an ever-present reminder. Chappell did not fancy the idea. Then he reconsidered, jotting down: 'My ambition is to captain Australia.' The slip of paper was still in his wallet twelve years later as he took out the money for a pub schnitzel on the afternoon he succeeded Bill Lawry. One soaring philosophical distinction split Ian and Kim. For Chappell, captaincy was something that happened when a cricketer reached the top. For Kim, it was not a by-product but the objective.

Ian Chappell was a man and a captain Kim strove to be like. 'I respect him more than any other player,' said Kim in 1979. 'To me the one thing a captain must do is rally the players around him, and players would run through a brick wall for Chappell.' Kim believed in two sorts of captains: 'The intellectual types whose tactics are their forte, and those who lead by example.' Himself he saw as an action man, not an intellectual man. He promised not to be an outspoken captain. But a discreet captain might vocalise one in every thirty thoughts, and this was one battle for which affable, anxious-to-please Kim was spectacularly ill equipped.

Halfway through the 1981 Ashes series he stopped defining his leadership style in terms of his predecessors. It was a fleeting moment of serenity never to be recaptured, the day before the Fourth Test, when only Botham's Headingley superheroics—unrepeatable, surely—had thwarted a 2–0 series lead. 'Kim was a bee's old fella,' as Hogg puts it, 'off going down as the guy who won back the Ashes.' In this mood a tracksuited Kim pondered aloud to Alan Shiell:

The great thing I have in my favour is I will never change. I hope I'll always be a likeable enough, easy-to-get-along-with type of person. Deep down I'd like to be a fellow like

Barassi or Marsh, the type who can get somebody by the throat in a corner and nail him. What I mean is someone like a good football coach, a great orator. Marshy does it very well. He can be very blunt. If I tried to copy it, it wouldn't be me. I have to do things my way. If a player says he's injured or can't bowl I believe him because I know I wouldn't mislead my captain. My philosophy is that I never expect any more or less from the players than I try to do.

If this was his way, not Ian Chappell's way, that Kim was struggling to shape into words, then he was also, without actually saying so, distancing himself from the Greg Chappell way. 'Some captains tend to be aloof or private,' said Kim. 'But I would find that difficult. I like being with the fellows.'

Kim's model captain became Brearley, the clear thinker who located Botham's on-switch. 'The art of being a good leader,' Kim would say later, with the certainty of a leader long since vanquished, 'is to develop a relationship with a person where you can find out what it is that makes them excited . . . To capture that dream in them.' Kim did not need hindsight to be a positive captain. That came instinctively:

I can remember being told I'd do silly things. I'd get out at 30 or 40 and they would say: 'Look, you can't afford to get out at 30 or 40. You've got to go on.' What that did in my mind was reinforce not getting out at 30, not making a mistake. So I'd bat really well up to 30 then I'd think: 'Rod's told me not to get out.' If all of a sudden you're thinking of what not to do, that's exactly what happens.

A Test XI of Kim's was by definition undermanned, for if Kim was captain that meant Greg Chappell was not there. Lillee, Thomson, Pascoe . . . Often some or all of these were absent too, whether for reasons bodily or mysterious. Then most of those players retired and Kim's teams were enfeebled all over again. In lobbed pups and journeymen, underdone, overwrought and surprised to be there. Kim set them at ease. He welcomed them, involved them, made them feel he believed in them, as if their selection was his idea. For many, starting out under Kim was a soothing experience in a traumatic era. 'I bowled to Gavaskar in my first game and I remember not feeling nervous,' says Murray Bennett. 'I came back from India saying: "This bloke, he's a great captain."' Bennett's past skippers included McCosker and Wellham. 'I'd put Kim in front of them all, just with his effervescence and personality. Heaps of personality.'

Kim's positivity was especially effective in tandem with another attribute of his: cricket-sense. Opener Steve Smith debuted in a 1982–83 one-dayer in Perth. Only after the players' warm-ups did he discover he was in the XI. Australia lost the toss. He would be batting in minutes. 'Mate,' said Smith, kitting up, 'can you give me a heads-up?'

New Zealand had won four straight thanks to a seam attack snarlier than it looked. Kim sat himself down, outlining in intricate detail the nuances of combating Ewen Chatfield, Lance Cairns, Martin Snedden. Finally he rose, patting Smith on the knee. 'Mate,' said Kim, 'all the best.'

Smith looked at him, eyes like medicine balls. 'Mate, what . . . what about Hadlee?'

'Oh, don't worry about him. He's just quick and bowls in

the right areas. Mate, you'll get used to that. Just play 'em the way you see 'em.'

Smith was still staring after Kim as he skipped away. Only later, out there, did Kim's wisdom sink in. 'He could have said: "Mate, he's one of the best bowlers ever to grace the earth." Kim took another option.'

Two summers later West Indies lost the first final, an ignominy so rare that their ears were steam-scorched. Rumour had it that Michael Holding was reverting to his 35-pace run-up for game two. To batsmen, the young Holding was a malevolent fleck on the horizon, a ten-pace trot the prelude to a soundless 25-pace glide to the popping crease. But for a year 'Whispering Death' had operated off a whistling amble—fifteen paces—to protect his left knee.

'Kim,' said Smith, 'is he off his long run-up today? That's the whisper.' By this time Kim had woes enough. He'd quit the captaincy, lost his spot and caught half a lifeline as thirteenth man.

'Yeah.'

'Mate,' Smith pleaded, 'any advice?'

Kim stopped what he was doing. 'Smithy, when Mikey gets to the top of his mark, look down, count to three and look up. By then he'll be half-way in.'

'Well . . . Why?'

'Because a lot of guys,' said Kim, 'get mesmerised by his run-up.'

Smith watched Holding's first delivery all the way. 'I thought, I've got to see what it's like. And sure, it was daunting. Then I did it Kim's way. And I was fine.' Smith and Wood put on 135 that day.

Sometimes Kim's need to help stretched to surreal lengths. Before the 1982–83 McDonald's Cup final he and Wellham finished their pitchside interviews and wandered off together. As they walked Wellham, a first-time captain of New South Wales, was conscious of potentially eavesdropping TV cameras. Kim launched uninvited into a crash course on the art of one-day field settings. 'That was Kim just trying to be helpful, giving me some helpful advice,' says Wellham. 'Classic Kim. He wasn't being patronising. He was being genuine—because we knew each other, you know? That's Kim.'

Rodney Hogg was born with a belief that he knew when, what and for how long to bowl and a suspicion of captains who did not trust their fast bowlers. 'I found I could talk to Kim on the same wavelength,' says Hogg. 'I don't think Kim's much smarter than me.' It's a funny compliment. Sagacity tends to count as a leadership strength, not a handicap. There is plenty to admire in a captain friendly with his players. And Kim would have known from his childhood perusals of *The Art of Cricket* that Bradman considered it essential for a captain to enjoy his players' confidence and respect. That is similar to, but not the same as, friendship.

'There was something about him,' says Adrian McGregor. 'He was almost too amenable, too nice a guy. He was great with the media, would answer all sorts of questions, never told people to piss off.' McGregor—biographer of Greg Chappell, runner Cathy Freeman and rugby league champion Wally Lewis—never met another like Kim:

It was almost like he didn't have the appropriate personality. Wally Lewis: led by example, never afraid to jump on people, never afraid to use his influence to get rid of them, nasty if need be. Mal Meninga was always giving people a hard time, he'd run roughshod over them. Allan Border: dark personality, led by example. Even Grant Hackett, the swimmer, he's just like Greg Chappell: strong, no doubts about himself, no attempts to be nice to everybody, just is what he is. Kim doesn't fit any of these. I've never seen an Australian sports captain like him.

•••••

FIVE MEN FESTOONED the leg-side for Ashley Mallett's first over under Kim's captaincy. Mallett wondered whether five were enough. The Trent Bridge boundary was short. He ripped an off-break and watched Clive Rice tap it: one bounce, into the fence. 'Shit,' Mallett realised, 'he's going to keep doing that.'

'Nah, nah, nah.' Kim was not flustered.

Mallett pointed out the gap at midwicket. 'I want you to plug that so we get him trying to hit against the spin on the off-side.'

'Nah, nah, nah.'

Mallett bowled. Four more. 'Look, you know what will happen. I'm going to bowl this ball, he's gunna go clock and it's going to be another four in the same spot. Can you plug it?'

'No,' said Kim.

The match, Australia's final hit-out before the 1980 Centenary Test, was short on pomp, sprinkled with pantomime. Born fine legs Lillee, Thomson and Pascoe were posted in slips, hands like ping pong bats. Nottinghamshire triumphed by an innings and plenty, Australia's heftiest county shellacking since 1888. And as Rice's third successive blow rattled the midwicket fence, Mallett enquired of the acting captain: 'Any chance of plugging that?'

Unconventional field settings, a shrewd change of bowler: the kind of manoeuvre likely to confound Kim the batsman seldom occurred to Kim the captain. Afternoons under the sun could drag. Bowlers were like sneakers: replaced when worn out. Batsmen were like socks: all basically the same. A new batsman did not necessarily demand adjustments in plan or field. The passing years made little difference. In South Africa, West Indies' rebels advised Australia's rebels to attack Graeme Pollock from around the wicket. Carl Rackemann noticed Pollock rocking from foot to foot as the bowler approached, feet spreading wider and wider, so wide that eventually they could not go forward or back. He just swayed. Altering the angle to around the wicket made Pollock reach. He had trouble covering his stumps.

But Kim would not have it: 'He's a left-hander. Bowl the ball across him and he'll nick it.' Pollock hit 108 in the first unofficial Test, doing a lot of walloping and not much nicking. The bowlers went around the wicket thereafter and removed Pollock comparatively painlessly. 'Anyway,' Rackemann recalls, 'we line up for the second season and Kim's back to insisting we bowl over the wicket.'

Team-mates wondered about the level of contemplation accompanying Kim's more creative moments. 'Little gut-feeling gambles,' Rackemann calls them. Often it could feel like he was supervising not influencing proceedings. When Kim got the Australian job, Inverarity did not rank him among the five top contenders for the Western Australian job. Himself, Brayshaw, Charlesworth, Mann and Serjeant were better credentialled.

'Any serious person would have had all five ahead of Kim as captain. Fact.'

Kim's intention to lead by example is a pledge made by Australian captains before and since. Do credentials much matter if the example set by your bat and demeanour is high enough? Tactics and tricks: can these not be learnt? Can temperament? 'Kim has a very good heart and was a very attractive player and a mercurial personality,' says Inverarity. 'Over the years in cricket there have been a lot of these uninhibited and mercurial personalities. In the end, on balance, it's better if they are unencumbered with the burdens of captaincy, that somebody else does that and they remain as uninhibited cricketers.'

Greg Chappell felt no doubt about what Kim's appointment meant. The new captain was someone he too knew to be 'a very mercurial character':

Captaining a cricket team is not the place for high emotion. There are times when you are bereft of ideas, when you can't see how you can change the game, when you don't feel you've got any options left. But you have to pretend you've got the answers. Bad feelings, negative thoughts are contagious. Body language is picked up by everyone. And Kim's body language was like the biggest neon sign up at Kings Cross. You only had to look at Kim and you knew exactly what was going on in that little head under those blond curls. And generally when he was nervous, unsure or worried, the right forefinger was at the back of the curly head, twirling away at his hair. In Test cricket there are a lot of times when it's a standoff and you need to play poker. And Kim didn't know what a poker face was.

The curls, of course, helped get him the job. He looked like the boy prince out of a picture book. What could go wrong? 'Giving Kim Hughes the captaincy was like giving an arsonist the key to the bloody match cupboard,' says Chappell. 'He wanted it for the wrong reason. They gave it to him for the wrong reason. And decisions like that can only have one outcome.'

•••••

THE LAST AUSTRALIAN captain to have taken a team to India, Bill Lawry in 1969, wrote a letter of complaint as pungent as Madras's Buckingham canal and with some of the Taj Mahal's fine detail. Team-mates who read it feared a hard-hearted board might speed up the expiry date on Lawry's job. As summer gave way to autumn the following home season, Lawry was sacked. Ten years on little had changed. Written accounts—books, diaries, disgruntled captains' reports—of cricketing life in India remained notoriously devoid of cricket. '[They] purport to be about cricket,' historian Ramachandra Guha observed, 'but actually tell more of the heat, the dirt, the diet—the last especially—of the trains that run late and the telephones that don't work, the rats in the airconditioning and the leaks in the plumbing, as if to say: how can one play *our sport* in conditions like this?'

Rats inside airconditioners were not so unnerving as cockroaches on dinner plates in 1979. Kim was the new leader of a party of newcomers to Asia. They drank 500 beers fewer than they were accustomed to and played many more games of 500. They met teetotallers, swindlers, shady umpires. Twenty-three to eight ran the lbw count against Australia. Srinagar shopowner Suffering Moses sold Kim an ivory chess set, dainty elephants for pawns, so 'priceless' promised Suffering that he'd rebuffed an offer from Nelson Rockefeller. The elephants turned to rubble upon leaving the shop. Madras was so hot that players wore cologne-laced neckerchiefs. Balls were so hard—all cork, no wool—that Yallop snapped five bats. Spectators flashed mirrors in batsmen's eyes in between hurling limes, onions, corn-cobs. In Kanpur, near the oval, a dead dog lay stiff for days, pecked at by birds and blanketed in flies. Water buffalo and cows roamed among people, thickets of people, surprising numbers of whom appeared to have withered limbs, or no limbs. Allan Border later recalled marvelling at the 'milling mass of humanity' from his Kanpur balcony:

We took to dropping rupees to them and watching them scramble. Unkind, I guess, but it was irresistible. We went a step further and started pouring water on to them as they fought each other for the rupees. We'd fill all available receptacles in the hotel room with water, drop the coins and whoosh! It's not the sort of caper I'd pull today and I'd discourage anybody in a touring party under my captaincy from doing anything like it. But it was a diversion and, remarkably, the Indians loved it. They reckoned it was a great joke. They enjoyed it so much that word spread quickly and the numbers outside our hotel actually increased. Everybody, it seemed, wanted to get into the raining rupee act.

Eleven weeks of culture shock had been preceded by three weeks' shellshock in England. Australia did nothing to upset the bookmakers who rated them 20–1 World Cup outsiders. But they left various others feeling miffed. Kim's first act as captain abroad was to be quoted—erroneously, he promised—as saying he would rather practise than attend the royal welcome. An apology helter-skeltered its way to Her Majesty's principal private secretary.

'No swearing,' instructed tour manager David Richards as the bus parked outside the palace.

'Does that mean we can't say fuck in front of the Queen?' replied Hogg, who on his next trip to England wisecracked 'nice legs for an old sheila' as Elizabeth II glided out of earshot.

If the Queen was put out, the King was fuming. Dennis Lillee's unannounced drop-in at Lord's resulted in the Australian dressing-room door closing abruptly in his face. Peace between Packer and the establishment was one week old, too newborn in some players' minds for them to be admitting a mercenary. Kim let Lillee in upon hearing he was stranded at the doorstep. But Lillee never forgot it.

Richards, the appointed hoser of bushfires, was only thirty-three himself. 'I was absolutely floored by the idea that I could manage a team, something I thought might happen much later in life.' When volunteer scorer Mike Ringham bought himself a green jacket, of similar shade to the players' blazers, the Trent Bridge gatekeepers assumed Ringham was manager and refused Richards entry. He was hardly less boy-faced than the captain. And the manager's job did not entitle one to a green blazer. Understaffing bothered Richards more than his wardrobe. 'In the end my sister, who was in London between marriages, found herself dragooned into doing some of the admin for me.'

Managing a World Cup expedition was an honour. For others, the end could not come too quickly. With Australia and India prematurely evacuated from the tournament, the Indians proposed a friendly match. A venue was arranged: Edgbaston. A team meeting was called and a show of hands invited. Graeme Porter's misty recollection is that he, Kim and vice-captain Hilditch were keen. Several hands stayed down. The vote in favour went 8–6, not enough for a game of cricket. 'Four or five of us spent a couple of days in Paris,' says Porter. 'We used it as our own travel time. I found it quite strange that we finished up not playing.' Some were wary that defeat might tempt the board to reinstate Packer players for the tour of India. And there was a certain aimlessness. 'We had an amicable discussion, there wasn't any great temperature in the room, and it was evident that I didn't have a consensus to play,' Richards recalls. Anyway, he adds, India's bus broke down between Manchester and Birmingham. It remains a highly unusual instance of an Australian cricket team choosing not to play an international fixture.

In testing circumstances, Kim's frankness with players and pressmen was refreshing. He did not get flummoxed or rummage for excuses. For the longer, mazier ordeal of India he was given a non-playing personnel of two: industrial relations specialist Bob Merriman—another first-time manager—and team physio Frank Hennessy, who worked nights as a rugby league club masseur. When Geoff Dymock's back creaked he turned not to Hennessy but to Pam Irwin, the physiotherapist wife of an Australian volunteer abroad who happened to be lodging in the same hotel. 'She saved my tour,' Dymock recalls. 'She came in and explained what she was doing, what she was pressing to fix it, and Frank had his books and charts out so he'd know what to do next time.'

Here the hurdles grew higher, and broader, from a terrorist bomb scare over the opening game to twenty-two spilt catches over six Tests. Kim's determination never to be an outspoken captain faltered on departure when he pronounced Peter Sleep of Penola 'the most exciting leg-spinning allrounder since Richie Benaud'. That was overconfidence talking. But Kim stayed upbeat and—to his toilet-hopping team-mates' consternation—healthy. He lived on curries, bananas, naan and a bottle of beer. How can you tell food's off, he'd say, unless you try it? Trailing 1–0, he roused his weary squad with a Carlton–Collingwood grand final replay over breakfast in Delhi. He followed up with a Stan Hughes-style exhortation, the kind that used to silence the crows in the Western Australian bush.

Hogg was a handful. Sustained by canned spaghetti and baked beans, he kicked down a stump, squabbled with umpires and overstepped forty-two times in the first two Tests, his no-ball tally ultimately hitting triple figures. Kim kept believing, kept handing Hogg the ball, no matter how unhappy the tidings:

I can't see how you could come up with the word 'happy' when you've bowled a hundred no-balls, taken no wickets and can't get anything to eat. There's nothing much happening off the ground. You've got to sign to get a drink. Oh, it was a nightmare. Nightmare tour. But Kim never gave up on me. He had faith, and I'm thankful for that. Most captains would have been hopeless under those conditions—hopeless. Kim led from the front that whole tour.

Commonsense teetered once, against Central Zone in Nagpur, where the umpires disallowed Australia's overnight declaration on the grounds that Kim, resting that match, had already requested a light roller. Sleep and Yardley materialised for one ball—minus gloves, pads, protectors—and skulked back. That sideshow would have a more sinister sequel in the town of Pointe-à-Pierre five years later. And Kim's wells of diplomacy finally ran dry during the tour's twelfth week and Sixth Test in Bombay. Amid Australian fantasies of drawing 1–1, the lbw laws were seemingly immobilised for Kapil Dev's stay. Kim was caught at silly point off a delivery that imprinted a cherry tattoo on his shoulder sleeve. 'I had to do everything,' he lamented on the tour's twenty-fifth anniversary. 'Diplomat, motivator, lead from the front, deal with the umpires. Then there was the lack of practice facilities, the homesickness . . . And five-star hotels meant you saw five stars through the roof. We did bloody well to lose 2–0.'

Kim's 594 runs were more than he'd muster in a series again. He always mentions, modestly, that Venkataraghavan was the sole, ageing survivor of India's hallowed spin quartet. Kim began with 100 in Madras. He finished, as Australia followed on 298 behind, with 80 in Bombay, one of the most majestic emasculations of an Indian spin attack in years, reckoned local expert Dicky Rutnagur. 'The sweep,' wrote Rutnagur, 'is regarded as an unchristian stroke because it is both unsafe and ungainly. But this is not true when Hughes plays it. He swept with such precision and such control as to make the shot look classical.'

When he didn't sweep he danced, bounding down to get at the ball before it landed, like it was a Frank Parry underarm.

For his first fifteen minutes Kim would feel anxious, choked by a necklace of fieldsmen silly and short. Then he'd attack, his hands soft, avoiding midwicket, skipping forward or else striding completely back, never hovering. One grainy photograph in David Frith's *Pageant of Cricket* preserves his panache: a metre out of the crease, perfectly balanced, head bent over the ball, cover driving Dilip Doshi.

The tour had a slogan. *To lose patience is to lose the battle.* Leg-spinner Jim Higgs saw it scrawled on a wall as the bus wound through Madras slums. 'To lose patience is to lose the battle' became the motto of subsequent journeys to the sub-continent. A generation of Australian cricketers never forgot it. Would Kim?

NINE

His Right Knee

TWO ROMANTIC SUPERHEROES of cricket's golden age, Charlie Macartney and Archie MacLaren, both dead for decades, reappeared in small intermittent flickers when Kim Hughes batted. Macartney was an aggressor, an improviser, who learned to play with the red wood of a cedar tree. 'By cripes, I feel sorry for any poor bastard who has to bowl to me today,' legend has him declaring one sun-filled Test morning. Like Macartney, and like few others in history, Kim had the ability to foretell the extraordinary off his own bat.

Similarities with MacLaren, beloved captain of England, revolved around bat swing. The resemblance lay not at the cusp of their swings—for MacLaren heaved his bat high like a woodchopper, all but touching his right ear—but in the final elongated flourish. Neville Cardus, most felicitous of MacLaren's enthusiasts in the press box, would reminisce: 'I can still see the swing of MacLaren's bat, the great follow-through, finishing high and held there with the body poised as he himself contemplated the grandeur of the stroke and savoured it.' Kim did that too. As ball scorched grass Kim would hold his pose, bat and elbow pointed skywards, watching the ball shrink smaller and smaller. 'What are you doing?' Mike Whitney used to say when it happened off his bowling. 'Holding it for the photographers? Wanker!'

And it was odd. Author David Frith once remarked of MacLaren's self-admiring standstill at the sight of his own majesty: 'To my credit, I hope, I never tried this. Such florid batsmanship is associated with the English amateur rather than the down to earth and usually victorious Australian batsman.' That was particularly so in Kim's era. Had the teams of Ian and Greg Chappell been any more down to earth they would have dined on mudcakes. Kim was different, a throwback. He did not shy away from MacLarenesque wallowing. He was pretty, arrogant, expressive, all things Australian men are encouraged not to be. When Whitney said *wanker!*, Kim would say nothing. But he'd hear all right. 'Next ball would be short,' Whitney recalls, 'and he'd be ready for it and hook me over the fence.' What Kim did not know is that Whitney wasn't really thinking *wanker!* Inside, though he never told Kim so, Whitney was thinking: 'I don't mind you hitting me through there, Kim. That looks so good.'

It looked nothing like anything most bowlers had seen. For when Kim gazed contentedly after the vanishing ball it was usually at the climax of his signature stroke, the cover drive off bended right knee. Viv Richards had might, Greg Chappell grace, David Gower butterfly-soft timing. But for a few short years no stroke was so thrilling to see or so geometrically pure as the Kim Hughes cover drive off one knee. It might appear once in a long innings. Invariably it defined that innings. Sometimes he cover drove and finished on one knee. Other times he would perch on that one knee, waiting, before the ball got to him.

Justin Langer was ten when he noticed Kim do it against New Zealand at the WACA Ground. 'The image was tattooed into my brain,' Langer later recalled. 'I vowed to learn how to play this shot if it was the last thing I ever did.' Boys badgered their fathers to buy them a Slazenger like Kim's. They stood hunched over copying the stroke in their backyards. Few, not even Langer, had the chutzpah or balance to try it in a match.

Balance: that was the virtue Frank Parry emphasised most relentlessly of all. Even as a grown-up Test cricketer, Kim's skipping rope still came out before an innings. He'd squint at the sky as he entered, like Ian Chappell and Allan Border, eyes adapting to the brightness. He gripped the handle high, though not as high as Greg Chappell did or Adam Gilchrist would. His feet rested apart, the popping crease between them. As the bowler closed in he tapped his bat loudly. For fast bowlers he tapped seven or eight times. His feet tended to make a little shuffle early, almost imperceptibly, before the bowler let go, and this sometimes necessitated a couple more shuffles in response to the actual delivery, leaving him on the move and off balance.

He liked using the whole crease, going sideways and backwards, boots nearly brushing the stumps. In the how-to manual *Skills and Tactics* he recommended: 'Every young cricketer could paste in his cap the word "footwork", because without it there is no way the youngster can make his way.' Cuts and sweeps were the shots Kim relished most. 'I believe a batsman, in Test or limited-overs cricket, must always try to carry the attack to the bowler. Otherwise why play the game?'

Home from India, Kim found himself out of the captaincy and out of mind. Heralding the peacetime summer of 1979–80 were three reworded versions of 'C'mon, Aussie, C'mon', one of which addressed the pickle of how to squeeze two Australian teams into one:

> *Will the wild and woolly new boys*
> *Beat the tested, tried and true boys*
> *'Cos there's only just eleven vacancies . . .*
> *There's Border, Hookes and others*
> *And the mighty Chappell brothers . . .*

Kim was unmistakably an 'other'. So began his uneasy relationship with Channel Nine, with Kim cast as a scab on Kerry Packer's marketing arm, Publishing and Broadcasting Ltd. Etiquette dissuading current players from pontificating about team selection was suddenly obsolete. 'Frankly,' commented Ian Chappell, 'I can't even see a place in the squad for Hughes.' Greg Chappell preferred Queensland colleague Martin Kent in his newspaper XI. None of eleven *Cricketer* experts could fit Kim in.

The selectors disagreed with the Chappells. Kim got the vice-captaincy. Border and Hogg were the only other survivors from India. International competition resumed with a Sydney one-dayer. Kim disliked the costumes. Clingy yellow stripes down their arms, ribs and thighs made them look like tennis players, he felt. In every other way he was not only in tune with but ahead of the times. His 60-ball 52 included a six off Viv Richards that almost burnt a hole in the Hill, unanimously acclaimed as the day and night's most exciting stroke. Excitement now mattered more than it used to.

Adult Test tickets rose from $3 to $5. Two touring sides signified a permanent departure from the time-honoured one or none. The Ashes were not at stake; three Tests, decreed fuddy-duddies England, did not an Ashes battle make. Instead players competed for the Palmolive Gold Strike Rate, the Pacific Film Shot of the Series, the GMH Classic Catches and the Benson & Hedges Golden Stumps Award. Commercial breaks ran between overs. Sometimes commercial breaks ran during overs, courtesy of tardy operators in master control. 'In a major step this season,' noted the London *Observer*'s Scyld Berry, 'the Australian Cricket Board introduced the six-ball over, but Channel Nine often go one ball better with a five-ball over.' Six wickets, 194 runs and fifty-four ad breaks on day one of Australia versus England made Berry feel like he was reading *War and Peace* with cartoons after every page.

Kim's third Test hundred, 130 not out, repelled what Michael Holding considered the most awesome of all West Indian foursomes. Roberts, Croft, Garner and Holding were all between twenty-five and twenty-eight, all canny, all seasoned, none of them slowing. Kim hooked ten of his eighteen boundaries. The hook was not just a run-fetcher but an ultimatum and a deterrent. Bounce me and I'll clobber you. It is a shot thought needlessly risky nowadays and seldom spotted. Modern batsmen, their supersonic bats propelling the daintiest nudges for four, are content to evade bouncers rather than retaliate. Inzamam-ul-Haq, Virender Sehwag and Chris Gayle have each erected Test triple hundreds containing not one hooked boundary.

Nine days later, on the last WACA Test strip Roy Abbott would ever prepare, Kim entered at 3–20 against England. He hit hard and without hesitation. He encountered quicksand in the nineties. Ninety-nine waddled up. Whoever dreamt of raising a hundred in front of his home crowd with a sensible single? Derek Underwood dropped short—'one of the worst balls I delivered in the series'. Kim pulled high, a triumphant clout, or it would have been, if not for the hands of Brearley who had placed himself on the fence moments earlier.

Australia clean-swept England and were themselves outslugged 2–0 by West Indies. Kim's runs tailed off, promising beginnings ending in pratfalls. It was more a case of overambition than underperformance. He went to Pakistan, where his first ball of the series from Tauseef Ahmed pitched a foot outside off and veered over his left earhole for byes. He recovered to make 85 on a Karachi turner that had the rest of the Australians toe-tied. He crafted 88 on a Faisalabad featherbed with all signs of life curated out of it, Pakistan monomaniacal about preserving their 1–0 lead. Seven times in twenty-five Tests he had got out between 80 and 99.

Soon a new comparison with a third cricketing Mac became popular. In the space of sixteen months, from September 1980 to December 1981, Kim played three innings fit to recite in the same sentence as Stan McCabe's 187 not out in Sydney, 189 not out in Johannesburg and 232 in Nottingham. Only one had the flailing-against-dark-destiny character of McCabe's trilogy. Two were constructed at moments in his life of high personal emotion. Two of them he foretold. He premeditated all three. And all three were products of Kim's fundamental philosophy to batting: 'There are plenty of safe shots in cricket, and it is a good thing to know how to play them all. It is also a good thing to know how to play the risky ones.'

•••••

McCABE, MACARTNEY AND MacLAREN were close to the hearts of the fifty giants from Australia's cricketing yesteryear as arthritic knees carried them to breakfast at London's Russell Hotel. But one famous name had special currency. That morning, Centenary Test morning, *Guardian* cricket writer Paul Fitzpatrick's pre-match blurb contained the following statement:

> It is an outrageous claim to make for him, I realise, but at the risk of incurring the derision of an older generation I would suggest that Hughes, if not the embodiment of Trumper, is at least a reminder of the great man. He has Trumper's clear gaze and good looks and a nature that one has yet to hear criticised: he has style.

Not Trumper. Not Victor. Words like that were blasphemy. But as the former Test players who had jetted over for the occasion stared out the window they saw no lightning bolts. All they could see was grey, a grey that hardly cracked all week, stealing from Lord's the twist and fizz that bespangled Melbourne's Centenary Test.

Allan Border did not want his friend, such jolly company, trying to be Trumper, Richards, Boycott or any of the others he eulogised. 'Forget about everybody else,' Border proposed before the game. 'Be yourself. You're a good player because you play your shots.' Old Test opener turned journalist Jack Fingleton wrote to Kim suggesting he stop sabotaging golden starts with flights of tomfoolery. Cutting against the spin had proved fraught back home. It was suicide in England. Fingleton said so because he cared, and was pleased when Kim sent a gracious reply. He and Bill O'Reilly were the last two alive who'd seen all three McCabe epics. Fingleton liked Kim's unordinariness, a quality in abundance that first afternoon at Lord's. Once, Kim crept a tiny step forward, almost motionless, and pulled Botham nearly into the Mound Stand, and as bat struck ball it emitted the sweetest pock.

He sped from 47 to 82 next day, darkness banishing the players at 12.45 p.m. The third-wicket stand raised 110, Kim scattering the cover fielders and Wood gliding through slips so territorially it was as if they had waltzed up from Trigg Beach. John Woodcock in the *Times* was grateful for the late-summer timing, which enabled holidaying British schoolchildren with corrupted techniques to watch Kim and learn. Brian Adair, Kim's old Watsonians captain, caught the night sleeper from Edinburgh to London with his son Robin. Over breakfast at the Waldorf, Kim announced to the Adairs that he would hit 'the Poms' for a century. The spirit of Macartney breathed again.

Breakfast was leisurely. There was warmth in the sunshine but two waterlogged patches delayed play for five hours. Peeved spectators, some in MCC ties, swore and shoved at the umpires. Kim gave 27,000 a reason for coming. Fourth ball of the day from Chris Old was short outside off. With a flap of his arms, Kim merely caressed it. It cleared the midwicket fence. Another pulled six was as casual as the first two, a swivel and a swing, except this one did not stop until it was inside the Mound Stand. 'A reasonable day for us boozers in the private boxes,' concluded big-match attendee Mick Jagger. 'But what about the geezers queuing and those blokes munching their sandwiches at the Nursery End?'

They had seen an innings exquisite but imperfect. Even as Kim trounced the bowlers he was tiptoeing, not striding. Sometimes he stabbed at the ball. A paddled three delivered his promised century. In acknowledging the clapping he yanked off his cap, as was his custom. It was only polite to give the people he was striving to entertain a good look at his face. They saw a small smile, not done yet.

Kim made 117, Australia 5–385 declared and England faced two balls before the murk returned, a draw a formality. On the rest day—sunny, balmy—Kim went drinking near Hyde Park with Border, Mallett and *Skippy* actor Ed Deveraux. 'The only good thing to do was to have a few drinks, which we did, all day,' Mallett remembers. 'We went down the pub and got absolutely smashed.'

Pascoe and Lillee jemmied out Englishmen swiftly enough on day four to renew mild interest. Australia were 203 ahead when Kim joined Greg Chappell at 2–28 in the second innings. He ran at Emburey, only to tickle a leg glance for four. Botham's knack for rolling down poisonous dross deserted him. By bludgeoning the dross, Kim neutralised the poison. He square cut and glanced Botham to be 38 at stumps. 'Smashed hell out of Botham—the way we should have played him a year later,' says Mallett. The day ended with Kim charging at Emburey, sweeping him high and watching the ball disappear from the finest vantage point in the house, his right knee.

A sunsplendent Lord's greeted the final morning. Patrick Eagar, in his ninth season on the Test match beat, unpacked cameras, tripods, rolls of film. Fireworks were likely and a declaration imminent, with Australia's lead 286. Resident scrooges Hendrick and Old offered the best bet of containment.

Kim entered with sleeves rolled high and shirt unbuttoned to the breastbone, glancing at the little hill in front of the pavilion boundary, so strange to Australian eyes, where balls trickled up and sometimes trickled back down. A four off Emburey was technically cutting against the spin. Really Kim arched away, opened up his body by sixty degrees and straight drove over cover from a metre down the pitch. It was a month when the unconventional was working, when no stroke was too preposterous. Against Hampshire he scythed the winning runs with a one-handed square cut off Mark Nicholas. In the one-day game at Edgbaston he performed two left-arm sweeps.

Now Old was galumphing in. Right line. Short of a length. Dangerous ball. Kim took one small step forward, then one large skip, bat rising behind him. His back foot pivoted. A puff of dust stirred. Freeze-framed, it was like a full-colour replica of George Beldam's photo of Trumper stepping out to drive. The ball nearly burst. The cameras lost it. Umpire Dickie Bird swivelled round. Non-striker Greg Chappell clapped his bat. Mike Gatting on the leg-side laughed. Voices cracked in the ABC commentary box.

'Down the ground again,' said Norman May. 'What a shot. That's six.' Beside him, Keith Miller murmured indiscernibly. Miller had been marvelling at Kim's timing all game. May continued: 'We'll nearly catch that. A magnificent hit. That almost finished in our broadcast box. Keith, have you ever seen a better hit at Lord's than that one?'

That Miller happened to be on air was a lucky break. It was like asking Jack if he had ever climbed a beanstalk so tall. 'Well,' said Miller, 'I hit a couple up there myself Norm, oddly enough. But not many have. That is one of the biggest hits I've seen for many, many a year. On top of the balcony.'

Those in the vicinity maintain the ball was rising still as it struck the top deck of the pavilion. Distance travelled was calculated at 125 metres; a couple more and it would have hurdled the roof. Only one man had done that, Albert Trott, putting a hand to his forehead and gawping at the ball's steepling trajectory after middling one in 1899. Miller did indeed go close, landing one on the top tier and another on the commentary box when the Dominions played England. But old England captain Gubby Allen could recall no straight hit more remarkable than Kim's. Several festive fellow old-timers missed it—or spied a glimmer in the mirror of the Q Stand bar. The board's David Richards was one who picked the right second to turn and look: 'Oh yeah, there's Hughesy, he's batting all right.' Then *clunk*. Kim had batted on all five days and swiped sixes on four of them.

Old's next delivery was on target again. Eminently blockable. Kim pirouetted, twisting to a foot outside off and scooping to the midwicket boundary in the style of a gravedigger shovelling sods. Later he remembered the bat feeling like a magic wand. 'I don't know why you're running in,' he thought about saying, 'because I know where you're going to bowl.' He advanced a couple of metres at Hendrick, intent on driving, found the ball not where he expected, changed his mind, adjusted his backswing and square cut—*square cut*—in front of point. 'Shot of the match—could well have been the shot of the century,' declared Fingleton in his autobiography. In Germany, Geoff Gallop listened gobsmacked via BBC shortwave. 'How do you spell repertoire?' Ian Chappell was heard to mutter in the press box. The Q Stand bar marathoners clanked down their glasses.

Patrick Eagar was seeing the ball as well as Kim. His black-and-white proof sheet from that morning could go in a museum. There's Kim's 'shot of the century', in all its implausibility: tongue out, kneeling, creaseline in the distance, ball a spinning blur, everything perfectly symmetrical. Another image has Kim cover driving off one knee and with one hand. He has backed away to leg, almost off the cut strip, left arm curled above his head and right arm thrusting his bat out like a dagger. A gladiator's pose. 'He always played a bit like that,' Eagar recalls. 'But this was something special. It was a joy to behold and to photograph.'

Botham's ball that ejected him lbw was probably missing leg, although the cameras were at one end and Kim's backside facing them. Eleven fours, two sixes, 84 runs, and this, not his 117, was the innings to savour, the couple of hours in his life when the impossible looked rudimentary. Greg Chappell, sentimentally, postponed his declaration until Kim was out. An otherwise stultifying draw ensued. John Arlott graced a Test microphone for the final time. Tiredness and bronchitis, Arlott's 'old wheezy chest which does sometimes sound like a pair of bagpipes full of dust', meant he'd had enough. An emotional goodbye ovation threatened never to end, and Kim had to wait several minutes before Arlott handed over his man-of-the-match award.

'I regard him as likely to become one of the all-time great batsmen,' trumpeted Richie Benaud's TV summary. 'Like Denis Compton at his best,' wrote Woodcock. 'The nearest approach to Stan McCabe in full flurry I have ever seen,' proclaimed R.S. Whitington. The *Daily Mirror* lauded 'The Handsome Young Hero of Australia' and presented Kim with £250.

After the game, sipping champagne, Mallett asked him about the straight six off Old. Mallett thought it incredible—more incredible, even, than anything he'd seen Graeme Pollock do. Kim replied:

I hit it on the rise, right in the middle. I thought: 'That's sensational! That's six in anybody's language.' I lost sight of it. I wasn't quite sure where it landed. Sometimes when you hit a ball like that you feel like waving your bat over your head and you think: 'What's the bowler going to do next to stop that?'

•••••

TWIN GEMS AT LORD'S were followed by twins. On 9 January 1981 Jenny gave birth to Sean and Simon, 2.25 kilograms each. Kim missed the birth by a couple of hours because of a limited-overs commitment. On the day they were born he flew from Sydney to Perth, marched into King Edward Hospital in his Australian blazer, patted his sons' heads and caught the midnight horror to Melbourne for another one-day game.

The Hughes family's expansion coincided with the cricket schedule's most crackbrained expansion ever known. That January, Kim cultivated a carbon footprint the size of Australia's skateboard-booted former captain Monty Noble: Sydney for a one-dayer on the 8th, became a father in Perth (9th), a Melbourne one-dayer (11th), more Sydney one-day games (13th and 15th), a McDonald's Cup clash in Hobart (16th), a Sheffield Shield match in Devonport (17th to 19th), another

Sydney one-dayer (21st), the Adelaide Test (23rd to 27th), then back to Sydney (29th) and Melbourne (31st) for the best-of-five finals against New Zealand. By summer's end he had endured six Tests, fourteen limited-overs internationals, eight Shield and four McDonald's Cup fixtures. In February he met his sons for the second time.

He had been thinking about them, though. He wanted to show them how much. On his second full day of fatherhood he trod Tullamarine tarmac at 6 a.m., shortly before the MCG's wooden benches began filling:

> There was a big crowd. And I felt, well, a fella's got twins, he's pretty pumped up. I remember going out there. I was batting with Graeme Wood. The scene was set for the father of twins to go out and score a double hundred. I could see it. I could picture it.
>
> But Woody hadn't read the script. I was at the non-striker's end thinking not too much can happen here when Woody smashed one to backward point and said: 'Yes.'
>
> And I said: 'Well, OK.'
>
> I got run out by five yards. Hadn't even faced a ball.

One-day cricket often made Kim frustrated and frustrating. He was an instinctive entertainer and natural hurrier. Put him in an artificially entertaining environment where he was expected to hurry and he struggled. They were the days when openers opened. Yet twice in 1980–81 Kim partnered John Dyson, a precursor to the era of the sweetest strokemaker, a Tendulkar or Mark Waugh, going in first. Kim hit 19 off 26 balls. He top-scored with 35 off 53 on an MCG dungheap better suited to half-day cricket. Alas, Greg Chappell abandoned the experiment and Kim never opened again. There were flickers of bold showmanship—how could there not have been?—but no hundreds, not in 125 official one-dayers for state and country, and his scoring rate was little more lustrous than his low-twenties average. People remember Kim's stroke range and wonder at the Twenty20 phenomenon who might have been. He might just as easily have been diabolical.

Diabolical looked like summing up that 1980–81 season. Kim made no contribution to Australia's slaying of New Zealand. Shirty team-mates, always 'senior' ones, were rumoured to be in his face and round his neck. One fifty in fourteen innings was his summer's stack coming into the Second Test against India. 'Hughes really does need to build up a big score here,' warned Ian Chappell as Kim took guard. 'People are starting to talk about him being dropped.' Just as the words spilled out of Chappell's mouth a dancing Kim manufactured a half-volley from thin air and carved Dilip Doshi through the covers.

The Adelaide wicket was true, Gavaskar's decision to bowl unfathomable and India's attack rich in mystique. Accompanying Kapil Dev was Karsan Ghavri's fickle left-arm outswing. Doshi bowled gorgeous, looping left-armers in whites crisply ironed, sleeves buttoned to the wrist and thick square glasses that he fingered before gliding in. Upon getting thumped he never seemed cross, merely puzzled, as if it did not compute. Shivlal Yadav, bearded and dishevelled, with a straight, bobbing run-up, turned the ball less extravagantly and looked like Professor Doshi's ragamuffin pupil. Only twenty-three, playing his first Test abroad, Yadav was reluctant to shout his appeals lest he cop a gobful of mysterious Australian blowflies.

It was two weeks to the day since the birth of the sons Kim had met once. He got to 85 not out at stumps, and a telegram from home followed him into the changeroom: 'Well done, Dad—keep it going—Sean and Simon.' Kim resolved to hit them a hundred each. That night he told Jenny and Frank Parry he'd get 200. To team-mates he mentioned 300.

Saturday was sweltering. Adelaideans in straw hats and stubbies slumped in their finest fold-up chairs. A 'SUPER KIM' banner was tethered to a chicken wire fence. Milestones were announced with exclamation marks: an along-the-ground-hook to go from 98 to 102; a cover drive off one knee, bat twirling lasso-like, to reach 150. The heat grew stickier. Doshi's buttons stayed fixed as insistently as Kim's sprung undone, skin browning over the course of 383 minutes' batting. When fast bowlers strayed he stood erect and dispatched them with backfoot drives, a shot that reminded older viewers of their childhoods. Against the spinners no inch of his half of the pitch was left untrampled. Three, four, five steps he took. Between boundaries, bouts of scorelessness did not bother him.

Last man Len Pascoe loped out with Kim on 193. On 199 the crowd's chatter rose, Yadav fidgeting with the ball, stalling. Three steps down traipsed Kim this time. A bullet off-drive sent gulls flapping. The camera panned to the dressing room. How much can be read into the following no one knows. But there sat Border, delighted, slapping hands above his head. Hogg, clad only in black undies, beamed. Walters, Marsh and Higgs, seated all in a row, applauded enthusiastically. Last to join in was Greg Chappell, who had been reading a newspaper, and was now clapping slowly but intently, unsmiling, while staring at himself on a TV monitor. Off came Kim's cap and down came a little bow, which he only half-heartedly tried to disguise by brushing some muck off the pitch.

Few innings gave Kim such joy as his 213. 'I hardly played a bad shot.' The second of his masterpieces was chanceless and rhythmic, fifties accruing in 80, 82, 64 and 67 deliveries. His theory that spinners, even skilful ones, are for slaughtering got its most exhaustive airing. His footwork was nearly as audacious as at Lord's and more precise, every boundary a mini-masterclass. Just as satisfying personally were the maidens he dead-batted and the reports of a happy crowd's appreciation. Then there was family. 'I feel,' said Kim, 'as if I'm doing something worthwhile for the time I've been away.'

India hung on in Adelaide and squared things 1–1 in Melbourne. Old habits of Kim's resurfaced as if Lord's and Adelaide had never happened. In his very next innings, 53 not out overnight became 53 out the minute Kapil Dev resumed. Stumps were spreadeagled in Melbourne when he cut at Doshi's arm ball—an unbreakable addiction, this one. Worse was his first-innings demise, a delectable 24 terminated with two kangaroo hops down the wicket and a slog to mid-on. Kim left beetroot-cheeked, stabbing the ground with his bat as he went. All that was missing from Bill Lawry's description were tears.

> Last over before lunch! That's unbelievable, Kim Hughes. Chauhan took the catch. But charging before lunch! Greg Chappell storms off. And you should hit the ground, Kim Hughes. Far too often we've seen this.

•••••

LIKE A SWAGMAN checking the ground for death adders, Greg Chappell glanced once at the MCG pitch as Michael Holding slithered in. Green splotches everywhere. Chappell didn't trust them. After three consecutive ducks he didn't much trust himself. 'Stumpy' Laird had succumbed down the leg-side the ball before. Now Holding arrowed outside off: wide enough to leave, close enough to tempt a man on tenterhooks. Chappell played and snicked. Four ducks. Andy Roberts speared one across and away from Wood as if by remote control, mugging the bat's edge. On Boxing Day 1981, first morning of the series, Australia were 3–8 before a half-full MCG. All they wanted for Christmas was a contest.

Lying seriously ill in hospital was Rix Davidson, Jenny's dad, Kim's beloved friend. If a contest was out of the question, Kim was determined to at least put on a show for Rix. But this looked like a horror show, *A Nightmare on Jolimont Street*, with Kim sleepwalking to a gore-spattered doom and unlikely to survive far beyond the interval. Border didn't. Nor Wellham, married four days earlier in the backyard to Barbara. Kim, anxious to be beside family, had not held a bat in a week. He hacked at a Garner no-ball. It slapped short leg's hands and bubbled out. Rix fell out of Kim's head.

He began that summer with 106—sedate early, scintillating to finish—against Pakistan, his solitary Test ton in Perth. Under Sydney's floodlights he defied the meanest and deepest attack known to mankind, Clive Lloyd upgrading his standard speed quartet to a never-before-seen quintet: Holding, Roberts, Marshall, Garner, Croft. Kim finished unconquered on 62 and Laird a sparkling, match-stealing 117, the alien chant of 'Lairdy, Lairdy' tingling in his ears. Today only four quicks circled. But this was a Test, so no bouncer limitations. And it was in Melbourne, so no hope of telling if a ball might rear, roll or skid.

In Kim's eyes, Holding was 'the Rolls-Royce', fast and sleek. Roberts was 'the closest I've seen to Lillee', bending missiles through air, off turf and at multiple undetectable speeds. 'Never said a word but you knew Andy didn't like batsmen.' As for Garner, Big Joel's hands were scarier than Big Joel himself.

'You know, Kim, I've never dropped a catch in my life,' Garner disclosed one day.

'Why wouldya? You've got baseball mitts for hands.'

Garner was nanoseconds slower than the others. Kim could get on the front foot. Croft he found hardest: unsmiling, unspeaking, unnerving, unflagging. 'Hit him with an axe and he'd still get up. All Lloyd had to do was wind him up, point him in the right direction and say: "Skitch 'em."'

Still alive on 24, Kim cut Roberts fortuitously short of Garner in the gully. Trams outside shuddered in their tracks as Garner's palm banged the grass in annoyance. This, Kim calculated, could not go on. Maybe he should swing harder. Maybe then their overpowering urge to maim him would distract them from the stumps.

He had wondered about sports psychology after his desolate 1981 Ashes tour. He visited Professor John Bloomfield at the University of Western Australia's sports department. Bloomfield had been to China. In table tennis psychology's bunk, Kim heard Bloomfield say. If a problem arises the Chinese practise and practise until it's fixed. Kim promptly took himself to the nets for days, cameras rolling, then pored over the video replays.

He flicked Roberts off his hip—a fate unfamiliar to Roberts. In the same over he rolled his wrists over a blistering off-drive. Now Channel Nine's replay machine was working overtime.

Old cricket footage can be anticlimactic. Half-volleys are offered up like scones. Paunchy fieldsmen avoid bending. You find yourself waiting for the speed-talking chap with the tinny accent to narrate shipboard games of quoits. How is it that everyone didn't average 99.94? But when Holding and company go *kapow* at Kim it's as if the producers jammed the fast-forward switch and hired David Lynch to draft in additional bleakness. The pitch looks short as a nature strip and less satisfactorily mown. The miniature red ball zigzags. Someone's put Kim's bat in the washing machine and forgotten to take it out.

'Concentrate,' he roared between deliveries. He roared it even as the bowlers stormed in. At slip, Viv Richards clapped Kim's half-century. Still Kim beseeched himself: '*Concentrate.*' He put on 56 with Marsh and 34 with Yardley. He hooked Roberts once and attempted an encore—only to realise, the seam shaving his skull, that the first bouncer was the slow sucker one. 'Roberts gave me a look that said: don't get too clever.' Lillee spanked a skyer to cover, looking for once like he'd rather be any place than the MCG. Holding yorked Lawson. Prospects of a heroic hundred vanished. On 71, Kim was joined by a man in a doormat-sized thigh pad.

Kim wished No. 11 Terry Alderman luck. 'You'll need it,' he thought to himself. Alderman was a scrapper with a trapdoor backlift who took nine first-class matches to break his duck and had a Test average of 6. Better treat this like a one-dayer, Kim decided. He jumped down the wicket at Garner. The ball was short and ribcage-bound. Kim pulled it away off the front foot: textbook-perfect, but for the maniacal dash. Next ball was short again. Kim leapt back and across, square cutting with gusto. Ian Chappell disliked Kim's habit of pre-empting bowlers' deliveries. On this occasion, Chappell sensed, he was reading their minds impeccably. 'In fact, Hughes seemed to have the bowlers in tune with *his* thought processes,' Chappell hypothesised decades later. 'The more he hooked, pulled and cut, the shorter they pitched. The harder he hammered the ball, the harder they ran in.'

Alderman was sticking. Smacked on the helmet and elbow, he straight drove Croft for four. He had once chaperoned Ian Brayshaw from 39 to 100 in a last-wicket rearguard for Western Australia. Now Kim crashed into the nineties. Rix re-entered his head. He knew Rix would be watching. Bowlers and fielders tried every trick to keep Kim off strike. But in 56 minutes Alderman faced only 26 balls. Two scampered runs to an empty midwicket—which Larry Gomes was supposed to keep to one—took Kim to 96.

Later, at game's end, the despised MCG pitch square was earmarked for ripping up. The charming old wooden scoreboard was pulled down. Australia won by 58 runs, and they threatened in Sydney too, until two wickets fell on the last morning and Greg Chappell instructed Dyson to give up chasing 373. Dyson's stoic 127 safeguarded the draw. 'But out in the middle,' recalled Dyson, 'I kept thinking to myself, we could have won.' West Indies tied the series with seventeen balls left on Marsh's regret-laden evening as captain in Adelaide. There, a stationary Kim pounded 84 with a broken left toe, a badly bruised right instep and a runner. 'The best series, the most enjoyable series, I ever played in,' said Kim. In early January, Rix Davidson died.

Back in Melbourne, Kim's scrambled two meant he was still on strike to Garner. He wound back his bat: a rainmaking backlift. He jabbed down. The force of the stroke made him topple backwards. The ball screeched past point. Uncharacteristically, he punched the air twice. His tears were for his father-in-law. One hundred not out in a total of 198. Nobody else passed 21. Even now Ian Chappell considers it the greatest postwar Australian knock. In Chappell's imaginings, only McCabe's 187 and Bradman's 334 could possibly be finer.

Striding off, Kim noticed Croft whirling towards him. Fear was Kim's first instinct. 'He's been trying to get me all day. Maybe now he's going to thump me.'

But for once, Croft spoke. 'Well played, man. Well played.'

TEN

'Bacchus Is Being Absolutely Obnoxious'

RUNS DID NOT stop trouble. Sample copies of four jigsaw puzzles released by PBL Marketing landed on the Western Australian Cricket Association's doorstep in November 1981. An Australian cricketer starred in each: Greg Chappell driving sumptuously, Rod Marsh swooping spectacularly, Dennis Lillee hovering high in his delivery stride, feet flying. Kim studied the fourth jigsaw. The only things flying were bails. PBL flunkeys— Packer's flunkeys—had unearthed a photo of him charging a medium pacer, Lance Cairns, and actually getting out stumped. They had turned two seconds of insanity and humiliation into a 560-piece jigsaw.

There was no puzzle. It was obvious—a vendetta. It was a trap too. Say nothing and he'd look a fool. Complain and he was a crybaby. He whistled up his lawyers. They appealed to Australian Cricket Board officials. That went nowhere. Memorabilia was the Packer people's domain. And it was too late. And it was a jigsaw. And what could be more trivial than that? Neither names nor jigsaws were mentioned in an interview with sportswriter Richard Sleeman. 'Maybe I'm too sensitive,' said Kim. 'I don't know. But people are gunning for me. They're in reasonably high positions too.'

After World Series Cricket, Kim had returned from India to find himself no longer Australian captain and not even WA captain. Chappell and Marsh filled those jobs. Yet Kim, not Marsh, got the Australian vice-captaincy. That added up to one too many compromises. Instead of everyone being happy, unhappiness was rife. The next season, 1980–81, Kim replaced Marsh in WA. That at least was logical: the national vice-captain was now running his own state. But unhappiness turned to foul fury. Lillee was miffed by the decision and ropeable about its leaking: Kim—'in his own cute way'—dropped it over a card game in Faisalabad. That evening, Marsh told Lillee it wasn't worth stewing over. Lillee's respect for his gumnut-tough buddy grew. Marsh, it would emerge, had quieter ways of signalling displeasure.

'Possibly the biggest moment in my life . . . every young kid's ambition,' said Western Australia's new captain. Marsh refused to be his deputy. So did Lillee. Feeling hurt, Kim tried to hide it. Their mere presence would be 'a great comfort'. But what if they were present in body only? Daryl Foster recalls the tenor of team meetings changing overnight.

'We're playing Victoria, we're gunna do this,' Kim would say. And then: 'Rod, have you got any thoughts?'

'You're captain. You control the meeting.'

Eyes flicked uncomfortably to the floor and around corners. 'Rod wouldn't participate in team meetings,' says Foster. 'He wouldn't cooperate in any Hughes-led ventures. Or if he did it was with a growl and a grump. People who know Rod know he's a fantastic team person; so it was the lack of that, him trying to make things harder for Kim.' Reaching out to Lillee proved equally fruitless. Foster tackled them. He got the old response: 'And how many Tests have you played?' Bruce Laird shouldered the twin posts of third-choice vice-captain and unofficial go-between.

'Stumpy,' Foster would say, 'Bacchus is being absolutely obnoxious. It's affecting the ten other blokes.' And Laird would go to Marsh. 'For a couple of weeks everything would be hunky-dory,' says Foster. 'Then if you needed it done again, he'd do it again. I had tremendous respect for Laird because he wasn't frightened. He wasn't reticent about telling Rod: "Listen, mate, pull your head in. All these young blokes, they don't know what they should be doing."'

Not every youngster minded. 'It was great being in the dressing room with them, whether they were fighting or not,' says Geoff Marsh. But the anxieties were real enough for Sam Gannon's temporary recruitment as manager of Kim's first eastern states expedition as WA captain. 'My job was to integrate people,' says Gannon. 'Some younger players, the future of West Australian cricket, were in a state of flux and confusion about where to show their allegiance. Because Rod was such a strong bloke and Kim was captain.'

In Sydney, Marsh spotted 70-year-old Alan McGilvray's familiar face: 'Come into the room and have a beer, Mac . . .' Instantly Marsh overruled himself. 'Sorry, I'm not captain anymore. I don't have any right to invite you in.' It was Marsh's quiet signal. McGilvray got the hint loud and clear. John Inverarity, who'd moved to Adelaide, detected uneasiness when he played against his old state. 'Rod was, in a sense, captaining through Kim. He had the better views on bowling changes, tactics, field placings. That created an awkward situation for all. It was clear to me on the field because I heard what was going on.'

For those off the field it was less obvious. 'The WA Sheffield Shield team is sick . . . torn apart from within,' huffed straightshooting *Sunday Times* columnist Doug Cunningham. Yet they won the Shield. They might even have pickpocketed the double, except in the McDonald's Cup final Kim fell first ball. Pure slapstick, that was: he hooked, missed and ran himself out attempting a madcap second bye. It earned him a Marsh bollocking, which Kim welcomed as a wonderful learning experience. 'A turning point,' Kim called it. Then he led Marsh and Lillee to England in 1981, and it became clear that this was no turning point, just another flashpoint.

Western Australia did not attempt to name a vice-captain the following season. Graeme Porter remembers Marsh's reaction when requested to stand in against Pakistan: 'No, no, no. Shippy [Greg Shipperd] can take over.'

Kim's parallel life as Test vice-captain would normally have seemed inconsequential. If captain of Australia ranks second only to prime minister in importance, as is commonly asserted, then vice-captain is like being odd-job man at the Lodge. But these were not normal times. The preferred Australian captain, Greg Chappell, was routinely unavailable for overseas tours, a situation unprecedented then and unrepeated since. Australian teams to England, Pakistan and the 1983 World Cup took— and occasionally didn't take—instructions from Kim. He was the hair in certain people's eyes. And if he couldn't be brushed aside, one alternative was to snip away at him.

•••••

NO ISSUE WAS TOO SMALL to squabble over. The Sheffield Shield bonus points system, which rewarded rapid scoring inside the first 65 overs, came up for review in 1981–82. Bonus points had operated for a decade and encouraged the innate dasher in Kim. Yet he felt future batsmen should be groomed to linger longer. Every other WA squad member voted to keep them. Kim reported to the board's cricket committee that Western Australians wanted them scrapped. Lillee and Marsh never mentioned their disgust. They didn't, Tim Zoehrer recalls, say a word:

> Kim was in the nets, no helmet on, and it was like war. Dennis was bouncing him. Kim was top-edging balls out of the ground. It was on. It was fearful. People were sitting back watching: 'Oh, Jesus. Kim's going to get killed here.' Nothing needed to be said. Dennis and Rod didn't openly express their disappointment. They were just letting him know, hey, we love you as a mate to have a drink with, but fuck, that hurt us.

Kim's head could be a popular target. Weeks later, Len Pascoe aimed a beamer at it. Kim had been hooking Pascoe bouncers all afternoon. 'That's four more, Lenny,' he'd say—'and that's as he's hitting it,' remembers Graeme Wood. Some saw Kim actually laughing at Pascoe as he hooked one delivery. Kim maintained he simply smiled. Some believe Pascoe's Yugoslavian heritage was canvassed. Others say that wasn't Kim's nature. After Pascoe's retaliatory beamer drew no blood and a ticking off from Kim, he visited the Western Australian rooms at teatime.

'Isn't this nice. Lenny's come to apologise,' thought Foster. 'Next minute he's got Kim by the scruff of the neck up against the wall.' Pascoe pushed Kim in the chest. Kim landed on a wooden bench in front of the lockers. Kim got up. Another shove. A sort of whimper, a squeak, came out of him. New South Wales team-mates suspended Pascoe for one game. Crook knees needed a rest anyway. And the season ended with Kim lamenting a lack of snarl in Australia's pace stocks. Maybe the selectors should trawl the beaches? 'Hughes,' replied Lillee, 'would be better advised looking at his own batting before pointing the bone.'

Six weeks in New Zealand felt like half a lifetime's drizzle. Kim's best in three Test innings was 17. He proved instrumental in the one-day decider. Greg Chappell, knowing the pitch was moist and his vice-captain a lucky tosser, sent out Kim, who performed a little jig when the coin landed the desired side up. Less auspicious was an acting captain's stint against Central Districts at postcard-perfect Pukekura Park. A 5.30 alarm bell, two flights and a breakfast eaten out of tinfoil gave the injury-mangled Australians little appetite for a day's cricket. Manager Alan Crompton was asked to keep wicket. Crompton declined. Marsh opened the bowling and batting. Wood went in last. Australia lost on the second-last ball. Kim, prompted by a journalist's $50 dare, batted in his Australian team tie for twenty minutes until Marsh informed him that the manager wasn't guffawing.

'Kim was an extremely likeable, approachable, friendly fellow,' says Crompton. 'Some senior players regarded him as a boy who hadn't grown up yet. In New Zealand I felt they not only regarded Kim as an immature boy but to some extent treated him as such. They were a little bit aloof, a bit dismissive of him, not as inclusive as they could and should have been.'

Equally striking was the way everyone buzzed around their boab-legged wicketkeeper in bars, buses, dressing rooms. 'The players,' sensed Crompton, 'would have died for Rod Marsh.'

Next stop was Pakistan, without Chappell. Abnormal times were about to get less normal. The captain's job went not to the incumbent vice-captain but to a vote of the fourteen Australian Cricket Board delegates. Ten of the fourteen are dead. The surviving four are aged between sixty-eight and eighty-five. Some have forgotten. Others wish to forget. The captaincy was one item on a long agenda. Details weren't recorded in the minutes. There might have been a show of hands. There could have been a secret ballot. No one's quite certain. But they met on 25 March 1982. The captaincy discussion lasted more than an hour. Silences were few. Everyone who wanted to talk talked. There were two candidates.

The board's composition was and is based on archaic power structures: New South Wales, Victoria and South Australia had three delegates each, Queensland and Western Australia two, Tasmania one. Two of the fourteen, Crompton and Fred Bennett, had managed Australia's two most recent tours. They'd lived with the team. They didn't consider themselves anti-Kim; they were pro-Marsh. They stated their case boldly. The third New South Welshman, Tim Caldwell, voted with them. Two more votes sailed Marsh's way—probably from South Australia, perhaps from a mix of South Australia and Queensland. And the chairman, South Australia's Phil Ridings, favoured Marsh. This was crucial. If there was a 7–7 deadlock Ridings's vote would become the casting vote and Marsh would be appointed captain of Australia. But there wasn't, it didn't and Marsh never. Kim won 8–6.

He owed it to WA's men on the board, Bert Rigg and Lawrie Sawle. 'I'm eighty-four years old, I've got no bloody memory and I've been through all that,' says Rigg. 'No factual recollection or recall on matters twenty-five to thirty years ago,' says Sawle, eighty-three. Both men were teachers. Sawle, quiet and sagacious, went on to become perhaps Australia's most respected chairman of selectors. He was probably less outspoken that day than Rigg, a Western Australian batsman of the 1950s, who wore thick black glasses and had been on the board a year longer. That mattered. John Rogers, the WACA's general manager, believes:

> Kim was like a son to Bert. That's how Bert saw him. And Bert would have pushed Kim's barrow very hard. Oh, he was proud of the fact he did. It did Kim a huge disservice. Really, it ruined the career of one of the all-time great WA batsmen. I don't know whether Bert saw it that way. But having promoted him to be Australian captain and to then see what happened would have been an incredible disappointment for Bert.

Marsh's larrikinism would have been mentioned. Ian Chappell's cowboy boots gave some long-serving board members blisters; they were reluctant to now elect his 'clone'. World Series Cricket, feelings of abandonment by Marsh and others, lurked in a few minds too. 'Vengeance is far too strong a word,' says Crompton. 'But there may have been a subconscious prejudice. That's possible.' Besides, children loved Kim. He was young, polite, attractive. He looked like the future. 'And heaven help us,' Crompton recalls, 'we were all trying to look to the future.'

To have both WA delegates favouring one WA candidate over another was impossible to ignore. Victoria's Bob Parish, Ray Steele and Len Maddocks backed Kim. Bob Ingamells probably voted with the Victorians because Tasmanian delegates invariably did. Among the others, Kim inspired sufficient hope to secure eight votes.

Had the conversation been less robust the fourteen men round the table might have heard destiny rapping on the door. So much swung on so narrow a margin. If one Kim supporter switched his vote, Marsh would have led Australia to Pakistan. If Marsh impressed, Greg Chappell might never have got his job back. Three years later Kim—worldlier, steadier—might have inherited it. Three years after that he might have bequeathed it to Border. Instead everything ended unhappily ever after.

•••••

MARSH'S QUIET SIGNALS of displeasure got louder. Named vice-captain to Pakistan, he declined the job. Days before departure he gave an interview to Russell Deiley of *Playboy* magazine. Marsh was at North Sydney Oval, filming an antihistamine commercial. He'd drunk a can of Tooheys and was feeling frank, chatty—enough to fill nine text-heavy pages.

'Kim is bloody good company,' Marsh told *Playboy*, 'but he's always liable to do silly things, whether he has a bat, a golf club or cards in his hand . . . That's not the sort of thing you need if you're a captain.' Kim was 'still learning'. Kim 'suffers a lot by comparison' with the Chappells, Inverarity and Lock. 'You don't deny,' said Deiley to Marsh, 'that you have challenged some of his on-field decisions?'

I don't agree with some decisions he makes and I feel it's my duty to tell him. He listens, but that doesn't overcome the real problem. You tell him something but a week later he's doing the same thing again . . . I don't think he resents advice. In many ways he's a very naive person and, like most of us, he works on adrenalin. When his adrenalin is pumping he makes decisions that aren't calculated . . . I'm very proud to be playing for Australia and I will play under anyone. But I honestly would prefer to play under several other players who I think would do a better job than Kim.

Books became almost annual: Lillee's *My Life in Cricket* (1982) and *Over and Out!* (1984); Marsh's *The Gloves of Irony* (1982), *The Inside Edge* (1983) and *Gloves, Sweat and Tears* (1984). Puns were not only painful but occasionally repetitive.

> Stacky . . . thought defence was something you build around de house! (*The Gloves of Irony*)
> Thomson . . . believes defence is something you build around de paddock to keep de sheep and de cows in. (*The Inside Edge*)

Kim references were plentiful and usually insulting. Often the tone was patronising, sarcastic or both, sometimes schoolyardishly so:

> He was thrown in at the deep end—and that was well over his depth . . .
> The man—or should I say young man—wasn't fully prepared . . .

Co-writer was Austin Robertson. His distant puppetmaster's presence in Kim's life was proving unshakeable. Whole chapters belittled Kim in *Gloves, Sweat and Tears* and *Over and Out!*. Marsh listed his team-mate's shortcomings in point form, a first for Australian cricket literature. Lillee, master of leg-cutters and off-cutters, exhibited a penchant for throat-cutters. The following is a small selection from *Over and Out!*:

I didn't like Hughes as captain.

I don't think he was even close to being a good captain.

A very mediocre leader of men.

I thought him a poor captain—and I was no orphan.

I had very little respect for him—and I wasn't Robinson Crusoe.

His lack of interest in what you had to say was bordering on the astonishing.

Kim would burst into print about how he should get the job. How stupid was that!

I didn't really give a dead prawn what he thought about me.

The books sit on fans' shelves today and raked in riches. And money mattered, more and more. When Lillee belatedly exposed the Headingley bet—itself a money-spinner—Marsh was not the only one perturbed. 'For him to deny having had the bet and to now admit it to sell a book, well I don't go along with that,' said respected West Australian elder Ken Meuleman. 1979–80 was memorable for Lillee's on-field marketing of his aluminium bat. In 1981 he had two lightning bolts—his personal logo—stitched on to his previously unadorned orange headbands and started raffling them. In advance of breaking Lance Gibbs's Test wickets record he sold exclusive rights to his post-milestone reaction to Sydney's *Sun*, before eventually making himself available to all comers 'for a short period'. The same newspaper later bought the scoop on Lillee's retirement.

In Pakistan, Australia lost all three Tests under Kim and won none of nine games on tour. Abdul Qadir's serpentine flippers and googlies would have flummoxed most sides. A team spooked by flying rocks, burning marquees and suspiciously scuffed balls stood no chance. 'For me,' wrote Pakistan captain Imran Khan, 'the disappointing aspect of the Australian attitude to Pakistan has been the inability to accept the country as it is—a third world country with its own culture.' As if to underline Imran's point, Marsh watched *The Sting* thirty-three times on video and lampooned the boredom, facilities and curries. 'Imagine what one of those devastating Pakistani concoctions could do to you as you stood behind the stumps all day. You'd be making more runs than Bradman.'

The team's homecoming coincided with *Playboy*'s November 1982 issue hitting magazine racks. 'If I've got team-mates like that,' said Kim, 'I wonder what I'd do for enemies . . . I'm not a Greg or Ian Chappell; I'm a Kim Hughes.' A Greg Chappell interview in October's *Cricketer* gave him another jolt. 'I'm a better captain now than five years ago,' said Chappell. 'I'm a better captain now than twelve months ago. I think last summer as captain I really did a good job . . . In a head to head contest between Kim and myself, I'm a better captain.'

It read a lot like Chappell had chosen the hustings over Pakistan. 'It was almost like he was running a campaign,' the board's executive director David Richards reflected. 'I've always felt he was a little indiscreet.' The board took some persuading; brother Trevor's underarm had left many feeling overwrought. Greg pipped Kim to the captaincy in 1981–82. Eight days before the 1982–83 Ashes series he was reappointed.

Kim was disappointed, not surprised. More shocking was his sacking as Western Australia's representative on the ACB's cricket committee. A meeting was arranged at state training while Kim was away helping pick the First Test team. Players plonked themselves down on the lush WACA grass. Nominations were called for and three received: Mann (nominated by Marsh), Serjeant (nominated by Lillee) and Kim. Hands went up. Mann won comfortably. Kim polled two votes out of about twenty-three, coach Foster's and rookie Subiaco fast bowler Brian Raven's. Nobody told Kim, about the meeting or outcome, for four days.

A sensitive man could have wept or made a fuss. But it all passed virtually unnoticed. Kim kept quiet. December's *Cricketer* consulted Len Pascoe for his views on the captaincy. 'Of the Tests I've played under Kim, the less said the better.' Yet Pascoe never played a Test under Kim. Again—silence from Kim. But of course he was sensitive. He was sensitive, everyone knew it and it only made things worse. The jigsaw business showed that. 'It would have been right for him to be upset but better for him to be man enough to cop it on the chin,' says Crompton. 'If you react all you do is reveal your underbelly.'

Kim did ask one person for help. He asked Don Bradman how he should handle Lillee. Bradman wrote back, unsure if he could assist but pleased to be asked, inviting Kim to dinner with himself and Lady Jessie. Bradman scooped Kim up at the airport and drove him out to their Holden Street home. Kim was nervous. He considers it one of his life's highlights. He still has the letter. Over dinner, Bradman related a story about how he himself dealt with a wilful Keith Miller. They talked about captains having the final say. And the outcome? Kim won't tell exactly—only that the name Kim Hughes lacked the aura and authority of the name Don Bradman. And that it did not work.

Allan Border called the Lillee–Marsh–Kim relationship a 'cold war'. Opponents sensed it. 'Something of a mafia,' noted David Gower of Lillee, Marsh and the Chappells. Umpires heard it. Controversy-shy Peter McConnell umpired more of Lillee, Marsh and Kim all together than anybody. Lillee gave him a stump after Melville's inaugural first-grade flag. McConnell likes all three, blames cricket's rulers for their predicament and gets riled by umpires who indulge in histrionics. 'The game is about the players, not umpires.' But McConnell will say: 'They were put into this, the three of them, but yeah, there was tension. You'll always get people disagreeing with things a captain does. Ninety-nine times out of a hundred they'll just walk away. Whereas here, there were a few things said.'

Those things they said entered one ear and swiftly exited the other. That was Kim's way. It infuriated Marsh and Lillee. But it was a blessing. Because the words did not eat at him—not yet. A batting crease is no place for self-doubt and Kim had none. He was twenty-eight. The world was as round and tameable as Bay 13's beach balls. Amid unwatered-down defamation from team-mates he produced the batting of his life.

Five sixes in five Tests against England were more than any Australian had clouted in a home summer since Keith Miller's eight sixes off the 1947–48 Indians. More remarkable than their frequency was the process. Kim pounced when well-set. He responded to the delivery, not the voice in his head. He radiated total control. In big stands he played the passive partner. Every game he contributed. A 62 in Perth was vintage, freewheeling Kim. A vigilant 39 not out in Brisbane—in partnership with another reformed wild colonial boy, David Hookes—made a tricky late-afternoon run chase simple. In Adelaide, Botham felt for the first time when bowling to Kim that he might not get him out at any given minute. Hesitation between wickets cost Kim a hundred. So serene was his state of mind that he shook off his disappointment, told batting partner Border it wasn't his fault and quietly departed for 88.

The team's wellbeing preoccupied Kim in Melbourne too. He hit 66 and 48 in a low-scoring humdinger. Last man Thomson joined Border on the fourth evening with 74 hopelessly required. Hookes, Lawson and Marsh retreated to the downstairs dressing room, unable to watch. Also, six o'clock beckoned. 'Time to tear the top from a can of beer,' as Marsh put it. 'It is as much a part of a day's cricket to me as putting on the gloves.'

The batsmen survived: edging, grimacing, bunting, galloping. Next morning Hookes, teetotaller Lawson and Marsh superstitiously reconvened downstairs. Border and Thomson had 37 more runs to knock off. Marsh and Hookes knocked off eight beers each. 'You could say we were drunk.' Four runs shy of the impossible, Thomson snicked Botham to second slip Chris Tavare, whose muffed catching attempt fended the ball to within swooping distance of a crab-clawed Geoff Miller. Marsh, Hookes and several Australian cities missed it; Botham, heart aflutter, had taken twenty-five instead of thirty seconds between overs and the ad break ran over the top. But Kim followed every beat. On a manila envelope he re-sketched his 'Mountain to Glory' that had tracked Australia's improbable Guyana victory of 1978. He crossed off every run and marked incisions up the mountain face. 'Today,' said Border, seeing the tattered, sweat-soaked scrap, 'we stumbled at the peak.'

Needing to draw in Sydney, Australia were only 190 ahead when Border, the last specialist batsman, joined Kim. Miller and Eddie Hemmings were not over-endowed with inbuilt menace. But they were making the ball judder on an SCG turner, twenty-two yards so inhospitable to Kim that he'd never topped 48 there in first-class circles. Six hours it took England to dismiss him. He used his feet, whittled away time, let Border outpace him. If that seemed unfeasible, Bill O'Reilly's first five words in the next day's *Sydney Morning Herald* were unforeseeable:

Kim Hughes, Australia's Mr Reliable . . .

He made 137—469 for the series.

'It's nice to think I played a part in winning the Ashes back when a lot of people thought I stuffed up in England,' said Kim. 'But for a bloke called Botham who walked on water for three matches we could have won that series 4–0. Maybe now I can forget about 1981.' Hughes enemies, even the persistent ones, said amen to that. 'After this series,' wrote Ian Chappell, 'not only should Hughes's conscience be clear but his slate clean in regard to the 1981 disaster.'

Fifteen hours after Kim's SCG hundred, Greg Chappell rang Phil Ridings to relinquish the captaincy—for the subsequent limited-overs series, and for good. He did so knowing who would take over. Kim at last was in command of a full-strength outfit at home. Forty-five thousand Melburnians clapped him all the way out in that opening one-dayer, then all the way off when he dabbed the winning run. Australia won three straight, a rarity, for the men in canary yellow treated 50-over cricket with the reverence an alcoholic reserves for soda. Lillee was missing after a knee operation. Was there a connection? He returned mid-series at quarter-throttle. 'Poor old Lillee trudging around,' sympathised New Zealand prime minister Robert Muldoon. 'He should be out to grass.'

The Kiwis met Australia in the first final in Sydney. Lillee was back—and fuming. He couldn't believe John Wright was still batting. Second-gamer Steve Smith had dropped him at midwicket, a sitter. 'Fot sort of went "Grrrr" and walked back to his mark,' Smith remembers. Home ground jitters, that was all. But then he dropped another. 'Kim just shook his head. But Fot blew up. I thought, oh no, what am I doing here? Is this ground going to open up and let me in or what?'

Playing for Australia was hard enough without antagonising Lillee. Smith had anticipated a welcoming nugget or two from Chappell. None was forthcoming. 'I never found Greg all that approachable,' says Smith. 'And he didn't go out of his way to help me. It was a fend-for-yourself-type job. That's fine.' Worse was the muttering when Kim made a field change. The wicketkeeper would shake his head. 'Glove straight over the face . . . Here I am, a young fella expecting everyone to get on, and it's completely the opposite. I'm not talking about everyone. I'm talking about three or four or five.'

The game continued. No more catches came Smith's way. Trouble did. Lillee wanted him moved straighter. 'Over 'ere.'

Kim was thinking the reverse: Smith should go squarer. 'Nah, I want him 'ere.'

They were yelling. 'I felt like a bloody yoyo,' Smith recalls, 'because this went on for a couple of minutes. And I was thinking, hey, any chance of you guys working this out?' Lillee pointed, gesticulated, threw up his hands and thundered off.

Glenn Turner, a cultured shotmaker who knew it and thus qualified as Australia's least favourite Kiwi, couldn't help noticing Kim's besieged, harried exterior at the crease. Champing, spitting, snorting—'sticking out his chest like a pouter pigeon and pulling back his shoulders like a man being prodded from behind'.

Kim won a gold tray and goblets for being named man of the finals, then more golden goblets as Sheffield Shield player of the year. Here was a cricketer in his prime who demanded respect. High in the SCG members' stand his picture hung above one of the dressing-room doors. The inscription read: 'Kim Hughes, Australian Captain'. But someone, the whisper went, had got at it with a Clag gluepot and a felt pen. They'd stuck a 'Clag' label on top of the word 'Kim', and in front of 'Australian Captain' they'd scribbled the word 'Pretend'.

•••••

SPECIAL TREATMENT in the nets was the other thing young Steve Smith found bewildering:

> I always thought a team environment was supposed to be: 'Good to see you, good luck, let's have a few throwdowns.' Uh-uh. Uh-uh, not happening. I remember Kim facing Fot

in Perth, the day before my first game, and Fot nearly killed him. Then he'd bowl to me and was nowhere near as quick. Kim didn't give a shit. It was part and parcel of what he had to put up with. If Fot bowled short Kim gonged him, the way he would in a game. Just in that one session Kim copped a couple on the shoulder—went to duck and didn't get down early enough. But he never once flinched.

There is always a certain pointlessness about a quick bowling at his own batsmen within a narrow net-rimmed rectangle. He must challenge without injuring while simultaneously polishing his own game. When Dennis bowled at Kim, it was something else again. At state training, Foster tried intervening: 'Come on, mate, he's had enough.'

'He's gotta learn,' Lillee would reply. 'He's gunna get bounced in the game, little fair-haired prick, so therefore he's gotta cop 'em in the nets.'

Foster felt it dangerous at times. Afterwards he'd say to Kim: 'It was a bit overdone today.'

'It's all right. No problem. He'll never get me out. Don't worry.'

The Australian team had no coach, no permanent support staff, no outsider inclined to put a clamp on Lillee. 'It was definitely not aired at team meetings,' says Lawson. 'It was whispered in corners of bars and hotel rooms. Because of the stature of Dennis and Rod.'

'They were Chappell, Lillee and Marsh,' says Mike Whitney. 'Man, this was the fucking royalty.'

And Kim was never badly hurt—not badly enough for the hoi polloi to revolt. 'It had a degree of amusement, like when someone gets hit in the box and their team-mates laugh,' says Lawson. 'When Kim got hit on the arm the day before the Ashes, we thought this is going too far. If Dennis broke Kim's arm the players, I think, would have come down heavily on him. But he didn't break Kim's arm. There was never that one step to pull it all back into order.'

Kim never squealed. It never made the papers. Even now, the pressure to keep safe the team secret is strong. Dennis headhunting Kim? Some smile cryptically. Others talk nervously, and only when assured that they are not alone, not blabbing. 'Someone should have sat them in a room,' Wood believes, 'and said: "Sort it out, or one or all of you have got to go." I think now that would happen. You wouldn't let it fester. But it was left to fester. There was this clique. You had the world's best bowler trying to knock your No. 4 batsman's head off.'

Without a coach, who could stop it? Of the three most experienced players, one was detonating the bouncers and another's thwarted leadership ambitions were a prime cause. The third was a man everyone respected. 'It used to disappoint me,' says Wood, 'that Greg at times pulled out of things.' Chappell is initially wary of discussing Lillee's bouncing of Kim:

There was never a point when you considered it inappropriate?

Oh, look, I wasn't there on those occasions so I can't really comment. The only time I was aware of any open dissent was the telecast from England [in 1981] when I saw Dennis and Rod openly disagree with Kim on the field.

Other players talk about net sessions in the '81–82, '82–83 and '83–84 home summers when Dennis, ball after ball, would aim at Kim's head . . .

I didn't see too many occasions. And to be quite honest, if I did see anything like that from time to time, when you have a bunch of highly motivated individuals occasionally there's going to be a short circuit. We weren't always all the best of mates. Teams often worked with some elements of dysfunction in them. Some personalities didn't go with other personalities. But provided you had a blend of personalities, that little bit of electricity could actually work in your favour. Occasionally you had a short circuit or a bloody power rush and there was an incident within the group. But, you know, we're not talking about a bunch of choirboys.

This theory is reminiscent of something Marsh told *Playboy*: 'It's not a bad thing when a little bit of aggro creeps in. If the people are big enough to bring whatever is bugging them out into the open, it's one of the greatest ways to knit a team.' Chappell continues:

A lot of them, all of us, had big egos and high opinions of ourselves. We had to. It's a tough environment. It's a survival of the fittest. There wasn't a lot of time to stop and bend down and pick people up. You'd bend down and pick 'em up a few times but from then on they were on their own, because by then you'd found someone else who didn't need picking up. There weren't bloody team chaplains. There weren't nurturing systems in place. There weren't permanent team managers. There wasn't a raft of fifteen support staff. The captain was it. You had a manager who joined you for each tour and most of those guys didn't have a clue. We spent more time managing them than they spent managing us.

Chappell's otherwise meticulous 1985 biography made no mention of Lillee's serenading of Kim with chin music. The lid stayed on the secret. 'Maybe they'—Chappell, Lillee and Marsh—'talked about it over their beers,' says Adrian McGregor. 'That's the sort of friendship those guys had.' It isn't Chappell's recollection:

Occasionally things bubbled over and burst out. And occasionally it was worthwhile sitting back and watching the outcome. It wasn't a matter of stepping in: 'Oh Dennis, don't do that, that's not very nice.' It may have been just the thing the guy needed. If he couldn't cope with it, he probably wasn't going to cope on the field. We weren't running a bloody kindergarten. We were trying to survive in a tough world. We needed guys in there with us who were tough and could survive as well.

That didn't mean everyone had the same personality. There were softer individuals, softer in the sense that their personality was different. And Kim was certainly different. Kim would cry. His emotions he wore on his sleeve. You knew exactly where he was. That's what we loved about him. There wasn't a lot of 'side' to Kim, other than the downside of some of his personality traits. There was no nastiness in him. But there were times when we felt he needed toughening up. A good workout in the nets occasionally was probably a good place to start. And the thing about it was Kim loved it, generally, because he loved playing hook shots.

Lillee had been bouncing Kim for years, since long before captaincy shenanigans. The boy could have been a world-beater like them if only he'd tempered that flamboyance, if only he'd listened. *But would he listen?* Bouncers were an attempt to cut through where words failed. As Chappell puts it: 'You're not listening to the verbal message—try this one.'

World Series Cricket came then went. Chappell played. Chappell skipped. He was mentally knackered. 'I needed those breaks otherwise I wasn't going to be able to keep playing.' Every time he abdicated he knew he may not return. 'I've read in many places that I picked and chose when I'd be captain. I had no say in it.' But the board kept reappointing him. 'An unsatisfactory position,' says Alan Crompton, later chairman, 'but one we were wearing. Following the peace the ACB and PBL were desperately keen to make the peace work. From the ACB's point of view we were more than happy to bend over backwards to accommodate the World Series players as they came back.'

Also, Chappell seemed the obvious leader. But so did Marsh in Chappell's absence. Reasons for targeting Kim's head grew more complicated. It was upsetting for Marsh. Fluffing his nest with Packer didn't make him selfish. Future cricketers would thank World Series Cricketers. Yet Marsh felt like he was being flogged. There was more to it, as we know, but flogged was how he felt. And Lillee felt furious on his mate's behalf. Men defended mates. Barely a cricketer in the country reckoned Kim likely to outdo Marsh in ingenuity or inspirational might. But there it was. The guy was captain. You were taught to back your captain. You got on with it. Proud as they were, tirelessly as they toiled, Lillee and Marsh did not always look like people getting on with it.

'Dennis and Rod didn't think Kim should be captain and probably had a logical view,' says Lawson. 'But to carry on about it was six-year-old's stuff.' Bob Simpson, still years away from the coaching reign that transformed the Test team's culture, watched with concern from afar. 'I certainly would have had an honest, open team meeting about it all . . . I remember being totally distressed by the situation.' Craig Serjeant felt almost embarrassed:

> Embarrassed's not the right word. You felt sorry for Kim. You really felt sorry. Senior players should have had enough respect for the position to not make their thoughts on the field so overtly obvious. I felt really uncomfortable about that. That wouldn't be tolerated at a lot of levels. But they were strong-minded, strong-willed . . . And it was Dennis more than anyone. If he were in the room he'd object to me saying that. But that's a fact. For Kim to have to control these competing egos when deep down he knew they didn't want him in that position . . . I don't know what his answer would be, or how he dealt with it. But, God, it wouldn't have been easy. Lots of people would have cracked and crumbled before he did.

Kim wasn't cracking yet. He still had his sense of humour. Favourite magazine was one question asked in a Q&A for *Australian Cricket* on 4 March 1983. Kim's answer? '*Playboy*.' For the articles, presumably.

ELEVEN

God Was His Nickname

GEOFF LAWSON'S PREPARATION for the 1983 World Cup consisted of him arriving home from university on a winter's evening, walking five hundred metres to Coogee Oval and bowling at a garbage tin in an otherwise empty net. There was no team get-together or acclimatisation camp in Maroochydore. No Greg Chappell either. Three days before the plane left for London, Chappell withdrew with a stiff neck that made batting uncomfortable and bowling unfeasible. Even this provoked discord. Kim wanted to take a '60 or 70 per cent fit' Chappell. Chappell pronounced himself 65 per cent fit—'and that's nowhere near good enough'. Little did the Australians know it but they would soon rewrite the medical books. Pains in the neck were about to prove contagious.

Thirty-One Days to Power was the name of a new book charting Bob Hawke's breakneck conquest of the Australian Labor Party and prime ministership. *Eleven Days to Purgatory* summed up the progress of another charismatic Westralian son. Kim's World Cup campaign began on 9 June and finished on 20 June. A practice game at Arundel Castle—hailed out, not rained out—set the tone. This would be a tournament of extremes.

World cricket was booming with an uncommon depth. Six countries were genuinely competitive and a seventh, Sri Lanka, rising fast. Never in one spot had so many current or soon-to-be giants clustered: Border, Botham, Crowe, Dujon, Garner, Gavaskar, Gower, Greenidge, Hadlee, Haynes, Holding, Imran, Javed, Kapil Dev, Lillee, Lloyd, Marsh, Marshall, Ranatunga, Richards, Roberts, Turner, Willis, Zaheer. None, promisingly, hailed from Zimbabwe, Australia's first-up opponent.

Reputations counted nought. The cup debutants and 1000–1 nonentities were 13 runs too good for a team garrotting every one-day by-law. Australia bowled first, spilt catches, leaked extras, squandered wickets. Recent Young Australia tourist Ken MacLeay had warned against underestimating a side handy enough to bench seventeen-year-old Graeme Hick. Nonetheless Marsh, long since recovered from a 45-can hangover after the flight over, felt Kim's approach too slapdash. Hogg was bothered more by the aftermath: 'Next day we should have been running roads, or fielding, or doing a bit in the nets—or something. And we weren't. It was a free day.'

Kim batted like a goose or a lord with nothing in between. Light was scant and the deck untrustworthy when he confronted West Indies at Headingley. Wood was already in Leeds Infirmary, en route to becoming history's first man to retire hurt after having his head clobbered on three consecutive England tours. Wayne Daniel said hello with a bouncer. Kim just stared. 'Sssssss.' Another bouncer. Kim hissed at him again. Daniel's wrath was foaming, his response predictable: two more at the skull. Kim deposited both over the fine-leg rope. 'You've got to bowl better than that,' he declared, 'to stop me hitting you for six.' He perished minutes later for 18. In the return bout he top-scored with 69 in the company of a runner and two strapped and battered thighs. Agony was the one foolproof way of making Kim concentrate.

Conceivably, Australia could cop a double drubbing from West Indies, take revenge against Zimbabwe, twice beat India and still reach the semi-finals as Group B runners-up. With one game to go the back-up plan was on track. India were pushovers in Nottingham thanks to two one-hit wonders: MacLeay's 6–39 (he never again managed 3–for) and Trevor Chappell's 110 (27 was his next best). A repeat victory in Chelmsford looked a formality. Lillee, out of sorts, was dropped. Kim was a late scratching, his barbecued thigh muscles stiffening on a pre-game jog. Marsh had again refused the deputy's job so Hookes captained.

The gates were closed, the small ground crammed with 9000 Indians—'loud-mouthed and in many cases sozzled,' noted the *Guardian*'s Matthew Engel. The atmosphere was electric, sometimes toxic. When Kim, perturbed by Hookes's field settings, sent twelfth man Kepler Wessels out with instructions, Marsh roared: 'Tell fucking Kim Hughes that if he wants to captain the fucking side, fucking play.' But Kim had sunny memories of Chelmsford. In his Scottish league days he once splashed a six into the nearby River Can for the Irish Leprechauns. India failed to last 60 overs, sputtering to 247. The pitch was flat, the sky blue.

In 38.2 overs Australia capsized for 129. The destroyer was Roger Binny, taking out a litter of transfixed Australians with mild-mannered floaters that swung sharper in imagination than through the air. First man overboard, Trevor Chappell, caught the spirit. After edging a Balwinder Sandhu straight ball to gully he performed an altogether more elegant sweep stroke upon entering the pavilion, sending an afternoon tea set flying. Next, he picked up a coffee cup, aimed for the window and instead shattered a drinks machine, unloosing rivers. Wood recalls:

> It reached a crescendo in England in '83. That's as bad as I've ever known a team environment. We should have at least made the semi-finals. You'd walk into a bar at night and there were definitely two factions. I tried to surf down the middle because, you know, they were all my friends. It's disappointing when you look back. You go away on a World Cup, which should be a great experience, but this wasn't. There were whispers and mutterings and it wasn't enjoyable. And at Chelmsford, it was as bad as it ever was.

Books by Marsh and Lillee materialised in shop windows, like twisted power cables after a cyclone. Blame was apportioned: Kim wouldn't talk, couldn't listen, didn't mix well, wasn't one of the boys. 'If you saw him at the back of the bus leading the singing you knew he had scored runs,' wrote Lillee. 'If he was down the front sleeping you knew he had failed. (The team beer was at the back).' Ifs piled on top of ifs. If only Kim hadn't batted at three. If only he'd played that last game instead of saving his leg for a hypothetical semi-final. If he'd just shown some respect. 'A few guys,' claimed Marsh, 'were talking behind his back and muttering things about what they'd like to do to him if they caught him in an alley on a dark night.'

Wood says: 'I definitely didn't hear that.'

Hogg says: 'I wouldn't even go down the path of talking like that . . . Australian cricket was crying out for a coach . . . It wasn't Kim's fault.'

Lawson says: 'It's not my recollection.'

Marsh's fiercest gripe was the pensioning off of Lillee. Twice it happened. The last time against India, dropping a champion matchwinner for a must-win match, cut deepest. 'Dennis left the ground, as I recall,' says Wood. 'Didn't get a game, didn't get picked and actually left.' Marsh's version of his mate's whereabouts was more charitable. Lillee, he said, went for a run to work off his anger and ran so far he got lost.

Men not only defended mates. Men returned favours. Lillee had long blown down houses in protest at Marsh's treatment. Now Marsh huffed and puffed. But Lillee's knee was troubling him. At Arundel Castle he let fly an estimated twenty-two bouncers in twenty-four balls at Glenn Turner yet still went for six runs an over. No trace of menace had been sighted since. 'Maybe Rod thought that because Dennis was a senior player everyone should be loyal,' says Lawson. 'Oh, your name's Dennis Lillee, it doesn't matter then. But you had to divorce the name from the guy out there bowling.' Lawson saw dropping Lillee as proof of Kim's strength. Mutterings quite different to the ones Marsh heard were reaching Lawson's ears:

> Everyone in the team agreed Dennis shouldn't be playing. He was the greatest bowler I've ever seen. Pain was no issue and he wanted to get out and play, but he just wasn't physically capable. Conversations I had with guys went along the lines of: 'God, Dennis has been dropped, he won't be happy.' Which he wasn't. But it was the right thing. We wanted to make the World Cup finals.

In the *Age*, Peter McFarline advocated that Lillee, at thirty-three, never be selected again. 'Pardon the unforgivable, but

Australia looks and is a much better team without Lillee and Thomson. That is akin to suggesting Sydney Harbour is better without the bridge.' India's giant-squashing passage all the way to Lord's soothed nobody. Dire days prompted dark ruminations. Even McFarline's favourites weren't exempt: 'In a leadership career not exactly studded with memorable decisions, Hughes's decision not to play [versus India] was lamentable . . . A collection of individuals without plan or forethought, this Australian team does not have a capable leader. Many older players have little faith in Hughes, whose communication lines within the dressing room are definitely Boy's Own stuff.'

Round the Waldorf bar, the players were drinking to get maudlin. The captain appeared at the entrance in his green blazer and tie. A function? 'No, I'm going home.' Kim hoisted his luggage and boarded a cab for Heathrow. It was either the night of the Chelmsford catastrophe or the day after; memories differ. But he'd secretly booked himself on an early flight to Perth. And he hadn't necessarily intended saying goodbye. 'He wants to put his side of the story to the ACB before we get back,' grizzled one player. For Hookes, it was 'the most staggering thirty seconds'.

Staggering times, they were. Kim didn't know it yet, but twenty-four hours after Australia's Zimbabwean meltdown Yallop and Wessels had dinner with the South African Cricket Union's Dr Ali Bacher. The day after Chelmsford six Australians— Yallop, Wessels, Wood, Hogg, Hookes, Thomson—slunk off to see Bacher at his brother-in-law's Mayfair flat. Nobody mentioned that either. Kim was fighting a losing war in which the boundaries kept changing.

•••••

BEING A GRACIOUS LOSER was not so appealing a characteristic after all in a leader who lost so regularly and spectacularly. Kim's early return home was time spent shrewdly. He rang Bob Merriman complaining of several bothersome anachronisms in Australian cricket. Merriman arranged a meeting with two board grandees, Bob Parish and Fred Bennett, each old enough to be Kim's grandfather. They were thoughtful men, Parish a timber merchant and Bennett an ex-ABC personnel officer, with eighty-one years of cricket administration between them. In Parish's downtown office Kim proposed what he called his 'masterplan': a national coach, support staff, player contracts, practice sessions with a whiff of verve and purpose, the way Daryl Foster ran things in WA. Bowl at garbage tins and you'll get rubbish on the pitch. 'An outstanding presentation,' recalls Merriman. 'Those two ACB chiefs were very impressed and hellbent on taking a lot of Kim's recommendations to the board.'

Alas, Kim was not the only one with a vision. And some people's visions did not involve Kim. Home from London, Jeff Thomson shuffled up to a TV microphone and went whang. No, he conceded, the leadership wasn't terribly inspiring. Yes, Marsh must be disappointed not to be captain: 'I'd like to see him there. Put it that way.'

More withering was Hookes on Ken Cunningham's 5DN drivetime show in Adelaide. Hookes was contracted to the station and knew his interrogator well. Years earlier, 'KG' had sledged the budding West Torrens wonderboy, inciting a flash of Hookes's blade and the retort: 'Listen old man, continue bowling those wobbly seamers and the next eight will go over the fence.' When KG asked Hookes to choose between Marsh and Kim he anticipated the deadest of bats. 'Maybe,' went Hookes's unexpected reply, 'Kim has got to be an apprentice to somebody everybody respects.'

If lazy feet were Hookes's supreme cricketing flaw, a whipcrack tongue cost him just as dear. Honesty was his unbending policy. 'Have you swallowed a pig?' he'd say by way of greeting Kerry O'Keeffe. Kim had irked him during their matchwinning Gabba stand against England, remarking to Botham after one hazardous Hookes hook: 'It's about time one of our players had as much arse as you.' Hookes never forgot it. He was also utterly convinced of Marsh's capabilities. Fined $1200 for his frankness, Hookes was flown to Perth under an alias—'I felt like Paul McCartney'—on a secret peacekeeping mission. He and Kim chatted in Kim's dining room and over beers at the Sheraton. Yet Hookes played not one Test against Pakistan that summer. Viral pneumonia would have kept him from the start; but the First Test team, minus Hookes, was picked days before sickness struck. In the previous six Tests Hookes had averaged 69. In his last knock in Kandy he blazed a century in a session. By the time he got another chance—against West Indies on their wickets—his moment had passed.

Kim was paying too. Abject disappointment had driven him on to the first plane out of Heathrow. But that didn't make it right, or popular. Bob Merriman copped 'a decent earful' from tour manager Phil Ridings. Two players came to Merriman brandishing misgivings. 'Then, to see where the hell it was at, I spoke to two others. They questioned Kim's leadership, his methodology of dealing with people.' Meanwhile Greg

Chappell led Border around Royal Queensland golf course. He chipped away at Border's well-known reluctance to be captain. If board delegates would not countenance Marsh they might contemplate Border, but only if he had some experience. That meant captaining Queensland.

Chappell teed up an orderly transition. He felt entitled to do so. With Chappell, the grandness of the office of Australian captain was no myth. Sometimes he really felt like his country's second most powerful citizen. He'd say so to people. Reporters used to ring him.

'What do you think of the situation in Pakistan?'

'We're not touring Pakistan.'

'No, but what do you think?'

Chappell had a sense of certainty. It went with him every-where. It was so rock-solid it verged on Bradmanesque. He'd ponder what was best for Australian cricket, decide, then organise it. He has an uncluttered mind, a pernickety memory. Those qualities made sculpting Chappell's memoirs pure pleasure for Adrian McGregor. 'You've just got to be around Greg long enough,' McGregor adds, 'and you start to believe him.' Eighteen holes did the trick on this occasion. According to Chappell, Border gave in with the words: 'Having seen the cock-up Kim's making of it, I might as well do it myself.'

On 18 August 1983 Border succeeded Chappell as Queens-land skipper. On 26 August the ACB's cricket committee met at Melbourne's Hilton Hotel. Chappell represented Queensland. Kim, now a deposed committee member, was there as Australian captain. Also present were the five other state representatives plus Ridings, Bennett, Richards and Merriman. Chappell, with that customary certainty of his, arranged to room with Kim.

Circumstances meant Chappell had seldom experienced or even witnessed Kim's captaincy himself. But others' gripes came as no surprise. He remembered that 1977 night with the overboiled waitress in the hick New Zealand town. Recent telephone interactions unsettled Chappell. 'Kim would agree to something then the next day we'd have a conversation as though the previous conversation hadn't taken place. Alarm bells were ringing for me. This guy needed help.'

The way Chappell saw it, to be a Test cricketer was to lead a tenuous existence in an uncoddled world. Certain personalities were required, special training. 'Batting against my brother—five years older than myself—as a nine-year-old, getting bounced with a hard ball, helped develop me to the point where I could stand up to a West Indian pace attack. We competed with our mates in parks, backyards, streets. That's where we got the tools and coping skills to deal with each situation, to make decisions in real time that were akin to the decisions we had to make in Tests and one-day internationals. And if you missed bits of that . . .'

Chappell's meditations culminated in a room-service break-fast for two at the Hilton. He did not want to risk interruption. It was 7.30 a.m. on a Friday. Chappell told Kim the team was not united. Players were 'at breaking point'. Most wanted a new leader. Marsh would be perfect—or, if the board kiboshed that idea, Border. It cannot be you. Stick with the captaincy and you will most likely lose it. Runs will dry up. Then you'll get dropped. The pressure is more than you can stand. If you truly care for Australian cricket, do as I say. Declare yourself unavailable. 'Do yourself a favour.' In a couple of years, maybe, you'll get it back.

Saying these words did not come easily to Chappell—'a terrible situation to be in':

Christ, I wasn't a counsellor. I was a bloody cricketer. I cared for the individuals. And when I say 'cared', I wasn't professionally trained to sit down with them and give advice. I could only give them advice from the heart and from my own life experiences. And what I told Kim was he needed help. He needed to get away from cricket, get some professional help and hopefully be able to resurrect himself and his career.

Chappell's wish to not be disturbed was fulfilled. Even Kim said nothing, ate nothing. Chappell spoke for half an hour. He feels Kim 'took it on board pretty well'. He believes Kim considered it well-meaning advice intended for his own good. He thinks Kim trusted him.

Yet when Chappell finished talking Kim stayed silent. After thirty seconds Kim got up. 'I'll go and see if Bob and the others are ready.' And with that, he left.

Chappell was dumbstruck. 'He either had to hit me or agree with me. But to just walk out of the room—*it was his room*. He was a shattered man. He was gone. He was an emotionally wrecked individual and it was tragic to see.' Items on that day's committee agenda included the World Cup wash-up, the itinerary, fluorescent uniforms, coloured balls. Emotionally wrecked or not, Kim said his bit. People could upset him but he would not cower. And in all the years since, other than the things he tells his family, he has never mentioned what happened over breakfast.

What Chappell did took bravery. And brazenness. He thought it the right thing for Australian cricket. But doing what you think is right is not quite the same as doing right. And how do you ever know the difference? Even when you do know you don't really; you only think you know. In Chappell's case, additional complications abounded. By no leap of anyone's imagination was he objective: Marsh was his mate. And he was Greg Chappell. 'God' was his nickname. Knowing God was not entirely on his side maximised Kim's degree of difficulty, should he persist.

Chappell says he consulted widely before ordering breakfast in on 26 August. 'I brought in the whole selection panel, Bob Merriman. Bob's background as an industrial advocate meant he had some experience in that area.' Merriman says he knew what Chappell was planning but not exactly when: 'He told me afterwards.' David Richards only found out later. It is possible that Chappell was no dispassionate observer of his own actions at this moment; that he was in the wrong headspace to distinguish between being right and thinking himself right. Adrian McGregor, with nearly a quarter of a century's hindsight, suggests:

I think he felt really guilty about not being there for the team in England. And I think that coloured his reaction. I think he had an overreaction. He'd ditched the team for his own good reasons, they suffered and he felt it incumbent upon him to right this wrong. The way he went about it was probably a bit over the top. I don't think he was undermining Kim in a malicious way. Greg was acting out of his own sense of guilt, or something like guilt.

The guilt could explain the haste. Still soft was the kiss of the Chappell family's blessing—Ian's thoughtful praise, Greg's bequeathing of the captaincy—two lovely and surprising sequels to Kim's Ashes-sealing 137. After that Kim led Australia in the limited-overs games. They polished those off. 'Go to it Kim,' wrote Greg in his newspaper column. 'Get stuck in and make it one of the greatest winning eras . . . I would like to see Kim captain the side in every match and on every tour from now on. I hope he captains for the next umpteen years—for as long as he wants.'

That was on 6 February 1983: 201 days earlier. Since then Kim had led Australia to three defeats in five one-dayers, none of which Greg played, all of which he followed from 10,000 miles away. *Declare yourself unavailable. Do yourself a favour.* Wasn't that advice a little impetuous? Impetuosity was the trait they despaired of in Kim.

Kim could walk out. But he could not walk away. Other people at the country's opposite end were puzzling over his welfare and arriving at the same answer as Chappell. 'We have to try to do this for Kim,' Daryl Foster told Sam Gannon. They made an appointment to see him. A week after the Hilton breakfast the three men met at Gannon's Outram Street office in West Perth. It was mid-afternoon. Gannon, respected in business and liked by all, did most of the talking. 'Concentrate on your batting,' he said. 'Become one of Australia's all-time greats. Score 8000 runs. Forget the peripheral stuff.'

Bluntness and flattery were Gannon and Foster's two prongs. With Marsh or Lillee they'd have camouflaged deepest thoughts and tiptoed through the back door. With Kim they knew he wouldn't slam it in their faces. 'You could be the equal of Viv

Richards,' proclaimed Foster. That wasn't just flattery. 'There were innings,' Foster believes now, 'that even Viv couldn't have played.' He recalls Kim listening politely, attentively. 'We virtually had him convinced,' says Gannon, 'to stand down as captain.' Kim departed at 5 p.m.

By chance, Merriman was dining at the Hughes household that evening. He was in Perth on Australian Conciliation and Arbitration Commission business. There were four at the table: Kim, Jenny, Merriman and Rob Parry, Frank's son and Kim's friend since their teens. Rob managed his accounts and guarded his affairs—'business adviser', Kim called him. The higher Kim went in cricket, the deeper Rob's influence.

Merriman arrived determined to discuss the complaints gathered from team-mates in England. The conversation started there and didn't stray far. They covered Kim's inconsistent batting as captain, whether he was happy, the inability of some players to support him. 'Rob was probing,' says Merriman. He cannot remember Jenny's feelings. This time, Kim spoke. For a week he can have pondered little else but the words he did not want to hear of men who said they cared. 'It was a night of a lot of thought and a fair bit of self-examination by Kim,' says Merriman. 'No angst or anger or untoward feeling. Just Kim talking about a problem confronting him.'

Four still sat round the table when Kim began writing. Merriman recalls: 'He comfortably worked through a letter explaining his concerns and where he felt he was going, saying he still wanted to serve Australian cricket. But he had come to the conclusion, very firmly, that it was in the best interests of his form and enjoyment to not have the responsibility of leadership.'

Do not consider me for the captaincy this season, Kim's letter said. He addressed it to the board and entrusted Merriman with delivering it to the chairman. Merriman left Kim's house late, with the handwritten letter, catching the red-eye to Melbourne and driving home to Geelong. He had a site inspection near Colac in the afternoon. His phone rang that morning:

There's no doubt that after I left Kim had conversations with Parry—and maybe Frank, I don't know—and obviously with his lawyer. Because the next morning's phone call wasn't a 'Hi Bob, how are you?' It was a very clear, precise, fairly legalistic statement. 'I will be captain of Australia. My family says I will be captain of Australia. My family includes my friends over here. I will be captain of Australia.' He said that if he didn't get the captaincy he would be changing his phone numbers and he wouldn't be giving them to me.

Oddest was this: not once did Kim say he had changed his mind. 'Is that really what you want?' asked Merriman. Kim repeated his message. Merriman ripped up the letter. He delved no deeper and told the board nothing. As cricket committee coordinator he felt an obligation to the players.

But something sinister had happened. Form and enjoyment were suddenly lesser considerations. Years earlier, Kim had left schoolteaching behind with visions of a cricketing afterlife in finance. He was a promotions officer with City Building Society, then an assistant manager of business development for Town & Country Building Society. The job involved marketing duties. And he'd ring big investors to tell them when their investments were coming up to maturity. 'One of the loyalest people I ever had working for me,' says Ray Turner, the Town & Country general manager who brought Kim to the firm. 'He was a great player, well presented, good-looking. He was a family man. He fitted the Town & Country mould admirably.'

In *Network News*, the in-house staff newsletter, one item went: 'Kim Hughes? The Australian Cricket captain? Yes, that's right. In "civilian" life Kim Hughes is a Town & Country WA executive.'

He posed with shirt unbuttoned, bat upraised in Town & Country ads. They gave him time off for cricket. He lent them pizzazz, prestige and wholesomeness. Only one cricketer in the land could possibly offer all those qualities. 'Town & Country wanted to be seen to be employing the Australian captain,' says Sam Gannon. 'He was told in no uncertain terms that he couldn't stand down.'

Ray Turner is a man Kim used to confide in and respect. 'He would only have been given advice,' says Turner, 'if he sought it. And I honestly can't remember whether he did seek advice . . . Even if I could recall it I wouldn't be disclosing the details of it, because that's pretty personal.'

Kim banned Rob Parry and Stephen Owen-Conway, his lawyer, from being interviewed for this book. Frank Parry died in 2003. Kim had let a lot of men into his life, men who watched him bat and saw possibility. His coach and his coach's son and his lawyer. His employer and his cricket board barrackers. His father. Too many men.

•••••

IF SECOND-GUESSING KIM'S true wishes was tricky, the intentions of the fourteen Australian Cricket Board delegates posed another mystery. A vote on the captaincy was scheduled for 2 November 1983. So began two months of front-bar prattle and newspaper tattle. Chappell ruled himself out. Border was too raw. That left Kim and Marsh, a re-run of last year's wild west showdown. The continent divided in two. Fifty-two per cent backed Marsh and 19 per cent Kim in a Sydney newspaper survey. Over in Perth a *Daily News* cut-out coupon beckoned readers to scrawl an X beside their preferred head. Kim polled 77 per cent, Marsh 16, Chappell 5, Hookes 2, Border zero. 'It is not easy being stabbed in the back by people who are supposed to be your mates,' noted letter writer Jerry Roberts of Highgate. 'Hughes has a quality not evident in those mentioned as successors. The quality is class.'

The WACA seemed to agree. A fortnight before the ACB vote, Lillee was unveiled as WA vice-captain. Was that a hint? Marsh, Test captain in waiting, was apparently unfit to be his state's second-in-command. On the first morning of Western Australia's new leadership regime, Lillee refused a newspaper request for a photo with Kim. Lillee was suspicious of media entrapment. Also, they had been tiffing again. He was still frothing over a one-on-one meeting at which Kim had flagged his desire to bowl Lillee first-change and into the breeze. Lillee promptly drove home, donned joggers and ran twelve kilometres. Asked by 6PR's Bob Maumill about the significance of him accepting the deputy's job, Lillee replied: 'If I go into a bar and have a drink with a bloke, it doesn't show my sexual preference, does it?'

Kim rose early on 2 November, boarding a train for the wheatbelt hub of Northam. Town & Country was sponsoring a WA Country XI against Pakistan. Kim wore a Town & Country hat. A waiting car propelled him to the company's Northam branch. There, he waited for new ACB chairman Fred Bennett's 10.45 a.m. phone call.

In Sydney, Ian McDonald watched fourteen faceless men debate who should be the public face of Australian cricket. McDonald was surprised they let him attend. He was coming to the end of his first week as the board's inaugural media manager, having previously performed the same trailblazing role for the Victorian Football League. 'I thought the board blokes were all nice gentlemen compared to the footballers. But Christ, they played the footballers on a break,' says McDonald. 'I didn't realise how much bloody politics there was, how much state rivalry.' The New South Wales faction lauded Marsh's attributes, again. Rigg and Sawle of WA were pro-Kim.

Kim hung up the telephone and headed to the local oval, Burwood Park, for a prearranged press conference in the ladies' self-defence room. Twenty journalists gathered expectantly. Kim drifted in on a cloud of melancholy—'as if he had just found weevils in his wheat silos', observed the *Australian*'s Phil Wilkins. Instantly, Wilkins and the *Daily News*'s Robbie Burns guessed that Marsh's long-cherished dream had been realised. Kim read from notes in a voice with the youth drained out of it: 'The team is Wessels, Phillips, Yallop, Hughes.' Pause. '*Captain*.' The boy with a neon sign for a face had learnt a thing or two about poker.

Twice in nineteen months Marsh's ambition had been slit by the skinniest of margins. Again Marsh had the chairman's potential casting vote—Bennett's, in succession to Ridings—but to no avail. This time he agreed to be Kim's deputy. The First Test started in Perth on the 11th. On the 5th captain and vice-captain were to chat with Ian Chappell on *Wide World of Sports*. Kim pulled out on the 4th, via a telex message sent by his lawyers. The 8th was hectic. Bennett lectured the players in their Sheraton team room on the need for loyalty and unity. Then he handed over to the man from the Australian Wool Corporation, official team tailors, who previewed the new summer's fashions before attacking the players with his tape measure. Mid-morning nets were followed by boat rides and a function at Royal Perth Yacht Club, the America's Cup's new residence. Notions of loyalty and unity got lost in a tidal wave of Swan Lager.

Trouble stirred over a trivial selection discrepancy. Kim and Marsh chatted on the clubhouse steps, in full view of players, scribes and assorted hobnobbers on the outside lawn. Chatting turned to shouting, gesticulating, jostling, shirt-pulling. 'Break it up,' David Richards ordered McDonald, who felt like saying: 'Do it yourself.' But it was only his second week. The players, he was learning, could be as ungentlemanly as the board dwellers. McDonald plopped himself between Australia's captain and vice-captain. Fisticuffs were forestalled. 'Instead of trying to punch each other,' McDonald recalls, 'I thought they were going to take me.' The story didn't seep out despite a full media contingent—and because of a *full* media contingent. 'They were all,' McDonald explains, 'drunk.' A giant marquee proved too giant for one reporter to navigate his way out. And Alan McGilvray's evening ended with him creeping to the edge of the jetty and into a telephone box, imagining it to be a cab.

Five Tests against Pakistan promised nearly as many fireworks. Australia's speed resources were rich and Pakistan's batting long. Sadly Mohsin Khan, Mudassar Nazar, Qasim Omar, Javed Miandad, Zaheer Abbas and Salim Malik were more explosive on paper than on pitches conducive to swing. Worse, Imran was shin-sore and Sarfraz at war with the selectors. Queensland rain kept Australia to a 2–0 victory. As for Kim's captaincy, even Greg Chappell—'an uneventful, happy series'—had no complaints. In the last four Tests Kim carved half-centuries or better, his feet less cobwebby by the day in response to Abdul Qadir's mischief and loop.

His best was saved for his country's five hours of crisis in Adelaide, with Qadir tossing into footmarks, five close catchers hovering and Australia scrabbling for a draw. Kim's chanceless 106 was a showpiece of circumspect precision. A week later he showed Queensland the flip side of his batting personality. Redheaded teenage gunslinger Craig McDermott—a long-time Kim admirer from the safety of his parents' Ipswich living room—suffered second-game stagefright. Kim pillaged 130, twenty of them off one McDermott over, several dozen from cover drives off his quivering right knee. 'As he hit the ball,' a humbled McDermott recalled, 'he said, "Shot, Claggy! That's fucking four, young fella." So in the same breath he was congratulating himself on a fine shot and pointing out to me where the ball was headed. He also called down the pitch more than once: "It's not so easy up here, is it young fella?"'

Kim's first marshalling of a full-powered Test XI was his last. Chappell, Lillee and Marsh bade cricket adieu amid a statisticians' nirvana of tumbling milestones. Marsh held nearly as many testimonial dinners as catches. At Sydney's Sheraton–Wentworth, 637 high-fliers paid $50 a head. Marsh auctioned a baggy green, two sweaters and the gloves he wore—the ones with more clang than cling—on his Test debut. Smoky Dawson sang and two Chappells spoke, Ian paraphrasing country singer Jerry Reed. 'Hughes got the goldmine,' said Ian, 'and Marsh got the shaft.' Two days later Australia played a one-day final at the SCG. Kim didn't inch towards Ian for the customary post-toss interview. Kim turned and walked off.

Ian Chappell recently summarised his approach to people who get on his goat like so:

> I have found as I get older that if I come across somebody who annoys me, or someone I don't like or respect, I don't particularly want to have anything to do with them . . . You think, shit, I've got less and less time here, I'm not going to waste it mixing with people who bore the shit out of me.

People who know Ian well call it a mellowing. Back in the Hughes mini-era, he remained deeply influenced by his father's chainsaw honesty. Martin Chappell once embarrassed wife Jeanne at a dinner function by advising the woman sitting opposite: 'Your hairstyle's terrible.' Ian shared his father's flair for verbal nunchukku. Often he combined pith, vitriol and a deadly analogy, as in the commemorative book *Ten Turbulent Years*. 'Yallop and Hughes,' wrote Ian, 'were the worst choice as leaders since Robert O'Hara Burke. Burke's expedition with Wills was a disaster and the only difference with Yallop and Hughes is that they got away with their lives.' Around Ian, Border always tried, usually unsuccessfully, to duck the subject. 'Ian and I got along pretty well but we argued a helluva lot about Kim . . . You could see Ian's hackles rise.'

Border never understood it. And in some ways, as cricketers,

Ian and Kim could have been brothers, right down to their habit of gazing skywards to adjust eyes to the light. Both were entertainers. Both pummelled spin bowlers. 'Against the average guys I thought there was four coming,' was Chappell's philosophy, 'and if I didn't get one that over there would be two the next over.' That was Kim's thinking too. Chappell goaded Kim on TV about his risky hooking of fast bowlers. Yet that was Chappell's own preferred strategy, his signature stroke. Did it reflect some subconscious, unspoken lament for the lost digits the hook shot lopped off his own batting average?

Sometimes you sensed Ian grappling aloud with their similarities, as in the SCG Test of 1979–80, their first together. Kim arrived in a fix, saw Australia to safety with a cool 47, then self-destructed with a mad dash at Willis moments before deliverance. 'I admire Kim's attitude of not playing for the average and looking to entertain the public,' wrote Chappell. And yet . . . 'Having seen out the hard part it was ridiculous to throw his wicket away. His motto should always be "aim to be in there at the kill".'

Kim lacked killer. That was the problem. 'Captaincy is a task best carried out by a dictator with a feeling for his comrades,' Chappell once remarked. That wasn't Kim. Chappell swore— sometimes on air. That wasn't Kim either. 'One thing I like about Kim,' says Hogg, 'is, he swears a bit now, but I've never heard him swear too much. I love bagging people, that's my caper, but I've never heard Kim really say a bad word about anyone.' Kim's wholesomeness made certain others choke. Englishman John Woodcock wrote of Ian Chappell: 'He was what Australians value most of all, a winner. His players swore by him. But, my hat, he was basic.'

At Marsh's testimonial dinner Kim arrived late, missing Chappell's goldmine sledge by minutes. His team-mates heard it though. Forty or fifty strangers tried to comfort him. He felt humiliated. But to stomp off from the microphone after winning the toss, a Channel Nine technician's cries dying on the breeze, confirmed every bad impression the Chappells ever had. He stomped right back out there minutes later and constructed an eleven-ball duck. That settled it. The kid was soft. It was a repeat of his untouched Hilton breakfast with Greg. Anyone else would have agreed, nodded, thanked Greg, fought or swore. But to walk out, fly home, quit to somebody else then cancel your resignation? Nothing manly in that.

They reckoned him narrow, too. Australian cricket was in a lull between the advent of professionalism and the players being treated like professionals. The monkeys were on a better grade of peanuts. But peanuts, relatively speaking, they were. The gap between gate receipts and player wages remained a chasm. Players were overworked and underappreciated. Some weren't even awake to it. Australian cricket needed a man who could walk tightropes, not walk away.

TWELVE
'Guys, I'm Going Into the Trenches for You'

A JOURNALIST AND A CAMERAMAN on his front doorstep at 6.30 a.m. could only mean good news, Carl Rackemann
reckoned. The Fourth Test team against Pakistan was due to be
announced that morning. Rackemann had blown away eleven
Pakistani batsmen in the First Test, five in the Second and
missed the Third with a strained hip. But he was fit again now.
Flinging open the door, he thought: 'You beauty.'

'Actually, well, you haven't been picked.'

'So what are you blokes doing here?'

'Oh we, well, want to do a story on, you know, how you're
probably disappointed, take a picture of you looking upset or
something.'

'Get outta here.'

To this day Rackemann has never received an explanation
from the selectors. Picked instead for his Test debut was John
Maguire, Rackemann's upwind Queensland buddy. Maguire
took nothing for granted. His custom on a Monday afternoon
was to buy the old Brisbane *Telegraph* to see if he was playing
that Friday's Sheffield Shield game. Selectors weren't ones
to let slip. During the 1982–83 World Series Cup he flew to

Brisbane with national selector Ray Lindwall after one bunch of games. The squad for the next bunch had just been picked. Lindwall sat in first class, Maguire down the rear. Only after they disembarked and were inside the airport did Lindwall say: 'There's a newspaper. It's in there. Now I can tell you.' Maguire had been axed. 'I had the greatest admiration for Ray, rest his soul. He was probably under instructions.'

To the players, nothing illustrated the board's indifference to their welfare so graphically as the way it dealt with—or couldn't be bothered dealing with—the termination of careers. That, though, was the oldest of sores. The 1980s brought new reasons to feel unloved. Only one hand on cricket's steering wheel was actually the board's. The other was Kerry Packer's. In the divvying up of peacetime spoils, Packer's PBL pouched a say in the programming and control over promotion and marketing, over how cricket presented itself to the public. *Thunder Down Under, Showdown for the Crown, Double Trouble, Clashes for the Ashes* . . . Suddenly it wasn't summertime without a new slogan.

PBL's managing director Lynton Taylor declared five-day cricket a dodo. Lo and behold, 1984–85 spawned the one-off World Championship of Cricket—aka *The Greatest Show on Turf*—and a record thirty-one one-dayers. Malcolm Marshall found it 'a real bore'. Allan Border sensed PBL 'worried first and foremost about the dollar'. Graeme Wood, in a PBL questionnaire, pinpointed excessive PBL control under 'dislikes', until Merriman quietly recommended a rethink—thereby underlining Wood's point. Most Australians knew nothing of this because most Australians' cricket intake consisted of watching it on telly. And Packer owned the broadcaster. 'It was a shame,' felt England wicketkeeper Bob Taylor, 'that such a chivalrous, attractive cricketer as Richie Benaud was hired to jack up the hype and give his seal of approval.'

Slo-mo replays chewed up airtime aeons, with no consideration of the consequences. Two umpires quit mid-season and without notice in 1982–83. Robin Bailhache felt dehumanised at having his screw-ups rehashed frame by frame when he could adjudicate only in real time. Rex Whitehead followed Bailhache into early retirement, dispatching Gower caught behind in what became Whitehead's final Test. 'At home I said yep, that's out, bang,' remembers umpiring colleague Peter McConnell. 'Then they showed it from the camera behind the wicketkeeper and he missed it by a mile. But Rex wasn't standing behind the wicketkeeper. And I felt so sorry for him.'

At packed grounds players would count heads in the crowd, multiply by the entry fee, divide by their own wages and wonder why the lucky post-Packer days didn't feel so lucky. 'The players were all aware we were getting the raw prawn,' says Rackemann. What they didn't know was the prawn's size—or whether the prawn might, in fact, be a whale. PBL's annual share in Australian cricket's profits was detailed in the mystical ten-year peace treaty. That document never left David Richards's safe. But it was no secret that in the World Series aftermath the board negotiated from a position of vulnerability. 'A very poor deal, commercially naive, inept, done under extreme duress,' eventual chairman Malcolm Gray would later admit.

'You only get one Australian Cricket Board in your life,' Packer might nearly have boasted in 1979. 'And I've had mine.'

Occasionally, players sought to initiate a conversation about money. Uncannily, officials' hearing aids would play up. 'A game of cat and mouse,' the ACB's administration manager Graham

Halbish called it, owning up to some selective presentation of figures: 'I suppose we cooked the pie. The books certainly weren't cooked, but the pie was from a recipe of the board's creation.' Alan Crompton considers PBL a craftier promoter of cricket than the board could have been back then. 'But we found Lynton Taylor difficult to deal with. Nice guy socially but a bit overbearing, a bit bombastic . . . Bullying, yes, I think he tried to bully us . . . PBL tried to have more influence than they actually had. I think we hosed them down.'

Players got paid, says Crompton, what money there was to pay them. Junior cricket, the states, the game's future all had to be looked after. And PBL had to get their cut. 'There came a time,' Crompton says, 'when we felt they were not so much screwing us, because we were going into these things with our eyes wide open, but we were certainly concerned that PBL were getting too much money, money that should have been going into Australian cricket.'

Some players were whispered to be receiving little pocketfuls extra. Nobody was exactly sure how much everyone else was on. The general restlessness did not amount to a conviction that anything would change anytime soon. It was the same with team selection. Players had been getting scrapheaped without explanation for generations. 'That was the mentality,' says Maguire, 'and we just accepted it.' One day a captain rated too soft and too narrow decided not to accept it.

•••••

ALTHOUGH HE NO LONGER relied on Tooheys promo stickers to conceal his car's rust spots, Geoff Lawson still liked to show a lawyer his contracts before signing them. Terry Buddin, now a Supreme Court judge, was second-grade captain at the University of New South Wales when Lawson handed him a document in late January 1984. 'Gee,' said Buddin, looking up. 'You really want to go to the West Indies, don't you?'

At law firm Corser & Corser's seventh-floor office on St George's Terrace, Perth's burgeoning toyland of skyscrapers, Stephen Owen-Conway said something similar to Kim. Generally speaking, the $15,000 contract for eleven weeks away was typical—'the media restraint rules, the ban on wives, the antediluvian language,' says Buddin. Clause 24 stuck out. It sought to tie the players to board-approved matches not until May 1984, when the West Indies tour ended, but May 1985. This was an unsubtle attempt to ward off South Africans lugging rand-stuffed suitcases. But it cut across the players' marketing contracts with PBL, which expired in September 1984. More disturbingly, in return for signing away their livelihoods for an extra year, the players were offered not one cent.

Owen-Conway addressed them before a WACA one-dayer against West Indies. The whole squad attended. Rob Parry was there. Rod Marsh, missing recent retirees Lillee and Chappell and preparing to say his own goodbyes, skipped some of it. The players authorised Owen-Conway and Buddin to represent them in discussions with the board. Buddin, who knew Bennett and Richards, would play the conciliator. Owen-Conway, who nobody knew, was to be the enforcer. He sat beside Kim on the team's flight to Sydney and roomed with him on arrival.

For around five hours, with barely a break, till past midnight, they talked: Owen-Conway, Buddin, Bennett, Richards and board solicitor Gerald Raftesath. And Kim. His lawyer worried about that. Kim was slipperily placed, likely to be branded a rebel should the night turn foul. Keep quiet, Owen-Conway instructed. The mood was at times cordial, heated, tense. It was loosely accepted that the contract system was perhaps overdue for a shake-up. They got bogged on Clause 24. 'The players don't care two hoots about Clause 24,' said Raftesath. In plunged Kim, coolly yet forcefully. That just wasn't so, he made plain.

'Some people around the table were more than a little taken aback,' Buddin recalls. 'I'm not sure they had ever seen Kim in that light. I think they saw him as a bit of a boy, frankly, rather than a man.' Only three months ago they'd elected him captain. Was this how he thanked them? Bubbling beneath the surface, unspoken, Buddin detected a patronising air. 'It's like when you give your children something and they show no gratitude and all they want is more.'

Strike was not a word that came out of Kim's mouth, nor Buddin's. But gradually, tantalisingly, the players' participation in that week's best-of-three one-day finals felt less than clear-cut. 'It was sort of draped across the table, without being put quite so bluntly,' says Buddin. Fred Bennett believed Owen-Conway, the enforcer, was trying to 'make a name for himself'. Bennett's recollection, disputed by David Richards, was that Richards grew loud: 'He abused Hughes.' Noises were made about the board recruiting eleven replacements who'd be rapt to play, not the first time that sentiment had been floated in the long and flyblown annals of player-administrator relations. The meeting finished at 1.30 a.m.

Underneath cricket's new glitz, some of the game's workaday rhythms were evolving more slowly. Old board secretary Alan

Barnes's twenty years beneath a paperwork avalanche were immortalised by twenty words: 'If they don't like the conditions there are 500,000 other cricketers in Australia who would love to take their place.' Even in the mid-seventies that didn't just sound antagonistic. It sounded anachronistic. Yet Barnes's spirit lived on.

'There are a hundred dozen youngsters waiting to take their place,' blustered Tasmanian Bob Ingamells at a board phone hook-up after the late-night lawyers' session.

'Hughes,' contended Ray Steele, 'is carried away with his own value.' If 'C'mon, Aussie, C'mon' symbolised cricket's new order, 'C'moff It, Aussies' could have been the board's motto.

Across town, Kim was telling Owen-Conway that players were treated 'like chattels', words redolent of the Ian Chappell generation. Kim may even have wondered: what would Chappelli do? That was easy. Chappelli would scrap for his players. They would barricade round him. Kim's men were younger, many of them unmoved, but Lawson, Border and Wessels believed strongly in the principle at stake. Kim was determined not to disappoint Border, especially. The board's lawyer was scheduled to address the players at eight o'clock on the morning after a day–night game. That suited the players' lawyers. 'You didn't need to think too hard about human psychology,' smiles Buddin, 'to realise the players would be a trifle grumpy.'

The dapper Raftesath wore a subdued blue suit. Rodney Hogg wore whites and banged down his cricket bag. Raftesath mentioned Clause 24, silken vowels sounding out the words 'fair' and 'proper'.

Hogg leapt up. *'Fair?'* Swollen, craggier vowels filled the room. *'Fair!'* Hogg embarked on his own shorthand sketch of that word's meaning in players-bosses folklore. As Hogg tells it: 'I get annoyed when people try to brainwash you. That's why I could never have followed Adolf Hitler or George Bush. I can't suffer crap. And this bloke kept saying the word "fair". I was happy just playing for Australia really. I wasn't trying to be greedy. But when people say we're gunna do this and that for you, and you can't do this and you can't do that, well, that starts to grate away.'

This wasn't how the board envisaged proceedings. These players of Kim's seemed united. It felt significant.

Compromise came after several more meetings and in time for the Caribbean. In exchange for signing on until March 1985, players were guaranteed a minimum sum: $4000, $8000 or $12,000, depending on seniority. Players would get paid even if injured or dropped. And the board pledged to establish one streamlined annual contract. It did not amount to riches yet. As late as 1989, Lawson was in a portable hut at Manuka Oval haggling with an official after Mark Taylor was offered a mere $9000 contract in reward for an 839-run Ashes series: 'Only Bradman's beaten this guy here. Oh, Graham Halbish, you are kidding.' In the early nineties Whitney was still tallying heads on the MCG terraces and saying: 'That's a million bucks they've made on the gate tonight. And we're getting thirteen grand between us. How's that right, AB?'

But what Kim and the lawyers initiated were the humble beginnings of the contract system as Australian cricket knows it. Last to sign in 1984 was Lawson, dropped off by his wife Julie at Sydney airport's international departures area, pressing pen to paper on the check-in counter and taking his seat on the plane to the West Indies minutes later. Lawson reflects:

The unfairness of the whole deal—it had to be stopped somewhere. And unfortunately we didn't stop it in 1984. It took until 1992 or '3 or '4. When we look back at history that ten years won't be a long span. For us who played through that period, got paid bugger all and got treated poorly, it will be. The guys from 1994 onwards have felt the benefit of what Kim Hughes started. I think the inequity of it all struck Kim, because he treated everybody equally. Greg Chappell didn't treat people equally. Rod and Dennis did—unless it was Kim. But Kim was fundamentally a fair guy.

The Kim who Terry Buddin met when their trails crossed for four days was a diplomat. He was appropriately reverential towards gentlemen who were his elders. He was strong, steadfast, dignified. He was not the Kim who Buddin had read about:

> There seemed to be some real inner steel. And that's the impression you don't necessarily get. It's almost like he was some blancmange: the captaincy was taken away from him and he cried. Now, the players weren't there to see what he really said behind closed doors, but it was as if he was saying: 'Listen guys, I'm going into the trenches for you.' And he was, palpably. Maybe he was even doing it to demonstrate to himself that he was a leader, a worthy leader. I think he went into it with his eyes wide open, knowing full well that this was not necessarily going to sit easily with those who bestowed the golden sword on him.

Few captains can have known four days more frantic. Kim's first conference with Buddin and Owen-Conway, on a Monday evening, clashed with Marsh's testimonial dinner. That was how Kim came to miss Ian Chappell's tale of the goldmine and the shaft. He returned to his room late, feeling upset. Tuesday was the day of his five-hour marathon with the lawyers and the board. He slept briefly, reported back to his team-mates, snubbed Chappell at the toss, played and lost the first final against West Indies, then went clubbing until 4 a.m. The phone rang at 8.10 a.m. Where was he? Raftesath was ready to address the players; everyone was waiting. Kim tumbled out of bed and into shorts and a T-shirt. He hared barefoot down the Sheraton's seventh-floor corridor, caught the lift to the fifth-floor meeting room, sat through the meeting, hosted an impromptu press conference, then skedaddled to the SCG No. 2 oval to film the 1984–85 season ads.

Saturday was the day of the second final and an unforeseen tie. Then, bedlam. Bob Parish and the umpires locked themselves in the MCG's tiny umpires' room—just a shower and a dunny—and decided that even though West Indies could not possibly lose the tournament, a third final was required. 'Bob called it a shithouse decision,' says umpire McConnell, 'just by virtue of where it was made.' Eleven indignant West Indians concurred with that. A third final was played, Kim top-scored, Australia got flogged and everyone departed for the Caribbean. Buddin recalls:

Kim's phone went on at six in the morning and there would be a flurry of phone calls. He'd finish one call, put the phone down, then pick it up again. There'd be ten or fifteen calls from members of the press. He didn't, I assume, have too many media skills. There was no coach. And I remember thinking, boy, this is a lot for a young man without much support who has just been given the Australian captaincy to have to handle.

•••••

AMONG THE GOOD and not so good turns that Greg Chappell, Lillee and Marsh did Australian cricket, none hurt more than the timing of their exits. They retired all at once and on the eve of ten straight Tests against Clive Lloyd's rib-cracking, picket-jarring West Indians. Commonsense swayed them more than chicken-heartedness. None was getting any younger. All three exhibited faint traces of decline. Hard-earned averages would have taken a beating. Their timing stunk though. The full-bodied team that had toppled Pakistan and which Kim had waited nearly half his adult life to inherit lost its brain, heart and hands.

Neil Harvey appraised Australia's sixteen-man Caribbean combination thus: no spinners, hardly any fast bowlers, no openers. 'It's going to be 2-for-next-to-nothing every time.' No Bob Simpson would sail to Australia's salvation this time either. 'The saddest and hardest lot for any captain,' Simpson observed, 'is taking over the remnants of a once great team. I wouldn't be in Hughes's shoes for quids.' Border and Kim could presumably be counted on for runs, Lawson and Hogg for some wickets maybe. Who else?

Improbable characters, as it happened. After two Tests it was 0–0. A pair of unlikelier draws Australian cricket has never known. In Georgetown, tenth-wicket partners Hogg and Tom Hogan ignored the whistling past their ears to put on 97. 'Slog. Get a few quick runs,' Kim told Hogg to tell the slightly more accomplished Hogan. Hogg passed on no such thing. 'Another ten minutes, another ten runs,' he urged between overs, a messenger boy turned mid-pitch preacher. 'What's the record? I don't know. Let's go for it anyway.' A first-innings lead was Kim's compensation for his orders going unheard.

More last-stand pigheadedness defied logic in Port-of-Spain. Border and Alderman—a familiar pebble in West Indian sneakers—survived the final 105 minutes on the greenest Test track Kim had seen. Debutant Dean Jones lived to tell of one of cricket's most harrowing introductions. Struggling to lay eyes or bat on Garner, Jones felt one ball nearly rupture his stomach, opened his scoring with a blow to the hand, watched partner Border dry-retch pitchside, and conversed disconcertingly with bat-pad Desmond Haynes. Haynes appeared to be cackling.

'What's wrong, Desi?'

'Man, you are shitting yourself.'

'Mebbe so, but don't tell Joel.'

'Man, I think he knows . . .'

Jones prizes his 48 more highly than his triumph of occupation over dehydration in the Madras tied Test. Border endured ten hours, not out 98 and 100, a battered pillar of unbowlability. After safely negotiating his 639th and final minute he took a call from Rod Marsh, who granted permission for a unique non-victory rendition of 'Under the Southern Cross I Stand'.

Pressmen praised the apparent bonhomie. Mishaps usually suggestive of team cracks—'Flipper' Phillips and 'Fat Cat' Ritchie oversleeping past the start of the opening tour game—were construed as harmony-builders. Lawson, with his sponsored JVC handycam, filmed Steve Smith waking the culprits. Commemorative T-shirts were presented: '*Missing in Action . . . St Kitts 1984*'. Players took to jogging to and from training. Youthful cricketing ignoramus Errol Alcott, a late signing as tour physiotherapist, graded them on their sit-ups. 'The fittest tourists for years, perhaps ever,' reported Peter McFarline. Kim's thoughtful assertiveness won plaudits. On his 1978 visit Kim's chief acquaintance had been with local health workers. Now he came to admire a fun-seeking people who lived with high unemployment amid widespread poverty yet could recite the home state of every Australian cricketer. Their favourites, Kim noticed, were the shotmakers.

Seldom one for modestly downplaying a situation, Kim threatened to run dry of superlatives. The Hogg–Hogan Show and subsequent shirtfronting of West Indies for 230 was 'the best day's play by an Australian touring side I have seen'. Border and Alderman trumped that. 'I have seen some inspirational events,' remarked Kim, 'but this was the greatest.'

The Third Test in Bridgetown flickered brighter still. 'Take up your positions on the balcony,' the outbound Phillips advised team-mates. Standing still and swirling sixes, like a hammerthrower in ill-fitting boots, Phillips smashed 120 of Australia's 429. West Indies retaliated with 509, another draw imminent. Assistant manager Geoff Dymock took Rackemann and Maguire for a net at a nearby club ground. 'We were keeping an ear out for the Test score,' Dymock remembers. 'Suddenly we had to stop, hitchhike a ride out in the street and get back.' Wickets were falling faster than wheels could go: 2–62 became 97 all out. Australia never recovered.

Kim's patriotic cry in Antigua for a baggy green on every skull rallied no one. First slip Hookes was seen turning his back on Roger Woolley when Australia's new wicketkeeper snatched at and grassed an elementary chance from Richie Richardson. Richardson proceeded to 154 and Australia to annihilation. 'Victory in a beach match against the hotel bellhops would be a welcome change,' concluded West Indian sage Tony Cozier. The 3–0 wipeout was sealed at Sabina Park, Marshall's five second-innings wickets utterly perfunctory—'devalued,' he felt, 'by the lack of heart and courage shown'. Australia dislodged not one second-innings wicket all series.

'Look,' explains Rackemann, 'we got out of those first two Tests by miracles.' Truth was, the Australians had only one eye on the ball. Three eyes mightn't have been enough against these opponents. Dymock's frustrations were cemented before departure: a job title that meant nothing and had everything to do with administrators' lip-pursing disbelief in coaches. 'I wasn't coach. I wasn't manager. I was assistant manager-cum-the person in charge of practice.' On arrival, Dymock found himself dollying catches to distracted men:

> I was a bit disgusted. They were talking about player payments, players getting more. They used to meet: 'The board's making all this and we're getting peanuts. When we get home . . .' They'd discuss it the day before a Test. We'd have a team meeting and they'd be discussing it. I'd think, hang on, there's a Test match about to start. Who gives a stuff?

Australian cricket's new friendship with the Australian Wool Corporation snagged. 'Kim was trying desperately to tell us that the players didn't like the shirts and pants,' Merriman recalls. 'The wool, the fibre, it didn't go too well in hot weather. It worked all right with some but with others it didn't work at all. It created a helluva problem when you're trying to play West Indies.' Stickiness turned suffocating against Trinidad & Tobago in Pointe-à-Pierre. Dodgy fibres and sulphur-roasted Guaracara Park's oil refinery location were only partly to blame. When Hogg took leave from the field without first seeking permission, Rackemann was dispatched to find and fetch him. Rackemann returned apologetically: 'He told me to tell you, captain, that he's passed away.' Dispatched once more, Rackemann again reappeared sans Hogg: 'He told me to tell you he's gone for a drive into town.'

When Trinidad captain Rangy Nanan left Australia only 20 overs and fifteen minutes to chase 189, Kim flipped. He opened the batting, refused obvious singles, dead-batted full tosses. Eight bowlers took turns. Kim bunted back to each of them their half-volleys and donkey-drops. Nanan proposed an early finish. Kim rebuffed him, rooted to the spot—and unsupervised. Manager Col Egar was out of town on a business meeting. Border was resting with Hookes at the Trinidad Hilton, watching the live TV coverage in wonderment and dread, until the cheesed-off local broadcaster yanked the plug and switched to an ice-skating movie twenty-five minutes before stumps. Phillips lounged at the non-striker's end, pads tucked under his arm through the dying seconds. And after 24 overs Kim finished 10 not out: a six, a four. He vacated the premises between two rows of policemen and informed reporters that Trinidadian cricket's welfare was no business of his.

It was no brainsnap; rather, a prolonged meltdown. Its methodical execution, Kim's imperviousness to outrage, his blankness to wrongdoing were reminiscent of Chappell's ordering of the underarm. His hometown *Sunday Times* editorialised: 'The blue-eyed boy of Australian cricket took the out-of-character step of displaying blatant petulance . . . Hughes is the world standard-setter in on-field manners. Hopefully his flirtation with a bad-boy image is merely fleeting.'

It wasn't Kim. But where was Kim? And would a smack around the ears bring the real Kim back? Six days later emerged photographic evidence of an Australian cricketer swinging a punch at his own Test captain.

Ray Titus's photo shows Hogg's eyes dancing and forehead furrowed, black fury palpable. It's the third morning of the Second Test. Hogg's right hand is clenched into a fist and arcing downwards: the climax, seemingly, of a front-on haymaker. Kim is back-pedalling, hands raised in the universal don't-hit-me pose. After play, they extolled their cosier-than-ever mateship and Hogg's innocence. He had merely been flapping his arms in an explosion of pent-up frustration and excitement at getting Gordon Greenidge's wicket. 'Sure I nearly knocked his head off but my eyes were spinning. I didn't know who it was. It is a case of a photograph telling a lie.' Those were Hogg's words then. In the press box, Cozier thought he saw a punch; Phil Wilkins a 'violent shove'. Now, whenever they meet, Kim asks Hogg about it.

Hogg explains: 'Look, I was pretty annoyed because I didn't have a—it wasn't his fault—but I didn't have a third man . . .'

Who else's fault could it be? Kim was captain.

'I kept getting snicked through third man and they kept getting fours . . .'

Kim's next mistake was to swoop in for the celebrations upon Greenidge's dismissal, planting his head within throttling range.

'And then I got a wicket and I was pretty fired up and he's come in to congratulate me and I'm throwing a punch at the same time. So . . . It was a good photo. A very good photo.'

It was not, however, a photo fit for a happy family's album. Fred Bennett asked Merriman to hotfoot it to the Caribbean on a fix-it mission. Merriman, knocked back for the tour manager's job and wary of stepping on toes, rang instead. Time differences and flaky phonelines thwarted him, until eventually he tracked down McFarline who handed Merriman on to Kim:

Basically I said, 'It's a bad look. OK, you can get frustrated because the other captain wouldn't declare, but frankly we should be good enough to bowl them out. For God's sake, you're doing yourself a lot of damage. You're going to have to make that up.'

His response was: 'Yeah, OK, I might have stuffed up.'

It's like his batting. He'll do things on the spur of the moment then give it some thought and say 'maybe I shouldn't have done that'. You know, he's an amazing character.

To get out between 18 and 33, the hardest graft done, is normally considered an oversight. To do so nine times in ten innings points to something more than carelessness: to a mind in a muddle. Kim's sequence of Test scores in the Caribbean reads like a bingo-hall burlesque. 18. 0. 24. 33. 20. 25. 24. 29. 19. 23. Marshall and Holding nabbed him three times apiece. Yet no particular bowler haunted him. Sometimes he thrashed at the ball like a desperado. Just as often he bided his time.

He invariably lingered an hour but never two. Eight times in a row he succumbed between the 58th and 100th minute. Only once did he fall hooking.

Inside, he did not feel good. All those late nights before departure hadn't helped. He battled within himself just to concentrate. It takes a special kind of talent to lose concentration against an attack whose modus operandi involves flinging five balls at your windpipe and trying to york you with the sixth. It is not the kind of talent necessarily conducive to a long, prolific Test career.

The faint beard he'd cultivated looked like it belonged on some other man's face. Weirder still was the sight awaiting team-mates near tour's end when a washed-out three-dayer with Jamaica offered some overdue R&R on Montego Bay. Rackemann recalls:

A few of us had been souvenir shopping down on the beach. We got back to our hotel late in the day, on sunset, and Kim's turned up with his hair braided—beads and everything. This was the Australian captain. I mean, it was a ludicrous thing to do. It was just something fanciful; he sort of took leave of his responsibilities for an afternoon. He looked ridiculous. I think it was very much a case of him showing the stresses he was under.

When Border saw him, Kim was half drunk, watching cartoons. He had four decent inches of hair to experiment with once he unwound his curls. Woven into golden plaits were tiny multicoloured baubles. For Border, it was a revelatory moment: 'I thought then, Kim, you've lost the plot.'

·····

KIM HAD STARTED THINKING of himself as a captain first, batsman second. It is generally agreed he led capably, if not inspirationally, enjoying his freedom away from the three wise but sometimes cantankerous men. One of his last acts on tour was to sit through an entire session at Sabina Park with Steve Smith, who'd had a hand mangled by Garner. 'Mate,' said Kim, 'you can't keep going the way you're going.' You need to develop a backfoot game, he added, and here's how. It revolutionised Smith's batting. 'I wish,' says Smith, 'I'd been taught that before. But I never knew any different.' Border— whose 74 series average was the equal of Kim, Smith, Ritchie, Wessels and Jones combined—reckoned the harmony levels 'simply fantastic'.

Others wondered. Rackemann wondered how he bowled 27 consecutive overs into the wind in the Fourth Test, netted 5–161, then didn't play the Fifth Test. The simmering grumpiness of Hogg and Hookes was another mystery. Kim's talk of a new era came too late for some old dogs. 'I've heard more inspirational speeches in under-14 football for Northcote,' pronounced Hogg, excusing himself from one team meeting.

Dean Jones found Kim helpful, others self-obsessed. 'As a very junior member of the squad I hated it,' Jones wrote afterwards. 'Some senior guys didn't offer one word of advice or encouragement . . . There were tantrums . . . I only hope no senior players in the present Australian side treat the young kids as shabbily.' Another first-time tourist, Greg Matthews, felt his team-mates 'did not like me as a human being'. Observing from afar was Merriman: 'There was a fair degree of hope that here was the first tour where Kim was not subject to this alleged difficulty with the two West Australians. And all of a sudden there were other problems. It wasn't Lillee and Marsh. That was a real disappointment—a real disappointment.'

But if Kim was anything, he was resilient. Winter was for fishing, Sunday afternoon drives and weeding with the twins: 'Usually they pull out the lawn instead of the weeds, but they think they're helping Dad and I think it's beaut.' In September he led a training camp at Canberra's Australian Institute of Sport. He and vice-captain Border interviewed every player about their motivations and future roles, their views on Australian cricket's ills. Fourteen fighting-fit, not fighting, men headed abroad for a one-day series marking the Ranji Trophy golden jubilee. They outclassed India 3–0, a feat beyond more gifted Australian combinations of later vintages. They inspected the Taj Mahal. Saddened at seeing limbless boys and girls, they gave a swag of their prizemoney to a crippled children's home in Ahmedabad.

Travelling scribe Mike Coward sensed compassion for and solidarity with their captain—'to a man'. Merriman, the new full-time team manager, who'd so nearly elicited Kim's resignation, dared to hope. 'Kim was ruling supreme, things were rosy, he was on top of the world. There was no question of anyone else being captain.' He wasn't so unlike a much younger, unscarred man who Merriman remembered befriending, also in India, years earlier.

Kim, Border and Merriman were unaware of certain seedy goings-on. In the West Indies there were whispers, code names and eerie phone calls. In Canberra seven players taxied in twos to the Embassy Motel, where they visited ex-Test opener Bruce Francis and contemplated the mind-blowing riches being proposed to play cricket in apartheid South Africa. After India nine players met Ali Bacher at Singapore's Paramount Hotel. They were supposed to rendezvous at the ritzier Marco Polo; that plan was headbutted when Kim, awaiting a connecting flight to Perth, checked in next door. He, like Border, knew zilch.

'I told AB I was going shopping or some bloody thing,' says Maguire. 'I read one of his books later on and he was pretty pissed off, and that's understandable. But what could you do?' Says Rackemann: 'Ahhh, I suppose, um, well, it had to be done. If you were going to be involved that's how it had to be.'

It was a reflective Kim who had arrived home from the West Indies. 'What I've gone through over the past five or six years is more than nearly any cricketer has gone through.' He was dead right. And he knew barely the half of it.

THIRTEEN

'Gentlemen, Before You Go . . .'

FOR MANY YEARS, virtually the only black faces seen on Channel Nine belonged to West Indian cricketers. And they were seen often—too often for the ripe health of Australian batsmen. Even Allan Border found their bowlers close to unplayable and verging on unspeakable:

> You're out there batting, battling really hard, then they get that good ball through you and you think, well, I've spent two hours getting 20. Whoopee-do! To stand at the other end of Joel Garner and Malcolm Marshall and these people . . . Watching from a distance, you can't pick up the variation in bounce or sideways movement. And the pace they're bowling at makes it very, very difficult. It's just . . . well, I can't properly explain it in words.

A batsman's nightmare was a TV mogul's dream. 'Kerry was in love with them,' says Merriman. 'Just the attractiveness of them; I think Kerry himself loved watching them. So we finished up with these programmes, agreed to by the board, which saw them here pretty frequently.' From 1977–78 onwards, Clive Lloyd-led West Indian teams pitched camp down under six

Christmases out of eight. The five Tests of 1984–85, coming so soon after five on their patch, threatened to be the ones that broke the Australian cricket team.

Gore was summer's unofficial theme. A series logo decorated promotional brochures: two red balls slamming into each other, seams splitting and blood spurting on impact. Rod Marsh, no longer at risk of getting sconed himself, bestrode the National Press Club podium preaching violence. 'Plan A,' declared Marsh, 'is to fight fire with fire . . . Try and crack a few skulls.' Some batsmen tried hypnotherapy. Schemes to lengthen pitches by half a metre aroused serious discussion. Lloyd's firing squad was fresh from terrorising Englishmen. Ageing off-spinner Pat Pocock, awaiting his turn at Old Trafford, divulged to the physio that he had brushed teeth and gargled, lest the kiss of life be required.

Kim's teeth and smile were intact and everywhere. He and celebrity chef Peter Russell-Clarke fronted a twelve-minute instructional video for Kanga Cricket, whose butter-coloured bats, stumps and balls would soon invade 93 per cent of primary schools. Kim hammed it up with a plastic bat—'might be able to score a few runs with that'—and said down the barrel: 'Playing cricket as a boy we had a bat, ball and tree trunk. That was about all we needed to have a lot of fun and play Test matches in our imagination.'

Kim was the latest star of Ashley Mallett's *Master Cricketer* series of children's mini-paperbacks. Previous subjects included the Chappells, Lillee, Marsh, Walters—and, after considerable negotiation, Bradman. 'Bradman knocked me back the first time because I don't think he wanted to be associated with the Chappells and Lillee,' Mallett explains. 'That was the inference.' Mallett would write to him, ending each letter with a question, however silly, thus guaranteeing a Bradman reply. 'In the meantime I'd done the Doug Walters one. I think he identified with Doug: country New South Wales, no coaching, self-taught sort of kids, naive. And some of Doug's innings were Bradmanlike. So he agreed to do it so long as it was in much the same tone as the Walters book.'

Through his traditionally rose-coloured glasses, Kim was having visions of purple. Michael Holding, he reckoned, bowled mostly 'half-pace'. The West Indian speed department lacked depth. Their batsmen were bouncer-shy. The middle and tail looked iffy. Seeing off Garner and Marshall was the key. 'West Indies have been winning because of those two bowlers—it's as simple as that!' His vice-captain was a fellow believer. 'We're thinking of beating them,' trumpeted *Australian Cricket*'s 'Borderline' column. 'Laugh all you want . . .'

Old foes delivered untimely knees to the solar plexus: the September publication of *Gloves, Sweat and Tears*; mid-October's *Over and Out!* Old friends still wished to see Kim unshackled. Wayne Clark sat him down on the WACA's public benches, two men gazing upon a field. 'Give the captaincy away,' Clark pleaded. 'Just play cricket. Just go and play. You'll play for another five years.' Again—Kim reacted calmly. Clark remembers:

I honestly believed that if he backed off then he would become one of the great players. But he'd set his mind. He wasn't listening . . . When you're under that mental strain you don't believe or trust anybody. It builds and builds and builds and it's going to explode at some stage. He ostracised himself. I don't know who he actually talked to—probably

Jen, and that's about it. He didn't know who to trust. And in the end he said: 'Fuck it, I won't trust anyone, I'll do it my way.' He would go down a path, right or wrong, and wouldn't waver.

Wood made multiple, less formal approaches: 'Just play. Why put up with all this bullshit?' Same response. 'He was hellbent on it,' says Wood. 'I think he thought about it but in the end the desire took over.'

There was no finer moment to not be captain. Ever since Tony Greig of England vowed to make Lloyd's men 'grovel', opposition captains had become the favourite bits of meat dangling off the end of West Indian speedsters' forks. Botham had already been chewed up and spat out: stripped of runs, deposed soon after. Howarth, Gower and Vengsarkar would all follow. Greg Chappell, after seven ducks in fifteen innings, kept his job but lost some of his aura. As Holding put it: 'The theory was, once the head goes, the body must wither.'

•••••

STILTS AND FLYSPRAY should have been presented to visiting batsmen upon landing in Perth. For the opening stanza of the hyper-hyped Showdown for the Crown, John Maley's WACA pitch was not merely bouncy but green-specked, a consequence of rare spring rain. 'We'll bowl,' said Kim with glee. Openers Greenidge and Haynes, supremely unflustered, batted two hours. After much deliberation Kim posted himself at an extremely short short-cover for the last over before lunch. Haynes wafted the ball straight to him. Tipping forward, unbalanced, Kim dropped it. Everyone stumped off to gnaw at their food, everyone except Kim, who had politely agreed to open the new Prindiville Stand with state governor Gordon Reid. For twenty-two minutes Kim stood out there while people laughed at him.

Rod Marsh got to the ground early, bringing his thirst with him. It was fourteen Novembers ago that he'd woken to the news of his Test selection and cracked open a celebratory 7 a.m. bottle of beer with WA room-mate Derek Chadwick. Now he wanted to be sipping a beer at the moment the first ball was bowled, to savour that feeling. Another earlybird was Terry Alderman, playing his first home Test in two years. So enthusiastic was Alderman that a policeman cautioned him for speeding on his way to the ground. He bent balls around and away from horizontal bats, West Indies sliding from 0–83 to 5–104. Then began a footloose riposte to Kim's taunts of middle-order feebleness.

Larry Gomes and Jeff Dujon erected hundreds. Nine catches went astray. 'Somebody hit a huge skyer down to fine leg,' remembers twelfth man Maguire. 'And I'd just come on the field and dropped it—of course. Never played again after that.' West Indies amassed 416. In late afternoon sunshine Wood, listed at No. 3, slipped on his left pad, then his protector, then draped over his leg a too-wispy thigh pad:

> I sat up in the old WACA seats. First ball was to Wessels. The ball hit the bat; bat didn't hit ball. And I thought, well, I'll be in soon. Then Dyso nicked one and I was in at the start of the second over. I remember looking back at Lloyd and the slips cordon—forty metres away. It was incredible.

Then I nicked one. Clive came forward, caught it and I wondered how the hell did it get that far back. I couldn't possibly nick it that high. That night was as quick as any bowling I ever faced.

Wood wasn't imagining things. 'One of the most brilliant' passages Holding ever experienced; the most sustained 'high pressure cricket' Tony Cozier ever witnessed. The colours heightened the drama. Red ball flying, green helmets bobbing, outstretched black arms prising half-chances from mid-air in a dazzling yellow light. Kim entered at 3–28, nineteen minutes before stumps, and survived. Two not out.

He was fresh from slaughtering Patrick Patterson and the Tasmanians for 183, balls clunking into gold Benson & Hedges signs and rebounding metres back. As well as weeding the garden over winter, Kim hacked at his technique. Feet were splayed wider, bat between them, so he could move faster into position. Before the Test he showed Greg Chappell. 'You always looked perfectly balanced, Kim, feet closer together,' said Chappell. But Kim felt confident. He'd learnt from Border's Caribbean successes. Grind, eliminate risk, score in front of the body. Reporters fishing for pre-Test quotes were informed: 'I won't be hooking at the WACA unless it is the second innings, I am 150 and we are 3–330.'

On the day Kim passed his nineteen-minute nose and throat examination, Xavier Herbert died. Herbert, author of *Capricornia*, was born in Geraldton and the town's most celebrated export. He gave his last interview under a gum tree outside Alice Springs. 'There are two kinds of Australians: Australians and West Australians,' Herbert told the *National*

Times that day, and 'We are a nation of liars and rogues, generally.' Kim told no lie, but the effect was the same. Holding, suspicious of pre-Test pledges rogues couldn't possibly keep, set a deep leg trap and waited. Twenty-eight minutes elapsed next morning before he offered his prey a bouncer. Kim hooked. Wonderful shot, thought Garner in the gully. It rocketed flat and hard. On the fence, the force jolted Marshall, who kicked one leg out high to stay upright. In modern times with roped-in boundaries it would be six. Instead it was out.

Kim made 4 and Australia 76, 'half-pace' Holding's figures 6–21. Assailed a second time, Kim was lbw for 37, offering no stroke, bat periscoping high in front of him like he meant to plunge the handle into his chest. Australia's defeat was gigantic. A Mike Willesee interview felt like an inquest. File footage was overlaid. One second Kim was pumping iron, an excerpt from a PBL promo; the next second he was hooking fatally. An insulted Alderman fumed: 'Willesee is a wizard in political and current affairs circles . . . But what right does he have to slip into the Australian side like he did?'

Cannier cricketing minds than Willesee worried about Kim's belated installation of a gully despite Gomes's countless airborne flutters. Kim had spent long periods at backward square leg. Hiding, was he? Even when he was around he wasn't. His icy response to a one-handed catch by Phillips shocked Ian Brayshaw: 'I watched in mild amazement as he walked slowly, head bowed, down to where some of his men were putting on a celebration party. His arrival and almost apologetic pat on the back for those concerned was a dampener, rather than an inspiration.'

And that was before Kim batted. Hooking was no sin. Hooking fetched you runs. But a public vow of abstinence was barmy. Greg Chappell remembered what he'd seen in the nets. With feet spread, Kim was sure to get pinned on his stumps. Also, he'd be driving off the back foot. The ball would balloon. 'Your footwork is a mirror of your mental state,' says Chappell. 'Kim's footwork was a muddle and his mental state was worse than a muddle.'

•••••

BOB HAWKE WAS in campaign mode and lodging at the Brisbane Sheraton, the Australian team's hotel, on Gabba Test eve. He'd called the election eighteen months early. Mischief-makers reckoned it a ploy to get in before a 5–0 Windies whitewash and the torpedoing of national morale. In between ribbing Opposition leader Andrew Peacock and getting mobbed by his usual posse of elderly devotees at Redcliffe City Bowls Club, Australia's prime minister found time to admonish Australia's most embattled public figure. 'Eschew the hook, at least for the first fifty runs,' said Hawke. 'And the other thing is spend all day today, and turn the lights on at night as well, Kim, if possible, and practise your catching.'

Five weeks earlier Hawke had been sporting an eye patch, his spectacles in smithereens, after an ill-considered hook during the Prime Minister's Staff versus Press Gallery cricket match. But no one was too unqualified to take potshots at Kim, star attraction at the national coconut shy. Test new boy David Boon found it all quite surreal. At practice, recently appointed selector Greg Chappell belted slips catches while wearing a tie.

The culture Boon entered was unrecognisable from the culture he would help sculpt over the following decade.

Kim was Chappell-addled, again. Ian had been itemising Kim's latest shortcomings on Channel Nine while saving several salvos for his *Sun-Herald* column: 'It is time for Hughes to stop talking about using a psychologist in the dressing room . . . To stop talking about the "new professionalism" . . . To stop talking about not hooking . . . To stop talking.' This time, Kim took Chappell literally. He decided he had participated in his last post-toss interview.

'Your contract requires you to do it,' Merriman instructed.

'Can't Channel Nine get somebody else?' said Kim.

Ian Chappell's televised chats with the two captains in the middle of the oval had come to seem as much a part of Test match morning as the toss itself. Ian McDonald, media troubleshooter, tried sweet-talking Chappell. 'How about easing off a bit?'

'He's captain of Australia,' came Chappell's reply. 'He's gotta be able to take it.'

David Richards confirms having 'a dip behind the scenes' too. Merriman came away believing an agreement had been struck. The post-toss interview would be 'a reasonable inter-view'. Merriman urged Kim: 'Go and do it. It's all right. Nothing will happen.' Grudgingly, Kim complied. 'And the first question Ian Chappell asked,' Merriman reflects, 'was *totally* unreasonable . . . It was a boomer.'

Chappell had swotted up. Three months ago, Chappell began, you claimed Australia possessed no Test-worthy leg-spinner. So what, he continued, is Bob Holland doing in the XI?

'I admired Kim for staying there,' says Merriman. 'I shouldn't have said anything,' McDonald acknowledges. 'It probably made Chappell go harder.' Kim trudged off distressed, filthy, yelling at the pair of them. *I'll never do that again.'*

Less than two hours later he was walking back out at 3–33. Sections of the Gabba booed him. That was a jolt. He cracked a few balls around, fleetingly at peace, rolling to 34 off 36 deliveries. Then Garner pounded short, predators loitering backward of square, and Kim did what came naturally. Chin jutting down, eyes could not bring themselves to monitor the ball's flightpath. Even the bowler took scant pleasure in targeting this opposition captain. 'It was a little depressing,' noted Garner, 'when it led to the total demoralisation of a player with Kim's talents.' Australia coughed up 175. Phillips got a standing ovation for 44.

On the second morning Kim spilled another sitter, Richardson on 40, which soon swelled to 138. On the third morning he caught Lloyd. Kim looked glummer than Lloyd did. He frowned, unclasping the ball from his right hand and resting it in his left. Joyful team-mates saw Kim's face and adjusted their grins to something more circumspect and in keeping. In the afternoon he was lbw for 4. He had played five thousand sillier shots in his life but none so meek. He went out in a thigh pad as big as a saloon bar's swinging door and a helmet with low-hanging earguards. They seemed to weigh him down, for his head was slumped rather than pointing up as he tapped away at the crease. He shuffled then jumped back. Both feet were in the air. His body twisted grotesquely. The bat jabbed down, a mile outside the line, and the ball stayed low. It got barely halfway up to his knee roll. He would not have hit it anyway.

Next day, 26 November 1984, Kim rang Merriman, who ordered breakfast to his room. 'Kim was as clear as I've ever seen him.' It had just gone eight o'clock.

'I want to quit as Australian captain.'

'Do you really want . . . Is that really where you want to go?'

'Bob, I don't want to hear it. I don't want advice from you. I've made my mind up. All I want you to do is get hold of Greg Chappell.'

Merriman phoned Chappell at home. Without being told exactly, Chappell guessed what was cooking. The trio met at the Gabba around nine in the Queensland cricket secretary's office. When Kim started talking, Merriman left the two of them alone with a wall of *Wisdens*. Chappell felt relief mostly, and sadness. Quitting was sensible, he told Kim. 'I can't say it was the worst day of my life but it was certainly one of my worst days in cricket,' Chappell recalls. 'Something had broken the camel's back. Until that point I think Kim hoped things would change. But he had no more fight left and no more hope left.'

After fifteen minutes Merriman returned. Kim was writing out his resignation.

'I've spoken to Greg and he understands. I resign.'

'Well, you better think about how you're going to do this.'

'I'll probably go and tell people at the Australian Cricket Board.'

'Well, let's plan it out. Yes, you'll have to tell them. But it's a matter of when.'

Merriman reminded Kim of the game in progress and an afternoon sponsorship announcement with Fourex: 'That's a pretty important thing.'

Kim's next words, according to Merriman, were: 'Well I don't want anybody, y'know, I don't want anybody talking about it till, till I handle it.'

To which Merriman replied: 'Greg and I will maintain the confidence.' They mapped out a procedure.

The morning was humid. Queensland in November. Before play McDonald entered the Queensland Cricketers' Club, where the Moreton Bay bugs wouldn't be wading in ginger sauce for a couple of hours yet. A large window faced on to the field and the seats in front. Something surprised McDonald. 'I just went in to say good morning to a few people. I looked out the window and on the other side, sitting, were Fred Bennett, Greg Chappell and Merriman, talking very earnestly. I had a view through the window. And I've often thought about it.'

Australia resumed at 5–134, still 115 shy of ducking another innings defeat. Phillips lashed lustily. Boon's white-knuckle 51 made Marshall see red: 'Boonie, I know this is your first Test, but are you going to get out or do I have to come around the wicket and kill you?'

It bought Kim extra scripting time. Border noticed that Kim seemed strangely chirpy. McDonald saw Kim sitting in the players' dining room—writing. He thought nothing of it. Twice McDonald walked past the grassy patch out front. Had Kim called over, McDonald would at least have made the spelling shipshape: innuendo was spelt *inuendo*, credibility *credability*, see *seem*, gentlemen *gentleman*. But Kim didn't call over.

Merriman read it. Two words were promptly inserted. Constant criticism from 'the media' became 'sections of the media'. 'Don't bag the lot,' Merriman recommended. 'Put the word "some" in there.' McFarline, Casellas, Coward and others had all treated Kim softly.

Something else bugged Merriman. 'There's too much there. It's going to be tough.' He meant it would be tough for Kim to get through it.

'No,' said Kim. 'That's what I want to say.'

'Well, you know, just think about it.'

In the dressing room, Kim handed it to Border. 'Mate,' said Border, 'what are you doing? You don't need to. This is ridiculous. We're playing a very good team. It's not your fault.'

'Mate,' Kim replied, 'I've had enough. It's not working.'

Minutes before lunch Marshall got his man, Boon, who observed Kim—'visibly upset'—in conversation with Merriman. West Indies sacrificed two second-innings wickets, their first in seven Australian encounters, in pursuit of 23. Haynes was seething, bowled by an exuberant Lawson and irked by Australian indifference towards the health of Dujon and Gomes, whose heads they'd banged with bouncers in Perth. After his dismissal Haynes reappeared with a large carving knife, stored in the Gabba dressing rooms to slice watermelons. 'I was out front of the Australian room as twelfth man,' Murray Bennett remembers. 'And Haynes had a sharpening stone. He was sitting on the dog track, in the sun, sharpening this knife. Clive came out and yelled: "Desi, get inside. *Get* inside." Desi walked past and I was the only whitefella within cooee.'

West Indies manager Wes Hall located McDonald. 'I need to speak to your chief,' said Hall. 'One of my players wants to kill Geoff Lawson.'

'You'll have to wait,' McDonald replied. 'The chairman's pretty busy with the captain.'

Kim was telling Fred Bennett and David Richards his news. Richards, pragmatic by nature, was shocked, disappointed and upset. He thought it the wrong thing for Australian cricket. Instinct told him to talk Kim round. But it was so late in the day. So much else was erupting. Kim strolled to a corner table in the players' dining room, where twenty or so men had assembled for the end-of-match press conference. Tables were piled with fruit and crockery. Pictures of the Queen Mother's 1958 visit adorned a wall. 'We could have been in Benalla for a Country Women's Association meeting,' says Mike Coward. 'Worn carpet and laminated tabletops. So different to the world we're used to now.'

Sipping at a lemon squash, Kim was still in his fielding attire, creams and a sleeveless sweater. Someone asked would he do anything differently. 'Yes, I'd win the toss, send them in and catch Richie Richardson when he was 40.' Droll self-deprecation was an old Kim trait. Blind exaggeration was another. 'Wessels,' he went on, 'will become one of the greats'—lavish praise for a man whose inverted stoop at the crease brought to mind a six-foot-tall platypus. Merriman sat to Kim's right. McDonald hovered behind. A young reporter's enquiry about leadership rumours was intercepted by Merriman and swatted away as board business. Small talk resumed. It could have been just another Kim Hughes press briefing.

Alan Shiell thought it was. So did McFarline. He skipped it, catching an early flight home to Melbourne. Coward expected something. 'Don't go too far tonight,' Greg Chappell, cornered in a Cricketers' Club corridor, had advised him. Questions petered out and the packing up of pads and cables began.

'Gentlemen before you go I have something to read.'

Kim glanced at Merriman, then down at the two pieces of notepaper he had fished from his flannels. They were slightly crumpled by now, having visited several pairs of hands, and they said:

The Australian Cricket Captaincy is something that I've held very dear to me.

However playing the game with total enjoyment has always been of greatest importance.

The constant speculation, criticism and inuendo by former players and sections of the media over the past 4–5 years have finally taken their toll.

It is in the interest of the team, Australian Cricket and myself that I have informed the ACB of my decision to stand down as Australian Captain.

I look forward to continuing my career in whatever capacity the selectors and the Board seem fit with the same integrity and credability I have displayed as Australian Captain.

Gentleman I wish not to discuss

PTO

this matter any further and I will not be available to answer any further questions.

Kim Hughes

The closing signature contained squiggles through the K and H and a longer extravagant squiggle underneath, trademark flourishes. Kim made it halfway to PTO. He read three sentences in a voice which wobbled before cracking to a whimper.

It is in the interest of the team.

Silence. Merriman leaned in: 'Go on.'

Australian cricket.

Kim was crying now. 'You read it,' he squeaked. He lunged for the doorway.

'The statement continues, gentlemen . . .' said Merriman.

Kim's very next words would have been *And myself.* Those two words—the ones that admitted being captain of Australia did him no good—were the ones he found unutterable.

The players hadn't all heard yet. Kim's next stop was the dressing room, where he cried again. 'Oh, look, fellas . . .' he began. He did not finish one sentence this time. He bolted, for the bench, between Hogg and Murray Bennett. 'He sat right next to me and he put his head in a towel and he sobbed,' Bennett recalls. 'I reckon he sobbed for over half an hour, his head in the towel.' Border got up, gave a summary, talked of courage and grim luck, sat down. Then no one said anything. Wessels stared at Kim. Boon felt confused. Wood was reminded of the underarm aftermath, that feeling of being in the dressing room, normally your sanctuary, and not knowing where to look or how to react. After twenty minutes Hogg spoke: 'It's a fucking great game this Test cricket, Murray.'

At last an uptight man emerged from the dressing room, his jaw clenched and head bowed. A polo shirt was tucked into pale slacks. In his hand was a brown stubby of beer. He stopped for no one, skirting the Gabba outer on his way to the beer tent, where the players were guests of brewer Castlemaine Perkins. Once there he mingled and joked, laughing. Not long after, around five, Wood spied him moping alone in the Sheraton's bottom-level bar. Kim was gutted. Wood hated to see it. For a couple of hours they sank beers. Wood chatted about the future, tried geeing him up. It was hard work. Slowly the melancholy budged. 'Whether he was putting on a front, I don't know,' says Wood. 'He seemed OK. But then you go to your room and you're on your own again.'

Landing in faraway Melbourne was McFarline, spikiest and most evocative of Australia's sporting pressmen. McFarline was gruff, blue-eyed, floppy-haired, a man of many opinions who propounded them with steel. His cricketing passions included Ken 'Slasher' Mackay and Kim, one a stone-waller, the other a wall-toppler, both somehow unfashionable, both middle-order members of the all-Australian XI McFarline would one day select to play 'if my life depended on it'. He was nine years Kim's senior. Kim would seek his advice. McFarline liked giving advice. They'd talk one to one, away from the other journalists. Reliant on no typewriter, McFarline could ring for the copytakers and spontaneously deliver fifteen muscular paragraphs. It was a handy skill to have when his wife met him off the plane that afternoon, filled him in on what had happened to Kim, and said something like: 'You've got a bit of work ahead of you.'

Murray Bennett was sitting beside fellow New South Welshman John Dyson as the Australians flew out of Brisbane. Bennett remembers it well.

I said to him: 'Mate, I feel so sorry for Kim Hughes.'
And he shot back: 'Mate, I don't. I reckon he's a cunt.'

Bennett sensed that was not an unusual reaction, and he could see how Kim could be annoying. Personally, he liked Kim's company. 'I just went: "Oh".'

While they were flying, after a 6 a.m. departure, Alan McGilvray was speaking ill of the vanquished on ABC radio's

AM. 'He's a little boy who hasn't yet grown up.' With more sleep McGilvray would have chosen a line less blatantly quotable. But Kim's dig at the media had annoyed him. Inside Sydney airport the media bit back. Sprinting backwards up escalators were photographers and cameramen. Some were overseas freelancers, hoping to hawk a shot or grab. One was a crime reporter deputising for the squeaky-clean sports hacks. Alderman pronounced it 'sickening'. A waiting car on the tarmac prevented more torture by flashbulbs in Perth. By afternoon Kim was in his backyard. There, Ken Casellas thought he saw relief—'a man with a millstone cut from his neck'.

Should he wish to wallow he had mailbags in which to do so. The first goodwill messages had arrived, and would keep coming, something like 1700 in five weeks, from all sorts, stay-at-home mums to mining magnates. One, a previously unpublished telex, lies forgotten in Kudardup among 94-year-old Pud Challis's belongings:

27/11/1984
FOR: KIM HUGHES, AUSTRALIAN CRICKET TEAM
Your gentlemanly and courageous behaviour in the face of constant undermining by several of your more recent teammates, past players in the commentary box and 'would be' players in the press is a wonderful example to all young Australians in these days of declining moral standards.

Considering the fact that you have always been sent overseas to lead a virtual 2nd eleven your performance as skipper has been meritorious.

Congratulations,
Lang Hancock

FOURTEEN

The Bulldozer Theory

'THE SHOP STEWARD' was Geoff Lawson's private nick-name among some board officials. It was a hangover from those tumultuous few days when he and Kim called time out and the lawyers in. Lawson remembers precisely where he was during the most famous press conference in Australian cricket history. He was on a dressing-room bench, peeling off his boots, tired but cheerful, reflecting on the most promising day's toil in several Tests, thinking how with fewer dropped catches and more batting grit not so much separated Australian and West Indian cricketers after all. That's when Border muttered: 'Oh, Claggy's resigned.'

Angry indignation was Lawson's first reaction. 'What? He didn't talk to me.' Then, wistful regret. 'Oh shit, I wish he had spoken to me. I'd have told him not to do that.' The two have not discussed it in twenty-four years since. To this day, Kim is unaware of what Lawson would have done if only he'd known:

> I would have held you back. I would have held you in that dressing room and not let you go. Why did you resign?

Why did you not ask me? You idiot. Because that was the wrong thing to do, mate.

After indignation and regret came suspicion:

I thought, he hasn't talked to anybody about this. There's got to be more to it. And I thought of all our contract negotiations. He put his head on the block—and it got chopped off. He was pushed. He didn't jump. My gut feeling was that this has got bugger all to do with playing cricket. This is about a captain backing his players and being difficult for the board. They've got a reputation. For a hundred years they have operated like this. Players cannot have any power. Players cannot be treated reasonably. A stand was made, led by Kim Hughes. And Kim Hughes, quite rapidly, was no longer captain of Australia.

The constant criticism, speculation and innuendo. Speculation and innuendo had it that there was more to this than speculation and innuendo. Those doing the speculating did so privately, their innuendoes spreading no further than the front verandah. McFarline, on the front page, was one who hinted publicly at skulduggery. 'Kim Hughes did not give up his beloved Australian captaincy voluntarily,' McFarline wrote. 'He was pushed into Monday's painful announcement as surely as a bulldozer would push him over a cliff.'

According to McFarline, Kim was warned that his leadership lacked Test polish and might not survive the series. This was said to Kim over five days in Brisbane by 'men associated with the running of Australian cricket'. Were the men acting independently? Or conspiring? That, McFarline did not know.

Presumably, Kim was his source. Presumably, Kim was vague. For McFarline, till the day he died, never named names or elaborated, aside from a 1991 allusion to 'unremitting pressure' imposed by 'at least one' selector and 'other officials'.

Bill Lawry's effervescent persona in the Channel Nine box used to grow a few extra decibels when Kim batted. Lawry loved an entertainer. He'd delighted in the 213 Kim took off Doshi and Yadav. Guest-speaking at the weekly gathering of Adelaide's Rotary Club, Bradman's club, Lawry declared: 'The demise of Kim Hughes in Brisbane in a manner equal to being dragged down like a dingo in the pack and devoured by your own, within and without, is a disgrace . . . If the Australian captain is not performing it is simple. You do what Sir Donald Bradman did to me in 1971 and you drop the captain. You do not pull him down from within.'

This was uncharacteristic. Lawry's volume generally rises in inverse proportion to his outspokenness. He is not, never was, a controversialist. Mentioning his own inglorious exit was also unlike him. The two eldest Chappells said 'Phanto' was dreaming. Australian cricket moved on.

Peculiarities from that Gabba Test dangle hazily. Two nights beforehand Greg Chappell addressed the team at the Sheraton. Motivational giddy-ups were in vogue that summer. Richie Benaud delivered one in Perth. Bradman yarned with the players in Adelaide. Chappell likens his Brisbane pep talk to one brother Ian gave in the Caribbean in 1973. *You've been run over, now get up*. As Merriman recalls it: 'Greg strongly supported Kim and really nailed a couple of players who he didn't think were doing the right thing by the captain. Greg, at that meeting, showed a helluva lot of support for Kim.'

Others saw it as career-changing, terminally so. McFarline mentioned days later that Chappell 'fired a broadside' at Kim; Lawry claimed Chappell 'tore strips off' him. Neither was present. Indeed McFarline and Ian McDonald were dining on the Gold Coast that night, chewing over what Chappell's words could possibly be. But Kim would have enlightened McFarline afterwards. 'There is no doubt in my mind,' wrote McFarline, 'that Hughes there and then began thinking about his role.'

Forty hours later came Ian's dagger at Kim—the last in a conga line. Ian's post-toss captains' chats were preceded by Tony Greig's pitch report and Dulux Weatherwall readings. 'If you're going to air live,' says Greig, 'there can only be one loser. The coin goes up, and if a guy says something like "you've got a problem with the hook shot", then you say something like: "Yeah, a bit like you had against John Snow." You can't allow people interviewing you to get to you. The answer to selection is: "I don't pick the team, the selectors do." What you do is you attack.'

Opinions inside the commentary box split. Lawry considered the post-toss interviews 'a PR job for cricket and country' and Chappell's Bob Holland query 'completely out of order'. Chappelli's Chappelli, the Australian players knew. Knows nigh on everything. Expresses nearly all of it. Deeply respected. Not to be taken to heart. Kim's heart was big. That made it a big target. John Maguire recalls: 'The Channel Nine commentary—we used to try not to listen to it—but it was this Chinese water torture dripping away at him, wearing him down.' Kim's loud, last words as he left Chappell pitchside were eloquent testimony to that. *I'll never do that again.* And he never did.

Was that it? Did the only Australian captain to give up mid-series in puddles of tears do so to escape Ian Chappell? Friends hope not. 'If that was a trigger point,' says David Richards, 'I'd be amazed.' What would be more amazing is if it wasn't. Kim was not invited into Chappell's club during World Series Cricket. His membership prospects dwindled every year after. He publicly praised Chappell, batted a bit like Chappell, tried approaching his cricket like Chappell. Desperate, in the days before Brisbane he pleaded with the game's highest authorities to reason with Chappell. That only brought more aggravation. It also brought a dead end. For Kim knew then that to stay captain would mean confronting unpleasantness again and again, all summer, every summer. The Bob Holland reference upset him. The subsequent sound of spectators booing him was something he'd heard in Pointe-à-Pierre, and on a few Caribbean islands thereafter, but not at home, not for him, who was the decent, chivalrous, honest, crowd-pleasing one. Wasn't he? Ian Chappell was just a man, one bane among several. It seems probable that none troubled Kim more at the precise moment when going looked less painful than staying.

ABC television duties brought Bob Simpson to Brisbane. Simpson felt something sharper than sorrow. 'Disbelief—that it should have gone to an open press conference. Obviously Kim wasn't mentally up to it,' says Simpson. 'I thought Merriman, as manager, should have been very much aware of that. It could have been handled so much better. It didn't have to be announced then. Kim should have been given time.' A similar thought occurred to McGilvray. Hadn't Botham been spared the trauma in 1981 of reading aloud his own death warrant?

With Kim, though, it could not truly have been otherwise. If he was not to be a gallant, rousing leader then he was determined to at least bow out with fine, stirring words. Captaincy was not a job or a burden, more a lover. He could no sooner slink away from it than he could let a long hop in the last over before lunch go unhammered. The possibility of him weeping, unable to speak, did not occur to him, just as he never thought the long hop might get him out.

When Merriman and Greg Chappell told no others of Kim's plan they say that too was how Kim wished it, a broken man's last desire. The ramifications were momentous. It meant there was no one to talk Kim out of it. Merriman had disagreed with Kim being captain fifteen months ago; Chappell had disagreed with it forever. McDonald, had he known, would have sought to change Kim's mind. And if that foundered—'I'd have gone and grabbed a few people.' McFarline did not know. Head selector Lawrie Sawle did not know. 'Lawrie was definitely a Hughes man and very upset by it all,' says McDonald. Nobody told David Richards. And Richards could be persuasive:

I would have talked Kim out of it, or tried to talk him out of it. I would have wanted to understand what was driving him. Were those factors permanent, or capable of change? Was it really what he wanted deep in his heart? And if he was absolute—'mate, this is what I want'—then we would perhaps have laid it out in slightly different circumstances. But I found out a couple of minutes before the press conference. No chance to intercede.

Kim informed Richards in the same breath as telling chairman Fred Bennett. Except that Richards sensed Bennett already knew: 'I would say he did. Yep.' Bennett had opposed Kim's captaincy whenever it went to a vote. If he did know, he wasn't about to protest Kim's going. Merriman is firm: 'I didn't tell Fred.' Bennett passed away in 1995. His knowledge or ignorance of Kim's intentions went with him. He did, though, give reporters a line on the afternoon Kim quit, a line which suggested either an enigmatic approach to facts or that he lived in a cave. 'I have not,' said Bennett, 'seen any unfair criticism of Hughes's captaincy.'

Could people in favour of Kim's leadership have been shut out for one simple reason—so that they could not talk Kim around? 'Don't know,' says Richards. 'I don't know enough to suggest that when you flesh that out, the suggestion that people were acting collectively—I don't know. If they were not acting collectively but were acting as individuals, they all knew me well enough to know where I was coming from. And if they felt that might have stopped the ship . . . It doesn't matter. It's the way it happened. I can't change the fact that the sun rose at 6.10 this morning.'

'My own feeling,' says McDonald, 'is they were keen to change the captain.'

Of course, one man could have altered history that day: the man making it. Maybe Kim kept quiet because he knew people would attempt to talk him out of it. Maybe he knew that if they tried, they'd succeed. Maybe he didn't know what he wanted.

He did not tell Jenny. Richards rang her during the press conference. Jenny was grateful for the call and worried about Kim. The people Kim dubbed 'the extended family'—the Parrys, his other Perth confidants—were not consulted. 'I urged him to ring Jenny,' says Merriman, 'and suggested he might want to call Parry. I said "Jenny and the extended family". He said no, he'd do that some other time. I don't know what he meant by that.'

The end result was this: not one person who might have been inclined to talk Kim out of quitting knew what he was planning.

Snap resignations followed by more considered about-faces are not unheard of. Border, Kim's successor, quit so regularly that McDonald learnt to say 'OK, Allan' and keep walking. Sawle joked that McDonald should store a resignation letter awaiting Border's signature on permanent standby in his pocket. In February 1985 the limited-overs jamboree swept the Australians to Perth, where McDonald and Kim lunched long and thoughtfully. 'We went through it all, whether things could have changed,' McDonald recalls. 'He said he'd made up his mind. But I sensed he could have been talked out of it.'

Not only that. McDonald got the feeling that Kim resigned *expecting* someone would seek to dissuade him, and expecting their attempt to work. 'If he'd known what was going to happen I think he might have hung on,' says McDonald. 'I think there was every chance. It was a huge decision, not one you make in the heat of the moment at the end of a match you've lost. Better to cool off, talk to a few people. And he talked to the wrong bloody people.'

Who he talked to, however, was Kim's decision, and Kim's alone. It was not always the way. Sometimes it felt like there was a decision-making committee: soothing Kim, propelling Kim, distracting Kim. 'The pressures of Perth, the pressures of home, not Jenny but others around him, saying *you must continue to be captain* . . . It might have been in the best interests of what they saw as his stature and standing,' says Merriman, 'but I don't think it was in the best interests of his longevity in cricket.' Merriman regrets flying home after dinner at Kim's on that September night of 1983. He regrets not waking up in Perth next morning, the morning his phone rang.

> To me, Kim was torn very deeply between what he knew the ACB wanted of him, what he wanted to do himself and what his extended family wanted of him. He was in a three-way tug of war. I could see a person who I thought was a terrific bloke being destroyed. And you were helpless to do anything, because every time you talked to him about things it was the opposite to what somebody else was putting to him. I think there were too many people in his ear.

Graeme Porter saw Kim and Frank Parry most Sunday mornings in the late sixties and early seventies. 'I often think back,' Porter reflects, 'and I can't understand why Kim pursued the captaincy. I always felt he got the wrong advice. Frank, and maybe Rob, I got the feeling they were encouraging him.' As lives grew cluttered Porter saw them less, and hardly at all when Kim was trying on the king's crown. 'He should have focused on his own game, on being part of the team, on being the best player in the world. I think we would have seen Kim Hughes as a genius. And I really do think Frank should have seen that. Look, maybe he did. Maybe he did and maybe Kim was driving it. I don't know.'

Key men of influence dismiss any connection between Kim standing up for his men and falling down himself. Nine months separated those two landmark happenings. During that period

Merriman became Australian cricket's first full-time home and away manager. That was the board trying to help Kim. Why would the board help an irritant? 'It's a long time ago,' says Alan Crompton, 'but I have no recollection of any conscious desire on the board's part to get rid of Kim. I've no memory of anyone being pleased or delighted or glad when he resigned.'

As for The Shop Steward, he took 8–112 in the next innings in Adelaide. His star twinkled a little duller ever after. One Test later Lawson was fined for refusing his sweater from umpire Steve Randell after having two lbw shouts rebuffed. Lawson maintains he was merely hot and so elected to leave the sweater with Randell, yet was denied any right to appeal the fine. 'Discredit Kim Hughes, discredit Geoff Lawson,' was how he read it. The following season his overworked back gave out. 'I bowled thirty per cent more deliveries than I'd ever bowled in a year. AB kept saying: "Here's the ball".' Lawson's reward was a board reluctant to fly him to Perth to see his preferred chiropractor. 'I was doing all this bowling, treated like a piece of soap and thrown out.'

The winter of 1989, and Australia's 4–0 Ashes conquest, loomed as a time of rebirth for the national team and Lawson. He returned shrewder, the late kick of his cutters undiminished, reaping 29 wickets in six Tests. Nine at Old Trafford, scene of the urn's handover, had him toasted man of the match. Three Tests later in Perth he was nearly the game-breaker again. But first slip Alderman dropped Mark Greatbatch, nearing the end of an eleven-hour blockathon. Keeper Ian Healy reprieved Martin Snedden. Lawson was the bowler both times. New Zealand drew. Then it was to Melbourne for cricket committee discussions about money and to Brisbane for a Test match. It was a stirrer's forty-sixth—'I would have played another twenty-odd, for sure'—and last. Sri Lanka batted once. Lawson's figures read 33–10–51–1. He was dumped for Greg Campbell.

> There might be a degree of paranoia, I'm not too sure. But to me all these things are related. I mean, for Kim Hughes to resign when he never should have, when there was no good cricket reason, and for all those things to happen in that particular sequence . . . Kim wasn't the kind who jumped. He wasn't the kind of guy who ran away from a challenge. Ever. He stood up face to face to Dennis. In 1981 he tore clothing off Dennis. Kim wasn't a quitter.

A conspiracy? Impossible to say. But on 26 November 1984, and in the days before, they could not possibly have done less to stop him.

•••••

THE BRONZED, MUSCULAR ALLROUNDER from Queensland cried uncontrollably after wrenching the hamstring that struck him out of the First Test against England in November 2006. Shane Watson really wanted to play that match. People sympathised. Sympathy flowed two decades earlier for the captain who cried at the vanishing of a dream. But sympathy had to jostle with ridicule, shame, mirth. 'It could be that Kim's cricket box was too tight,' theorised Barry Humphries. Australians of old, Humphries went on, 'would simply chunder'.

Yet more comparisons were drawn with the unhappy hooker. Prime Minister Hawke had wept only weeks earlier for his daughter's heroin addiction. 'Australian men are not as cold-hearted as Englishmen,' Germaine Greer decided. 'They are great big softies underneath.' Male culture was raked over, high-flying literary analogies proposed. 'Kim and Mr Hawke felt immense personal anguish,' commented the well-read rugby coach Alan Jones. 'Shakespeare wrote sonnets about this kind of thing.'

Upon surrendering, Kim's hurt went deeper and dragged on longer than he expected. He felt bogged, in limbo, forlorn. He grieved. 'It was almost like losing your wife,' he said. He couldn't find his old self. Friends, in truth, had noticed his old self go missing some while ago. Nowhere was the boy who got the captaincy and laughed in the faces of seventeen kinds of doom in India in 1979. 'He'd gone from an outstanding leader,' feels Merriman, 'to a guy continually being questioned and questioning himself, who was very much frayed at the edges.' Old colts comrade Wayne Clark believes: 'He got so paranoid about people trying to knock him off. He was paranoid and in the end I think he had a little breakdown. He was trying to run cricket, trying to set the rules—fuck, it's my way or the highway. He wouldn't listen to criticism.'

That was not so surprising. For no longer could he discern the constructive from the malicious. He couldn't tell friends from enemies. Perhaps he is still unsure, so endemic was the muck-making, so overgrown were the protagonists' trails. Soon he would take to discreetly recording and scribbling down phone conversations with officials. It might have been more extraordinary if he hadn't cried.

Sportsmen and women cry rivers now after races, rounds, sets, finals. Winners weep for the enormity of all they have achieved, losers for the chance that may never be recovered. Often when they cry they are lauded for their sweaty knowingness, for the emotional maturity lurking in bodies so tender. That's if their tears are noticed amid everyone else's. Teardrops have become part of the sporting narrative.

Kim's tears are still seen through a 1984 prism. He is a batsman to be reckoned with in the reminiscences of those who watched 1980s Australian cricket and valued exotic strokeplay. Among all others, if he is remembered at all, it is as the sook, the crybaby, the effeminate cricketer. 'One inadequate captain getting life so out of proportion as to make a complete clown of himself'—so ran a recent line by British sportswriter Kevin Mitchell.

Kimberley. A girl's name.

A secret has long been harboured by Australian cricketers. They cried too, even in Kim's day, even the toughest of tough, sometimes when nothing was lost or gained, when there was no enormity, just a boy falling for a girl. This we now know thanks to a 2003 episode of Andrew Denton's *Enough Rope*:

DENTON: You're considered a man's man. I think most men would say that. Do you ever cry?

LILLEE: Oh yeah. Um, I cried when I saw *Love Story* . . .

DENTON: Ahhh.

LILLEE: Nice story it was.

DENTON: That is.

LILLEE: And a few other times. I mean, I'm . . . I'm as susceptible as anyone.

DENTON: You're a big gooey lump basically.
LILLEE: Yeah, I think so.

'Don't do a Kim Hughes,' a father was once overheard telling his disconsolate boy, a harsh epitaph for someone whose real mistake was to do it in a room full of men with the lights on.

•••••

A MAN ON THE EDGE played out the rest of that 1984–85 summer. The Third Test was in Adelaide, where people were celebrating a century of Test cricket. A dinner was held in the Hilton ballroom. The stage was done up to look like the old scoreboard. Perched on the equivalent of the grassy mound that backs on to the bar underneath the scoreboard was compere Mike Coward, introducing twenty-two old-time Test skippers. Magic filled the room. Kim got a standing ovation. The visiting West Indians clapped hardest. People rose from their seats on the Sunday, too, as Kim strode out in sunshine. He had scarcely known failure beneath the spires of St Peter's: 213, 53, 5, 84, 88, 30, 106. All were chanceless, all in a row. On his happiest hunting ground he became the unhappily hunted. He lasted one ball and seven balls, felled by a straight one and a shooter, for 0 and 2.

The team was improving, flogged again but detaining their tormentors five days. Border's ascension had been less straightforward than it now seems. The press wheeled out ten candidates. McFarline backed Hogg ('has an extraordinary understanding of the game'). Coward and Wilkins liked Hookes. McGilvray pushed for Wessels and Mossop for Thomson.

Greig, Blofeld and Burns nominated Inverarity. 'I'd have loved it,' says Inverarity. 'But I was forty. I read the articles as if they were about somebody else and shrugged my shoulders.' Rounding out the card were Wellham, Phillips, Hilditch and Rod Marsh, Old Skullcracker himself. And Border—judged favourite by all, yet the personal favourite of almost none. Too introspective, they fancied. Too unimaginative. For the next four years they were probably right.

Captain and ex-captain tossed immediately after Adelaide, for Queensland were hosting Western Australia. 'You could see it in Kim's face. He wasn't the jovial fella,' remembers Geoff Marsh. Perhaps Border contemplated donating some fraternal half-volleys. But it was hard to help a man determined not to help himself. Kim was run out for 1 then self-destructed for 14, unsheathing an outlandish pull at Jeff Thomson in the shadow of stumps. Worse than a trot, this was resembling a curse.

To drop a man in whom so much hope had so recently been invested would have felt precipitous and looked ungrateful. And so Kim headed to the Fourth Test in Melbourne, city of bright omens, scene three years before of the last West Indian Test comeuppance. Viv Richards, previously out of kilter, staged a two-day skyshow. Two-hundred-and-eight he butchered. The third-day hopes of a quarter-full MCG were crystallised in a Bay 13 banner: 'IF VIV CAN DO IT, SO CAN YOU KIM.'

Two balls he faced this time. Courtney Walsh angled one away, and Kim made no attempt to leave it without ever looking like he wanted to hit it. Dujon, outstretched, caught it. Nought again.

Christmas Day was a rest day. Lunch was at Kim's rented North Melbourne townhouse. Jenny, the twins and baby Bradley flew across. Wood and his wife Angela stayed in the same block. 'A good place to relax, away from the hotel environment,' says Wood. 'Kim seemed OK.' Murray Bennett remembers a fun afternoon and a high-spirited host. 'But he had a ball and chain dragging along behind him, really. He was a shot duck.'

Australia managed 296, slightly better than half their opponents' 479. Bashfully, Lloyd batted on fifteen minutes into the final morning until the lead was 369. Five and a half hours of survival didn't sound so onerous. Less pressurised atmospherics might save Kim yet. Then Garner began a new over. The first ball would have had Wood playing pick-up-sticks to retrieve his ribcage, had he not nudged it to a low-flying Dujon. The stupendous fifth ball pitched outside leg and sent Wessels's off stump somersaulting. Australia were 2–17 with five hours to go and Garner's over unfinished.

Helmetless for the first time all summer, cracking hardy, out came Kim. To a ball neither full nor short he shuffled but went nowhere. He presented a high elbow and an impeccably straight bat. But the ball was thirty centimetres away, whistling in. A golden duck; a humiliating pair: what kind of an ending would that be? Something must have alerted Kim to the danger. Because across jerked his bat. Too late. As the ball rapped his front knee-roll he tipped forward like a tall man being backslapped. Of all the world's cricket commentators, the job of describing it fell to Ian Chappell:

Garner really charging in. And it's out. First ball. He's got him lbw.

Watching had stopped being fun. All but 11,325 seats were empty. The decade-old love affair between the Australian public and West Indian cricketers was up, never to be rekindled, not the way it was. Non-striker Hilditch looked mournful. He hadn't played a Test in five years and would later that day rescue one. Away hurried Kim, in his cap and his gold-and-green wristband, through the dressing room and into the indoor nets to practise. Selectors Sawle, McCosker and Chappell did the only thing practical. 'Your mind plays games when you're not scoring runs,' Kim would rue afterwards. 'Against West Indies you don't get a half-volley or full toss you can clip off your toes. The first ball's a screamer.'

Within a week he was down among the cast-offs and hopefuls, just another fossicker in the fishpond. A 45-over arm wrestle featuring WA's second-stringers and Sri Lanka's medium pacers was too inconsequential even for *Wisden* to record. Passing motorists would not normally have turned their heads to peer through the gap in the stands. Yet 1484 turned up. Every run brought rapture. Kim's third ball sizzled past point. 'I felt like doing a lap of the oval when I reached 10.' He danced and straight-drove Ravi Ratnayeke, twice. Forty-seven not out—a start. 'I know my best years are in front of me.'

In Adelaide for the McDonald's Cup, biffing a cover drive, Kim's cap flew into the stumps. The bails stayed on. Had the curse lifted? He middled a pull. Midwicket Stephen Wundke swooped, knocked the ball up with his right hand, reverse-swooped, and plucked it on the way down in his left. An aeronautical miracle—so wondrous that it went on high rotation in that summer's Classic Catches, rarest of honours for a domestic grab. Fate hadn't finished fooling with Kim yet.

A 111 against South Australia in the Shield radiated enough of his old self for a call-up to Australia's one-day squad. It was the WACA's last game before its dread-inducing old white pitch was dug up. Kim's twelfth man stint entailed more standing ovations, one for every change of hats and jumpers. A spot in the XI materialised when Steve Smith fractured a finger before the third final. Jogging Sydney streets in preparation, Kim stepped in a pothole, turned his ankle and withdrew on match morning.

What next? A place in Australia's party for the World Championship of Cricket, a seven-nation extravaganza marking Victoria's 150th birthday. Roy Abbott, the man who built the WACA pitch and thus had a hand in creating Kim, was flown over for the final by radio station 96FM. Abbott had never seen the MCG. No one ever saw it like this: clowns, skydivers and fireworks, black warpaint streaked along players' cheekbones to ward off the glare from six new light towers. Australia and England opened festivities before 82,000. 'COME ON KIM!' pleaded the *Sunday Times* back page. Fifty-two days it was since Garner pinned him lbw. Border showed a mate's faith and sent him out at three. The bowling was hospitable and Australia handily placed, 1–57 chasing 214.

He had bathed in grand applause all summer, this nigh-on runless man, but nothing like this, from the second the loudspeaker called his name until Richard Ellison pottered in to bowl. If only the mob could bat for him. He survived his first ball, so they stood and cheered again. He could do this. His third ball he pushed into the covers.

'Yes,' said Kim, and away he and young Robbie Kerr bolted.

'Cripes,' thought Kim, for there, a blur in blue, was Gower.

Kim panicked, turned, scampered. Suddenly two batsmen were headed for one end and Gower's throw was missing the stumps and Chris Cowdrey was backing up and the bails were gone. 'It's just one of those summers for Kim,' said Border. Except no one ever had a summer like this. Dab and run: Kim's Kanga kids couldn't muck up that.

Pakistan were next. First ball, Kim dabbed and kept running, a single, waving his bat to the crowd. The next twelve deliveries he defended. A real handful was Wasim Akram, a college student from a Lahore laneway wearing his first pair of bowling boots. In seventy Tests and more one-dayers than he could remember Kim had encountered few left-arm quicks: Lever, Ghavri, Gary Troup, Azeem Hafeez. Akram was something else. He was zigzagging it on a pudding. But Kim kept him out OK. Akram consulted mid-off. 'A bouncer,' suggested Imran. 'He won't be able to resist it.' Kim spooned it as far as mid-on's hands.

In seven innings for his country, spanning 38 balls, he had scored 4, 0, 2, 0, 0, 0, 1. It made Greg Chappell's blue period of 1981–82 look like a purple patch. Kim sat and he plotted. He was due to fly home with everyone else the next day. Instead, within fifteen minutes of the game's conclusion, before the first beer, without telling his captain, he was out of the MCG and on the evening flight to Perth. Even Border was peeved. Few are so shameful as the boy who takes his bat and goes home.

The public's loyalty was fraying. A letter to the *West Australian* asked: 'How many times must Hughes be out for a duck before Ken Casellas feels his omission is justified?' The pressmen could not imagine a 1985 Ashes squad without him. Almost all—Wilkins was an exception—had Kim in their personal seventeens. Ashley Mallett was working for Adelaide's afternoon paper, the *News*. The squad was to be announced a couple of hours after last edition. Greg Chappell was sworn to secrecy but Mallett called him anyway:

> Remember *All the President's Men* and Bob Woodward ringing up Deep Throat? That's the way I did it. I told Greg: 'As I read through my list, you just say yes, and if you don't say anything then I'll know.' And I didn't mention Kim Hughes. I just assumed there's no way in the world he won't be in the side. I mentioned every other fucking bloke, I wrote the story and we had it on the front page. Kim was out and I didn't even *mention* him. Greg must have been laughing: 'Silly bastard hasn't asked the obvious question.' Looking back, I think it's pretty funny too. But it wasn't funny the next day when the editor said: 'Greg's done ya.'

It reads now like a vindictive, improbable trick. But on the day the team was named, Kim was packing his whites into his cricket coffin. He was bound not for England but Arabia: a one-day junket in Sharjah. 'I could never come to grips with why,' says Merriman. 'For the selectors to pick him for Sharjah and drop him for England—for Dirk Wellham or somebody—was an appalling act to perpetrate on a great Australian servant.'

The rationale, whatever it was, is lost forever. 'A short tour? One-day games? Nup, don't remember,' says Chappell.

Ten days they were gone. They sunbaked, swam, played squash and scoffed cheese, for the Australian Dairy Corporation were sponsors. They were paid in cameras, watches, gold ounces and cash, bewildering heaps of the stuff. They played twice, meeting England and India. Kim made 14 and 11. Neither effort was fluent. 'Chose a bat with no middle,' reported the *Guardian*'s roving scallywag Frank Keating. There was one boundary: one last exquisite cover drive. Apt was the ending, an uncertain stroke to an unthreatening medium pacer, caught and bowled Mohinder Amarnath.

When Bennett was run out without facing a ball, Kim blasted him. 'Mate, you've got to look around before running.' Bennett wondered what that was about. A gentle ribbing about Wessels always being injured ended with Kim bleeding above the ear, face rubbed in the grass, until he and Wessels were separated and exchanged sorrys. Watching Kim poolside at the hotel was Keating, an intrigued outsider. One unnamed colleague told Keating: 'When the magnificent mafia returned Kim had to presume to be one of the boys, else he was a goner. He would join the mob in rubbishing the opposition in the bar and in being generally loud, raucous and overconfidently Australian. He turned into a rugby player, which he just is not.'

Around the pool he seemed like one of the boys. Keating tried for an interview. 'Sorry,' said Kim. 'If I've refused one, I've refused a hundred.' He proceeded to offer a hundred apologies: 'No troubles? Fair enough? You see my point, don't you?' That was the old Kim.

At home, the longest summer ended in familiar surroundings, Floreat Oval, where Subiaco–Floreat were hosting Bayswater–Morley. The Ashes bombshell was still three days away. Kim made 9 and 7, bowled in the second innings by one of young brother Glenn's harmless dobbers. Said Glenn to a team-mate: 'I feel sick in the stomach.'

FIFTEEN

Cape Crusader

WITH TANNED, LEATHERY FOREARMS and an afro hairstyle that made baggy green caps a tight fit, Mike Whitney was a peculiar sight in Australian cricket teams and an even odder one on the beaches of Cape Town. One day in 1984, clad in bathers and nothing else, he stepped past the 'Whites Only' sign and on to the sand. Trouble ran up to him. A bunch of local men, hectoring the stranger in Afrikaans.

'Hey hey, whoa,' said Whitney. 'I'm Australian mate.'

'What?'

'Australian. On holiday.'

Whitney turned his back, tugged down his bathers and showed them the only part of his body that was lilywhite.

'Happy?' he asked.

'Sorry. Sorry. So sorry, man.'

Temptation had been Whitney's first instinct when Bruce Francis rang promising the dollars of daydreams. Curiosity followed close behind. Whitney wanted to see this land so mystical that it made cricket bosses' wallets spring wide open. Also, there was a girl on a Contiki tour, Sandy, from Durban; he hadn't seen her in eighteen months. A busted knee early in the

1983–84 season gave him his chance. A ravenous traveller was Whitney. South Africa fed him with little longing to return.

Regularly, entering buildings, Whitney provoked uproar. 'Are you half-coloured? Or coloured? Or what are you? Man, you go in the other door.'

Always he answered the same way. 'Australian. On holiday.'

His assailants would look at Sandy and her friends. They'd nod. 'You feel alienated,' says Whitney. 'It's demeaning. I might have some colour in me; my sister thinks we have some Aboriginal blood on my father's side. I'd be quite proud if that was a fact. But I'm a white man as far as I know, and just because I was really suntanned and had this big curly mop I got a hard time.'

In the pretty seaside village of Fish Hoek he witnessed a cop whipping three black men. Their crime was to stand together on a street corner, talking. 'I made my decision right then. I had a moral problem with it. I couldn't go and earn money in a place where the blacks were so badly treated. After that I went to India, and it changed me forever. India's a place that cleanses your soul. It doesn't matter if they offer me a million dollars, I thought. I can't go.'

A neat million was the sum Malcolm Marshall rejected over breakfast at a Wimpy's grease joint in Southampton. That so astounded Marshall's suitor, Ali Bacher, that he spilt coffee down his shirt. Other black-skinned cricketers, Michael Holding and Viv Richards, said no, not for whopping riches, would they flout governments' wishes and tour a country where the black man was not 'a free bird'. 'I would rather die,' decided Richards, 'than lay down my dignity.' Whitney's troublesome knee ensured no formal offer ever came. His actions read now like the plainest horse sense. He was sounded out, took a look at the place and people, and thought better of it. What made Whitney's actions extraordinary was that he was the only Australian cricketer who decided against going to South Africa on moral grounds.

Others stayed put for different reasons—desire to play Tests, fear of a life ban, or because they weren't asked. Among the latter were Australian cricketing royalty. 'I was on the farm one day when I got a call saying to sit near the phone,' Geoff Marsh recalls. 'I didn't leave for about four days. Didn't sleep for four days. Never got the phone call.' Allan Border was presumed uninterested and never invited but has since confessed: 'I'd have thought very hard about it . . . And the higher the offer, the longer I'd have thought.'

Batsman Peter Clifford decided he wouldn't go out of respect for his dead father and the thousands of balls he'd devotedly tossed at his son. Dean Jones agreed to go but was cajoled out of it by his ropeable and very alive father Barney. Jeff Thomson's astronomical asking price was rebuffed. David Hookes felt obliged to see out his jumbo deal with South Australia. The moral question was never answered. The moral question was never asked.

As clearly as Whitney and Viv Richards viewed things, it was possible to think the opposite with equal clarity. Bacher had been captain of South Africa when the country was exiled in 1970. The way he saw it, whites-only cricket was the cause of their expulsion and multiracial cricket the prerequisite for their return. That, he believed, had been achieved. Of course he didn't like his country's politics. But how did continuing to block cricket help end apartheid? To keep the game ticking he arranged rebel tours by Englishmen, Sri Lankans, West Indians. Francis was a student of the country and a believer in Bacher's strategy. He had long been convinced that he himself would be the orchestrator of an Australian rebel squad. The players Francis recruited felt they would be doing no harm and perhaps some good. And they were to be paid $200,000 for two tours. This detail was their first, last and overwhelming reason for saying yes.

When South Africa beckoned, Steve Smith was moonlighting as a Woolworths storeman. Graham Yallop ran indoor sports centres. Both would rather have been practising. The Rackemann family farm needed a new tractor. A $25,000 signing-on fee took care of that. Carl laced ribbon round the steering wheel, put a blindfold round his dad and led him over a hill to the new tractor's hiding place.

Their $200,000 came tax-free and thus seemed all the more unknockbackable. But players had ways beyond their legitimate financial gripes of reassuring themselves that they were in the right. Smith had been pigeonholed as a limited-overs specialist and Rackemann as bung-hoofed. The future felt slight. Mike Haysman was overlooked for an under-25s trip to Zimbabwe. Wayne Phillips was a world-class batsman who the selectors were turning into a halfpenny wicketkeeper. Steve Rixon was a world-class keeper who wasn't being turned to at all.

There were sixteen variations on these tales. Some players were seething. Most were at least mildly disgruntled. None felt any pang of loyalty to their employer. But the Australian Cricket Board was only their world. It was not the world. This distinction was never drawn by the players. The notion of a wider loyalty was barely contemplated. It was not until after he signed his contract that Haysman opened an atlas and looked up where South Africa sat on the world map.

Murray Bennett's case was unique. A PE teacher in between cricket hours, he consulted his mentor, the old New South Wales opener Warren Saunders. Unknockbackable, they concluded. Upon signing, Bennett's troubles began. 'I couldn't sleep,' he recalls. 'I went for about two weeks without sleep. I'd played all my cricket for nothing and suddenly I was making a decision based purely on money that was probably going to end my cricket career.' Bennett telephoned his mentor.

'I can't go ahead with this. It's just not me.'

'Jeez I'm glad you rang,' Saunders replied. 'I haven't been able to stop thinking about it.'

Bennett told Francis. A day later the mailman delivered a $25,000 cheque. Bennett rang Francis again. Francis said hang on to it. 'I never put the cheque in my bank account,' says Bennett. 'For a long time it sat on the sideboard at home. I kept wanting instructions on where to send it.' Most of his would-be rebel team-mates were furious. One out could lead to more out and ultimately all out. Then the media got wind of Bennett's withdrawal. 'I'm not a person who likes the limelight,' he says quietly. 'I don't like having a birthday party for myself.'

All of this coincided with the fulfilment of Bennett's lifelong dream: his first two Tests against West Indies. Did it cloud his thinking at the bowling crease? 'Possibly it did,' he concedes. 'I know that by the time I started missing out on the one-day side I was actually quite relieved. I was mentally and physically drained.' One Test on the 1985 Ashes tour and figures of 1–111 were the last international cricket saw of him.

The rebels stated with admirable honesty and frankness that they were going for the money. Some, as a secondary consideration, cited annoyance with their current paymasters;

others, such as Trevor Hohns, suspected unofficial Tests in South Africa were the closest thing to real Tests they'd ever play. There was no other reason. This was almost unanimous. Almost.

'I am going to South Africa with an open and, I hope, intelligent mind,' announced Kim Hughes. 'I believe I have the ability to judge right and wrong. I also believe I will be able to comment and suggest ways in which the situation can be improved.' He said this at the press conference revealing his captaincy of the rebels, broadcast live on Channel Nine from Perth's Sheraton boardroom. Outside demonstrators chanted 'Shame, Kim, shame'. Inside were more microphones than he had ever seen. 'When I stand up in front of schoolchildren and business groups I [will be] in a better position to let the people at home know how the rest of the world lives.'

Later Kim would call his men 'ambassadors for sport, ambassadors for humanity'. He would tell TV interviewer Jana Wendt: 'We are supporting those people who are fighting the government to end apartheid . . . We are fighting the South African government.' On tour's eve he would profess:

I honestly believe the athletes of the world do more to break down the barriers than anybody else. Maybe it's for a split second. But during a sports event the world can forget about the Russians, the communists or whatever and just appreciate somebody's God-given talent. The religious leaders and the political leaders of the world build barriers. I say to them, spare us your hypocrisy, your double-dealing, your discrimination.

Was he trying to persuade the world? Or himself?

•••••

KIM WAS NEARLY THE LAST to say yes and the most likely to say no. This was the boy who wore his Australia Day birthdate as proof of his Australianness. Bruce Francis first mentioned South Africa to him in November 1982. Kim told the press about their conversation and thereafter Kim was told zilch. Of the twelve men he led into slaughter against West Indies on day one of summer 1984–85, nine had South African contracts signed on their behalf. The paperwork had been sorted in secrecy at seven o'clock that morning. Not until Sharjah, his Test career well and truly pitchforked, was Kim filled in by team-mates. In effect they were letting him know that they'd betrayed him. They had been betraying him since the 1983 World Cup, almost from the moment, in fact, that the captaincy became his and his only. Instead of decking them, Kim thought about joining them.

Everybody else's disgruntlement with the board looked like mere pique beside Kim's. He had been so confident of an Ashes spot that he booked a London flat and looked into a nanny for the kids. Selectors were Sawle, McCosker and Greg Chappell: Kim's long-time champion, his first Test batting partner and his first skipper. 'I spoke strongly,' says Chappell, 'in favour of leaving him out. I'd been witness to his mental state probably more than anyone.'

Chappell's haste in accepting a selector's job—six months after his final Test—bewildered fellow retirees Lillee and Marsh. Hadn't Greg been pleading exhaustion? Unfinished business seems a plausible explanation. That Hilton breakfast with Kim. Australian cricket's boils that required pinpricking.

'There was an element of that,' Chappell agrees. And he enjoyed the involvement, the sitting with players, identifying talent. England '85 was the first Test touring squad he helped pick. He felt Kim needed time and Border space. 'Kim could not have sat quietly in the corner and probably would still have had some supporters within the group. That would have made it very hard for Allan as captain. Kim wouldn't have led anything, I can promise you. But to send him to England was going to destroy him as a player. He needed to regroup his emotions and his mental state.'

Before long, the freewheeler of old would come dancing back. Chappell says Kim was to be given exactly that assurance. Despair not of the now. Look to the future. Here, the mist turns to murk:

> My understanding was that when we left that meeting Lawrie, being from Perth and knowing Kim well, was the man who was going to pass on the message to Kim that he was still in our vision in the big picture. I found out some time later—many years later, in fact—that Kim's understanding was that no one passed that message on. But, you know, knowing the state of mind he was in, it may well have been another one of those discussions. As I say, we had a lot of them around that time that he wouldn't recall.

Chappell describes the aftermath as 'one of the tragedies of life . . . He got the shits, didn't understand the decision—and understandably so—and took the first opportunity to say, well, stuff you.' Sawle says he cannot recall. McCosker declined interview requests for this book. Was it a 2–1 vote, with Sawle backing Kim? Chappell remembers it as unanimous. Some observers point out that Chappell and McCosker were ex-World Series. Kim was Establishment. All those years later, two into one still would not go. The wound refused to scab.

Kim's world was shrinking and becoming a more brutish place. Word reached Sharjah that Rod Marsh was challenging for a selector's gig in Perth. Frank Parry, sixty years old and his zeal unquenchable, wrote the WACA a letter: 'In the event that Marsh is elected a WA selector then Kim Hughes will continue his playing career over my dead body.' A year ago Kim had been speaking of freedom and a life without the big three. And here they were again. One had him by the big toe and another was grabbing at his ankle. It was like he was being pincered. 'I wonder,' mused Ian Brayshaw, 'if Hughes would make such a dramatic response over such an issue, however abhorrent the prospect of working in tandem with his old adversary.' Where Kim's own trepidation ended and the extended family's influence began was no easy thing to pinpoint.

On 9 April 1985 the *Daily News* front page had Rob Parry seeking a $30,000 guarantee—$12,000 was the standard Sheffield Shield player's income—or else Kim would flee interstate. Officials from four states greeted that idea with reactions varying between reluctance and squeamishness. Even import-friendly Tasmania, their players as likely to hail from Boggabri as Burnie, said they wanted a bowler not a batsman. Owen-Conway's people contacted the *News*'s people and a retraction of sorts was printed. There had been no ultimatum, merely a request to talk, and their client was embarrassed.

Dollars were certainly being discussed—with Francis. He thought Kim desperate still to play for Australia and the unlikeliest of rebels. On 11 April the tour became public knowledge. Kim knew that those who'd signed were forfeiting their Ashes spots. Replacements—himself, say—would be required. Of this he was certain. He was England-bound after all. On 20 April he turned down Francis, politely. The next day Bacher rang. 'You can always leave the door open,' said Kim. 'But, mate, I'm not going.'

Francis chatted regularly with myriad cranky cricketers clutching grudges. Any tawdry anti-board or anti-Packer scraps he fed to Kim. On 22 April one journalist supposedly overheard a selector tell another journalist that Kim was disruptive and past it. Francis informed Kim. He sounded dismayed, Francis thought. Kim was down all right. But his well was deep. On 25 April, Anzac Day, he resolved to return to the Test XI and 'stick it up a few people'.

Around this time Kim phoned Border at home to pledge wholehearted loyalty. But Border was out and his wife Jane picked up the phone. Kim's mind was swinging between extremes. The day after Anzac Day he discussed with Merriman and Richards the bid by Packer, protective of his investments, to entice various signed-up rebels back. They talked about why, how and how much. Shattered, Kim turned to Jenny: 'I've had a gutful.' And then he called Ali Bacher.

Steve Smith was on Packer's shopping list. 'I was in the shower when Francis rang. He told Jo that Tony Greig was going to ring our house and try to get me to change my mind, so don't answer the phone. And that's what happened. I was a man of my word.' Packer's minions did track down Wellham, Phillips and Wood. Wellham cheerfully recalls his brief meeting with Packer and Lynton Taylor.

'What do you need?'

A job was the issue. Options were canvassed.

'What about sales at PBL?'

'Yep, fine.'

Wellham's title was sales manager and his job description broad: on-ground sponsorships, magazine production, organising patches on grand prix jackets. Hours were nine to five at Park Street HQ, then off to the SCG for training. 'I remember Kerry Packer getting in the lift occasionally and the lift going deathly quiet,' says Wellham. 'And Kerry Packer knew of course that everybody was deathly quiet because he was in there. It was quite funny, an interesting place. The Christmas hamper everybody got was a wonderful gesture.'

Tony Greig will confirm only that he was involved. Was Kim ever on Packer's shopping list? 'No comment.' Almost certainly, Kim was not.

Kim was feeling disillusioned, nauseous, ashamed of officialdom. But he hadn't yet told Bacher yes. Nor had he surrendered his dream, as Merriman reveals:

Kim rang me the morning before we were due to leave. 'Listen, Bob,' he said, 'I still want to go on the Ashes tour. If there is a vacancy make sure people know I want to go.'

So I spoke to Greg Chappell. 'We've got this terrible mess. How's it going to unfold? And,' I said, 'I've had a call from Kim.'

The result was that the three players did go to England and Kim went to South Africa. And I, quite frankly, don't blame him. That phone call was the last time I spoke to Kim for a couple of years. That was my fault as much as his. I could have rung. I just felt so bad. I couldn't deliver for him. Couldn't help him. I wasn't a selector. Here I had a great friend and good colleague asking for help at his moment of heartbreak. I didn't enjoy it. And I still don't enjoy it.

Later that fateful day the board met in Melbourne. The players' unanimous verdict was that Wellham, Phillips and Wood were not welcome on the plane to England. The board's advice was that any attempt to exclude them was legally doomed. The players lost. Three streets away at the Hilton, agitated team-mates interrogated the tainted trio. 'Does Packer own the Australian team?' was one missile Wellham recalls dead-batting. It's a rancid memory: 'I was sat down in a chair and grilled by eighteen adults in a small room.' The plane left next day with Wellham, Phillips and Wood all aboard.

A little of Kim's hope died. His instinctive disgust knew no bounds. Now another instinct surfaced: self-preservation. Packer was paying five additional youngsters $15,000 a year to keep out of temptation's way. They were five more Packer investments which Kim guessed would need safeguarding. About the time the Australian team's plane was commencing its descent, Bert Rigg invited Kim for a late-afternoon drink at Yokine Bowling Club, 9000 miles from Heathrow and a million metaphorically. The drink lasted three hours. Kim heard Rigg grouch about Packer gluttony and cricket's pollution by politics. When Kim got home David Richards rang. According to Kim, Richards predicted a 'shitty tour' to England and agreed the game stank. The most telling words uttered were Kim's own: 'Kerry Packer runs the game. He's not going to be doing me any favours. Who's going to be looking after me? What assurances have I got?'

Long and mazy were the notes Kim was scrawling at this time after conversations with officials. Excerpts went to South African Cricket Union lawyers and materialised in *Guilty: Bob Hawke or Kim Hughes?*, Francis's take-no-prisoners book. One of Kim's jottings went:

I can remember sitting down and thinking that throughout the whole of my cricketing career I seemed to have been opposing people. Because of my stand against World Series Cricket there were axes to grind and the situation just went from bad to worse. Later as captain of Australia I was involved in opposition to the administration in my attempts to improve the lot of players. All I seem to have done is oppose people. Gradually it had eaten away my confidence. In the end I did not know who to trust.

He could see past and present clearly now. As David Frith has observed, the idea of South Africa 'took on the guise of rehabilitation'. 'He was not a happy chappie at the end, not at all,' confirms Richards. Without telling Kim, and going beyond his CEO's remit, Richards phoned a selector—probably chairman Sawle, he thinks—and floated Kim's possible appointment as guest captain of Australia's under-25s to Zimbabwe. 'Yeah,' says Richards, 'I'd own up to that call. I felt strongly that Kim still had something to contribute.'

The suggestion fell flat. Rod Marsh became a WA selector on 6 May and Kim reached Johannesburg on the 12th, accompanied by Rob Parry and Jenny. They travelled under a false name—the Smiths—and savoured the delights of Sun City resort. A dry three-paragraph letter announced Kim's unavailability for Australian selection. To the last, Kim's knack of innocently rubbing his elders up the wrong way remained intact. The letter, signed by Stephen Owen-Conway and bound for board chairman Frederick William Cecil Bennett, was addressed to the attention of Mr T.W.C. Bennett.

•••••

HIS TIME as the golden boy was up. 'So long, Kim, it's been good to know you,' mocked the *Sunday Times* editorial. 'Presumably South Africa may even launch its own version of the Ashes. Steve Biko's, perhaps.' Desire for a guaranteed game, not megabucks, swayed Kim, in Francis's opinion. And it was true that $200,000 felt thinner than it might have thanks to lost superannuation entitlements, airfares for family members, months away from Town & Country and a gruelling court action over his right to play club cricket. But mega it was when piled beside a scrapheaped cricketer's lot. Kim was a dad under pressure. 'He was our biggest problem, always asking for money, even when the tours were over,' South African Cricket Union president Geoff Dakin would later reminisce. Money anxieties can be shameful to own up to, even to yourself, which perhaps explains why Kim preferred talking about humanity.

People who had never entertained a thought about Kim Hughes monstered him. Hypocrite, hollered Archbishop Desmond Tutu. Has-been, reckoned Gough Whitlam. Comforter of racists, lamented Bob Hawke.

Other critics were as familiar as sunburn. No black person was allowed into Berea Park, Pretoria, when Ian Chappell hit a hundred there in 1969–70. Fifteen years on Chappell disagreed with Australians playing in South Africa and interpreted as pro-government propaganda a picture of Kim and Bacher pointing thumbs up. Francis couldn't help but highlight Chappell's two Test trips, his subsequent Wanderers and double-wicket forays to South Africa, and his enthusiasm for South Africa's reinstatement in books he'd written. With Ian and Kim, contradictions did tend to abound. Chappell roved amiably among Australia's Test tourists in England, where scatological visions were borne out and the Ashes squandered 3–1. Batsman Greg Ritchie, an eager inhaler of Chappellian wisdom, exclaimed: 'It is one of the biggest tragedies ever for Australian cricket that people like Ian Chappell have not been called in to help us.'

The knockers rattled Kim. Not being liked always had. 'People think I'm a racist,' friends heard him mutter disbelievingly. When Clive Lloyd voiced gentle support for cricketers' right to choose, Kim called him 'the black Jesus', which just sounded batty, especially when Lloyd had been the opposite of Kim's saviour in the summer just gone. Respect, reverence actually, was only continents away. Journalist Les Carlyon visited a land where Kim was 'a hero, larger than a Reagan . . . our most exotic African export since Breaker Morant . . . a cult figure'. And that was before the rebels got there.

It became known as the Hughes tour of South Africa. ('It wasn't his tour; he came with us,' team-mates half joke.) It began under three hundred chandeliers at Johannesburg's Carlton Hotel, where bigwigs gathered for the welcoming banquet. Kim gave his Australian Test blazer to South Africa's captain Clive Rice—a gifted salesman's first masterstroke. His effervescence and quotability seldom waned, his lustre taking some of the potential shabbiness out of proceedings. Talkative, relaxed, jolly: team-mates recognised the old Kim, and then some. He showed author Chris Harte his back. 'Look,' he said, 'no knives.' Never before could Kim remember having a room to himself on tour. Jenny came for Christmas. So did Jenny's mum, Kim's mum, Sean, Simon, Bradley and Rob Parry.

A billboard advocated the players' murder. Security tarzans hovered. In nearly every other respect it could have been any other tour. 'You were going from airport to five-star hotel to cricket ground,' recalls 'Sheff' Shiell, whose ten weeks away ranked among his most pleasurable. 'The hotels were very good, the food was very good, the beer was just like ours. If you shut your eyes you could be completely oblivious to what was happening in the country.'

Soweto was a daytrip for some. Game parks were a more common excursion.

Any other tour meant the same old uncontrollables. 'Kim still had the same problem,' observes the thoughtful Maguire, Australia's last full-bearded fast bowler. 'Blokes were trying to white-ant him.' Kim found Yallop a listless, largely runless deputy. Wessels's inclusion for the second season was reportedly opposed 14–0 by the players but insisted on by Bacher. 'So that's how they vote in South Africa,' quipped one anonymous quick.

Hogg describes them as unpressurised tours. 'You've got a contract for two years,' he says. 'You can sit back and relax, or you can have half a go, but at the end of two years you're not striving to still be in a side.' It was noticeable that if some players sat back and relaxed any further they might fall out of their chairs. No media manager went: another familiar scenario. Little, avoidable aggravations weren't avoided, such as Kim's unasked-for dissertations on local umpires and batting techniques, or his two-day fishing trip to Namibia, a diamond-dusted war zone whose South African-run status defied Australia's pro-independence foreign policy.

In his farewell hook at Australian cricket, Kim had savaged a culture at big business's mercy. Big business, he avowed, drove him out: 'The commercial interests have been successful.' He thought he could escape them in South Africa. But there he was, arms round two Yellow Pages babes, the babes in skimpy shorts, all posing for sponsors' photos. Was it the sun making Kim's eyes crinkle? Or embarrassment? For one-day games the rebels dressed in mustard yellow and mismatched headgear. Stumps were orange and umpires Adidas blue. 'The South Africans,' reported the *Guardian*'s Matthew Engel, 'have out-Packered Channel Nine.'

When the rebels played Transvaal, Engel sized up the 29,000 Wanderers cricket-goers: 'A homogeneous crowd, speaking English, rather than Afrikaans; emphatically white, not black, mostly I would guess old boys from the local colleges that still model themselves on the English public schools of twenty and thirty years ago, with whackings and prefects and initiation rites.' The day before, 40,000 attended a funeral of slain blacks in Mamelodi. 'Except for the odd journalist,' wrote Engel, 'it seemed most improbable that anyone was present at both events.'

If the knives were out of Kim's back, the scars still smarted. His after-dinner speeches—and these were plentiful—arrowed in on the shambles back home, the faceless board egotists, the all-powerful marketing men, the paucity of bat-wielding Aboriginal people. Between tours, addressing Sturt Football Club, Kim added:

> I have a tremendous gift to please people. Nothing would give me greater pleasure than to walk back on to the WACA Ground. I want my three boys to see me play for WA and Australia . . . I just happen to work for a different boss at the moment. Greg Chappell and Rod Marsh worked for Kerry Packer during World Series Cricket. Now Greg is a national selector and Marsh is a WA selector. Maybe I might end up chairman of the ACB.

One last characteristic distinguished the rebel expeditions as typical Australian cricket tours of the 1980s: the result. The unofficial Australians, as they called themselves, lost both 'Test' series 1–0 and their mustard outings more comprehensively, a match for but never masters of ageing men clawing back time stolen: Jimmy Cook, Ken McEwan, Peter Kirsten, Clive Rice, Garth le Roux. And Graeme Pollock, forty-two. One Pollock wallop seemed comfortably fielded by boundary rider Mick Taylor, only for the might of the blow to buffet Taylor over the rope. 'Pollock played like a busted arse till he got about 30,' Maguire remembers. 'Then, once he started seeing the ball, he was scary.'

Pyrotechnics and perversity were hallmarks of Kim's batting. So there was no change there either. Poised in Cape Town to add an unofficial Test hundred to his nine regulation ones, Kim scavenged five runs in the last fifteen overs to maroon himself

on 97. In Johannesburg he made the seemingly impossible—
three first-ball ducks—as simple as falling lbw, caught-behind
and then appointing himself runner for an incapacitated Hogg,
who was dismissed instantly. Kim averaged 45 the first season,
42 the next, and when he was good he was scintillating. The
worriless backstreets of youth were roamed in a Port Elizabeth
one-dayer. Cover drives erupted off one knee and both heels, as
Kim stepped away and smashed, the rebels running down 316.
He donated his wicket with victory a breath away and they lost
eight for 12, another road he had wandered before.

Kim was among the quickest to offer congratulations when
South Africa picked a non-white spinner. 'The pioneer, the
pathfinder,' Omar Henry joyously anointed himself. Death
threats ensued. A guard monitored Henry's mother's home for
five days. Bacher now admits he misunderstood the anti-apartheid
campaign. Bacher thought apartheid would outlive him.

The games went off hitch-free. Protests by blacks were illegal,
and so there were none. President F.W. de Klerk changed that
law in time for Mike Gatting's 1990 English rebels. Only then
did Bacher see the offence caused, the anger harboured, the
damage done. He told the ABC's Warwick Hadfield in 2004:
'Had I known in retrospect their [black people's] abhorrence
of these tours, I believe we would have thought twice about
entertaining those tours.' Little was black and white about the
happiness Kim's men spread. Most of it was white.

'It's a bit of a grey area,' says Rackemann, who nonetheless
regrets nothing. The cricket was fierce and bowling to Pollock a
thrill. Yallop felt ill-informed once he got there. 'But we couldn't
get out of the decision. We were under contract and it was
something I had to complete,' he confessed to *Wisden Australia*

on the rebels' twentieth anniversary. 'After we returned that made for some difficult moments of conscience.' For Maguire, two productive stints with Eastern Province meant four seasons in South Africa overall, ample time for rumination:

> My conscience tells me one thing—now—but at the time I probably didn't have all the information. I think I have a better understanding of what really happened there after spending that time there. I don't know. It's a hard one. Sometimes I think: I shouldn't have gone. I should have had more principles and that sort of thing and not gone. But then other times I think, well, I owed it to myself and my family to make the best of the profession I was pursuing.

The uncertainties of Bacher, Yallop and Maguire are minority ones. When contemplating the moral question, most think now as then that perhaps they helped. 'I believed through my discussions with Ali Bacher that I would be involved in some way in the political discussions,' says Wellham, 'which really appealed to me, because I thought I could maybe assist.' That was probably naive, Wellham says now. Kim, too, believed he could assist. Kim believes he did assist. In mid-2007 he said: 'Cricket was at the forefront of trying to break down barriers, and when you look at how cricket has developed in South Africa I was very pleased to be involved.'

Kim found a lot to like in South Africa. Children and frisbees were welcome on fields at lunchbreaks. Young men underwent compulsory military training. 'They come back desperate, very disciplined, very proud and very patriotic.' Black cricket was making progress. But soccer was their passion. Seeing Bacher give township children fruit, drinks and a fare home was touching. Sporting sanctions were not. 'People sell their coal, wheat, sheep . . . But because a cricketer goes you're a bad cat.'

Once exile was over, Kepler Wessels brought an official South African fourteen to Australia for the 1992 World Cup. Kim wore his rebel tour blazer to the team's cocktail reception. In the WACA press box he encountered Mike Coward for the first time in years.

'Maaate, glad to see you.'

'Oh. Hi Kim.'

Coward, no fan of the rebel tours, was bewildered. 'It was as though nothing had happened—that we would resume the matey, casual relationship we had in 1978.'

In the Caribbean, visiting reporters with a day off between matches sometimes enquire after the damnation of the 1983 West Indian rebels—blacks who were reckoned to be shafting fellow blacks. Lawrence Rowe and others moved to America. Among those who stayed, Richard Austin is said to beg, sleep and do drugs on Kingston's streets. David Murray and Herbert Chang have found money short and friendships elusive. All received life bans. Sri Lanka's rebels got twenty-five years. As the unofficial Australians' homecoming flight neared Perth, the South African Airways captain offered thanks for touring his beautiful country. 'Good luck for the future,' he proposed, 'and God bless.'

And blessed, it seemed, they were. Two seasons out of Sheffield Shield cricket—the terms of an out-of-court settlement—merely covered their time in South Africa. They had to do a year's penance before playing Tests. And, presto. Alderman flashed back into the XI. Rackemann followed. Hohns won a

Test debut and his country's thanks as a steel-nerved chairman of selectors. Jobs as state coaches or in commentary boxes seemed almost effortlessly attained. Three coached foreign Test teams. As for Kim, well, what happened next was another improbable tale.

SIXTEEN

'I Just Remember the Shenanigans Up on the Tenth Floor'

KIM'S COMEBACK TO AUSTRALIA took place on a wet field in front of five hundred people against a Scarborough attack of Henderson, Schlegl, Tomlin . . . and Lillee. The flowing, storybook action that looked like the work of a roomful of clockmakers could be nobody else's. Neither could the nasally growl, the order that no questions be breathed about Kim Hughes. It was Lillee's comeback day too. Border had complained of a fast bowler shortage, and Lillee's comeback would take him as far as Tasmania and Northamptonshire but not quite the Test team. Here at Floreat Oval, the pitch was greasy and the ball did little but skid. Lillee was thirty-eight. He'd grown a pepper-specked beard. He glared at Kim and huffed, and when Kim pulled and missed Lillee clapped hands teasingly. Kim did not miss often. Lillee bowled him for 100.

Could runs bring forgiveness? Some of Kim's colleagues were indignant. They had resisted South Africa's loot, anticipating a life ban not a feather duster for punishment. Traditionalists resented Kim for depleting Australia's playing stocks. When WACA committeemen moved to outlaw the rebels from club cricket, general manager John Rogers urged: 'Don't pursue

Kim. You're missing the feeling of the Western Australian public who absolutely adore him.' Pursue him they did, a chase which ended up in the Federal Court, where Kim alleged a conspiracy against him and a restraint of his trade, and won on the latter. The WACA lost several hundred thousand dollars in court costs and—it seemed—any lingering inclination to see Kim ever again.

One sunray heralded season 1987–88. Rod Marsh, a busy TV commentator, gave up selecting teams. When Western Australia needed an opening batsman on a green seamer against New South Wales, Kim was it. In the field beforehand, he felt nauseous. The proposition had unnerved him once before, in Junior Country Week, when Mr Carr pressed him into opening and Narrogin took hours dislodging Kimmy. Under his helmet and sweater he looked stockier than spectators remembered. He batted slowly, stoically, for 76. No one else passed 40. The noise when Kim reached 50 made his batting partner Tom Moody think WA had won the Shield.

Soon after, Kim invented a new saying. 'Claggy boy,' he'd say, 'back in town. Back in town, Claggy boy.'

'I can still hear it,' Tim Zoehrer recalls. 'I can see it. It was one of his great sayings when he hit a six, or after he got out. *Back in town, Claggy boy*. He'd joke and laugh and you loved seeing it.'

Scores of 22 and 3 at the Gabba, where he renewed contact with old friend Border, were trumped by 21 and 62 in Adelaide. 'Hughes's bid to win a Test cap again,' rejoiced Alan Shiell in the *Advertiser*, 'will be one of the most fascinating aspects of cricket this year.' The old swagger was back against Victoria, the helmet discarded. Kim survived an attempted beheading first ball then top-edged Merv Hughes for six. 'Forget it, Merv,' a familiar voice sang out. 'You're bowling to the big boys now.' He went lbw for 7 an over later, outsmarted by Merv. Hooking at Rackemann, Kim pouched a pair of ducks against Queensland and was sent back to Perth's log-fenced suburban parklands.

Big, belligerent hundreds at Kingsway Reserve and Tompkins Park landed him back at the WACA Ground for the Shield final with Queensland. Late on the second evening, 11 not out, Kim padded one away. Wood roared. At backward point crouched Rackemann, who felt sometimes that batsmen disrespected his throwing arm. 'If you're hitting the ball to Viv Richards, you're wary about taking a run; and they weren't wary enough running to me, were they?'

Rackemann demolished the bowler's stumps. 'That's just lost us the match,' spat Kim, back in the rooms, and not to captain Wood's face, though Wood heard about it later. 'You feel shithouse,' Wood admits. 'You feel bad about any run out.'

Over five seesawing days Western Australia edged to within 29 of victory. Kim was 21, six wickets standing, the Shield nearly won, when in his final deed on the ground where he made memories he hooked Botham to deep square leg two minutes before lunch.

Out of the team—and he fretted. A new season began. A team hunting three straight Shields had no pressing vacancy for a 34-year-old with a teenager's street-smarts. But club trundlers could not contain him. With the Test men away, Kim returned as vice-captain against New South Wales at Newcastle Sports Ground. It wasn't the SCG. But *vice-captain*. He chattered to reporters about new daughter Claire, about how Bradley, now five, had been thumbing his old Bradman book. One day Bradley trotted up to Kim and demonstrated his favourite stroke. 'He got down on his knees and hit through the covers. And he's never even seen me bat.'

Kim was drinking less, sleeping more, he explained. The season before he'd been on the Perth stock exchange floor soon after dawn, working as a dogsbody clerk for a stockbroking firm. It blunted his concentration. After the market crashed he gave that up for some brickie work with his brother-in-law. The crash made him a poorer man. But he felt fitter, he reckoned, more relaxed. The old optimism hinting ever so faintly at delusion was intact. 'Sure I'd like to play Test cricket again,' he told the *Sydney Morning Herald*'s Phil Derriman. 'I'm batting as well as ever. So who knows?'

There was a comedy of mishits. Out for 5 in the first innings, he looked a curious sight in the second. 'Hughes hunched over his bat,' the *Australian* reported, 'revealing a two-eyed, open-chested stance and a strange rocking on his feet as the bowler approaches.' Timing still awry, he got to 26 before feathering one. Jigging twenty-two yards to say farewell was bowler Greg Matthews: 'Clag was giving me his usual supercilious grin all the time I was bowling at him. I said, "You're not smiling now, Claggy." He told me to grow up. I'd like a dollar for every time he has mean-mouthed me.'

By a quirk of the itinerary, the Test men were available for all but three games. Finally granted another chance in Brisbane, Kim made 14 and 10, neither of them convincing.

Again he struck a dead end, nowhere to play. Again South Africa beckoned. Natal were the owners of eighteen Currie Cups and a home ground, Kingsmead, within hooking range of the Indian Ocean. Kim arrived in September 1989 as captain of one of Natal's drabber line-ups. Two tyros, both goers, appealed. Andrew Hudson, an opener, would later compose 163 on debut against West Indies and pinpoint Kim's coming as his personal turning point: 'Kim instilled a positiveness and a self-belief in me.'

The other goer was a second-year player from Pietermaritzburg, Jonty Rhodes, aged twenty, who'd struggled for acceptance but whose running and fielding were ferret-like. 'Ferret', Kim nicknamed him. Rhodes stayed in Kim's Durban house during home games. Never had Rhodes known anyone to play with Kim's joy, to issue grand proclamations like: 'No spinner in this country can bowl to me.' He related to the risk-taking and revered Kim's passion. 'That was what I wanted to be,' Rhodes recalled during his own Test pomp. 'There are too many robots . . . Kim was emotional because he cared. I wanted to be the same.'

Natal flopped, and Kim averaged 13. His second season began against Eastern Province and John Maguire, whose strategy against Kim always went: 'Just bowl straight—he'll miss one eventually.' Many rated Maguire the least punishable bowler in South Africa. Let's see about that, Kim told Rhodes, and blazed 74. More often Kim's braggadocio was his undoing. Beating Transvaal at the Wanderers snapped a 28-year hex. Tellingly, it was Natal's maiden first-class win under Kim. Patience was cracking. Someone put it to Rhodes that he should take over. Unshakeably loyal, Rhodes turned and walked off. Kim was dropped mid-season and Peter Rawson of Zimbabwe named captain.

Once more Kim promised redemption: 'Just watch my smoke in club cricket.' What smoke there was came out of

Kim's ears, for he was left out of Natal's B team, one final slight too unbecoming for belief. Once more he railed at mal-administration and injustice. Once more he had reason to. But in fourteen games under his watch Natal won once. Four post-rebel summers yielded four fifties and an average of 18. On 25 February 1991 Kim came home. He'd retired. Scarcely a newspaper in Australia mentioned it.

'It all caught up with me. All those years of facing the West Indian quicks had me thinking about the short ball.' That was Kim's explanation, and probably too self-deprecating. For he'd been batting in the old familiar way. Shots he attempted, others fantasised about. But the degree of difficulty had jumped with age. 'He could see different shots and visualise them coming off,' Rackemann believes. 'And lots of times he did play the shot he'd concocted in his mind. It was achievable. But not always.'

Kim's last game was against Transvaal at Kingsmead. He made 4 and 9, unlamented and almost unseen. Steve Smith, playing for Transvaal, the one Australian who was present, cannot remember it.

•••••

HE HELPS OUT sometimes at his daughter's surf lifesaving club: odd jobs, fundraising, serving the chips on a Sunday. Walking through Karrinyup shopping centre with his three grown-up sons recently, Kim was stopped by a boy of six with delight in his eyes. 'I know who you are.'

It happens a lot less often than it used to. Kim was chuffed. He still had something—and in front of his own lads. He wasn't a forgotten figure. Well, this six-year-old hadn't forgotten.

'And how do you know me, son?'

'You're the chip bagger.'

A kind of post-Natal depression settled over Kim's cricketing life upon his return. No TV commentator's job—a retirement village for all regular Australian captains since Benaud and except Yallop and Waugh—was offered. Kim stayed in official-dom's bad books. His was among the last names turned to in journalists' black books. It was as if everyone wished to forget. One sleepy afternoon at Latimer Road, west London, *Wisden Cricket Monthly's* young editorial team took an unusual phone call: 'Kim Hughes here, former captain of Australia, and I'd really like to talk to someone about . . .'

When Dean Jones was dumped, Kim claimed selectors favoured players with 'one bag, two bags, three bags full sir' mentalities. When the Western Australian team's fortunes dipped, he called for a public inquiry. The estrangement was bitterest at home. There, administrators were not like lovers scorned but lovers habitually jilted. No captain can match Kim's 50 per cent winning record in twenty-six Shield–Pura Cup games, not Lock, Inverarity, Wood or Gilchrist, not Rod Marsh either. Yet by the mid-1990s Tim Zoehrer could find little trace at the WACA Ground that Kim had ever existed. 'Just a photo of him batting which hangs in the backwater of the Farley Stand.'

He got involved in network marketing: cosmetics, kitchen goods, an imported magnetic gadget to trim fuel bills. He dabbled in plasterboard, and in auctioning cricket memorabilia. A way back opened in 1999 when Western Australia appointed him chairman of selectors. That lasted twenty-two months. 'There were still people within administration who made life difficult. I thought, I don't need that.' Some felt he picked players the way he picked balls to hit. One look, then bang. 'The skin at the edges of his eyes and mouth is sparrow-footed, creased in the squint of assessment, concentration.' So wrote John Benaud of Lawrie Sawle. That was never Kim.

Cricket's outskirts have been his home ever since. Irregular expert commentary spells on radio. Opinionated. Humorous. Weekend chat sessions on the local ABC with the much-missed Wally Foreman, who sold ice-cream as a boy to get into the 1962 Commonwealth Games. More opinions. Hilarity. A WACA Ground dining area is now the Kim Hughes Room. President Lillee did the ribbon-cutting. Old Scottish chums were charmed anew at Watsonian Cricket Club's end-of-season dinner in 2006. Kim was guest speaker. It was the thirtieth anniversary of perhaps his one blissful trip as a professional cricketer.

Nowadays he gets asked what he thinks about things. Wives attending the early part of tours concern him. 'You don't want blokes worrying about their other halves and children.' He wonders whether players are too comfortable, whether wealth obliterates passion. 'How do you keep that raw ingredient? Players now are paid irrespective of performance. I have a real hang-up with that. The Australian adage has been you should get a fee but your biggest amount of money should be paid on how well you perform.' 1984 can seem several lifetimes ago.

He plays celebrity games, charity days, beach bashes— enough to reveal a couple more leaps in the degree of difficulty. He gets bulky. Then his weight comes down. He swears—something people never expected of Kim; often after a drink, and sometimes more than he probably should, when children and women are watching.

Brother Glenn played four seasons with Tasmania. 'Quick hands, inventive—his best shot was a slog-sweep,' says old Tasmanian captain Mark Ray. Bradley is a professional body-boarder. Jenny and two children work in real estate. Kim and Jenny have homes in Perth, Mandurah and the Cocos Islands, halfway to Sri Lanka, where coconut palms outnumber people. In a TV campaign promoting insurance for pensioners-to-be, Kim sat on a panel of formerly famous people and swapped getting-old yarns. Less long-running was his appearance on *Australia's Brainiest Cricketer*. He and Rodney Hogg were first-round evictees.

He set up business with former footballer Ken Judge. They give corporate presentations on leadership, motivation, teamwork and goal-setting. One workshop, Mates and Mentors, focuses on Australian men, their tendency to not talk, not seek help, heap stress on themselves at work, die younger than they should. 'You never know,' goes Kim's philosophy, 'I might just say something that, for someone, at that time, might change their lives.'

Asking for help is hard. Knowing when others need help is hard. Although nobody remembers seeing Kim fade from sight in South Africa, his last day as a first-class cricketer in Australia is not totally forgotten. It was a muggy January afternoon at the Gabba, a place where Kim and heartache had met once before. Western Australia polished off a simple run chase against Queensland. Unsettled by the short ball, Kim fell lbw for 10. Wood was in Perth with the Australian team: 'There was a photo in the paper, I remember, of him hooking, and he had long sleeves on, he looked quite pudgy, a bit old. When you look back you think, yeah, it was probably time.'

Wood's recollection of the photo is almost unerring. Two things he missed. First, the massive gap between ball and bat, the sluggishness of the stroke. Second, the expression of horror on Kim's face, his mouth open, collar upturned. Coach Daryl Foster's memory is of the aftermath:

> Hotel security had to come up and quieten him down and whatever. He was a mess . . . I just remember the shenanigans up on the tenth floor. It was three o'clock in the morning and he was still going strong, yelling and screaming. He obviously knew he was near the end. It's only natural to reflect and think, well, if I'd taken a different path, would I be happy? But I guess you've got to accept your lot. He had some highlights nobody else will ever have—that shot at Lord's. He had some moments that will live forever. But I think he felt he could have left an even bigger mark.

No wonder he yelled.

EPILOGUE
Old Men in a Bar

WHEN IT WAS OVER, Kim Hughes went back to where it began, Kudardup, on the virgin bushland Pud Challis cleared and in the house that he built, where Kim was cuddled as a baby. Pud led a working life more varied than any Australian may ever know again: possum snarer, farm labourer, fisherman, teamster, horsebreaker, sleeper cutter, hod carrier, miner, soldier, builder, barber, bookmaker, bulldozer driver, ferry skipper. That day on the verandah, by the Blackwood River's banks, the things Kim said surprised Pud. Mostly Kim talked, without bitterness, and only after being prodded, about four people, all old team-mates. Pud Challis, in his ninety-fifth year, will no longer speak their names. 'I just hate their names. Even when I hear them mentioned—I detest them.'

Now Kim, Dennis and Rod will have a drink together. Greg and Ian are Kim's friends. 'I am sure if I got into difficulty, financial or whatever, they are the first four blokes I would ring.' Dennis says their differences were exaggerated. Kim does not say that. But he does say they are 'great' mates, 'tremendous' mates, 'fantastic' mates, 'best' mates, as if fifteen years of his life never happened.

Kim says he blocks out the bad times. Even when he was playing, even when bad times were at their worst, he would come home to Jenny, see that she had three kids under four underfoot, and try to think about something else. He did not talk about it. He does not talk about it. Not one person interviewed for this book has had a conversation with Kim about those moments of direst wretchedness. Bob Merriman says they discuss funny times. They have not discussed 26 November 1984. 'We've talked about things,' says Greg. 'But in a boys' way not a girls' way—you know?' Bits go unsaid.

Since settling in Sydney via the Eastern Cape and Sussex, Tony Greig has noticed something about senior Australian cricketers of the seventies and early eighties. 'Those guys tried to dictate—and still do, I think, there's an element of dictation of history . . . In Australia, it seems to me, it's like there's a self-promotion brigade trying to dictate who was good at what, and why people could and couldn't play.'

For a man to whom much awfulness happened, Kim uses the word 'tremendous' a lot: sixty-nine times in one after-dinner speech at the Melbourne Cricket Club. Once, when Kim was running in the line of the stumps to stop himself getting run out, Joel Garner threw anyway and clocked Kim on the back of the head. He didn't rub it. He ran an overthrow. Ken MacLeay, the first time he touched the ball for Australia, skidded in a wild return that spat off the turf, through the man backing up's hands and put an egg on Kim's forehead. He didn't quail, or go off. Years later, on charity days, safely retired, Kim noticed—everyone noticed—how one particular bowler, he had a moustache and a bald spot, tore in extra hard whenever Kim was batting, as though lodging a ball in those golden curls was his life's last unfulfilled mission. Kim did not try to get off strike. Kim hooked.

Rodney Hogg thinks of courage not a crybaby when he thinks of Kim. Daryl Foster thinks of a rubberman. 'He had many shocking days. But he would bounce back. There was no weepin' in your beer with Kim.'

There's resilience, there's being brave, and there's pretending. People say deep hurt can heal if you do not let yourself think about it. But Kim nearly cried again five years ago when Mike Coward interviewed him for a cricket-in-the-eighties documentary. At a restaurant in Yallingup, on the south-west tip of Australia, Barry Nicholls thought he recognised the overweight fifty-or-so-year-old at a nearby table as his old Linden Park Primary School teacher. Nicholls reintroduced himself, and they agreed to meet up later that week. Kim chatted about team-mates letting him down, about how his average plunged from 41 to 37 in a trice. And in Kim's hand was a printout of all his Test scores that a friend found on the internet.

Hard as he tries—to forget, to get on—still he is not in the club, not quite. When Kim said Shane Warne would have made an embarrassing captain of Australia, Warne said the comment might bother him if it came from someone he respected. Warne admires Ian.

Something about Kim seemed to bring out the wicked in four cherished Australians. That, they would say, is in Kim's—our—head. Subtle put-downs, patronising asides, mutterings in meetings, public flailings in books, resisting orders, refusing vice-captaincy posts, backstage politicking, on-field quarrelling, bouncers; things they did, they did to help someone with a personality too mercurial to handle the fix he was in. 'And I tell you,' Greg says, 'the reason Kim Hughes and Dennis Lillee and Rod Marsh are still mates is because he knows they cared about him. Those two guys bloody did a lot of work behind the scenes trying to help Kim Hughes. And sometimes, when you love someone, you've got to be tough with them. It's not just about being nice and friendly.' Love? They had an odd way of showing it—and, in the end, an indefensible way.

Few departed cricket so sad as the one whose wish was to make the people watching happy: to 'give them that one hour of delight'. If Kim let himself think about it, he might realise that one person watching—watching Kim's right knee, in particular—was a youngster growing up between Geelong, Ballarat and Charters Towers. Today Andrew Symonds, like the Australian he admired most, chooses the extraordinary shot over the safe one every time. 'Take a lead from Kim,' coach Alan Abraham would tell his Perth juniors, Justin Langer and Damien Martyn among them. Langer stashed away his pocket money for a Kim Hughes black Slazenger. With an old SS Jumbo of Kim's, nicked from his father's study, he hit his first hundred. Far away in Launceston, Ricky Ponting and six friends would be arriving at the local park, where a sign said something like 'Tennis-Ball Cricket Only', and where Ponting would imagine he was Kim Hughes batting. If Kim stopped to think, to talk, he might see that he is making the people watching happy even now.

'Don't do a Kim Hughes,' a father once said to his boy. We can only hope the boy was not listening.

Statistics

FIRST-GRADE CRICKET, PERTH (132 matches)

INNINGS	N/O	RUNS	HIGHEST	AVERAGE	100s	50s	CATCHES	BOWLING
154	18	5526	205	40.63	13	19	54	2–100

FIRST-CLASS CRICKET (216 matches)

INNINGS	N/O	RUNS	HIGHEST	AVERAGE	100s	50s	CATCHES	BOWLING
368	20	12,711	213	36.52	26	69	155	3–97

ONE-DAY INTERNATIONALS (97 matches)

INNINGS	N/O	RUNS	HIGHEST	AVERAGE	100s	50s	CATCHES	BOWLING
88	6	1968	98	24.00	–	17	27	0–4

TEST CRICKET (70 matches)

INNINGS	N/O	RUNS	HIGHEST	AVERAGE	100s	50s	CATCHES	BOWLING
124	6	4415	213	37.41	9	22	50	0–28

TEST CRICKET: CAPTAINCY (28 matches)

WINS	DRAWS	LOSSES
4	11	13

Interviews

Alan Abraham, Brian Adair, Graeme Beard, John Benaud, Murray Bennett, Bob Blewett, Ian Brayshaw, Terry Buddin, Jeff Carr, George 'Pud' Challis, Greg Chappell, Ric Charlesworth, Wayne Clark, Gary Cosier, Mike Coward, Alan Crompton, Bruce Duperouzel, Geoff Dymock, Patrick Eagar, Sir Rod Eddington, Daryl Foster, Geoff Gallop, Sam Gannon, Howard Gliddon, Malcolm Gray, Tony Greig, Rodney Hogg, David Hourn, Graham House, Verdun Howell, John Inverarity, Daryl Lambert, Geoff Lawson, David Lord, Peter McConnell, Ian McDonald, Adrian McGregor, Len Maddocks, John Maguire, Ashley Mallett, Tony Mann, Geoff Marsh, Julia Matthews, Bob Merriman, Jeff Moss, Ian and Marianne Murray, Barry Nicholls, Stewart Oliver, Peter Philpott, Graeme Porter, Carl Rackemann, Mark Ray, David Richards, Austin Robertson, John Rogers, John Rutherford, Rudy Rybarczyk, Lawrie Sawle, Craig Serjeant, Yvonne Shaw, Alan Shiell, Bob Simpson, Keith Slater, Steve Smith, Norm Tasker, Con Tsokos, Ray Turner, Terry Waldron, Dirk Wellham, Mike Whitney, Graeme Wood, Roger Wotton, George Young, Tim Zoehrer.

Bibliography

Allen, David Rayvern, *Arlott: The Authorised Biography*, Harper Collins, London, 1994.

Barker, Anthony, *The WACA: An Australian Cricket Success Story*, Allen & Unwin, Sydney, 1998.

Beecher, Eric, *The Cricket Revolution*, Newspress, Melbourne, 1978.

Benaud, John, *Matters of Choice*, Swan Publishing, Dalkeith, 1997.

Benaud, Richie, *Benaud on Reflection*, Collins, London, 1984.

Benaud, Richie, *My Spin on Cricket*, Hodder & Stoughton, London, 2005.

Benaud, Richie and others, *Ten Turbulent Years*, Swan Publishing, Birchgrove, 1987.

Benaud, Richie (ed.), *Test Cricket*, Lansdowne, Sydney, 1982.

Benaud, Richie (ed.), *World Series Cup Cricket 1980–81*, Lansdowne, Sydney, 1981.

Berry, Scyld (ed.), *The Observer on Cricket*, Unwin Hyman, Hemel Hampstead, 1987.

Blofeld, Henry, *A Thirst for Life*, Hodder & Stoughton, London, 2000.

Boon, David, *Under the Southern Cross*, Harper Collins, Pymble, 1996.

Border, Allan, *Allan Border: An Autobiography*, Methuen, Sydney, 1986.

Border, Allan, *Beyond Ten Thousand*, Swan Publishing, Nedlands, 1993.

Botham, Ian and Jarrett, Ian, *Botham Down Under*, Collins, London, 1983.

Botham, Ian, *The Incredible Tests 1981*, Pelham Books, London, 1981.

Boycott, Geoff, *Put to the Test*, Arthur Barker, London, 1979.

Bradman, Don, *The Art of Cricket*, Hodder & Stoughton, London, 1958.

Brearley, Mike, *Phoenix from the Ashes*, Hodder & Stoughton, London, 1982.

Briggs, Simon, *Stiff Upper Lips and Baggy Green Caps: A Sledger's History of the Ashes*, Quercus, London, 2006.

Brittenden, Dick and Cameron, Don, *Test Series '82*, Reed, Wellington, 1982.

Bromby, Robin (ed.), *A Century of Ashes: An Anthology*, Resolution Press, Sydney, 1982.

Browning, Mark, *Rod Marsh: A Life in Cricket*, Rosenberg, Dural, 2004.

Butler, Keith, *Howzat!*, Collins, Sydney, 1979.

Byrell, John, *Thommo Declares*, Horwitz Grahame, Cammeray, 1986.

Cameron, Don, *Someone Had to Do It: A Sports Journalist Remembers*, Harper Sports, Auckland, 1998.

Cashman, Richard and others (eds), *The Oxford Companion to Australian Cricket*, Oxford University Press, Melbourne, 1996.

Challis, George, *Seventy-Five Quid and an Axe: The Story of George Challis*, self-published, Kudardup, 1994.

Chappell, Greg and Frith, David, *The Ashes '77*, Angus & Robertson, London, 1977.

Chappell, Greg, *The 100th Summer*, Garry Sparke & Associates, Melbourne, 1977.

Chappell, Greg, *Unders and Overs*, Lansdowne, Sydney, 1981.

Chappell, Ian and Jenkins, Viv, *Test of the Best*, PBL Marketing, Sydney, 1985.

Charlesworth, Ric, *The Coach: Managing for Success*, Macmillan, Sydney, 2001.

Coward, Mike, *Cricket Beyond the Bazaar*, Allen & Unwin, Sydney, 1990.

Coward, Mike, *Rookies, Rebels and Renaissance*, ABC Books, Sydney, 2004.

Cozier, Tony and Jameson, Neil, *Supercat's Summer*, ACCA Sporting Publications, West Melbourne, 1985.

Davis, Charles, *Test Cricket in Australia: 1877–2002*, self-published, Melbourne, 2002.

Doust, Dudley, *Ian Botham: The Great All-Rounder*, Cassell, London, 1980.

Down, Michael, *Archie: A Biography of A. C. MacLaren*, Allen & Unwin, London, 1981.

Eagar, Patrick and Ross, Alan, *A Summer to Remember*, Collins, London, 1981.

Egan, Jack, *Extra Cover*, Pan Books, Sydney, 1989.

Fingleton, Jack, *Batting From Memory*, Collins, London, 1981.

Fishman, Roland, *Greg Matthews: The Spirit of Modern Cricket*, Penguin, Ringwood, 1986.

Fitzhardinge, L.F., *The Little Digger, 1914–1952: William*

Morris Hughes, A Political Biography, Volume 2, Angus & Robertson, Sydney, 1979.

Foot, David, *Harold Gimblett: Tormented Genius of Cricket*, Heinemann, London, 1982.

Foot, David, *Wally Hammond: The Reasons Why*, Robson, London, 1996.

Forsyth, Christopher, *The Great Cricket Hijack*, Widescope, Melbourne, 1978.

Francis, Bruce, *Guilty: Bob Hawke or Kim Hughes?*, self-published, Coolangatta, 1989.

Frindall, Bill, *Frindall's Score Book: The Centenary Test at Melbourne and England Versus Australia 1977*, Lonsdale Press, Birmingham, 1977.

Frindall, Bill (ed.), *Limited-Overs International Cricket: The Complete Record*, Headline, London, 1997.

Frindall, Bill (ed.), *The Wisden Book of Test Cricket: Volume 1, 1877–1970 and Volume 2, 1970–1996*, Headline, London, 2000.

Frith, David, *The Ashes '79*, Angus & Robertson, London, 1979.

Frith, David, *Caught England, Bowled Australia: A Cricket Slave's Complex Story*, Eva Press, London, 1997.

Frith, David, *Pageant of Cricket*, Macmillan, South Melbourne, 1987.

Frith, David, *Silence of the Heart*, Mainstream, Edinburgh, 2001.

Frith, David, *Thommo*, Angus & Robertson, Sydney, 1980.

Garner, Joel, *Big Bird Flying High*, Arthur Barker, London, 1988.

Gascoigne, John (ed.), *Over and Out: Cricket Umpires Tell Their Stories*, Penguin, Camberwell, 2002.

Gliddon, Joan, *Joan's Story*, self-published, Kalbarri, 1992.

Gower, David and Johnson, Martin, *Gower: The Autobiography*, Collins Willow, London, 1992.

Griffiths, Edward, *Jonty: Fruits of the Spirit*, CAB, Auckland Park, 1998.

Griffiths, Edward, *Kepler: The Biography*, Pelham Books, London, 1994.

Guha, Ramachandra, *A Corner of a Foreign Field*, Picador, London, 2002.

Haigh, Gideon, *The Border Years*, Text, Melbourne, 1994.

Haigh, Gideon, *The Cricket War*, Text, Melbourne, 1993.

Haigh, Gideon and Frith, David, *Inside Story: Unlocking Australian Cricket's Archives*, News Custom Publishing, Melbourne, 2007.

Haigh, Gideon, *One Summer, Every Summer*, Text, Melbourne, 1995.

Haigh, Gideon, *The Summer Game*, Text, Melbourne, 1997.

Halbish, Graham, *Run Out*, Lothian, Melbourne, 2003.

Hamer, Michelle, *How it Feels …*, New Holland, Frenchs Forest, 2006.

Harte, Chris and Hadfield, Warwick, *Cricket Rebels*, QB Books, Cammeray, 1985.

Harte, Chris, *The Fight for the Ashes 1982–83*, Cathedral End Publications, Adelaide, 1983.

Harte, Chris and Whimpress, Bernard, *The Penguin History of Australian Cricket*, Penguin, Camberwell, 2003.

Harte, Chris, *Two Tours and Pollock*, Sports Marketing, Adelaide, 1988.

Hartman, Rodney, *Ali: The Life of Ali Bacher*, Viking, Johannesburg, 2004.

Henry, Omar, *The Man in the Middle*, Queen Anne Press, Harpenden, 1994.

Herbert, Peter and Sando, Geoff, *Parade to Paradise: 100 Seasons of East Torrens Cricket and Cricketers, 1897–98 to 2002–03*, East Torrens District Cricket Club, Adelaide, 2003.

Holding, Michael and Cozier, Tony, *Whispering Death: The Life and Times of Michael Holding*, Andre Deutsch, London, 1993.

Holmesby, Russell, *Heroes with Haloes: St Kilda's 100 Greatest*, Playright Publishing, Caringbah, 1995.

Hookes, David and Shiell, Alan, *Hookesy*, ABC Books, Sydney, 1993.

Hopps, David, *Free as a Bird: The Life and Times of Harold 'Dickie' Bird*, Robson, London, 1996.

Imran Khan, *All Round View*, Chatto & Windus, London, 1988.

Jaggard, Ed, *Garth: The Story of Graham McKenzie*, Fremantle Arts Centre Press, South Fremantle, 1993.

Jones, Dean and Brindle, Terry, *Deano: My Call*, Swan Publishing, Nedlands, 1994.

Keane, Patrick, *Merv: The Full Story*, Harper Sports, Pymble, 1997.

Knox, Malcolm, *A Private Man*, Vintage, Milsons Point, 2004.

Knox, Malcolm, *Taylor and Beyond*, ABC Books, Sydney, 2000.

Langer, Justin, *The Power of Passion*, Swan Sport, Isle of Capri, 2002.

Lawry, Bill and Main, Jim, *Skippers and Screamers*, Wilkinson Books, Melbourne, 1995.

Lawson, Geoff, *Henry: The Geoff Lawson Story*, Ironbark, Sydney, 1993.

Lillee, Dennis, *Lillee: An Autobiography*, Hodder, London, 2003.

Lillee, Dennis, *My Life in Cricket*, Methuen, Sydney, 1982.

Lillee, Dennis, *Over and Out!*, Methuen, Sydney, 1984.

Local Studies Department, *Geraldton: 150 Years, 150 Lives*, Geraldton Regional Library, Geraldton, 2001.

Macartney, Charles, *My Cricketing Days*, William Heinemann, London, 1930.

McDermott, Craig, *McDermott: Strike Bowler*, ABC Books, Sydney, 1992.

McFarline, Peter, *A Game Divided*, Marlin Books, Melbourne, 1978.

McFarline, Peter, *A Testing Time*, Hutchinson, Melbourne, 1979.

McGilvray, Alan and Tasker, Norm, *The Game Is Not the Same*, ABC Books, Sydney, 1985.

McGregor, Adrian, *Greg Chappell*, Collins, Sydney, 1985.

Main, Jim and Holmesby, Russell, *The Encyclopedia of League Footballers*, Wilkinson Books, Melbourne, 1994.

Mallett, Ashley and Chappell, Ian, *Chappelli Speaks Out*, Allen & Unwin, Sydney, 2005.

Mallett, Ashley, *Kim Hughes: Master Cricketer Series*, Hutchinson, Melbourne, 1984.

Marlar, Robin, *Decision Against England*, Methuen, London, 1983.

Marsh, Rod, *The Gloves of Irony*, Lansdowne, Sydney, 1982.

Marsh, Rod, *Gloves, Sweat and Tears*, Penguin, Ringwood, 1984.

Marsh, Rod, *The Inside Edge*, Lansdowne, Sydney, 1983.

Marsh, Rod, *You'll Keep*, Hutchinson, Melbourne, 1975.

Marshall, Malcolm and Symes, Patrick, *Marshall Arts: The Autobiography of Malcolm Marshall*, Macdonald, London, 1987.

Martin-Jenkins, Christopher, *The Complete Who's Who of Test Cricketers*, Macmillan, South Melbourne, 1987.

Murphy, Patrick, *Botham: A Biography*, J. M. Dent, London, 1988.

Murphy, Patrick, *The Spinner's Turn*, J. M. Dent, London, 1982.

O'Keeffe, Kerry, *According to Skull*, ABC Books, Sydney, 2004.

Philpott, Peter, *A Spinner's Yarn*, ABC Books, Sydney, 1990.

Piesse, Ken (ed.), *The A to Z of Cricket*, Wedneil Publications, Melbourne, 1983.

Pleydell, Ian, *From Limestone and Sandhills: The Story of the Development of City Beach and Floreat*, self-published, Mooroopna, 2003.

Pollard, Jack, *Australian Cricket: The Game and the Players*, Hodder & Stoughton, Sydney, 1982.

Ponting, Ricky and Staples, Peter, *Punter: First Tests of a Champion*, Ironbark, Sydney, 1998.

Prior, Tom, *The Sinners' Club: Confessions of a Walk-Up Man*, Penguin, Ringwood, 1993.

Randall, Derek, *The Sun Has Got His Hat On*, Collins, London, 1984.

Ray, Mark, *Border and Beyond*, ABC Books, Sydney, 1995.

Richards, Viv and Harris, Bob, *Sir Vivian: The Definitive Autobiography*, Michael Joseph, London, 2000.

Rielly, Cam, *The Graylands Story*, Graylands Teachers College, Perth, 1979.

Robinson, Ray and Haigh, Gideon, *On Top Down Under*, Andre Deutsch, London, 1997.

Roebuck, Peter, *Sometimes I Forgot to Laugh*, Allen & Unwin, Sydney, 2004.

Simmons, Jack and Bearshaw, Brian, *Flat Jack: The Autobiography of Jack Simmons*, Macdonald, London, 1986.

Spender, Barney (ed.), *Ground Rules*, Dakini, London, 2003.

Spillman, Ken, *Diehards: The Story of the Subiaco Football Club 1896–1945*, Subiaco Football Club, Perth, 1998.

Steen, Rob, *Desmond Haynes: Lion of Barbados*, H. F. and G. Witherby, London, 1993.

Steen, Rob and McLellan, Alastair, *500–1: The Miracle of Headingley '81*, BBC Books, London, 2001.

Stow, Randolph, *A Counterfeit Silence: Selected Poems*, Angus & Robertson, Sydney, 1969.

Swanton, E.W., *As I Said at the Time*, Collins Willow, London, 1983.

Symonds, Andrew and Gray, Stephen, *Roy: Going for Broke*, Hardie Grant Books, Prahran, 2006.

Taylor, Bob, *Standing Up, Standing Back*, Collins, London, 1985.

Turner, Glenn and Turner, Brian, *Opening Up*, Hodder & Stoughton, Auckland, 1987.

Tyson, Frank, *War or Peace*, Garry Sparke & Associates, Melbourne, 1980.

Underwood, Derek, *Deadly Down Under*, Arthur Barker, London, 1980.

Various authors, *Remembering Hookesy*, Swan Sport, Isle of Capri, 2004.

Various authors, *Skills and Tactics: The Australian Test Team Cricket Book*, Lansdowne, Sydney, 1982.

Wasim Akram, *Wasim: The Autobiography of Wasim Akram*, Piatkus, London, 1998.

Waugh, Steve, *Out of My Comfort Zone*, Viking, Camberwell, 2005.

Webster, Ray, *First-Class Cricket in Australia: Volume 1, 1850–51 to 1941–42 and Volume 2, 1945–46 to 1976–77*, self-published, Glen Waverley, 1991 and 1997.

Wellham, Dirk, *Solid Knocks and Second Thoughts*, Reed, Frenchs Forest, 1988.

Whitington, R. S., *Australians Abroad*, Five Mile Press, Melbourne, 1983.

Yallop, Graham, *Lambs to the Slaughter*, Outback Press, Melbourne, 1979.

Zoehrer, Tim, *The Gloves Are Off*, EMW Publications, Dianella, 1995.

Annuals
Allan's Australian Cricket Annual, Cricket in Australia, WACA Yearbook (Western Cricketer), Who's Who in Australia, Wisden Cricketers' Almanack, Wisden Cricketers' Almanack Australia.

Newspapers and Magazines
Advertiser, Age, Australian, Australian Cricket, Australian Cricket Tour Guide, Australian Playboy, Bulletin, Courier-Mail, Cricinfo Magazine, Cricketer (Australia), *Cricketer* (UK), *Cricket West, Daily News* (Perth), *Geraldton Guardian, Guardian, Herald* (Melbourne), *Inside Edge, Inside Sport, National Nine Tour Guide, National Times, Network News* (Town & Country), *News* (Adelaide), *Observer, Sun* (Melbourne), *Sunday Times* (Perth), *Sun-Herald, Sydney Morning Herald, Times, Watsonian* (George

Watson's College), *West Australian*, *Wisden Asia Cricket*, *Wisden Cricketer* (UK), *Wisden Cricketer* (South Africa), *Wisden Cricket Monthly*, *World of Cricket Monthly*.

Websites

www.abc.net.au, www.cricketarchive.com, www.cricinfo.com.

Index

Index